DATE DUE

EFFECTIVE SCHOOL INTERVENTIONS

The Guilford School Practitioner Series

EDITORS

STEPHEN N. ELLIOTT, PhD
University of Wisconsin–Madison

JOSEPH C. WITT, PhD
Louisiana State University, Baton Rouge

Recent Volumes

Behavior Change in the Classroom: Self-Management Interventions
EDWARD S. SHAPIRO and CHRISTINE L. COLE

ADHD in the Schools: Assessment and Intervention Strategies
GEORGE J. DuPAUL and GARY STONER

School Interventions for Children of Alcoholics
BONNIE K. NASTASI and DENISE M. DeZOLT

Entry Strategies for School Consultation
EDWARD S. MARKS

Instructional Consultation Teams: Collaborating for Change
SYLVIA A. ROSENFIELD and TODD A. GRAVOIS

Social Problem Solving: Interventions in the Schools
MAURICE J. ELIAS and STEVEN E. TOBIAS

Academic Skills Problems: Direct Assessment
and Intervention, Second Edition
EDWARD S. SHAPIRO

Brief Intervention for School Problems:
Collaborating for Practical Solutions
JOHN J. MURPHY and BARRY L. DUNCAN

Advanced Applications of Curriculum-Based Measurement
MARK R. SHINN, Editor

Medications for School-Age Children:
Effects on Learning and Behavior
RONALD T. BROWN and MICHAEL G. SAWYER

DSM-IV Diagnosis in the Schools
ALVIN E. HOUSE

Effective School Interventions: Strategies for Enhancing
Academic Achievement and Social Competence
NATALIE RATHVON

Effective
School Interventions

STRATEGIES FOR ENHANCING ACADEMIC
ACHIEVEMENT AND SOCIAL COMPETENCE

◆◆◆

Natalie Rathvon

◆

THE GUILFORD PRESS
New York   London

© 1999 The Guilford Press
A Division of Guilford Publications, Inc.
72 Spring Street, New York, NY 10012
http://www.guilford.com

Printed in the United States of America

This book is printed on acid-free paper.

Last digit is print number: 9 8 7 6 5 4 3

Library of Congress Cataloging-in-Publication Data
Rathvon, Natalie.
    Effective school interventions: strategies for enhancing academic
achievement and social competence / Natalie Rathvon.
        p.   cm. — (The Guilford school practitioner series)
    Includes bibliographical references (p.   ) and index.
    ISBN 1-57230-409-X
    1. Inclusive education—United States.   2. Classroom management—
    United States.   3. Behavior modification—United States.
    4. Academic achievement—United States.   5. Social skills—Study and
    teaching—United States.   I. Title.   II. Series.
    LC1201.R38   1999
    371.9'046—dc21
                                                                98-34856
                                                                CIP

About the Author

♦

Natalie Rathvon, PhD, is a clinical psychologist and school consultant in private practice in Maryland and the District of Columbia and an assistant clinical professor of psychology at George Washington University. She provides staff development and consultation services to a variety of schools and agencies, including the Archdiocese of Washington Schools, the Response-ability Teacher Service Program, and the Capital Children's Museum Options Public Charter School, where she serves as chair of the board of trustees. She is the author of *The Unmotivated Child: How to Help Your Underachiever Become a Successful Student* and numerous articles on school-based consultation and counseling services.

Preface

◆

Today's schools are struggling to cope with an increasingly diverse student population and an increasing number and proportion of students with learning and behavior problems. At the same time, special education services are undergoing a revolution, spurred by burgeoning enrollments and a growing body of research documenting the unreliability of the diagnostic and placement process, the overidentification of students, limited positive outcomes, and the failure of traditional assessments to provide meaningful help to teachers. As special education delivery systems shift from a refer–test–place to a refer–consult–intervene paradigm, the number of placements available to serve these children is being drastically reduced. Moreover, with the growth of the Regular Education Initiative (REI) movement, which emphasizes educating mildly disabled children in the mainstream, children previously placed in special education are returning to the regular classroom.

These developments have created a tremendous need for interventions that can help children with learning and behavior problems achieve success in the regular classroom. In the early days of special education, there was little emphasis on designing classroom strategies that could prevent students from being labeled and placed in pull-out remedial programs. In fact, placement in special education *was* the intervention. Today, the majority of states now require or recommend prereferral interventions before students can be considered for special education services, and many districts are implementing school-based intervention assistance teams to provide leadership roles in this effort.

Although school psychologists, special education teachers, counselors, and social workers are endeavoring to help teachers cope with the greater diversity among students, these professionals often have little training in consultation, much less in the process of designing, implementing, and evaluating school-based interventions. Moreover, as students' needs increase, so do the skills required for effective school consultation. Today's school consultants need much more than a few behavior modification techniques directed toward a single ineffectively behaving child. They need information about a broad range of strategies that can enhance teachers' capacity to create productive learning environments and students' capacity to benefit from instruction. In particular, they must be knowledgeable about strategies that can be used effectively with an entire classroom group but still accommodate diverse learners.

Although the last two decades have witnessed the publication of many useful, empirically validated interventions in the professional literature, these interventions are relatively inaccessible to busy practitioners, who have little time to sift through the ever expanding array of journals and books to find a strategy that matches the problem they are attempting to solve. Even if practitioners locate an intervention targeting the problem, other obstacles to implementation remain. Because of space limitations, interventions in these resources are seldom described in sufficient detail to permit effective implementation. Moreover, all too many interventions are so time-consuming, costly, or complicated that they are impractical for regular classroom teachers. As a result, consultants wishing to try out a particular strategy must first locate the original research article or text and then attempt to adapt the intervention to the exigencies of the classroom environment. Given these constraints, it is not surprising that even when prereferral interventions are attempted, consultants tend to rely on a limited range of strategies, and teachers often report that the referral problem remains unsolved.

Effective School Interventions: Strategies for Enhancing Academic Achievement and Social Competence is designed to bridge the gap between research and the practical realities of consulting in today's schools by providing a handbook of empirically based interventions that have been translated from the original source and adapted to the realities of the regular classroom environment. Each of the 76 interventions is presented in a brief, standardized format that provides step-by-step implementation procedures to facilitate treatment integrity and maintenance. Designed specifically for use within a consultation framework, the format has been developed and refined in the context of numerous staff development workshops, intervention assistance team meetings, and teacher consultation sessions. To meet the increasing demand for accountability in educational programming, each strategy includes an evaluation component that provides several different methods of assessing effectiveness. The interventions have been undergoing field testing for several years in the Archdiocese of Washington, DC, Schools and other public and private schools, with modifications based on feedback from teachers, administrators, counselors, students, and parents.

This book is designed to serve not only as a one-volume handbook in its own right but also as a resource guide to the rapidly expanding field of school-based interventions. In addition to the citations for the selected interventions, each chapter includes an annotated list of supplementary readings to assist consultants in locating other useful materials. This book is written for practitioners in school psychology, child clinical psychology, regular and special education, counseling, educational administration, and school social work, and for graduate or preservice students in those disciplines. It should be particularly useful to school psychologists, special education resource teachers, and intervention assistance teams responsible for designing accommodations for diverse learners and mildly disabled students in the regular classroom. It is also intended to serve as a resource for practitioners who conduct psychological and psychoeducational evaluations of children and adolescents. Using this book, they can locate interventions targeting a wide variety of referral problems and discuss those interventions in the recommendation sections of their reports, thus enhancing the instructional relevance of their assessments. The utility of this aspect of the book has been field tested for several years with George Washington University clinical psychology predoctoral students conducting school-based assessments as part of their training program.

The book consists of five chapters. Chapter 1 presents an overview of the recent developments in special education delivery systems and introduces the intervention assistance approach to helping diverse learners achieve success in the regular classroom. It also describes the criteria used to select interventions, the intervention format, targets of interventions, and suggestions for using the book. Emphasis is placed on an ecological, proactive approach to problem solving and the use of group-oriented interventions that can improve the functioning of entire classes rather than case-centered strategies focused on individual students. Chapter 2 describes guidelines for maximizing the success of intervention assistance programs; steps in the intervention assistance process; legal and ethical considerations in selecting, implementing, and evaluating interventions; issues in reinforcement selection; and strategies for evaluating intervention effectiveness. Two case examples are presented to illustrate how several interventions can be combined to create a comprehensive assistance program for an individual student or an entire class.

Chapters 3, 4, and 5 present the interventions. In keeping with the book's ecological perspective, the chapters follow a logical progression from proactive classroom management strategies to academic interventions to behavior management strategies. Chapter 3 presents 14 proactive interventions designed to create a productive, disruption-free classroom environment. Initial use of these strategies, which promote high levels of student engagement, should reduce the need for subsequent interventions addressing poor academic performance and disruptive behavior, which often result from ineffective instructional and behavior management systems. The chapter begins with descriptions of two basic methods of assessing the learning environment. Interventions target six key classroom management tasks: (1) organizing the classroom environment; (2) establishing classroom rules and procedures; (3) managing transitions; (4) managing independent seatwork; (5) communicating competently with students; and (6) teaching prosocial behaviors.

Chapter 4 presents 38 interventions designed to improve academic performance and includes an introduction to curriculum-based measurement for use in evaluating intervention effectiveness. Intervention targets include academic productivity (classwork and independent seatwork); homework; and performance in four academic areas (reading, mathematics, written language, and the content areas of social studies and science).

Chapter 5 presents 24 interventions targeting student behavior and social competence. Sections include strategies for increasing on-task behavior and reducing disruptive behavior; interventions for special classes and less structured situations, such as the media center, recess, and the lunchroom; and interventions to decrease verbal and physical aggression and increase cooperative behavior.

Acknowledgments

◆

I would like to express my sincere appreciation to the authors, journal board members, and publishers for permitting me to adapt their work into the intervention format and to all of the authors cited in this book for their contributions to the field of school-based interventions. My thanks go also to Sharon Panulla, former senior editor at The Guilford Press, for her support and assistance throughout the process of preparing this book.

I would also like to thank the educators, mental health professionals, and graduate students who have participated in the field testing of the interventions included in this book. I acknowledge with gratitude the ongoing support provided by the Archdiocese of Washington Catholic Schools Office, including Larry Callahan, superintendent; Trudy Sampangaro, assistant superintendent; Marcella Schraml, director of professional development; Mary Anne Stanton, former director of professional development; and Sister Delia Dowling, executive director of the Center City Consortium. I owe a special debt of gratitude to the Center City Catholic schools, especially to Sister Owen Patricia Bonner, principal of Holy Name School; Sister Carol Ann Knight, principal of Immaculate Conception School; William Eager, principal of St. Anthony's School; and Sister Brenda Cherry, principal of St. Benedict the Moor School, and their faculties for their efforts during the piloting of the Intervention Assistance Teams and for hosting George Washington University graduate students and psychology interns from the District of Columbia Commission on Mental Health in practicum placements.

I also wish to thank Jackie Lacinski, director of the Response-ability Teacher Service Program, which places recent college graduates in inner-city parochial schools across the country and in the Dominican Republic and Chile, and those inspired and inspiring new teachers. My appreciation also goes to the counselors of the Christ Child Society School Counseling Program, which serves the Center City parochial schools, and to its director, Susan Ley. Special thanks go to counselor Josie Rattien, who has served on two Intervention Assistance Teams since their inception, and to former counselor Dana Czapanskiy, who first suggested that I explore consultation projects with the parochial schools. My thanks also to the staff and trainees at Northwest Family Center in Washington, DC, especially its acting director, Aminah Moore, for her leadership in school-based mental health services in the District of Columbia public schools. I also want to express my appreciation to the faculty and students of The George Washington University's Department of Psychology, especially Robert Holmstrom, Department Chair; Rolf Peterson, Director of Clinical Training; and David Silber, Meltzer Center Director.

  Finally, my gratitude now and always to my husband, James—a loving and secure base for all of my life's endeavors.

Contents

♦

CHAPTER 1 **Introduction**   1
Challenges Facing Today's Educators   1
The Intervention Assistance Movement   6
Criteria Used to Select Interventions   10
Intervention Format   14
Targets of Intervention   16
How to Use This Book   17
Supplementary Readings   18

CHAPTER 2 **The Intervention Assistance Approach to Solving**   20
Classroom Problems
Guidelines for Maximizing the Success of Intervention
  Assistance Programs   21
Steps in the Intervention Assistance Process   23
Legal and Ethical Considerations in Selecting,
  Implementing, and Evaluating Interventions   35
Selecting Reinforcers for Interventions   40
Evaluating Intervention Effectiveness   44
Intervention Case Examples   54
Supplementary Readings   57

CHAPTER 3 **Proactive Interventions: Strategies That Create a**   60
Productive, Disruption-Free Classroom Environment
Overview   60
The Importance of Proactive Classroom Management   61

Evaluating the Effectiveness of Proactive Interventions   63
Assessing Available Instructional Time, 64; Assessing
Student Engagement Rates, 67
Proactive Classroom Management Interventions   68
Promoting On-Task Behavior with a Circular Desk
Arrangement, 71; Active Teaching of Classroom
Rules, 74; Say Show Check: Teaching Classroom
Procedures, 76; Teaching Transition Time, 78;
Speeding Up Transitions: Beat the Buzzer, 80;
Peer-Monitored Transitions, 82; Checking Stations, 86;
The Coupon System: Decreasing Inappropriate
Requests for Teacher Assistance, 88; The Study Game:
Improving Productivity during Seatwork, 90; Improving
Achievement and Behavior with Contingent Praise, 94;
Short, Soft, and Close: Delivering Effective
Reprimands, 99; Promoting Positive Behavior through
Attribution, 102; Problem-Solving Student
Conferences, 104; Sit and Watch: Teaching Prosocial
Behaviors, 108
Supplementary Readings, 111

CHAPTER 4   *Interventions to Improve Academic Performance*   113
Overview   113
Targets of Academic Interventions   114
Evaluating the Effectiveness of Academic Interventions   115
Interventions to Improve Academic Productivity   117
The Daily Assignment, 119; Classwide Peer
Tutoring, 122; Join the Team: Reciprocal Peer Tutoring
to Raise Achievement, 126; Increasing Academic
Performance by Reinforcing Correct Answers, 128;
Winning the Recess Game: Raising Class Averages
with a Free-Time Contingency, 131; Stop the Clock:
Improving Productivity during Small-Group
Instruction, 133; Improving Academic Productivity
with Performance Feedback, 136; Self-Monitoring to
Improve Work Completion, 138; Encouraging Academic
Achievement with Principal Praise, 140
Interventions to Improve Homework Completion   143
Improving Homework Submission with School–Home
Notes, 144; Improving Homework Compliance with
Public Posting and Group Contingencies, 150;
Self-Managed Teams to Monitor Homework, 152;
Self-Instruction to Improve Homework Completion, 155

Interventions to Improve Reading Performance   158
    Curriculum-Based Oral Reading Probes, 161; *Repeated*
    Readings, 165; *Listening Previewing,* 168; *Peer*
    Tutoring in Sight Words, 171; *Reconciled Reading,* 175;
    Group Story Mapping, 177; *Using Story Grammar to*
    Aid Comprehension, 181; *Story Retelling,* 183
Interventions to Improve Mathematics Performance   186
    Curriculum-Based Mathematics Probes, 188; *Cover,*
    Copy, and Compare: Increasing Math Fluency, 191;
    Improving Math Performance with Explicit Timing, 194;
    Reciprocal Peer Tutoring to Improve Math
    Achievement, 195; *Improving Math Performance with*
    Reciprocal Peer Tutoring and Parental Involvement, 199;
    Improving Math Completion Rates and Accuracy with
    Free Time, 204
Interventions to Improve Written Language
    Performance   206
    Curriculum-Based Spelling Probes, 208; *The Peer*
    Tutoring Spelling Game, 210; *Increasing Spelling*
    Performance with Group Contingencies, 214;
    Curriculum-Based Written Expression Probes, 217;
    Increasing Writing Productivity with Self-Monitoring, 219;
    Peer Editing, 222; *Improving Writing Revision Skills by*
    Monitoring Comprehension, 226; *Composition Strategy*
    Development in Writing, 229
Interventions to Improve Social Studies and Science
    Performance   233
    Improving Social Studies Homework Compliance with
    the Tic–Tac–Toe Game, 236; *Improving Understanding*
    of Textual Material in Social Studies with a Critical
    Thinking Map, 238; *Improving Participation in Social*
    Studies Classes, 243; *Using Cover, Copy, and Compare*
    to Improve Geography Accuracy, 246; *Improving Science*
    Test Grades with Public Posting, 249; *Using Response*
    Cards to Improve Participation and Achievement in
    Science, 251
Supplementary Readings   254

CHAPTER 5 ***Interventions to Modify Behavior and Enhance***   256
    Social Competence
    Overview   256
    Evaluating the Effectiveness of Behavioral Interventions   257

Interventions to Increase On-Task Behavior and Reduce
Inappropriate Behavior in the Classroom   258
  *The Good Behavior Game, 260; Red Light/Green Light, 263;
  The Good Behavior Game Plus Merit, 266; The Response
  Cost Raffle, 269; Countdown to Free Time, 272; Public
  Posting to Decrease Disruptive Behavior, 275; The Star
  Chart, 277; Using Peer Monitors to Improve On-Task
  Behavior, 279; Reducing Disruptive Behavior with Self-
  Managed Response Cost, 282; Self-Managed Behavior
  Ratings, 284; Reducing Rule Violations with Good Day
  Awards, 288; Enhancing the Effectiveness of School–
  Home Notes with Response Cost, 291; Group Contingencies
  to Reduce Stealing, 295*
Interventions to Improve Behavior in Special Classes and
Less Structured Situations   296
  *Charting to Improve Behavior during Specials, 298;
  Improving Media Center Behavior with the Good
  Behavior Game, 301; Reducing Aggressive and
  Inappropriate Behavior in Physical Education Classes with
  Sit and Watch, 303; Eliminating Disruptive Lunchroom
  Behavior with Mediation Essays, 302; Brag Sheets:
  Improving Behavior during Rest Time, 309*
Interventions to Decrease Verbal and Physical Aggression
and Increase Cooperative Behavior   314
  *Using Verbal Instructions to Reduce Aggressive
  Behavior, 318; Decreasing Inappropriate Verbalizations with
  a Peer Confrontation System, 321; Increasing Cooperative
  Behavior with Sharing Time, 323; Reinforcing Cooperative
  Play for Preschoolers, 325; Using DRL to Decrease
  Negative Verbalizations, 328; Decreasing Inappropriate
  Verbalizations with a Group Timeout Ribbon, 330*
Supplementary Readings   333

REFERENCES   335

INDEX   358

EFFECTIVE SCHOOL INTERVENTIONS

CHAPTER 1

♦♦♦

Introduction

♦

Joseph is a 7-year-old second grader. His teacher reports that his oral reading is slow and hesitant, and he has trouble remembering new vocabulary. Over the course of the year, Joseph has become more inattentive and unproductive, especially during reading instruction and independent seatwork. He often fails to complete his classwork, complains that school is "boring," and is falling behind the other students. His teacher worries that he will be unable to cope with the demands of the third-grade curriculum.

The students in Mr. Allen's seventh-grade social studies class have always been talkative, but recently they have become noisier and more unruly. Each day it takes them several minutes to settle down before Mr. Allen can begin the lesson, and even then, some students continue talking and joking among themselves for most of the period. The teacher also notices that the class as a whole is becoming less productive. Many students turn in their homework late or fail to complete it at all. Although Mr. Allen has talked with the seventh graders several times about the importance of behaving appropriately and completing homework, these discussions have had little impact on their behavior or academic performance. Requiring the most disruptive students to serve afterschool detention has also failed to solve the problem.

CHALLENGES FACING TODAY'S EDUCATORS

As school consultants know all too well, today's teachers are encountering increasing numbers of students who, like Joseph and the seventh graders, have problems with academic performance, behavior, or both. In recent years, there has been a dramatic increase in the needs and diversity of the student population, especially in what have been called the "new morbidities," such as substance abuse, depression, family violence, teen pregnancy, low motivation, and truancy (Reynolds, Wang, & Walberg, 1987). Whether these students are termed mildly disabled, difficult-to-teach, or at-risk, they fail to respond to traditional instructional and management methods and perform poorly as a result. How can school consultants help teachers improve the capacity of these students to succeed in school?

Failure of Special Education Programs to Meet Student Needs

At the same time that schools are facing increasing numbers of difficult-to-teach students, an accumulating body of research is questioning the effectiveness of the special education programs that were designed to help them (Carlberg & Kavale, 1980; Gartner & Lipsky, 1987; Gerber & Semmel, 1984; Kavale, 1990; Madden & Slavin, 1983; Reynolds et al., 1987). Criticism of traditional special education delivery systems has focused on five major problems: (1) a lengthy, costly, and unreliable referral, diagnosis, and placement process; (2) the overidentification and misidentification of students; (3) limited positive outcomes for students; (4) lack of meaningful assistance for teachers; and (5) an internal deficit approach to student problems.

Lengthy, Costly, and Unreliable Referral, Diagnosis, and Placement Process

Current special education procedures for referring, assessing, and placing students in special education programs are time-consuming, expensive, and lack reliability and validity, especially for learning disabilities and other mildly handicapping conditions (Carter & Sugai, 1989; Reschly, 1988; Ysseldyke, Thurlow, et al., 1983). Teachers' decisions to refer students are arbitrary and idiosyncratic, depending as much on the characteristics of the teacher as on those of the child (Christenson, Ysseldyke, Wang, & Algozzine, 1983; Gerber & Semmel, 1984; Pugach, 1985; Ysseldyke & Thurlow, 1984). Precious material and human resources are devoted to identifying and classifying children rather than to developing interventions to solve the referral problem (Curtis, Zins, & Graden, 1987). On the contrary, rather than searching for solutions, special education decision-making teams tend to search for pathology (Sarason & Doris, 1979), and the milder the problem, the more they test (Algozzine, Ysseldyke, & Hill, 1982). Moreover, many of the assessment measures commonly used in the diagnostic process have been criticized for their poor reliability and validity (Galagan, 1985; Reschly, 1980, 1988; Ysseldyke, Thurlow, et al., 1983).

Even the most psychometrically sophisticated instruments, such as the Wechsler scales, are designed to be used for making decisions about classification, not decisions about interventions (Thurlow & Ysseldyke, 1982).

In addition, the special education decision-making process itself lacks reliability, in large part because of the lack of consensus as to what learning disabilities (LD) are and how to identify them. After 5 years of researching the referral, assessment, and placement process for LD, Ysseldyke and his colleagues concluded that the current criteria for determining eligibility for LD services fail to discriminate learning-disabled from low-achieving students (Ysseldyke, Algozzine, Shinn, & McGue, 1982) and that there is no empirically defensible way to classify students as LD (Ysseldyke, Thurlow, et al., 1983).

Overidentification and Misidentification of Students

A second criticism of current special education practices is the identification and placement of too many nondisabled students (Algozzine, Ysseldyke, & Christenson, 1983). The problem of overidentification is particularly acute for the mildly disabled categories, where categorical differentiation is unreliable (Edgar & Hayden, 1984–1985; Reynolds et al., 1987; Ysseldyke & Christenson, 1988; Ysseldyke, Thurlow, et al., 1983), and as many as 85% of normal students can be classified as learning disabled using one or more of the current operational definitions (Ysseldyke, Algozzine, & Epps, 1983). Moreover, African-American students are overrepresented in classes for the educable and trainable mentally retarded and the seriously emotionally disturbed and are assigned to these categories at twice the rate that would be expected, based on their proportion in the population (Chinn & Hughes, 1987).

The rush to placement began after the implementation of Public Law 94-142 in the 1970s, when funding based on specific handicapping categories encouraged the identification of students as disabled to receive additional educational services. Teachers were thus reinforced for referring students for special education programs and came to expect that a referral would result in placement (Ysseldyke, Thurlow, et al., 1983; Zins, Curtis, Graden, & Ponti, 1988). As a result, children who could have been accommodated in the mainstream have been placed in pull-out programs, and resources that could have been used to help teachers work more effectively with students in the regular classroom have been depleted by the costly referral process and the creation of a second, separate educational system. Despite the criticisms leveled at special education practices, the number of children in special education has increased dramatically in recent years, especially in programs for mildly disabled students (Gartner & Lipsky, 1987; Reynolds et al., 1987).

The burgeoning number of referrals of difficult-to-teach children for special education services has also been fueled by the recent emphasis on higher standards in general education and by pressures for accountability for students and staff alike generated by national educational assessments and reports (Gentile, 1992; Mullis, Campbell, & Farstrup, 1993; Mullis, Dossey, Owen, & Phillips, 1993; Mullis & Jenkins, 1988; National Commission on Excellence in Education, 1983). Thus, at the same time that more students are having difficulty achieving success, higher academic standards, in response to national reform movements in education, have created an increasingly narrow definition of what constitutes normal or "regular" and intensified pressure on teachers to move more rapidly through more complex curricula, often leaving the difficult-to-teach students behind (Gartner & Lipsky, 1987; Lipsky & Gartner, 1987; Shepard, 1987).

Limited Positive Outcomes for Students

A third criticism of traditional special education programs has centered around their failure to achieve positive outcomes for many, if not most, of the students they were designed to serve. Studies (Carlberg & Kavale, 1980; Glass, 1983; Madden & Slavin, 1983) reviewing the efficacy of special education have failed to demonstrate that it has achieved its original goal of helping disabled youngsters catch up with their nondisabled peers and return rapidly to the mainstream. On the contrary, most children who enter special education programs stay for long periods of time, many for the rest of their educational careers (Clarizio & Halgren, 1993; Lipsky & Gartner, 1987; Stainback & Stainback, 1984). The goal of providing instruction specifically tailored to student needs and differentiated from that of the mainstream has also been unrealized. Information collected during the assessment process fails to ensure that students placed in special education will receive instruction that differs significantly from that received by regular education students (Ysseldyke & Thurlow, 1984). Observational studies have found few meaningful differences in the nature of instruction or learner involvement between disabled versus nondisabled students and among students with different categorical labels (Ysseldyke, Christenson, Thurlow, & Bakewell, 1989).

Lack of Meaningful Help for Teachers

A fourth criticism that has been leveled against traditional special education delivery systems is their failure to assist classroom teachers. As Reschly (1988) has observed, "The gravest difficulty with current assessment practices is the near total emphasis on eligibility determination and the relatively little emphasis on interventions" (p. 464). Because current psychoeducational assessment procedures are useful for categorical deci-sion making rather than designing interventions, special education evalua-tions often provide little instructionally relevant information for teachers (Thurlow & Ysseldyke, 1982; Ysseldyke & Christenson, 1988; Zins & Bar-nett, 1983). In fact, assessments are so lacking in instructional utility that despite the time and resources already consumed in the diagnostic process, special education teachers typically administer another series of tests for use in instructional planning when students are placed in resource or pull-out programs. The situation for children who are tested but found ineligi-ble for services is bleak. Because assessment reports often provide few sug-gestions for teachers about how to improve students' academic or social competence, no classroom interventions may be implemented on their be-half (Graden, Casey, & Christenson, 1985). Whatever problems prompted their referral are likely to remain unaddressed. Moreover, because of the lengthy nature of the special education referral process, much of the school year may have passed since the initial teacher request for assistance, limiting the time still available for designing, implementing, and evaluat-ing the effects of interventions in the regular classroom.

An Internal Deficit Approach to Student Problems

Finally, the use of categorical labels and placement in special education programs outside the mainstream has reinforced the belief that the prob-lem resides within the child alone rather than in the interaction between the child's characteristics and the characteristics of the systems in which the child functions, including the classroom, peer group, school, and com-munity (Gerber & Semmel, 1984; Pugach, 1985; Skrtic, 1991). Research demonstrates that teachers (Christenson et al., 1983; Medway, 1979) and school psychologists (Alessi, 1988) alike overwhelmingly attribute the cause of student problems to deficits in the child or problems in the family rather than to variables in the classroom. The attribution of problems to internal student deficits rather than to classroom or other school-related factors strengthens the notion that regular education teachers are power-less to remediate those problems. As long as teachers attribute student problems to factors beyond their control, they are likely to continue to re-fer difficult-to-teach students at high rates rather than attempt to imple-ment instructional or behavior management interventions prior to referral (Christenson et al., 1983; Zins et al., 1988).

The Revolution in Special Education Delivery Systems

Dissatisfaction with traditional special education practices and the recog-nition that the increasing numbers of at-risk students cannot be served by the current system have created a revolution in special education from a refer–test–pull-out placement model of service delivery to one that focuses on instructional and behavioral consultation. Spurred by a series of major reports and position statements from government and professional agencies (e.g., National Association of School Psychologists/National Coalition of Advocates for Students, 1985; National Coalition of Advocates for Students, 1987; Will, 1986, 1988), school districts are placing greater emphasis on including students with disabilities in the regular classroom and providing services to students without categorical labels or pull-out programs. As a result, many students with learning, behavior, and emotional problems are returning to the classroom, while other difficult-to-teach students are not being removed at the rates of previous years. If school consultants are to meet the challenges posed by this revolution, they will need expertise in helping teachers create effective instructional environments that promote academic productivity and appropriate social behavior for an increasingly diverse student population. In particular, they will need information about the process of designing, implementing, and evaluating interventions and about a broad range of strategies useful for classroom application (Elliott, Witt, & Kratochwill, 1991; Reschly, 1988).

THE INTERVENTION ASSISTANCE MOVEMENT

The combination of this special education paradigm shift and the growing diversity and needs of the student population has led to the increasing use of school-based intervention assistance programs (IAPs). IAPs are based on a consultation model of service delivery designed to help teachers provide interventions within the regular classroom to help difficult-to-teach students become more successful. Although this form of consultative assistance was originally described as a *prereferral intervention model* (Graden, Casey, & Christenson, 1985), the term *intervention assistance program (IAP)* is used in this book to dispel the notion that classroom interventions occur only in conjunction with referrals to special education. When consultation services are delivered by a school-based team rather than an individual consultant, that team is referred to as an *intervention assistance team (IAT)* (Zins et al., 1988).

Current Status of Intervention Assistance Programs

In recent years, IAPs have become widespread, with a majority of state education agencies now requiring or recommending interventions prior to referral for special education (Carter & Sugai, 1989; Wood, Lazzari, Davis, Sugai, & Carter, 1990). Several IAP approaches based on collaborative consultative models of service delivery have been developed with the goal of meeting the needs of difficult-to-teach students in the regular classroom. These models fall into two general categories, depending on whether special education personnel are involved. Teacher assistance teams (TATs; Chalfant, Pysh, & Moultrie, 1979; Hayeck, 1987) were developed as an alternative to traditional inservice training programs. TATs differ from other intervention assistance approaches in that these groups do not usually include nonteaching staff, such as administrators or special education personnel, and function primarily as informal peer support and self-help groups for teachers.

The second category of collaborative problem-solving models, which originated in the work of Graden and her associates (Graden, Casey, & Bonstrom, 1985; Graden, Casey, & Christenson, 1985) at the University of Minnesota's Institute of Research on Learning Disabilities, emphasizes a formal, data-based process of behavioral consultation. In these IAPs, special educators serve as individual consultants to regular classroom teachers or as members of a multidisciplinary team to design, implement, and evaluate interventions to assist students with learning or behavior problems (e.g., Fuchs, Fuchs, & Bahr, 1990; Idol, 1993; Rosenfield & Gravois, 1996). The primary goal of these IAPs is to increase teachers' ability to deal effectively with students in general education and thus prevent inappropriate special education referrals and placements.

Characteristics of Intervention Assistance Programs

Although there are several different models of IAPs, they share a set of core characteristics. First, they create a collaborative problem-solving process at the school level designed to provide consultative help to teachers. Because assistance is provided through indirect services to teachers rather than direct services to students, larger numbers of children can be helped. Second, they facilitate compliance with the least restrictive environment (LRE) principle of Public Law 94-142. Instead of labeling children and removing them from the regular classroom, IAPs seek to strengthen the capacity of regular education teachers to meet the needs of diverse learners in the mainstream. Third, IAPs serve both remedial and preventive functions. In addition to providing interventions on behalf of students already experiencing academic or behavior problems, they have the potential to reduce the need for special education placements and prevent future problems by enhancing teacher competence in creating effective instructional and behavior management systems (Fuchs, Fuchs, Gilman, et al., 1990; Zins et al., 1988).

Fourth, in contrast to the internal deficit attributions implicit in traditional special education practices, IAPs are based on an ecological perspective that views student problems as arising from the characteristics of the teacher, classroom, peers, curriculum, and other variables in addition to the characteristics of the child and the home environment. Such an ecological perspective is empowering for teachers because many of the factors influencing student performance are under their control. As a result, IAPs not only expand the context for analyzing the causes of student problems but broaden the range of possible solutions to those problems. In fact, IAPs have tremendous potential to shift the focus of teachers and other educators from searching for pathology in individual students to designing and implementing environmentally based strategies that can improve the functioning of entire classroom groups (Curtis et al., 1987).

Fifth, IAPs emphasize finding solutions rather than diagnosing problems. In the traditional special education paradigm, when a student experienced difficulty in the classroom, efforts were directed toward answering the question, "Is this student handicapped and if so, by what condition?" With the intervention assistance approach, the question becomes, "What can be done to help teachers improve the performance of this student in regular education?" (Flugum & Reschly, 1994). Assessment now focuses on gathering information for use in designing interventions, not classifying student problems as one of a group of "pathological" disorders. Finally, rather than requiring a lengthy referral and assessment process, IAPs provide immediate assistance to teachers. As soon as teachers make a referral, individual consultants or school-based teams can offer consultative help to address the problem, strengthening the preventive aspects of IAPs (Fuchs, Fuchs, Gilman, et al., 1990).

Studies of the Effectiveness of Intervention Assistance Programs

An increasing body of evidence supports the efficacy of IAPs in reducing the numbers of students referred for special education evaluations (Chalfant & Pysh, 1989; Graden, Casey, & Bonstrom, 1985; Graden, Casey, & Christenson, 1985; Fuchs, Fuchs, & Bahr, 1990; Fuchs, Fuchs, Bahr, Fernstrom, & Stecker, 1990; Gutkin, Henning-Stout, & Piersel, 1988; Ponti, Zins, & Graden, 1988) and improving teachers' attitudes toward diverse learners (Fuchs, Fuchs, & Bahr, 1990; Fuchs, Fuchs, Gilman, et al., 1990). To date, however, relatively few studies (Fuchs, Fuchs, Bahr, et al., 1990; Fuchs, Fuchs, Gilman, et al., 1990; Fuchs, Fuchs, Harris, & Roberts, 1996) have documented that IAPs produce measurable gains in student performance.

Moreover, despite the increasing use of IAPs and their potential for improving teacher effectiveness and student functioning, several studies have reported problems in the delivery of these alternative services. First, the interventions offered to teachers are frequently low in quality and lack variety (Flugum & Reschly, 1994; Fuchs & Fuchs, 1989). In a survey of 41 general education teachers in Kansas (Harrington & Gibson, 1986), only 5% believed that intervention assistance teams provided them with any new intervention ideas. Moreover, teams tend to emphasize recommendations that focus on factors outside of the classroom, such as individual counseling or temporary placement in resource rooms (Meyers, Valentino, Meyers, Boretti, & Brent, 1996).

Second, IAPs are often unable to assist teachers in solving referral problems. In the Harrington and Gibson (1986) survey, approximately half of the teachers reported that the intervention assistance team was unable to help them solve the referral problem, and only half indicated that they would continue referring students to the team. Success rates were similar in a survey of 201 regular classroom teachers in a large southeastern school district (Brown, Gable, Hendrickson, & Algozzine, 1991). Of the teachers responding, 43% reported frequent success with the use of prereferral strategies, and 47% reported occasional success. Third, even when teams offer recommendations, teachers frequently fail to implement those recommendations in the classroom. According to Harrington and Gibson (1986), a sizable number of the teachers surveyed either made no effort to implement team recommendations (15%) or were unsure if they had done so (27%). Teachers at the junior and senior high school level are especially unlikely to implement interventions prior to referral (Brown et al., 1991). As Sindelar, Griffin, Smith, and Watanabe (1992) have observed, "Regardless of the quality of the plan that the team develops, its implementation by the classroom teacher remains the most crucial step of the process" (p. 255).

Finally, a common problem among IAPs is the lack of systematic evaluation to determine whether interventions are effective in addressing referral problems. Intervention assistance teams spend too little time gathering and reviewing information to help define problems and move too rapidly to discuss intervention alternatives (Meyers et al., 1996). Once interventions have been implemented, teams and teachers alike often fail to employ objective evaluation procedures to assess changes in student performance (Bahr, 1994; Flugum & Reschly, 1994; Fuchs & Fuchs, 1989; Harrington & Gibson, 1986; Meyers et al., 1996; Ysseldyke, Pianta, Christenson, Wang, & Algozzine, 1983). Without collecting and analyzing data to document intervention effects, consultants and teachers will be unable to determine which, if any, strategies are successful in producing positive gains in student performance.

Many of the problems associated with IAPs are in all likelihood related to consultants' and teachers' lack of knowledge of effective school-based interventions. In a national survey of state directors of special education, Wood et al. (1990) found that approximately 25% of states requiring or recommending prereferral interventions failed to provide training in specific intervention strategies for professionals responsible for developing and implementing those strategies. Only three states reported that prereferral intervention training was provided for regular educators at the preservice level by universities and colleges. Training for school consultants is also lacking. In a survey of 210 National Association of School Psychology members, respondents rated their training in intervention skills as highly inadequate (1 on a scale of 1 to 10; McKee, Witt, Elliott, Pardue, & Judycki, 1987).

To help meet the need for information in this critical competency, this book includes a wide variety of empirically validated interventions that have been adapted to the exigencies of the regular classroom environment and presented in a teachable format specifically designed for use in consultation sessions, staff development workshops, and intervention assistance team meetings. Appropriately selected, implemented, and evaluated, classroom interventions offer the potential of meeting the major goals of IAPs: reducing inappropriate placements in special education and, by enabling teachers to meet a broader range of pupil needs, enhancing the education of all students.

CRITERIA USED TO SELECT INTERVENTIONS

The interventions included in this book were located by searching data bases, journals, and books in the consultation, behavioral sciences, and teacher effectiveness literature. The strategies have been modified from their original sources to facilitate implementation in regular education settings. In cases in which an intervention has been substantially modified and presented in a subsequent study, both sources have been cited, and the most effective and practical features of each version have been retained. In a number of cases, elements of several related strategies have been combined to create a single intervention (e.g., *Short, Soft, and Close: Delivering Effective Reprimands; Improving Homework Compliance with Public Posting and Group Contingencies; Red Light/Green Light*). The seven criteria used to select interventions for inclusion in this book are described below.

Documented Evidence of Effectiveness

Only interventions with empirical evidence of efficacy in improving the behaviors they were designed to address were considered for inclusion. This meant that the original source had to include some systematic method of documenting concrete, observable changes in student performance. Many studies employed single-subject designs, such as ABAB, reversal, alternating treatments, or multiple baseline methods, using data from direct classroom observations of behavior, or academic measures, such as classwork accuracy or homework completion rates. A sizable number of the interventions have been replicated or adapted across various subjects and settings, providing additional evidence of their effectiveness.

Consistent with an Ecological Perspective

Focusing on internal child deficits as the sole cause of ineffective student behavior provides little information or direction for designing classroom interventions. In contrast, an environmentally based approach that views student problems as arising from student–environment mismatches not only expands the analysis of factors that may be contributing to those problems but also yields a broader range of targets for classroom-based interventions (Johnson, Stoner, & Green, 1996). In keeping with an ecological perspective, the interventions are designed to be minimally intrusive so that they can be implemented in regular classroom settings without singling out individual students or unduly disrupting instructional and management routines. Interventions that require major alterations in classroom organization and procedures or cumbersome reinforcement delivery systems are unlikely to become integrated into regular education routines or to have the desired effects on student performance (Witt, 1986; Witt, Martens, & Elliott, 1984). Instead, interventions have been selected that capitalize on the human and material resources already present in school ecosystems, including teachers, peers, administrators, and the regular curriculum. Several interventions involving parents are also included, but these, too, are designed to require minimal alterations in either parents' or teachers' current routines.

Emphasis on a Proactive Approach to Classroom Problems

Priority has been placed on strategies that help teachers create learning environments that prevent problems from occurring rather than on strategies that are applied after problem behavior has already occurred. Many published interventions have focused on contingency management, that is, the manipulation of consequences to control behavior. In contrast, proactive strategies emphasize manipulating antecedents, that is, modifying the classroom environment to promote high levels of student engagement and thus prevent academic failure and disruptive behavior. An entire chapter is devoted to proactive management strategies drawn from the teacher effectiveness literature and interventions with proactive features that have been adapted from research in the behavioral sciences. Another chapter consists of strategies that were originally designed to enhance academic performance but also have the potential to reduce the likelihood of inappropriate behavior resulting from student frustration at lack of success with school tasks.

Capable of Classwide Application

Traditional case-centered consultation approaches directed at a single ineffectively behaving student are of limited utility in helping teachers become more effective problem solvers (Witt & Martens, 1988). Instead, given the growing diversity of the student population, teachers need strategies that enhance the academic performance and social competence of entire classes of students. Moreover, when a teacher refers an individual student because of some learning or behavior problem, consultants often discover that the problem extends beyond the referred child to several students or to the class as a whole. Although the teacher is focusing on one student, the referred child's dysfunctional behavior is embedded within an ineffective organizational, instructional, or behavior management system that is interfering with the optimal performance of many or all of the children in that classroom.

In keeping with this group-oriented perspective, interventions have been selected that were either originally designed to be implemented on a classwide basis or could be readily adapted to that format while at the same time accommodating mildly disabled students within that group. Thus, rather than focusing on a single student, they target entire classes or the classroom environment as a whole. Group-focused strategies have several advantages over interventions directed at one child. First, they are efficient in terms of time and labor, especially in classrooms with more than one ineffectively behaving child. Second, they avoid the problem of singling out individual students for either positive or negative attention. Third, group strategies are more acceptable to teachers, who often complain that it is unfair to allocate special attention to one student at the expense of others (Elliott, Turco, & Gresham, 1987). Finally, by incorporating peer influence into the intervention, they are especially effective in modifying group behavior (Crouch, Gresham, & Wright, 1985).

Capable of Being Easily Taught through a Consultation Format

Interventions requiring large amounts of consultant or teacher time to ensure accurate implementation are unlikely to find their way into consultants' repertoires or teachers' routines, regardless of their documented effectiveness in solving the target problem. For this reason, only interventions that can be quickly and easily taught to teachers in a consultative setting have been included. Strategies whose implementation or evaluation procedures as described in the original source were unclear or overly complicated have been modified to enhance their practicality and facilitate a high degree of treatment integrity. The format used for all the assessment methods and interventions presented in this book has been designed specifically for use in consultation sessions. Interventions judged to be so complex that modifications to accommodate the realities of the regular classroom would have substantially altered the nature or effectiveness of the original strategy were excluded from consideration.

Capable of Implementation Using Regular Classroom Resources

All the interventions in this book can be delivered by regular classroom teachers using resources that are already present in the typical classroom or can be prepared with minimal cost and effort. Even the most carefully designed intervention will fail to remediate a problem if it is never implemented in the classroom. Teachers are much more likely to use interventions that are relatively simple to implement and require little time and few material resources (Elliott, Witt, Galvin, & Peterson, 1984; Witt & Martens, 1983; Witt, Martens, & Elliott, 1984). In addition, because involving more than one treatment agent is likely to result in lower treatment integrity (Gresham, 1989), strategies requiring the participation of more than one teacher were either modified or excluded. Thus, classwide peer tutoring and reciprocal peer tutoring, which are designed for implementation in a single classroom, have been included, but cross-age peer tutoring, which matches students from different grade levels, has been omitted. For similar reasons, most interventions with a home-based component had to be excluded. Although school–home strategies often appear in the literature, many require a substantial investment of teacher and consultant time for accurate implementation, target only one or a small group of students, and even then, sometimes fail to achieve the desired outcome (e.g., Budd, Leibowitz, Riner, Mindell, & Goldfarb, 1981). Here, only the simplest school–home interventions that were originally designed for classwide application or could be readily adapted to that format have been selected.

Strategies requiring substantial additional human or material resources, such as extra staff, special services personnel, or supplementary curricular materials, or requiring the removal of students from the regular classroom were also modified or excluded. This eliminated individual and small-group training or counseling programs, as well as commercially published academic enhancement, social skills, or behavior management curricula. This criterion also reflects the goal of intervention assistance programs of enhancing the capacity of regular classroom teachers to meet the needs of difficult-to-teach students rather than relying on special services personnel or supplementary curricular programs. A surprising number of interventions had to be eliminated from consideration because they involved significant expenditures for equipment or materials. A notable example is an intervention that rewarded positive student behavior with time playing an electronic "pong" machine and a commercial electronic pinball machine (Robinson, Newby, & Ganzell, 1981). Interventions using money as a reinforcer were also eliminated or modified to incorporate other kinds of rewards. Although money can have a powerful effect on behavior, at least temporarily (e.g., Kelley & Stokes, 1982; Shapiro & Goldberg, 1986), classroom strategies based on money are unacceptable to many teachers, who consider the money to be a bribe for appropriate behavior. Moreover, most teachers and consultants lack access to school funding that would permit the regular use of monetary rewards.

Capable of Being Evaluated by Reliable, Valid, and Practical Methods

To meet the increasing demand for accountability in school psychology and special education services (Gresham & Kendell, 1987; Shapiro, 1987; Zins & Fairchild, 1986), the interventions in this book target concrete, observable behaviors that can be objectively measured over time. In addition to the evaluation procedures described in Chapter 2, each intervention includes at least two and as many as five different methods of gathering information on baseline performance and evaluating intervention effectiveness. Observational and evaluation measures are designed to be as practical as possible so that they can be easily implemented by regular classroom teachers or school consultants. Although efforts have been made to match the methodology of the original sources as closely as possible, evaluation procedures have been modified for many interventions to accommodate the exigencies of the regular classroom setting and to approximate more closely the typical data-gathering methods of regular classroom teachers. Moreover, because many of the interventions were originally directed at only one student or a small group of students, observational and evaluation methods suitable for classwide application have been substituted for or added to the individually focused methods for these strategies.

INTERVENTION FORMAT

The remainder of this book consists of 76 interventions grouped into three chapters (Chapters 3, 4, and 5) that present proactive, academic, and behavioral strategies, in that order. Each intervention has been adapted from the original source or sources into a uniform, structured format designed to be as brief and nontechnical as possible while still including sufficient detail for accurate implementation and reliable evaluation. All of the materials required for implementation, such as samples of student notes and parent letters for school–home interventions, have been included. The format is designed to facilitate the intervention assistance process in consultative and staff development settings and has been extensively field tested in numerous workshops, teacher consultations, and intervention assistance team meetings. The eight components of the intervention format are described below.

Overview

The overview provides a brief description of the intervention, a rationale for its use, and a summary of the anticipated results.

Purpose

This component presents the specific purpose or purposes of the intervention in terms of concrete, observable student behaviors.

Materials

This component lists all of the material resources required for successful implementation. Many interventions require minimal materials, such as posterboard for classroom charts, and some require no material resources at all. For contingency-based strategies, suggestions for tangible or activity reinforcers are included in the procedure component.

Observation

The observation component presents methods of obtaining baseline measures of the target behavior(s) for use in analyzing the nature and extent of the problem. At least two and as many as five different data-gathering strategies are included for each intervention, varying along a continuum of complexity from naturally occurring classroom assessments, such as grades, to observational methods that require special recording forms, examples of which are provided in Chapter 2. Although emphasis is placed on measures that gather information about target behaviors for an entire classroom, methods for observing the behavior of a small group of students that can be readily adapted to single-subject observations are also included for many interventions.

Procedure

This component provides step-by-step implementation procedures. In many cases, procedures have been amplified or modified from those in the original studies to enhance clarity, practicality, and nonintrusiveness. Every effort has been made to accommodate the realities of the regular classroom environment without sacrificing treatment efficacy.

Evaluation

The evaluation component describes a variety of measures that are linked to the baseline assessments described in the observation component. Teachers or consultants can use one or more of these methods to obtain reliable, objective information for assessing the relative effectiveness of the interventions that have been implemented.

Variations

This component describes one or more intervention variations. Some of these variations consist of adaptations of additional experiments or variations presented in the original source, whereas others have been developed during the field testing. By providing additional intervention alternatives for consultants to offer to teachers, these variations increase the likelihood that some of the suggested strategies will be acceptable and will be implemented in the classroom.

Notes

The notes component describes implementation issues or problems, if any, reported by the original authors or observed during field testing, along with suggestions for overcoming those problems. Other notes reflect the reactions and recommendations of the teachers, parents, administrators, graduate students, and pupils who participated in the field testing.

TARGETS OF INTERVENTION

The organization of chapters, presenting proactive interventions first, then academic interventions, and finally behavioral interventions, is intended to underscore the book's ecological perspective that views student ineffective behavior as often resulting from inadequate classroom management, lack of success with academic tasks, or both. Because of the interrelated nature of human behaviors, however, the categorization of interventions is necessarily artificial. Every proactive intervention is designed to set the conditions for high levels of academic responding and low levels of off-task and disruptive behavior. Similarly, academic interventions have the potential of enhancing positive social behavior because active academic responding is incompatible with misbehavior. Moreover, improving academic competence is likely to reduce student frustration and foster positive attitudes toward school. Finally, behavioral interventions designed to reduce classroom disruptions can increase instructional time and make students more available for learning.

HOW TO USE THIS BOOK

From the perspective of this book, school-based interventions should emphasize building academic and social competence rather than simply reducing negative behavior. Readers are therefore encouraged first to consider the proactive strategies presented in Chapter 3 when selecting interventions to address problems. Properly implemented, these strategies can create a classroom environment that maximizes opportunities for high levels of academic productivity and positive behavior and minimizes the need for interventions to remediate learning or behavior deficits. Readers may also use the table of contents and index to locate strategies for specific targets, such as homework completion, reading vocabulary, or disruptive behavior during special classes. Chapter 2 presents strategies designed to maximize the success of intervention assistance programs, including guidelines for selecting reinforcers, evaluating interventions, and developing intervention "packages" to address classroom problems. An annotated list of supplementary readings is provided at the end of each chapter to direct readers to additional resources in the consultation and intervention literature.

Cautions

As school consultants know only too well, no intervention works equally well with every student, with every teacher, or in every situation. Intervention selection should be a collaborative effort between consultant and teacher, or, in the case of intervention assistance teams, among team members and referring teachers. Parent involvement is also an important element in enhancing intervention effectiveness. In contrast to traditional school–home communication systems that simply provide parents with information, often negative information, about children's performance, the intervention assistance approach actively encourages parent participation in analyzing and solving problems. Finally, whether consultants are working with individual teachers, school-based teams, or parents, they can enhance their own acceptability and effectiveness by offering a variety of empirically based intervention alternatives for consideration and facilitating the decision-making process rather than advocating a particular strategy. Thoughtful selection, accurate implementation, and careful evaluation and followup enhance the likelihood that interventions will be successful in addressing target problems, but as in any area of human endeavor, no guarantees are possible.

SUPPLEMENTARY READINGS

Barnett, D. W., & Carey, K. T. (1992). *Designing interventions for preschool learning and behavior problems*. San Francisco: Jossey-Bass.

Written from an ecobehavioral perspective, this book presents a framework for designing interventions for preschoolers who are difficult to teach, are difficult to parent, or have peer relationship problems. Emphasis is placed on research-based interventions that can be used in natural settings with individuals or small groups of children.

Cohen, J. J., & Fish, M. C. (Eds.). (1993). *Handbook of school-based interventions: Resolving student problems and promoting healthy educational environments*. San Francisco: Jossey-Bass.

This book presents nontechnical summaries of research articles describing interventions with demonstrated or potential utility for school application. Interventions are included for the areas of classroom management, externalizing responses, internalizing responses, cognitive and social competence, peer relationships, relationships with adults, and health management. Commentaries at the end of each summary provide suggestions for extending interventions and enhancing effectiveness.

Graden, J. L., Zins, J. E., & Curtis, M. J. (Eds.). (1988). *Alternative educational delivery systems: Enhancing instructional options for all students*. Washington, DC: National Association of School Psychologists.

This edited volume is organized into three parts: (1) the need for alternative delivery systems for special education and at-risk students, (2) frameworks for alternative delivery systems, and (3) strategies for facilitating the change process. Seven chapters review intervention practices, including classroom management, direct instruction, reading, peer-mediated, learning strategies, behavioral, and social interventions.

Maher, C. A., & Zins, J. E. (Eds.). (1989). *Psychoeducational interventions in the schools: Methods and procedures for enhancing student competence*. New York: Pergamon Press.

This edited collection of articles covers a wide variety of intervention domains, including prereferral intervention programs, substance abuse prevention, peer-mediated academic interventions, school-based counseling, interventions for discipline problems, social skills training, behavioral self-management, and crisis intervention.

Stoner, G., Shinn, M. R., & Walker, H. M. (1991). *Interventions for achievement and behavior problems*. Silver Spring, MD: National Association of School Psychologists.

This is a one-volume, state-of-the-art guide to intervention-oriented school psychological services. The book is divided into six sections: an introduction to the interventionist approach; evaluation issues; general intervention strategies regardless of age and grade; interventions for target areas by level (preschool, elementary, and secondary); interventions for specific problems; and training issues.

Zins, J. E., Kratochwill, T. R., & Elliott, S. N. (Eds.). (1993). *Handbook of consultation services for children: Applications in educational and clinical settings*. San Francisco: Jossey-Bass.

Articles by national leaders in the field summarize current theoretical, practical, and research perspectives on child consultation. Sections review conceptual foundations and approaches; the consultation process; methods of evaluating consultation process and outcome; applications in schools, hospitals, the community, and the business sector; and training issues. Included are appendices listing books on human service consultation and special issues of journals devoted to consultation.

CHAPTER 2

♦♦♦

The Intervention Assistance Approach to Solving Classroom Problems

♦

> "I tried what you suggested, and it didn't make any difference."
> "I can't do all that for just one child! What about the other 24 students in my classroom?"
> "I already tried everything, and nothing works. He needs to be in special education."

How many times have school consultants heard these kinds of comments as they attempt to help teachers deal with difficult-to-teach students? How can consultants maximize the likelihood that teachers will implement appropriate interventions to assist students with learning or behavior problems and do so with accuracy? To be successful in helping teachers create productive, disruption-free classrooms, today's school consultants must be familiar with a wide variety of strategies designed to improve classroom behavior, academic performance, and social competence. At the same time, however, knowledge of effective, research-based interventions is a necessary but insufficient component of the complex process of creating positive change in classrooms. On the contrary, it is only one of a broad range of skills that school consultants must possess if they are to be able to use their expertise in ways that are genuinely helpful to teachers and students. To be effective, consultants must be astute observers of individuals, groups, and systems; skilled problem solvers; and tactful diplomats, capable of matching interventions not only to the needs of students but also to the classroom ecology, including the needs and style of the teacher and the various systems within which that teacher functions.

Curtis et al. (1987) have identified four sets of skills that are needed to implement a consultative service delivery model: (1) problem solving, (2) communication and human relations, (3) content expertise, and (4) systems analysis and change strategies. Although the emphasis in this book is on content expertise, even consultants armed with an array of empirically validated strategies will be unsuccessful if they cannot apply their knowledge to everyday classroom problems, communicate with teachers, administrators, and support personnel, and negotiate among the interrelated systems of classroom, school, home, and community. The importance of communication and interpersonal skills in the intervention assistance process cannot be underestimated. The personality of the consultant is inevitably the medium for interactions between consultant and teacher, so that the teacher may reject an intervention offered by one consultant but accept the identical strategy when it is suggested by a different consultant. Readers are encouraged to explore the supplementary readings at the end of this chapter that review other important consultation competencies. The following guidelines are designed to maximize intervention assistance success and are drawn from the consultation and intervention literature and observations from the field testing.

GUIDELINES FOR MAXIMIZING THE SUCCESS OF INTERVENTION ASSISTANCE PROGRAMS

Guideline 1: Understand Teachers' Perspectives on Student Problems

Much has been written about teacher resistance to consultation in general and to classroom interventions in particular (Friend & Bauwens, 1988; Harris & Cancelli, 1991; Piersel & Gutkin, 1983; Wickstrom & Witt, 1993; Witt, 1986). Dealing effectively with teacher resistance begins with understanding teachers' perspectives on student problems and their past history of reinforcement for referring students for special education services. As noted earlier, teachers tend to attribute student problems to internal, dispositional causes or to home factors that they believe they have no power to remediate (Brophy & Rohrkemper, 1981; Medway, 1979). If problems are viewed as arising from the characteristics of the child or the child's home environment, it makes little sense for teachers to attempt to modify their current instructional or behavior management systems in an effort to improve the child's performance. Instead, it is more logical from teachers' perspective to seek assistance in removing the "sick" child from the "healthy" classroom or persuading the family to obtain treatment at some agency outside of the school. Teachers are therefore likely to refer a child with the goal of removing the student from the classroom rather than implementing interventions that will enable that student to remain.

Another factor contributing to teacher resistance to school-based interventions is teachers' expectations based on traditional special education practices. When teachers refer students, past experience has taught them to expect that most of those children will be tested and placed in a special education program. They do not expect that they are going to be asked to alter their classroom routine to accommodate a student for whom they believe that they have already tried everything. As a result, teachers may resist implementing interventions or fail to implement them as planned and then declare these interventions unsuccessful (Gutkin & Curtis, 1990; Ysseldyke, Christenson, Pianta, & Algozzine, 1983). In addition, because of school psychologists' traditional role as assessors of individual children, teachers have come to view them as the gatekeepers of special education services. If consultants offer interventions rather than testing as solutions to student problems, teachers may initially view an intervention assistance program (IAP) as preventing students from accessing needed services. Consultants can also inadvertently contribute to teacher resistance by failing to acknowledge teachers' previous efforts to address student problems. Equipped with a knowledge of interventions and the desire to be helpful, consultants may initiate the problem-solving process too soon, making recommendations prematurely to overwhelmed teachers and unwittingly increasing their feelings of ineffectiveness. Sometimes listening empathically to a frustrated teacher's concerns is the most helpful intervention a consultant can offer.

The best strategy for addressing teacher resistance to IAPs is educating teachers, administrators, and parents about the purpose of IAPs and the manner in which they function, a process that is likely to extend over the first several years of implementation. Before teachers can fully invest in the IAP approach, they may have to experience its utility in their own classrooms. Because success reduces resistance, consultants participating in the development of IAPs should make every effort to work first with teachers who request assistance and to focus on problems that appear solvable. Teachers who have positive results with intervention assistance approaches are likely to share their experiences with their fellow teachers, thus increasing program acceptability (Ponti et al., 1988). On the other hand, no news spreads faster than a failed consultation, and even a single failure can solidify teacher resistance (Conoley & Conoley, 1992).

Despite the obstacles to teacher acceptance of IAPs, adopting an ecological approach to student problems can be empowering for consultants and teachers alike. When problems are ascribed not solely to the child's characteristics but to mismatches between the child's needs and the characteristics of the learning environment, the consultant's role is no

longer that of helping an ineffective teacher obtain an out-of-class placement for a dysfunctional child with a teacher with greater expertise (the
special education teacher). Instead, the consultant's task is to enhance the
referring teacher's professional skills by helping that teacher create a more
effective instructional environment, not only for the referred student, but
for all of the students in the classroom.

Guideline 2: Be Prepared to Take an Active Part in Intervention Design, Implementation, and Evaluation

School consultants seeking to help teachers accommodate diverse learners in the regular classroom must be prepared to provide support with
many aspects of the intervention assistance process. Although the teacher
must implement the strategy, the consultant should be available to provide hands-on assistance in the form of demonstrations, modeling, and
observing during the implementation phase. Unfortunately, busy consultants often focus on presenting an intervention and neglect to provide followup support for teachers' efforts to modify their instructional or behavior management practices. Because research indicates that teachers seldom make systematic efforts to evaluate changes in student behavior after
classroom interventions have been introduced (Ysseldyke, Pianta, et al.,
1983), consultants should be available to help collect accountability data.
Although the observation and evaluation methods for the interventions in
this book have been designed to be as simple as possible without sacrificing reliability and validity, even the simplest observation can be more easily performed by someone other than the teacher, who must be continually responding to the multiple demands presented by students and the
routines of everyday classroom life. For this reason, consultants are encouraged to offer assistance in gathering baseline data and evaluating intervention effectiveness, especially when initiating a consultative relationship.

Active participation by consultants in the intervention assistance
process also helps to ensure accurate implementation. Many interventions
are characterized as ineffective and discarded prematurely because they
were never correctly implemented in the first place. For example, after the
author conducted a workshop presenting a variety of interventions designed to reduce disruptive behavior, a teacher implemented *The Good Behavior Game Plus Merit*, a strategy that provides group rewards for positive
student behavior. Several weeks later, the teacher reported that the intervention had been unsuccessful in improving the behavior of her unruly
students. During a subsequent classroom observation and consultation session, the author discovered that the teacher had not only failed to specify
the desired positive behaviors but had never delivered any rewards, prob-

lems that could have been detected and resolved if an observation had been conducted during the initial implementation phase.

Guideline 3: Encourage Administrators to Support Teachers in Implementing Classroom Interventions

Administrator support has repeatedly been identified as critical to the success of consultation and IAPs (Bossard & Gutkin, 1983; Chalfant & Pysh, 1989; Harrington & Gibson, 1986; Kruger, Struzziero, Watts, & Vacca, 1995). In fact, a teacher's failure to use an intervention may reflect a perceived lack of support from administrators or the community rather than discomfort with the intervention itself (Broughton & Hester, 1993). Consultants should make every effort to encourage the building principal to participate in planning and implementing IAPs. Principal participation in staff development programs presenting the IAP and reviewing classroom interventions is especially important. In addition to demonstrating administrative support for teachers, principal involvement in training activities ensures that administrators are exposed to the same set of learning experiences as are teachers and thus are able to reinforce teachers' efforts to apply what they have learned (Allen & Forman, 1984).

Consultants can also promote principals' investment in IAPs by expanding their role in the intervention process itself. This book includes a strategy (*Encouraging Academic Achievement with Principal Praise*) in which the principal serves as the primary reinforcing agent for academic productivity or positive social behavior. Principal-delivered attention is included as a reinforcer for variations of several other interventions (e.g., *Promoting Positive Behavior through Attribution; Red Light/Green Light*). In addition, some interventions, such as *Problem-Solving Student Conferences* and *Eliminating Disruptive Lunchroom Behavior with Mediation Essays*, can be delivered by principals as well as by teachers. Including the principal as an active participant in interventions not only capitalizes on the influence of the most powerful individual in the school but can also increase administrator commitment to IAPs by providing opportunities for the principal to assume a positive rather than punitive role with students.

Guideline 4: Use a Variety of Staff Development and Consultation Formats to Provide Training in the Intervention Assistance Process and Specific Classroom Interventions

Lack of training for teachers has been repeatedly identified as a major barrier to successful implementation of IAPs (Bahr, 1994; Brown et al., 1991; Meyers et al., 1996). Given the time constraints of the typical consultation session and intervention assistance team meeting, consultants need to explore a variety of formats for providing information to teachers about the intervention assistance process and specific interventions for solving common referral problems. Options include preservice and inservice staff development programs, small-group workshops, small-group consultation, and individual consultation. Training during preservice days is a particularly good alternative because teachers have not yet established classroom routines and expectations. Even a single half-day or full-day preservice workshop, supplemented by a followup workshop during the fall semester, can have significant positive effects on teachers' classroom management skills and on student achievement and behavior throughout the entire school year (Evertson, 1985, 1989b; Evertson, Emmer, Sanford, & Clements, 1983). Workshops that include small-group activities not only provide opportunities for teachers to share effective strategies for enhancing student achievement and behavior with their colleagues but can also increase staff cohesion and collaborative problem solving. Providing opportunities for collaboration among regular and special education teachers is especially important, because their schedules often give them little time to interact during the school day.

When intervention assistance teams serve as the delivery system for an IAP, the consultant's role in staff development training becomes more diverse. Consultants can meet with teams to provide information about alternative interventions to address common referral problems, demonstrate specific strategies, and conduct workshops on topics identified by the teams as priorities for student and teacher needs. Training for team members in consultation, team-building, and IAP implementation will also need to be provided.

Suggested Sequence for IAP Implementation

Based on field testing and the IAP literature (e.g., National Association of School Psychologists, 1986; Zins et al., 1988), the following sequence for implementing an IAP at the building level is recommended.

Step 1: Administrative Support. Whether the IAP is being developed by an individual school or as part of a districtwide effort, obtaining administrative sanction at the appropriate levels is essential to its success. If consultants are unable to obtain full administrative support, achieving staff acceptance and participation is unlikely. Although an extended discussion of the IAP planning and development process is beyond the scope of this text, interested readers are invited to consult the supplementary references at the end of this chapter for further information on this aspect.

Step 2: Teacher and Parent Workshops. The next step in implementing an IAP should consist of an all-faculty workshop to introduce the consultant (if not a school-based staff member) and provide an overview of the IAP. Rather than presenting any one intervention in detail, this workshop should present a rationale for the IAP, goals, and anticipated outcomes. For schools developing an intervention assistance team (IAT) model, the workshop should introduce team members, describe times for team meetings and procedures for making referrals, and invite faculty questions and concerns. Presenting a typical student referral and using it as a case example to go through the IAP process step by step is the best way of making the IAP process meaningful to teachers. A similar, although less detailed, presentation sponsored by the PTA or Home–School Organization should be conducted to inform parents and enlist their support and participation. To ensure that all parents are aware of the IAP or IAT, a notice should also be placed in the school newsletter, with regular updates on program or team activities throughout the year.

Step 3: Needs Assessment. In this step, the consultant or school staff development committee collaborates with the principal and key staff members to prepare a needs assessment of topics for inservice training. The needs assessment can be distributed at the initial teacher workshop described above. Teachers are asked to rank order topics according to their degree of interest and to list additional suggestions for training. As part of the survey, teachers should be invited to share their knowledge about useful classroom strategies with their colleagues. Such an invitation helps to validate teachers' previous intervention efforts and encourages support for the IAP. The survey should also ask teachers to list their free times during the week to meet with the consultant or IAT members. A sample of a needs assessment survey for inservice topics is presented in Idol (1993). Results of the needs assessment can then be shared with the staff development committee or IAT members and used to plan training activities that support IAP goals.

Step 4: Small-Group Workshops and Individual Consultation. Although some principals prefer that every teacher attend every staff development workshop, supplementing all-faculty programs with small-group training for teachers who have expressed an interest in interventions addressing particular concerns is strongly recommended. Scheduling workshops for a few teachers is much easier than attempting to find times when the entire faculty can attend. Making workshops voluntary also helps to ensure that the participants are genuinely interested in learning about the interventions presented and increases the likelihood of classroom implementation. The best public relations tool for an IAP is a teacher who has successfully introduced a strategy into the classroom. Another effective option is to alternate classroom observation and consultation with individual teachers with small-group or whole-faculty workshops. In this format, the consultant observes in classrooms at the request of teachers and then presents relevant interventions in subsequent workshops. With this option, interventions can be directly targeted at observed classroom problems, thus continuing the needs assessment process throughout the school year and ensuring that training is relevant to teachers' concerns. Weekly or biweekly observations and individual consultations can be combined with monthly workshops, a format that lends itself to the typical staff development schedule in many districts.

Guideline 5: Be Creative in Finding Time for Consultation

Finding time to consult with teachers is a perennial problem faced by practitioners (Johnson, Pugach, & Hammitte, 1988; Marks, 1995; Rosenfield & Gravois, 1996). In many elementary schools, teachers do not have regular daily planning periods when they are free of the responsibility of supervising their students. More often, teachers have several free periods a week on different days while their students participate in physical education, art, or other "specials." Finding time to consult with teachers at the middle and high school levels can be even more difficult. Although teachers generally have one regular planning period per day, it can take days or weeks to find a time when all the staff responsible for a particular student or classroom group can meet together.

Scheduling consultation sessions can be even more problematic for consultants serving more than one building because their time allotted to a particular school may not coincide with any of a referring teacher's free periods. Although consultation sessions can be scheduled before or after school, teachers often have other duties or meetings at those times. Strategizing with administrators and staff to find time for teacher consultation is essential to the success of IAPs. If a teacher is experiencing problems with a student or classroom group, however, the principal also has a problem, and principals are often willing to arrange for support staff to cover classes or to cover classes themselves to provide consultation time for teachers.

Eating lunch with teachers can create time for consultation, but problems of confidentiality arise if conversations about students can be overheard by other staff or pupils (Marks, 1995). Arranging to eat lunch with teachers in their classrooms on a day when they do not have lunch duty is a better alternative and can help create an informal, collegial atmosphere conducive to problem solving. Other strategies include doubling classes to free teachers for consultation time. For example, two classes can meet in the auditorium or media center for a presentation by a community resource speaker or a video presentation. Aides, support staff, or substitute teachers can also be used to cover classes so that teachers can meet with the consultant or attend IAT meetings. Rosenfield and Gravois (1996, p. 71) list 10 creative ways of finding time for consultation, including hiring a permanent substitute one day a week throughout the year.

Effective consultation takes time—time to observe in classrooms, talk with teachers, develop intervention plans, assist with implementation and evaluation, and provide followup support. A consultant who breezes through a school and rattles off intervention recommendations without first establishing a relationship with teachers making referrals for student or classroom problems is likely to be ignored initially and regarded as an intrusion ultimately. Regardless of the time constraints that beset every consultant, personal receptiveness and availability to assist teachers are very important. Consultants who appear harried and overwhelmed send out signals that they are too busy to listen to teachers' concerns and are unlikely to be approached for assistance (Rosenfield, 1987). Similarly, consultants who merely suggest strategies without taking time to provide help with implementation can undermine teachers' sense of self-efficacy and reinforce the notion that only "experts" can deal with difficult-to-teach children.

On the other hand, teachers can be tremendously creative in carving out time from a busy school day to talk with a consultant who appears to be genuinely interested in helping them solve classroom problems. Provided that the teacher and consultant can talk quietly together without being overheard, effective consultations can be conducted at recess, in the hall during class changes and restroom breaks, outside the building at dismissal time, and in the classroom while students are having snack breaks, resting, performing independent seatwork, or working in small groups. When teachers and administrators believe consultation to be valuable, they will find time for consultation where no time seemed available before.

Guideline 6: Make Intervention Design and Selection a Collaborative Effort

Teachers need to feel that they have ownership of the solution to the problem, not just ownership of the problem. The gap between what a consultant recommends and what the teacher actually implements in the classroom often arises from the fact that the consultant is the only party invested in the intervention. No intervention is effective in and of itself. It is an interactional process among the teacher, the student, the classroom and school environment, and the nature of the strategy itself. Consultants must bear in mind that, despite their good intentions, the helping process is not always helpful to the recipient. In some situations, help can actually undermine recipients' competence and control by implying that they are incapable of solving problems on their own or by creating confusion about who should receive the credit or blame for the outcomes of the help (Coates, Renzalgia, & Embree, 1983).

Consultants who have no teaching experience may fail to realize how intimidating the intervention assistance process can be to teachers or how vulnerable teachers can feel when their best efforts to help students become successful learners seem ineffective. Discussing instructional and behavior management concerns with a group of colleagues, as in an IAT meeting, can be even more threatening, especially for veteran teachers, who are often less comfortable than beginning teachers in seeking assistance. Being observed in the classroom can also be a threatening experience for teachers. Although consultants may assure teachers that they are observing to assist rather than to evaluate, few of us enjoy being observed when we believe that our performance leaves something to be desired.

A collaborative approach to intervention design is also important because, although consultants are knowledgeable about interventions with documented efficacy in addressing the referral problem, teachers are experts on their own teaching strengths and weaknesses. A large part of a consultant's skill in the intervention assistance process lies in the ability to match interventions to a teacher's style and to the classroom ecology in which he or she functions. Rather than insisting that a particular intervention must be implemented, consultants can increase teachers' self-efficacy and investment in the intervention assistance process by suggesting several appropriate interventions from which to choose. The rapid disappearance of a university-sponsored IAP using a prescriptive consultation approach in which behavior contracts were the primary intervention (see Fuchs et al., 1996) may be due in part to the lack of flexibility in intervention selection.

Guideline 7: Offer Interventions That Balance Treatment Efficacy with Treatment Acceptability

Even an intervention with a documented history of effectiveness in solving the referral problem will be unsuccessful in improving student functioning unless the teacher implements it. Assessing treatment acceptability is therefore an important aspect of intervention selection. In addition to intervention efficacy, factors influencing intervention acceptability include the language with which it is described (Witt, Moe, Gutkin, & Andrews, 1984), the time and human and material resources required, and its ecological intrusiveness (Elliott, 1988; Witt, 1986; Witt & Elliott, 1985; Witt, Martens, & Elliott, 1984). In general, positive interventions, such as praise, token economies, and home-based reinforcement, are more acceptable than negative interventions, such as ignoring, response cost, and timeout (Elliott et al., 1984; Witt & Martens, 1983; Witt & Robbins, 1985). On the other hand, the more severe a student's problem, the more likely it is that any intervention will be considered acceptable (Martens, Witt, Elliott, & Darveaux, 1985; Witt, Martens, & Elliott, 1984). Treatment acceptability is also related to teaching experience. In general, highly experienced teachers find interventions less acceptable than do less experienced teachers (Witt, Moe, et al., 1984; Witt & Robbins, 1985).

Because ecological intrusiveness is a major factor in teacher resistance to interventions (Witt, 1986), consultants can enhance acceptability by matching interventions to teachers' existing classroom organization and procedures as closely as possible. For very overwhelmed teachers, interventions should be as simple as possible and require minimal modifications in current instructional and behavior management routines. Suggesting that a teacher with severe classroom management problems begin by implementing *Join the Team: Reciprocal Peer Tutoring to Raise Achievement,* an intervention that involves organizing the class into groups of four students and having them work collaboratively without direct teacher supervision, is likely to increase rather than solve those problems, at least initially. Moreover, the teacher would be likely to resist such a recommendation out of fear of losing control of the class.

Evaluating Intervention Acceptability

In matching interventions to teacher preferences and classroom ecosystems, consultants may wish to use one of several instruments that have been developed to assess intervention acceptability. The *Behavior Intervention Rating Scale* (BIRS; Von Brock & Elliott, 1987) is a 24-item scale that uses a 6-point Likert format to measure teachers' perceptions of treatment acceptability and the perceived effectiveness of classroom interventions. The BIRS has three factors (Acceptability, Effectiveness, and Time of Effect) and a Cronbach's alpha of .97 for the total scale (Elliott & Treuting, 1991). The BIRS has been used as a pretreatment measure of acceptability in analogue investigations (Elliott & Treuting, 1991; Von Brock & Elliott, 1987), as well as actual treatment programs (Sheridan, Kratochwill, & Elliott, 1990; Turco & Elliott, 1990).

In addition to assessing teacher acceptability of interventions, consultants may wish to measure students' reactions to classroom treatments. Thus far, only one published scale has been designed to assess children's judgments of treatment acceptability, the *Children's Intervention Rating Profile* (CIRP; Witt & Elliott, 1985). Written at a fifth-grade readability level, the CIRP is a seven-item, 6-point Likert scale of children's acceptability ratings. It has been validated on more than 1,000 students in grades 5 through 10 and used in several investigations to measure children's acceptability ratings for behavioral interventions (Elliott, Turco, & Gresham, 1987; Elliott, Witt, Galvin, & Moe, 1986; Shapiro & Goldberg, 1986; Turco & Elliott, 1986). Both the BIRS and CIRP are reproduced in Elliott et al. (1991).

Guideline 8: Assess and Maximize Treatment Integrity

Treatment integrity is the degree to which a planned intervention is implemented as it was intended. Assessing treatment integrity is important to help distinguish between interventions that are ineffective in addressing the target behaviors and those that are potentially effective but are inaccurately implemented (Gresham, Gansle, Noell, Cohen, & Rosenblum, 1993). Failure to assess treatment integrity is a common problem in the development and maintenance of IAPs. All too many practitioners employ what Gresham (1989) calls the "consult and hope" strategy, meaning that they consult with teachers and hope that teachers will implement interventions with integrity. As a result, teachers may implement an intervention inaccurately or inconsistently, only to report later to the consultant, "I tried what you suggested, and it didn't work."

A major threat to treatment integrity is the frequent failure of IAPs to develop written plans guiding implementation (Fuchs & Fuchs, 1989). Even in cases in which written plans are developed, treatment integrity is often assumed rather than assessed (Gresham, 1989). Unfortunately, building in adequate assessments of treatment integrity can greatly increase the complexity of the intervention design and the time required for implementation. Gresham estimates that three to five classroom observations of 20 to 30 minutes each are sufficient to provide a "reasonable" idea of treatment integrity. This means that an hour to an hour and a half of consultant or IAT member time may need to be devoted to assessing treatment integrity for a single intervention. Moreover, the presence of the consultant or IAT member in the classroom is likely to have some effect on teacher behavior, so that implementation may differ depending on whether observation is occurring. Gresham offers several suggestions for solving this reactivity problem: (1) spot checking on a random schedule, (2) observing as unobtrusively as possible, (3) observing without communicating that the purpose of observation is to assess treatment integrity and then providing feedback, and (4) using self-report or behavior ratings that do not require an observer's presence. Several methods of assessing treatment integrity for *The Response Cost Raffle*, including a direct observation form, a self-report measure to be completed by the teacher at the end of each day, and a behavior rating scale to be completed by the consultant after observing the entire intervention, are presented in Gresham (1989).

Strategies for Enhancing Treatment Integrity

The following recommendations for maximizing treatment integrity are drawn from Gresham (1989) and observations made during field testing.

1. Develop a written intervention plan that specifies implementation and evaluation responsibilities for participants and dates for reviewing the plan. Facilitate accurate implementation by providing detailed descriptions of interventions, supplemented by demonstrations, guided practice, and feedback.

2. Provide training for students as well as teachers in the intervention procedures. Consultants should demonstrate for teachers how to introduce an intervention to an entire class, a group of target students, or an individual student by means of a format similar to that in *Say Show Check: Teaching Classroom Procedures*. That is, teachers should first explain the purpose of the intervention; review and practice the intervention procedures, first with a few students and then with the entire class for a classwide strategy, or with the target student(s) for a small-group or individual strategy; and then provide positive feedback when students are following the procedures correctly. Specific training guidelines are also built into the procedure section of many interventions. Student training sessions are especially important for interventions that involve major changes in organizational and instructional systems, such as whole-class peer tutoring (e.g., *Classwide Peer Tutoring; Join the Team: Reciprocal Peer Tutoring to Raise Achievement; Peer Tutoring in Sight Words*) and strategies requiring disruptive students to move to a different location (e.g., *Sit and Watch: Teaching Prosocial Behaviors; Reducing Aggressive and Inappropriate Behavior in Physical Education Classes with Sit and Watch; Eliminating Disruptive Lunchroom Behavior with Mediation Essays*).

3. Build an observation component into the intervention plan to monitor treatment integrity and provide corrective feedback. Many interventions fail because teachers do not continue the strategies long enough to permit positive change to occur. Intervention research (e.g., Proctor & Morgan, 1991; Smith, Young, West, Morgan, & Rhode, 1988; Witt & Elliott, 1982) and field testing alike document that teachers have difficulty consistently consequating students for inappropriate behavior. Having a consultant or IAT member observe the teacher during the initial stage of implementation and providing feedback relative to this aspect can be critical to the ultimate success of an intervention.

4. Avoid complex and ecologically intrusive interventions that unduly disrupt current instructional and behavior management routines. Not surprisingly, treatment integrity is negatively associated with the complexity and time required to implement treatments (Gresham, 1989; Yeaton & Sechrest, 1981). The goal of any intervention is to increase teachers' pro-

fessional effectiveness in meeting student needs, not to increase teachers' burden in the classroom.

STEPS IN THE INTERVENTION ASSISTANCE PROCESS

The steps in the intervention assistance process described below are adapted from procedures developed during field testing and from several sources (Graden, Casey, & Christenson, 1985; National Association of School Psychologists [NASP], 1986; Zins et al., 1988) and are intended to apply to individual consultants as well as to IATs. Examples of forms for documenting IAPs can be found in NASP documents (1986) and Rosenfield and Gravois's (1996) book on consultation.

Stage 1: Problem Definition

1. *Requesting assistance.* The intervention assistance process begins with a request for help from a teacher to the consultant or a referral to the IAT. In the case of IATs, referrals are screened by the team chairperson to determine if all the necessary information has been included. If necessary, additional assessment information is obtained at this point. A record is maintained of the initial referral and subsequent parent conferences, consultation sessions, and/or IAT meetings.

2. *Conferring with parents and/or students.* In the case of an individual student, the referring teacher and the consultant or one or more IAT members meet with the student's parents (and the student, if appropriate) to inform the parents of the referral and invite parent and student assistance in analyzing the problem and generating possible solutions. Parents and groups of students may also be involved in the case of group or whole-class referrals.

3. *Clarifying the problem.* Collaborative problem solving between the teacher and consultant or IAT team members takes place to clarify the problem and define it in measurable terms. At the IAT meeting, members review the referral information and reach a consensus regarding the nature of the problem and the desired outcomes. The team develops a behavioral definition of the target behavior(s) and the desired outcomes. A case manager from the IAT is assigned at this point to serve as the major resource for the referring teacher for the remainder of the process and to assist with progress monitoring.

4. *Obtaining baseline data.* The referring teacher, consultant, and/or IAT members obtain one or more direct measures of the target behavior(s). These data are used to help define the discrepancy between the student's or group's current level of performance and the desired level of

performance. Data gathering may include a classroom observation by the consultant or IAT member.

Stage 2: Problem Analysis

5. *Conducting an ecological analysis of the problem.* The teacher and consultant and/or IAT members analyze factors that may be contributing to the problem, including student, peer group, classroom, curriculum, and home variables. Information obtained from parents and students is also analyzed in this step.

6. *Exploring alternative intervention strategies.* The teacher and consultant and/or IAT members explore alternative intervention strategies that may help reduce the discrepancy between current and desired performance. Students and parents are also involved in generating possible school- and home-based interventions. Strategies are evaluated for acceptability, efficacy, cost in terms of human and material resources, and closeness of match with classroom and home ecosystems.

7. *Selecting interventions.* One or more strategies is selected. Final intervention selection rests with the teacher and/or parent who will be responsible for implementing it.

8. *Clarifying implementation procedures.* Human and material resources needed for implementation are identified. A written intervention plan is developed that describes the selected strategy or strategies, the necessary material and human resources, and timelines for implementation. The plan clarifies the roles and responsibilities of the individuals involved in implementation, including teacher, parent, and/or student roles; assistance to be provided by the consultant, IAT members, and/or school staff; duration of the intervention; and strategies for evaluating effectiveness. The plan also includes a date for reviewing the effectiveness of the interventions in reducing the discrepancy between present and desired performance.

Stage 3: Plan Implementation

9. *Implementing the intervention plan.* The teacher and/or parent implement(s) the agreed-upon plan. Progress is monitored by the teacher with the assistance of the consultant or IAT case manager. Another classroom observation occurs at this point to assess treatment integrity and provide feedback and support.

Stage 4: Plan Evaluation

10. *Evaluating intervention plan effectiveness.* Postintervention performance is compared with baseline data. Additional evaluation data may be ob-

tained from the parent and student, if appropriate. If the plan is successful and no further assistance is needed, the case is closed, with followup consultation as needed. Records are kept to document outcomes.

11. *Continued problem solving and possible referral.* If the plan is not successful, another consultation session or IAT meeting date is set, at which time the referring teacher and the consultant or IAT members review the original plan and cycle through the process a second time. Additional information for use in solving the problem is obtained, and a date for review of the new plan is established. In the case of an individual student, when the teacher and consultant or IAT members agree that everything possible has been done and the problem is still not solved, the student is referred for a special education evaluation or for some other form of assistance. Signed parent permission is necessary at this stage. Data obtained from Stages 1 through 4 should be used in the evaluation, and, if the student is found eligible for special education services, to develop the Individualized Education Plan (IEP).

LEGAL AND ETHICAL CONSIDERATIONS IN SELECTING, IMPLEMENTING, AND EVALUATING INTERVENTIONS

Despite the increasing use of IAPs and IATs across the country, there has been surprisingly little discussion in the professional literature of the legal and ethical issues involved in the intervention assistance process. Nevertheless, consultants must take care that interventions provided through staff development, individual or small-group consultation, or IATs conform to federal and state regulations, local district guidelines, and the ethical principles and practice standards of relevant professional groups, such as the American Psychological Association (APA; 1981, 1992) and NASP (1992a, 1992b, 1992c). The major issues in this area include intervention targets, possible undesirable side effects, intervention efficacy, parental notification, documentation, evaluation, and provisions for referral for additional services if interventions are ineffective in solving the problem.

Intervention Targets

Ethical practice requires interventions to be directed toward building students' competencies and enhancing their capacity to benefit from instruction rather than focusing merely on reducing unwanted behavior (Winett & Winkler, 1972) or what Conoley and Conoley (1992) call "dead-person targets," meaning behaviors best performed by dead people, such as sitting still and being quiet. Moreover, an ecological perspective requires that targets should include not only student behaviors but environmental variables affecting student performance. The sequence of interventions in this book, beginning with strategies targeting the classroom environment, followed by interventions to enhance academic performance and finally interventions to reduce disruptive behavior and increase cooperation, is intended to emphasize the order in which targets should be considered.

Intervention targets should also be reviewed in terms of their *social validity*. Social validation is concerned with three basic issues central to the intervention process: (1) the social significance of intervention goals, (2) the social acceptability of the intervention procedures designed to achieve those goals, and (3) the social importance of the effects of the intervention (Gresham & Lopez, 1997; Wolf, 1978). For example, increasing on-task behavior may be less socially significant as an intervention goal than enhancing rates of academic responding because increasing on-task behavior does not necessarily result in higher student achievement. Gresham and Lopez present a 21-item semistructured teacher interview that assesses each of the three social validation concepts and can also be easily adapted for gathering information from parents on the validity of proposed intervention goals and procedures.

Possible Undesirable Side Effects

Many of the interventions in this book rely on group contingencies to enhance positive academic or social behavior. Although group contingencies can have powerful effects on student behavior and are usually more acceptable to teachers than individually based contingency programs, consultants should be aware of the potentially negative social consequences associated with some of these interventions. Because under certain group contingency systems, the poor performance of one student or a few students can result in the loss of rewards for an entire group, peer harassment may occur when these interventions are used (e.g., Bear & Richards, 1980). Consultants suggesting strategies that rely on group contingencies should advise teachers of this possibility and help them take preventive measures, such as modeling appropriate behavior during loss of privileges, selecting interventions with built-in opportunities to earn back lost rewards (e.g., *The Good Behavior Game Plus Merit*), and placing uncooperative pupils in a separate group so that their behavior does not reduce other students' chances to earn rewards. Other suggestions for dealing with possible group contingency problems are presented in the section on reinforcement issues below. Strategies for minimizing peer harassment are also provided in the Notes component of interventions for which this is a potential concern.

Intervention Efficacy

Early in the history of school-based interventions, consultants had limited access to empirically validated interventions and often relied on their own subjective judgment or personal repertoire of strategies. With the growing research base on effective interventions, however, consultants have a responsibility to use this information in recommending strategies that have demonstrated utility in addressing the referral problem. Indeed, part of their ethical responsibility is to make an effort to keep informed about a variety of interventions with solid empirical support of their effectiveness (Newman, 1993). The importance of considering efficacy in intervention selection is underscored by the recent NASP (1995) position statement on students with emotional/behavioral disorders, which stipulates that interventions for emotional and behavior problems should be empirically based and have documented effectiveness in dealing with the identified problems.

Parental Notification

Unfortunately, many local school districts have not developed explicit policies regarding whether parental permission is necessary for consultation or intervention assistance programs. When the consultant is a regular school employee, such as a school psychologist, written parental permission is generally not necessary to consult with teachers. Similarly, interventions that do not involve major changes in an individual student's regular educational program, especially classwide interventions that affect all of the students in a group equally, have usually been interpreted as not requiring parental notification or permission (Zins et al., 1988).

There are, however, several situations in which legal regulations or ethical practices require parental notification and/or permission. Questions and input from parents and the community should be encouraged when an IAP is first introduced at the building level. Parents should also be notified whenever a nonschool employee, such as an external consultant, will be providing consultation or intervention assistance services. This information may be provided through a notice in the school's newsletter, a letter from the principal, or a brief presentation at a PTA meeting. Moreover, if the consultant is not a school employee, written parental permission must be obtained for school staff to provide the consultant with personally identifying information about a student (Zins et al., 1988).

As noted above, parental permission is typically not required for interventions that affect all students in a class unless those interventions involve some unusual contingency. Written parental consent should always be obtained for interventions that involve providing additional services to a child, such as a psychological evaluation, counseling, or a major change in the child's educational program, especially if it involves removing the child from the classroom or treating the child differently from other students in some way. Even with classwide interventions, however, informing parents and soliciting their input and support can increase the effectiveness of academic or behavioral interventions (Brantley & Webster, 1993). An ecological perspective encourages involving parents, not only to obtain their permission for interventions but also to seek their assistance in collaborating to understand and solve problems. Several interventions in this book either invite parental participation or include parents as treatment agents (e.g., *Improving Math Performance with Reciprocal Peer Tutoring and Parental Involvement; The Daily Assignment*). For similar reasons, involving students in selecting target behaviors and designing interventions to address them is highly recommended, especially for students beyond the primary grade years.

Intervention Assistance Documentation

Documenting the intervention assistance process is important not only to provide accountability data regarding program or team activities but also to monitor the progress of the students being served (Ross, 1995). Interventions directed toward an individual student should be documented in that pupil's record, in a separate record of IAP activities, or both. If interventions are delivered through an IAT format, they should be documented in the notes for that team. An advantage of maintaining a separate set of IAP or IAT records is that all the data are together for use in program evaluation. If this latter option is selected, however, the 1974 Family Educational Rights and Privacy Act (FERPA; Public Law 93-380), also known as the Buckley Amendment, requires a brief note to be included in the student's record indicating where more detailed information may be found. Examples of forms for documenting IAP activities and interventions may be found in Fuchs et al. (1989), NASP (1986), Rosenfield and Gravois (1996), and Zins et al. (1988).

Consultants and IAT members should bear in mind that under FERPA, parents have access to essentially all of a child's school records, including records of classroom observations, consultations, and interventions. Exempted from this requirement are notes that remain the sole possession of the individual making them, are not shared with any other person, and are not used to make decisions about special education placements. If consultants share their notes with other personnel, such as teachers, principals, or IAT members, however, these notes are reclassified as educational records and become accessible to parents. Moreover, under the Education of All Handicapped Children Act of 1975 (Public Law 94-142), now the Individuals with Disabilities Education Act (IDEA; Public Law 101-476), parents have the right to review their child's records that have been collected as part of the special education decision-making process (Prasse, 1995).

If interventions are directed toward an entire class of students and do not involve major changes in educational programming, documentation in IAP or IAT records is probably sufficient in most districts, although notifying parents by means of a letter is recommended. Several interventions (e.g., *Improving Homework Submission with School–Home Notes; Brag Sheets: Improving Behavior during Rest Time*) include letters informing parents about the interventions and inviting their input that can be easily adapted for use with other strategies.

Evaluation

Ethical practice requires that consultants evaluate the effectiveness of the interventions they offer to ensure that students are being provided with optimal services. The importance of assessing intervention efficacy has been underscored by the NASP (1995) position statement on students with emotional/behavioral disorders, which states that interventions for emotional and behavior problems should include a plan to evaluate the effectiveness of those strategies in achieving the desired outcomes. In addition, the 1997 amendments to IDEA shift the emphasis of the legislation from simply providing services to students with special needs to evaluating the effectiveness of those services (Clay, 1998). Although consultants and teachers alike often fail systematically to collect accountability data in the intervention assistance process (Brown et al., 1991; Fuchs & Fuchs, 1989), their failure to do so means that they have no objective basis for determining the relative efficacy of the interventions that have been implemented. To facilitate accountability, all the interventions in this book include a variety of built-in strategies for evaluating their effectiveness, ranging from measures already in place in regular education classrooms, such as grades on homework and classwork, to observational methods for assessing the behavior of an entire classroom group.

Provisions for Referral for Additional Services If Needed

The intervention assistance process described in the previous section includes provisions for referring students for special education evaluations or other services if the interventions are not successful. Documenting interventions is important not only for assessing intervention effectiveness in improving the target behavior but also for maintaining a record of the strategies that have been implemented prior to referral for additional services. Including parents as participants in planning and evaluating the effectiveness of interventions not only facilitates home–school communication about student progress but also ensures that parents are kept informed of the intervention assistance process in the event that a psychological evaluation or another type of service is recommended at a later date.

SELECTING REINFORCERS FOR INTERVENTIONS

For many difficult-to-teach children, the usual rewards available in the classroom environment, such as grades and teacher praise, are insufficient to maintain appropriate behavior. As a result, many of the interventions in this book include some form of incentive to promote academic productivity and positive social behavior, such as public recognition by parents, teachers, or peers; opportunities to participate in team competitions; and material and activity rewards. Although reinforcers can contribute to a positive classroom climate and can be highly effective in motivating positive behavior change, there have been persistent concerns over the use of rewards in school settings, with some researchers suggesting that external reinforcement may undermine the intrinsic motivation to perform a task (Deci & Ryan, 1987; Levine & Fasnacht, 1974; Schwartz, 1990). According to this view, when individuals are reinforced for performing activities that they already enjoy, they lose the motivation to engage in the activity once the reward is withdrawn (Deci, 1971; Lepper, Greene, & Nisbett, 1973). Despite these concerns, the results of a recent meta-analysis (Cameron & Pierce, 1994) reviewing research on the influence of reinforcement on intrinsic motivation indicate that extrinsic rewards have no detrimental effects on intrinsic motivation in terms of willingness to work on tasks or attitudes toward those tasks. Negative effects are limited to situations in which external rewards are offered without requiring a particular standard of performance, and even in these cases, the negative impact on intrinsic motivation is minimal. Moreover, many classroom tasks, such as seatwork, which occupies the largest portion of the school day (Anderson, 1981; Durkin, 1978–1979), involve drill and practice activities that students often find boring. Finally, the interventions in this book that make use of incentive systems have been empirically demonstrated to be effective in enhancing students' academic productivity, achievement, or social behavior.

Despite the efficacy of rewards in promoting positive behavior, consultants should be aware of several potential pitfalls in implementing contingency-based interventions, including teacher resistance to the use of rewards, reward satiation, and delivery problems in situations in which only a subset of students in a classroom earns the reward.

Dealing with Teacher Resistance to Rewards

Although teachers have long used social reinforcers such as public recognition and praise to encourage academic productivity and appropriate behavior, some teachers are reluctant to implement interventions that involve delivering material rewards in the belief that such rewards constitute bribes for behaviors students should exhibit naturally. Resistance is especially likely if teachers are asked to implement strategies that provide rewards for only one or a few unproductive or disruptive students while appropriately behaving classmates are unrewarded. The interventions in this book avoid this problem because all the strategies are designed to be applied to an entire classroom group and, even for interventions that create intraclass team competitions, permit all teams to win and obtain the reward.

Another frequently encountered teacher concern relative to the use of material reinforcers is the amount of time and effort required to dispense rewards. Many of the behavior management programs described in the early intervention literature relied on elaborate token economies in which teachers administered tokens at frequent intervals to individual students while instruction was occurring and later delivered rewards in accordance with the number of tokens earned by each student. In contrast, the reinforcers for the interventions in this book were either originally designed or have been adapted to permit maximum ease of delivery and minimum disruption to ongoing instruction. In addition, a variety of material or activity rewards are suggested for these strategies, permitting teachers to select reinforcers that fit best into their own classroom ecologies.

Reducing Satiation Effects

A second potential pitfall for interventions involving reinforcement is reward satiation, in which rewards lose their ability to motivate behavior with continued use. There are several strategies that can reduce satiation effects. First, students can be involved in selecting rewards or privileges. Many of the interventions in this book that rely on tangible or activity rewards make use of a *Reinforcement Menu* to assess student preferences (see Figure 2.1). Additional examples of reinforcement surveys with open-ended, multiple-choice, and rank-order formats are presented in Raschke (1981).

Another strategy for reducing satiation effects is to make the rewards, the reward delivery schedule, or both, unpredictable. The element of unpredictability can be incorporated in a daily or weekly classroom reward structure by permitting students to draw from a grab bag or "surprise sack" containing a variety of small rewards, such as inexpensive school supplies,

REINFORCEMENT MENU

Directions: Below is a list of possible rewards our class could earn. Please circle the number that matches your level of interest in each reward. Your ratings will be used to help select the rewards.

	Level of interest		
Possible rewards	Low	Middle	High
Extra recess	1	2	3
Good note home	1	2	3
Classroom games	1	2	3
Special art project	1	2	3
Free time	1	2	3
Watching a video	1	2	3
Listening to tapes	1	2	3
Homework pass	1	2	3
Class computer time	1	2	3
Trip to school computer lab	1	2	3
Media center time	1	2	3
School supplies	1	2	3
Class field trip	1	2	3
Class party	1	2	3
Group games in gym	1	2	3

FIGURE 2.1. Reinforcement menu.

fast-food certificates, and wrapped candy. A variation of this procedure for delivering rewards at a later time involves filling the grab bag with slips of paper, each with a description of a reward written on it (e.g., *Stop the Clock: Improving Productivity during Small-Group Instruction*). A popular reward in this format is the "homework pass," a note exempting the student from homework in a particular subject for that day. Numbered slips of paper can also be used, with numbers designating various rewards. If a number system is used, posting a classroom chart that lists the rewards associated with each number not only facilitates efficient reward delivery but provides a visual reminder to students that positive behavior has positive consequences.

A third strategy to reduce reward satiation is to use a lottery in the context of a group contingency system, with eligibility to participate in the lottery based on satisfactory performance of the target behaviors. At the end of the day or week, the names of all students achieving the criterion are placed in a hat, one name is drawn, and the selected student receives the reward. This strategy not only enhances unpredictability and limits any expenditures on material rewards to a single student but is especially appropriate for rewards that involve reducing academic tasks, such as homework passes, because teachers are usually reluctant to permit entire classes or large groups of students to omit homework assignments (e.g., *Self-Managed Teams to Monitor Homework*).

Finally, using public recognition and relationship-based rewards rather than tangible rewards can help minimize reward satiation. Examples of recognition rewards include public posting of student performance (e.g., *Improving Academic Productivity with Performance Feedback*), parental recognition through school–home communications (e.g., *Increasing Homework Completion with a Daily Report Card*), and principal attention for improvements in achievement or behavior (*Encouraging Academic Achievement with Principal Praise*). Relationship-based rewards, in which the reinforcement consists of an opportunity to interact with another individual, are also likely to be less subject to satiation effects. These rewards can include eating lunch with the teacher, reading to other students, participating in school or community service programs, or coming early or staying after school to help the teacher with a special project.

Managing Reinforcement Delivery

Because the interventions in this book have been designed or adapted for use with entire classes rather than individual students so that all students have an equal opportunity to earn rewards, most of the problems associated with delivering a reward to some students while others remain unrewarded have been eliminated. Even with classwide interventions, however, reinforcement delivery problems can occur with interventions involving competition among teams. In many of the original studies using team contingencies, nonwinning teams were required to continue performing school tasks, often in the same classroom as their victorious peers. Field testing and research alike (e.g., Wolfe, Boyd, & Wolfe, 1983), however, indicate that students may become disgruntled and disruptive if they must watch their classmates enjoying a reward or privilege they have failed to earn. Supervising a group of nonrewarded students under these circumstances can be especially problematic for teachers with poor classroom management skills and can increase resistance to the intervention assistance process. Although the team-based interventions in this book permit all teams to win and receive the reward if each meets the criterion, every team may not meet the criterion on a particular day or on enough days to earn a weekly reward. Moreover, teachers may occasionally prefer to direct an intervention toward a single student or a small group of students rather than the entire class.

Several ways of managing reinforcement delivery exist when not all students receive the reward. One strategy is to send students who have earned the reward to another teacher to receive the reinforcement. For example, the reward can be an end-of-the-day video in another classroom or extra time in the gym or media center. Teachers implementing the same or similar interventions can collaborate in supervising students, with winners from the two classrooms going to one room to receive the reward while students who did not earn the reward go to the other room to continue working on their assignments (e.g., *Public Posting to Reduce Disruptive Behavior*).

A second strategy is to replace activity rewards with small tangible rewards that can easily be delivered to individuals, such as positive school–home notes, stickers, fast-food coupons, or miniature candy bars. Delivering these reinforcers at the very end of the school day minimizes opportunities for disruptive and unproductive behavior among students not receiving the rewards. Third, reinforcement for appropriate academic or social behavior can be provided at home rather than in the classroom. Several interventions use home-based social or material rewards to motivate positive behavior (e.g., *Improving Homework Submission with School–Home Notes; Increasing Homework Completion with a Daily Report Card; Reducing Rule Violations with Good Day Awards*). Finally, the behavior of an individual student can be consequated with a reward for the entire group (see *The Response Cost Raffle*).

EVALUATING INTERVENTION EFFECTIVENESS

This book incorporates assessment into every intervention but not in the sense of searching for pathological conditions in students with school problems. Instead, emphasis is placed on assessing changes in target behaviors in the context of the regular classroom environment, using measures designed to be as nonintrusive and practical as possible without sacrificing reliability and validity. The importance of documenting student outcomes during the intervention assistance process cannot be overemphasized. After intervention implementation, consultants may hear teachers report, "I tried what you recommended, and it didn't work," only to discover that no objective assessment of intervention effects on student performance has been conducted. Systematically evaluating behavior change not only provides information useful in monitoring and improving intervention effectiveness but contributes to teachers' maintenance of interventions by demonstrating that positive change is indeed occurring. Documenting change is even more critical for interventions targeting social behavior than for those focusing on academic achievement. Because grades and measures of productivity, such as homework completion rates, are part of the regular data-gathering process in classrooms, teachers can readily monitor and observe changes in academic performance. In contrast, teachers are much less likely to use objective methods of monitoring social behavior and thus may fail to detect small positive changes and prematurely abandon an intervention.

Barriers to Evaluation

Failing to evaluate the effects of their services is unfortunately common among school consultants, including psychologists (Zins & Fairchild, 1986) and counselors (Fairchild & Zins, 1986). Despite frequent calls in the literature to document the effects of interventions (Shapiro, 1987; Shapiro, 1996a; Sindelar et al., 1992; Zins et al., 1988), studies of IAPs indicate that consultants, teachers, and intervention assistance team members alike often neglect to conduct reliable assessments of target behaviors prior to intervention and changes in those behaviors after implementation (Flugum & Reschly, 1994; Fuchs & Fuchs, 1989; Nelson, Smith, Taylor, Dodd, & Reavis, 1992; Schumaker, Hovell, & Sherman, 1977; Smith, Schumaker, Schaeffer, & Sherman, 1982). As a result, it is often unclear whether an intervention was unsuccessful in solving the problem or whether it was simply terminated too soon.

Given the benefits of assessing intervention effectiveness, why is this so often the case? Lack of time is the factor most frequently cited for consultants' failure to collect accountability data (Zins & Fairchild, 1986). Given the constraints on both consultant and teacher time, the pressure to create changes in the performance of an unproductive, low-achieving, or disruptive student or classroom group is likely to take precedence over systematically evaluating the efficacy of those change efforts. As a result, teacher and consultant time tends to be allocated to implementation rather than evaluation, and evaluation often consists of the subjective impressions of the teacher and consultant, which may not coincide with each other or with actual changes in student performance.

Teachers' resistance to evaluation is also linked to the increased demands placed on them by the intervention assistance process. Teachers who refer students to IAPs are typically asked first to document current student performance, then to alter their instructional or management system by implementing one or more interventions, and finally to collect additional data assessing student behavior change after implementation. If the interventions are successful in solving the referral problem, documenting student outcomes may seem even less of a priority for teachers. If student achievement or behavior does not appear to be changing in a positive direction, teachers may become discouraged with the intervention assistance process and resist collecting data or gather it half-heartedly, especially if evaluation methods do not fit readily into the classroom ecology.

Lack of training also contributes to the failure to assess intervention effectiveness (Zins & Fairchild, 1986). School psychologists rate their training in evaluating service delivery and educational programs as highly inadequate (McKee et al., 1987). Especially in light of their perceived training deficiencies, consultants may be intimidated by the complexity of the evaluation methods used in many published studies. A sizable number of the interventions described in the literature rely on evaluation strategies that are impractical for both school consultants and classroom teachers, such as multivariable environmental rating systems requiring specially trained observers or special observational equipment not found in most schools (e.g., Acker & O'Leary, 1987; Greenwood, 1991).

Rationale for Intervention Evaluation

Despite these obstacles, integrating accountability into the intervention assistance process is essential for several reasons. First, evaluation is needed to assess changes in the target behavior of referred individual students or classroom groups. Without systematic accountability methods, consultants and teachers will be unable to determine what kinds of interventions are effective with which kinds of problems, and interventions will continue to be implemented primarily on the basis of familiarity or ease of implementation rather than treatment efficacy (Zins et al., 1988). Second, documenting IAP effectiveness contributes to program success by helping to reduce resistance, increase administrative, staff, and community support, and enhance teacher and parent participation. Accountability data can provide encouragement to IAP participants, including teachers, principals, parents, students, and consultants, for implementing innovative practices and effecting positive change. Providing feedback to students is probably the most neglected aspect of the evaluation process, despite the fact that research indicates that giving pupils frequent information about their progress significantly enhances performance (Thorpe, Chiang, & Darch, 1981). Several of the interventions provide systematic feedback to students about changes in their academic performance or behavior as a critical treatment component (e.g., *Increasing Writing Productivity Using Self-Monitoring; Public Posting to Decrease Disruptive Behavior; Charting to Improve Behavior during Specials*).

Commonly used measures of IAP effectiveness include the following: (1) number of referrals for special education and placements in special education programs; (2) changes in the achievement and behavior of referred students and groups; (3) teacher, parent, and student satisfaction with IAP activities and interventions; (4) changes in teachers' instructional or behavior management skills; and (5) number of requests for intervention assistance. Although a detailed discussion of program evaluation methodology is beyond the scope of this text, strategies for evaluating IAPs may be found in Rosenfield and Gravois (1996) and Zins et al. (1988).

Finally, as noted above, ethical practice requires that consultants recommend interventions with demonstrated efficacy in addressing referral problems and assess the effectiveness of those interventions on student performance. Conducting systematic evaluations of intervention effectiveness may be time consuming, but it remains the best way of ensuring that IAPs will be successful in achieving the purpose for which they have been developed—enhancing the quality of education for students in the regular classroom.

Evaluation Methods and Measures

The observation-evaluation component of each intervention in this book describes at least two and up to five assessment strategies for documenting changes in classroom environment variables, academic performance, or behavior. Because the interventions are group-focused, evaluation measures are primarily designed to assess aspects of student engagement, academic performance, or social behavior for an entire classroom. Most of these measures can be easily adapted for use with individual students or small groups, if desired.

To encourage the regular collection of accountability data, many of the evaluation measures rely on naturally collected information, such as grades or homework completion rates. Naturalistic evaluation that fits readily into current classroom routines is not only less ecologically intrusive but also enhances the acceptability and social validity of interventions. Assessing changes in academic achievement is especially desirable because student success is ultimately defined by the degree to which children are able to master the "business" of school—learning.

Evaluating Changes in Academic Performance

Evaluation strategies for many of the academic interventions rely on *curriculum-based measurement* (CBM), a type of assessment that directly links evaluation data to instructional interventions (Shinn, 1989). Theoretically neutral, CBM can be used to measure student growth over time with any type of instructional methods or curriculum. Because CBMs can be administered frequently, they yield a pattern of scores that indicates if the student is making progress. Moreover, a qualitative analysis of the types of errors made by students can provide information for designing the most appropriate interventions to target the observed problems. With CBM, consultants and teachers can examine student progress and evaluate the effectiveness of interventions at many points during the year, not merely in the fall or spring when standardized achievement tests are typically administered. Although CBM was originally designed for individual student assessment, CBMs in mathematics, spelling, and written expression can easily be administered to groups. Chapter 3 presents an overview of this type of assessment and describes procedures for conducting CBMs in reading, mathematics, spelling, and written expression.

Another useful method of assessing changes in academic performance involves calculating *percentage gain* (Menlo & Johnson, 1971). Originally designed to measure change for individuals, percentage gain scores can be combined to yield group averages so that classwide progress can be monitored in targeted academic areas. Percentage gain scores have several advantages over simple change scores. They correlate more highly with posttest scores and, unlike simple change scores, do not place initially high-scoring individuals at a disadvantage by reducing their gains below those of initially low scorers. To calculate percentage gain in cases in which the final score exceeds the initial score, the percentage gain score is defined as

$$PG = \frac{X_2 - X_1}{R_p} \times 100$$

where X_2 is the final score, X_1 is the initial score, and R_p is the highest possible score minus the initial score (i.e., the maximum possible gain). To calculate percentage gain in cases in which the final score is less than the initial score, the percentage gain score (which will be negative) is defined as

$$PG = \frac{X_2 - X_1}{R_n} \times 100$$

where R_n is the initial score minus the lowest possible score (i.e., the maximum possible loss). For example, a student's average reading test grade prior to implementing *Classwide Peer Tutoring* was 35 out of a possible 100 and 75 after implementation. The percentage gain for that student is 61.5% ([(75 − 35)/65] × 100 = 61.5). By adding the percentage gains for each student and dividing by the number of students in the entire group, the average percentage gain for the class can be calculated.

Evaluating Changes in Student Behavior

In assessing the effectiveness of interventions targeting social behavior, it is important to select measures that are capable of detecting small changes in student behavior. Although numerous teacher rating scales have been developed to assess student behavior, most of these measures were originally designed to screen for childhood disorders rather than to detect behavior changes subsequent to classroom interventions. In a study with the Achenbach Teacher Report Form (TRF), a frequently used child behavior rating scale, Harris, Wilkinson, Trovato, and Pryor (1992) found that TRF scores did not reflect observed behavioral differences between experimental and control groups of students. Similarly, although a wide variety of methods have been developed for observing student behavior in classroom settings, many published examples are so complex and require such extensive training and practice time that they are more appropriate for university researchers than school consultants or classroom teachers. Moreover, most of these observational methods have been designed to monitor the behavior of a single individual or a very small number of students rather than an entire classroom group. The observational strategies included in the interventions in this book are designed to be as simple to use as possible while still providing reliable and valid measures of relevant classwide behaviors. Three basic observational recording forms, a *Group Event Recording Form*, a *Group Interval Recording Form*, and a *Classwide Scanning Form* are used for most of the strategies, in accordance with Alessi's (1980) recommendation that school districts develop their own standard observation protocols to make data collected on students consistent, facilitate training new staff, and permit easy interpretation of results. The forms incorporate three methods of direct observation: event recording, momentary time sampling, and classwide scanning.

1. *Event recording* consists of tallying the number of times one or more target behaviors occurs. The *Group Event Recording Form* (see Figure 2.2) is designed to monitor the frequency of occurrence of between one and six positive or negative target behaviors for an entire class for up to 7 days or observational sessions. Behaviors that are most appropriate for monitoring by event recording are discrete, that is, they have identifiable beginnings and endings, such as call-outs, out of seats, contributions to class discussions, or hand raises. The data yielded by this method are frequency counts of the target behaviors, whether desired or undesired, displayed by the class, group, or individual student.

2. *Momentary time sampling*, a variation of interval recording, consists of observing a student at predetermined intervals and recording whether or not the student is exhibiting a target behavior at the moment of observation. The *Group Interval Recording Form* (see Figure 2.3) is designed for consecutively recording the behavior of all of the students in a class or group at predetermined intervals, such as every 5, 10, or 15 seconds. The observer records whether the student is displaying one of several mutually exclusive behaviors, such as being on-task, off-task, or disruptive, at the moment of observation. The data collected by this method are classwide rates of each of the target behavior categories. Although the emphasis in

GROUP EVENT RECORDING FORM

Teacher _____ School _____
Description of class or group _____
Number of students in group _____ Number of students observed _____
Dates of observation _____ Time(s) of observation _____
Observer _____ Class activity _____

Directions: Select one or more target behaviors (desired or undesired) to monitor. Place a check or tally in the box for each occurrence of each target behavior for that day or observation session. Sum the tallies in each box to obtain the frequency of each target behavior during the observational period.

Target behavior	Day 1	Day 2	Day 3	Day 4	Day 5	Day 6	Day 7	Totals

FIGURE 2.2. Group event recording form.

this book is on classwide observation methods, the *Group Event Recording Form* and the *Group Interval Recording Form* can also be used to monitor the behavior of a small group of students or an individual student.

3. *Classwide scanning,* a version of momentary time sampling, involves rapidly surveying an entire class and tallying the number of students in each of several mutually exclusive behavior categories, such as on-task, off-task, or disruptive (see Figure 2.4). Classwide scanning differs from momentary time sampling in that student behavior is monitored at longer in-

GROUP INTERVAL RECORDING FORM

Teacher _____ School_____

Description of class or group _____

Number of students in group _____ Class activity _____

Date of observation _____ Time of observation _____ to _____

Observer _____ Length of observation interval _____

Directions: Beginning at the left side of the room, glance at each student at the designated interval (e.g., 5, 10, or 15 seconds) and code that student's behavior as on-task (+), off-task (–), or disruptive (×) at the moment of observation. Record behavior for each student in turn and then begin again with the first student.

1	2	3	4	5	6	7	8	9	10	11	12	13	14	15	16	17	18	19	20
21	22	23	24	25	26	27	28	29	30	31	32	33	34	35	36	37	38	39	40
41	42	43	44	45	46	47	48	49	50	51	52	53	54	55	56	57	58	59	60
61	62	63	64	65	66	67	68	69	70	71	72	73	74	75	76	77	78	79	80
81	82	83	84	85	86	87	88	89	90	91	92	93	94	95	96	97	98	99	100
101	102	103	104	105	106	107	108	109	110	111	112	113	114	115	116	117	118	119	120
121	122	123	124	125	126	127	128	129	130	131	132	133	134	135	136	137	138	139	140
141	142	143	144	145	146	147	148	149	150	151	152	153	154	155	156	157	158	159	160
161	162	163	164	165	166	167	168	169	170	171	172	173	174	175	176	177	178	179	180

$$\text{Percent target behavior} = \frac{\text{Number of intervals in that category}}{\text{Total number of observation intervals}} \times 100$$

Percent on-task behavior　　= _____

Percent off-task behavior　　= _____

Percent disruptive behavior = _____

FIGURE 2.3. Group interval recording form.

CLASSWIDE SCANNING FORM

Teacher _____ School_____

Description of class or group _____

Number of students in group _____ Class activity _____

Date of observation _____ Time of observation _____ to _____

Observer _____ Length of observation interval _____

Directions: Scan the class at the designated interval (e.g., every 3, 5, 10, or 15 minutes) and tally the number of students in each behavior category. Tally marks for each interval should sum to the number of students in the entire group.

Interval	On-task	Off-task	Disruptive	Totals
1				
2				
3				
4				
5				
6				
7				
8				
9				
10				
11				
12				

$$\text{Percentage of students per category} = \frac{\text{Total number of students per category}}{\text{Number of intervals} \times \text{total number of students}}$$

Percent on-task behavior   = _____

Percent off-task behavior   = _____

Percent disruptive behavior   = _____

FIGURE 2.4. Classwide scanning form.

tervals, such as every 10 minutes, rather than coded sequentially every few seconds. Suggested intervals for classwide scanning range from 3 to 15 minutes. Although shorter intervals yield more reliable data, longer intervals permit teachers to monitor student behavior without unduly interrupting ongoing instruction. The data collected by classwide scanning are the percentages of students falling into each behavior category. Another classwide scanning form designed to monitor up to five behavior categories is presented in Chapter 3 and is especially appropriate for assessing the effectiveness of proactive interventions (see Figure 3.2, *Classwide Engagement Rate Recording Form*).

In considering which evaluation strategy to recommend, consultants should consider the demands on teacher time required by the different methodologies. Classwide scanning is especially suitable for teacher use because observations can be distributed at wide intervals. Event recording methods, which monitor discrete behaviors, are also relatively easy for classroom teachers to use. Momentary time sampling methods that involve rating behavior several times a minute are more easily conducted by an observer other than the teacher. Involving teachers in selecting evaluation strategies as well as interventions helps them to perceive evaluation as documenting their own increasing professional effectiveness rather than merely adding to their classroom duties.

Assessing the Reliability of Behavioral Observations

Given the realities of the typical school environment, in most cases, observations will be conducted by a single individual. Using two or more observers yields more reliable information, however, and is necessary to obtain interrater reliability data. The two observers can consist of the referring teacher and the consultant or IAT case manager, or teams of special education personnel, such as the school psychologist and a special education resource teacher. Alternatively, consultants can train student interns, aides, or other paraprofessionals to conduct observations. A common formula for calculating interrater reliability for two observers that can be used for event recording and time sampling procedures is as follows:

$$\text{Interobserver agreement} = \frac{\text{Number of agreements}}{(\text{Number of agreements} + \text{Number of disagreements})} \times 100$$

In general, interobserver agreement percentages should be 80% or higher in order to conclude that measurements of behavior are reliable and valid (Steege & Wacker, 1995).

Home-Based Evaluation Strategies

Although most of the interventions rely on classroom-based methods of evaluating academic and behavioral change, home-based evaluation strategies can also be useful in assessing intervention effectiveness. With school–home notes (e.g., *Increasing Homework Completion with a Daily Report Card; Reducing Rule Violations with Good Day Awards*), parents serve as reinforcing agents to deliver feedback to their children based on their academic performance or social behavior. Conducting conferences or telephone interviews with a sample of parents after implementation can provide useful information regarding parents' assessments of intervention effectiveness. Written parent questionnaires, sent home with students after implementation, are another option. An example is the survey soliciting parental feedback on the effectiveness of *Brag Sheets: Improving Behavior during Rest Time*. Even when interventions are classroom-based, consultants are encouraged to obtain parent input regarding intervention effectiveness and acceptability through satisfaction surveys, telephone contacts, or interviews.

INTERVENTION CASE EXAMPLES

Although in some cases, a single intervention will be sufficient to solve a classroom problem, field testing indicates that many of the students and classroom groups referred for assistance have not one but multiple problems that interfere with their capacity to benefit from instruction. In these cases, designing and implementing *intervention packages*, consisting of several strategies targeting the set of problem behaviors, enhances the likelihood of positive outcomes. The following case examples illustrate the use of intervention packages in addressing identified problems. These examples have been selected because they exemplify two key characteristics of the intervention assistance approach to classroom problems: (1) early intervention to help prevent future problems as well as remediate current difficulties and (2) group-focused intervention to assist not just one ineffectively behaving student but an entire classroom.

Aggressive and Defiant Prekindergarten Student

Jerome, a bright but very aggressive and noncompliant prekindergarten student, often hit or threatened his classmates with little provocation, got out of his seat without permission, and defied his teacher's efforts to control his behavior. He also had trouble waiting in line, sharing materials, and cooperating in group activities. When reprimanded, he would either ignore the teacher's directions or retreat to a corner of the classroom to sulk.

Intervention Targets and Components

Intervention targets were as follows: (1) increasing compliance with teacher directions, (2) reducing verbal and physical aggression, and (3) increasing cooperation with both adults and peers. Interventions were taught through a combination of workshops for beginning teachers and individual consultations subsequent to classroom observations. Classroom observations often included a coaching component, in which a consultant provides direct assistance to the teacher in using a strategy at the moment when the strategy is needed. For example, when Jerome resisted complying with teacher instructions, the consultant would quietly prompt the teacher to follow through with the planned consequences to ensure that his inappropriate behavior was consistently consequated.

An intervention package consisting of four strategies selected from the proactive and behavioral categories was implemented. In addition, to enhance preacademic competencies and reduce "down time" and opportunities for disruptive behavior, classroom prereading activities, such as singing, storybook reading, and rhyming games, were expanded. To address Jerome's noncompliant and aggressive behavior, *Short, Soft, and Close: Delivering Effective Reprimands*, which combines the features of effective reprimands into a single proactive intervention, was implemented. Another proactive intervention, *Sit and Watch: Teaching Prosocial Behaviors*, which provides a classroom timeout with an incidental teaching component, was implemented to help Jerome learn and practice more socially appropriate behaviors. To capitalize on peer influence for positive behavior, *Red Light/Green Light* was introduced, a team-oriented intervention that uses visual cues to indicate when children are eligible to receive rewards for following the classroom rules. All of these interventions were implemented on a classwide basis. In addition, a variation of the school–home intervention, *Reducing Rule Violations with Good Day Awards*, listing three classroom rules and rating Jerome's level of compliance from 1 (low) to 3 (high) was implemented on an individual basis. After a conference was held with his parents to explain the purpose of the intervention program and invite their involvement, the note was sent home every day. Over the course of the year, Jerome's behavior improved dramatically. He was particularly responsive to the school–home notes, and the teacher was able to prevent minor misbehavior from escalating by reminding him that she was "looking for him to have a '3' day," a goal that he achieved regularly toward the end of the year.

Disruptive and Unproductive Seventh-Grade Science Class

The teacher of this seventh-grade class was in her first year at a school serving a student population with a high proportion of diverse learners. Although she was experiencing management problems with all of her classes, the seventh-grade science class was especially disruptive and unproductive. As the fall semester progressed, it took the students longer and longer to enter the classroom and settle down to work, and they were so slow in getting their materials together at the end of the period that they often kept the next class standing outside in the hall for several minutes. The students were also very diverse in terms of academic skills and productivity, with some pupils participating frequently in class discussions and others seldom contributing. Fearful of losing further control, the teacher kept hands-on activities to a minimum and spent most of the period lecturing behind a podium.

Intervention Targets and Components

Interventions for this class were taught in the context of a monthly staff development program, supplemented by classroom observations and individual consultations. The consultant made written notes during each classroom observation and then shared them with the teacher to provide positive feedback and offer suggestions for intervention design and implementation. Intervention targets included the following: (1) increasing academic productivity, (2) reducing transition time, and (3) encouraging more positive attitudes toward learning. Because it was evident that the most disruptive students also had the greatest academic skill deficits and were having difficulty reading their textbooks and completing written assignments, emphasis was placed on interventions that increase available instructional time and maximize opportunities to respond actively to academic material.

A package consisting of three interventions—one from each of the proactive, academic, and behavior categories—was implemented. First, to increase available instructional time and reduce opportunities for disruption, the teacher introduced *Teaching Transition Time*, which provides direct instruction in making smooth and rapid transitions between activities. To encourage peer pressure for following classroom rules, she also implemented *The Good Behavior Game Plus Merit*. Field testing has demonstrated that this and other interventions that divide students into teams that compete for rewards based on appropriate classroom behavior are particularly helpful in creating a positive learning environment and combatting negative peer group attitudes and behaviors. As disruptive behavior gradually diminished, the teacher implemented *Classwide Peer Tutoring* (CWPT) several times a week, using skills exercises from the science workbook as the tutoring materials, to increase active responding and provide additional practice for low-achieving students. To facilitate the use of CWPT, she rearranged the classroom into rows of paired desks.

Over the course of the semester, the seventh graders learned to make quicker and more orderly transitions in and out of class and became more actively involved in class discussions and their academic tasks. The level of disruptive behavior declined considerably, and the teacher reported that the classroom atmosphere was much more positive. In fact, she indicated that it was now her favorite class.

SUPPLEMENTARY READINGS

Conoley, J. C., & Conoley, C. W. (1992). *School consultation: Practice and training* (2nd ed.). Needham Heights, MA: Allyn & Bacon.

This book provides an overview of school consultation based on an ecological perspective. The authors discuss the purposes of consultation, consultation skills and targets, entry problems, evaluation issues, and staff development. An appendix includes annotated transcripts of actual consultation sessions between a consultant and teacher, consultant and principal, and consultant and teacher committee.

Fuchs, D., Fuchs, L. S., Reeder, P., Gilman, S., Fernstrom, P., Bahr, M., & Moore, P. (1989). *Mainstream assistance teams: A handbook on prereferral intervention.* (Available from the MAP Project, John F. Kennedy Center, Box 40, George Peabody College, Vanderbilt University, Nashville, TN 37203)

This handbook presents a comprehensive description of a Mainstream Assistance Team (MAT) project implemented in the Nashville schools. The MAT project uses a prescriptive behavior consultation model of assistance, with teacher–student contracts as the basic intervention. The handbook contains the complete set of materials used by MAT consultants, including written scripts to guide interactions with teachers, checklists for classroom visits, and a variety of monitoring procedures and forms.

Gutkin, T. B., & Curtis, M. J. (1990). School-based consultation: Theory, techniques, and research. In T. B. Gutkin & C. R. Reynolds (Eds.), *The handbook of school psychology* (2nd ed., pp. 557–611). New York: Wiley.

In this one-chapter overview of school consultation, the authors present the core characteristics of consultation, rationale for consultation, major theoretical approaches, and critical issues. A detailed description of the step-by-step problem-solving consultative process is included.

Jacob-Timm, S., & Hartshorne, T. (1994). *Ethics and law for school psychologists* (2nd ed.). New York: Wiley.

This comprehensive sourcebook on ethics, law, and professional standards is specifically designed for school psychologists. Two chapters with particular relevance to intervention assistance programs (IAPs) review ethical and legal issues in counseling and therapeutic interventions (with individual students) and ethical issues in consultation. Numerous case examples, some from case law, some fictitious, illustrate various principles.

Marks, E. S. (1995). *Entry strategies for school consultation.* New York: Guilford Press.

The author presents practical guidelines for achieving entry in school consultation, including gaining access to principals; obtaining support from district-level administrators; enlisting teacher, staff, and parent assistance in consultation; and overcoming teacher resistance. An appendix reviews critical communication techniques and includes a variety of forms for assessing communication and process skills in consultation sessions.

National Association of School Psychologists. (1986). *Intervention assistance teams: A model for building level instructional problem solving.* Silver Spring, MD: Author.

Prepared by the Ohio Department of Education, this handbook provides a comprehensive set of guidelines for developing, implementing, and maintaining intervention assistance teams. An appendix includes samples of forms for monitoring student and team functioning.

National Association of School Psychologists. (1997). *Professional conduct manual* (3rd ed.). Silver Spring, MD: Author.

This publication contains NASP *Principles for Professional Ethics* and *Standards for the Provision of School Psychological Services.* The Association reviews the manual every 5 years to insure that the principles and standards reflect current conditions.

Rosenfield, S. A., & Gravois, T. A. (1996). *Instructional consultation teams.* New York: Guilford Press.

Instructional consultation teams are based on a model that synthesizes collaborative consultation strategies with knowledge about instruction to develop interventions for at-risk students. In this book, the authors present a plan for initiating, implementing, and institutionalizing this form of consultation-based service delivery system. Appendices with forms and materials for evaluating team process and effectiveness as well as student performance are included.

Stoner, G., Shinn, M. R., & Walker, H. M. (Eds.). (1991). *Interventions for achievement and behavior problems.* Silver Spring, MD: National Association of School Psychologists.

This comprehensive one-volume guide to intervention-oriented school psychological services includes state-of-the art articles on the intervention assistance movement. The book is divided into six sections: an introduction to the interventionist approach; evaluation issues; general intervention strategies regardless of age and grade; interventions for target areas by level (preschool, elementary, and secondary); interventions for specific problems; and training issues.

Zins, J. E., Curtis, M. J., Graden, J., & Ponti, C. R. (1988). *Helping students succeed in the regular classroom: A guide for developing intervention assistance programs*. San Francisco: Jossey-Bass.

The authors provide detailed guidelines for developing, implementing, and evaluating IAPs offering consultative support to teachers. Included are chapters on the step-by-step intervention assistance process, interventions for individual students with common learning and behavior problems, and legal and ethical issues related to IAPs.

CHAPTER 3

Proactive Interventions: Strategies That Create a Productive, Disruption-Free Classroom Environment

♦

OVERVIEW

Proactive classroom management refers to strategies that simultaneously promote high levels of academic engagement and prevent disruptive behavior. Proactive classroom management is distinguished from other management approaches by three characteristics (Gettinger, 1988). First, it is designed to be preventive rather than reactive by establishing an instructional program that minimizes opportunities for inappropriate behavior. In his classic observational study of 80 elementary school classrooms, Kounin (1970) found that the key behaviors distinguishing effective from ineffective classroom managers were not their reactions to student misbehavior. Rather, they were distinguished by their ability to maintain student engagement in academic tasks and limit classroom disruptions by *preventing* misbehavior. Second, rather than treating instruction and management as separate domains, proactive classroom management integrates both into a comprehensive classroom system. Academic and social task structures are interrelated, with effective instruction setting the conditions under which students develop and maintain appropriate behavior (Weade & Evertson, 1988).

Third, proactive management focuses on group aspects of classroom management rather than on individual student behavior (Gettinger, 1988). The power of the group to influence the behavior of the individuals within it is well-documented. As Hobbs (1966) has observed, "When a group is functioning well, it is extremely difficult for an individual child to behave in a disturbed way" (p. 1112). Interventions that apply consequences to the behavior of a single student or a few students in the context of a disorderly, poorly managed classroom are inappropriate and unlikely to be effective. For maximum benefits to teachers and students alike, consultants should focus on helping teachers establish the antecedent conditions that reduce the possibility of academic failure and misbehavior in the first place (Witt & Martens, 1988).

In keeping with a proactive approach to classroom management, the interventions in this chapter are designed to set the conditions for high levels of academic engagement and appropriate social behavior for an entire classroom group. Strategies have been drawn from the effective teaching literature as well as from the behavioral sciences literature. As Evertson (1989b) has noted, creating and maintaining an effective classroom environment requires more than a collection of isolated techniques, such as token economies or timeout. Fortunately, research has consistently identified a core set of effective teaching strategies that target critical areas of classroom management and can be taught within a consultative framework.

THE IMPORTANCE OF PROACTIVE
CLASSROOM MANAGEMENT

The importance of helping teachers create an environment that fosters active academic responding and decreases disruptive behavior cannot be underestimated. Observational research (Moskowitz & Hayman, 1976) attests to the fact that once teachers lose control of classes, it is increasingly difficult for them to regain it. In addition, the more time teachers must allot to correcting misbehavior rather than to instruction, the lower the rate of academic engagement (Berliner, 1988; Brophy & Good, 1986). In contrast, the more time teachers devote to implementing proactive classroom strategies at the beginning of the year, the more students are engaged in their academic tasks throughout the rest of the year (Emmer, Evertson, & Anderson, 1980; Evertson & Emmer, 1982).

Proactive interventions are also critical to maximizing the amount of time available for learning. Academic achievement is significantly related to the amount of time allotted for instruction and to *academic engagement rates*, the proportion of instructional time in which students are engaged in learning, as demonstrated by behaviors such as paying attention, working on assignments, and participating in class discussions (Berliner, 1988; Brophy, 1986; Fisher et al., 1980; Gettinger, 1988; Greenwood, 1991; Greenwood, Delquadri, & Hall, 1984). The importance of increasing available instructional time and academic engagement rates is underscored by studies reporting that only about 50 to 60% of the school day is actually devoted to instruction. Moreover, observational studies have found that student engagement rates vary as much as 40% from class to class (Fisher et al., 1980). Engagement rates also vary dramatically among students in the same classroom. When differences in engagement rates are extrapolated to a school year, hours of academic learning time per year may range from 46 hours to 280 hours in a single classroom (Smyth, 1985).

Proactive Strategies and Diverse Learners

Although all students profit from proactive strategies that increase instructional time and academic engagement, these interventions are especially important for diverse learners, including low-achieving, disabled, and low-socioeconomic-status (SES) students. Research (Greenwood, 1991; Greenwood, Delquadri, & Hall, 1989; Stanley & Greenwood, 1983) has consistently documented significant differences in instructional time and academic engagement between low-SES students in urban schools and their high-SES counterparts in suburban schools. Stanley and Greenwood (1983) reported that engagement in academically oriented activities was 11 minutes a day less for minority students in Chapter 1 schools than for non-Chapter 1 groups, placing already vulnerable youngsters at greater risk for failure. When these daily rates are extrapolated to the entire school year, Chapter 1 students would need to attend school for an additional month and a half to obtain an equivalent amount of academic practice. Classwide interventions that increase instructional time and raise levels of academic engagement are also important for learning-disabled students. Learning-disabled children not only display lower rates of attending in the regular classroom than in resource rooms but are significantly affected by group behavior, with engagement rates significantly higher when the engagement of the entire class is high (Friedman, Cancelli, & Yoshida, 1988).

Providing training in proactive classroom management interventions is most helpful during the preservice days before teachers have encountered their students and set expectations for academic and social performance. Research (Brooks, 1985; Emmer et al., 1980; Evertson, 1989b; Evertson & Emmer, 1982; Evertson et al., 1983; Moskowitz & Hayman, 1976) attests to the critical importance of teachers' very first contacts with students in establishing effective behavior for the rest of the year. As Brooks (1985) has observed, "There is only *one* first day of school" (p. 69; emphasis in the original). It is especially important to help beginning teachers acquire a repertoire of proactive strategies because they have usually received their practical training in a classroom in which another teacher has already established instructional and behavior management procedures (Veenman, 1984).

EVALUATING THE EFFECTIVENESS
OF PROACTIVE INTERVENTIONS

Evaluation methods for the interventions in this chapter include a variety of assessments of classroom functioning that have been designed to be as simple and practical as possible and still yield reliable and valid information. Although many of the evaluation strategies can be adapted for use in assessing the performance of a single student or small groups of students rather than an entire class, documenting classwide behavior is especially important in planning and evaluating proactive interventions because they are designed to improve the effectiveness of the learning environment as a whole. Measures assess learning-related behaviors, such as the number of discussion comments, questions, and hand raises, and task-management behaviors, such as the amount of time spent in transitions. Measures of relevant teacher behaviors, such as number of reprimands delivered during various classroom routines, are also included.

Several instruments have been developed to gather information about classroom variables affecting learning, notably the Code for Instructional Structure and Student Academic Response (CISSAR; Greenwood & Delquadri, 1988). The CISSAR, which has been used in numerous studies to evaluate the effectiveness of the *Classwide Peer Tutoring* intervention presented in Chapter 4, is a 53-code system assessing six categories of classroom ecological variables (Academic Activities, Nonacademic Activities, Task, Structure, Teacher Position, and Teacher Behavior) and three categories of student behavior (Academic Response, Task Management, and Competing Response). Although the CISSAR has yielded a wealth of classroom ecology data, its complexity makes it impractical for school consultants, a problem shared by many other classroom observational systems.

More practical for consultants is the Behavioral Observation of Students in Schools (BOSS; Shapiro, 1996a, 1996b), an observational code that assesses two categories of academic engagement (active engaged time [AET] and passive engaged time [PET]), and three categories of nonengagement (off-task motor, off-task verbal, and off-task passive). The BOSS also includes an additional category to identify the type of instructional setting, such as independent seatwork, teacher-directed small group, or teacher-directed large group. Although the BOSS is designed to assess the academic performance of a single student, data are collected on classroom peers as well as the target pupil. On every fifth interval, observations are conducted on a different randomly selected peer, and the data are combined to derive a peer comparison score for the behaviors sampled. Teacher-directed instruction is also coded every fifth interval to provide a sampling of the time in which the teacher is directly engaged in instructing individuals or the class. Data from the BOSS can provide information about rates of on- and off-task behavior, rates of academic engagement in different instructional settings, and opportunities to respond (AET level vs. PET level), as well as the extent to which the target student's behavior differs from classroom norms.

In addition to the evaluation methods built into each strategy in this chapter, procedures for assessing two critical classroom environmental variables are presented below using the same structured format as that for the interventions: (1) available instructional time and (2) student engagement rates. Using these procedures, consultants can help teachers collect data for use in identifying intervention targets and evaluating the effects of interventions designed to maximize productive learning time.

Assessing Available Instructional Time

Assessing Available Instructional Time provides a structured method for gathering information about the amount of time allotted to various activities, including instruction in different subject areas. Teachers can calculate the amount of time devoted to each subject or activity, rank the activities in terms of time allotted, and compare this information to standardized test data for a particular classroom group to help determine whether time is currently distributed according to their instructional priorities and identify areas in which interventions that enhance learning time are most needed. Conducting this form of classroom assessment is highly recommended as the first step in the intervention assistance process.

ASSESSING AVAILABLE INSTRUCTIONAL TIME

Overview

Assessing the use of available instructional time is critical to effective planning. This self-monitoring procedure enables teachers to conduct a precise analysis of their schedule to determine how they are currently using the instructional time available during the school week, assess whether time allocations match students' needs, and modify instructional time as desired.

Purpose

To provide an analysis of the use of instructional time available during the school day and week.

Materials

1. Copy of current weekly schedule
2. *Schedule Analysis Form* (see Figure 3.1)

Procedure

1. Review your current weekly schedule or construct one with as much detail as possible. Including transition times will make the schedule more accurate.
2. Compute the number of minutes in the school week as follows: (number of complete hours × 60 + number of extra minutes beyond the last full hour) × 5; for example, (5 × 60 + 35) × 5 = 1,675 minutes.
3. Enter this number (which will probably be between 1,600 and 2,400 minutes) in the Minutes/week space and on the blank next to School Time on the *Schedule Analysis Form.*
4. From your schedule, determine the number of minutes for each activity and enter that figure in the Time column next to the appropriate curriculum area.
5. Determine the number of times each week that the activity occurs for that length of time and enter this number in the Days/week column.
6. After you have entered all scheduled activities on the *Schedule Analysis Form*, multiply the number of minutes an activity lasts by the number of times it takes place each week. Enter the number for each line in the Minutes/week column.
7. Subtract the number for Lunch/Recess in the Minutes/week column from the total School Time and enter it in the space marked Class Time. This figure is the amount of time students spend in your classroom each week.
8. Subtract the number for Organizational in the Minutes/week column from the Class Time and enter it in the Instructional Time space. This is the amount of time you have available for teaching your students every week.
9. Divide each of the figures in the Minutes/week column by the amount of Class Time you have each week. Enter these percentages in the % column. These are the percentages of available class time you devote to each of the activities on your schedule.
10. Rank each of the activity areas from "1" for the highest percentage, to "2" for the next highest, and so on. These rankings reflect your current priorities for time use.
11. If available, enter the group achievement test scores for your class in the Achiev score column opposite the curriculum areas. You can evaluate whether there is a relationship between test scores and the time allotted to various subjects.
12. Check your calculations by looking at the space that reads ___/100 near the right center. The percentages in the % column should total 100%.
13. Use the bottom part of the form for comments and ideas about possible schedule modifications.

Source

Paine, S. C., Radicchi, J., Rosellini, L. C., Deutchman, L., & Darch, C. B. (1983). *Structuring your classroom for academic success* (pp. 79–82). Champaign, IL: Research Press. Copyright 1983 by the authors. Adapted by permission.

SCHEDULE ANALYSIS FORM

School _____ Minutes/week _____ Teacher _____ Grade _____

Area	Time	Days/ week	Minutes/ week	%	Rank	Achiev score
Reading						
Spelling						
Language Arts						
Writing						
Math						
Science						
Social Studies						
Health/PE						
Art/Music						
Other						
Organizational						
Lunch/Recess						

____/100

Total   _____ (School Time)
               _____ (Class Time)
               _____ (Instructional Time)

Comments/Recommendations

_____

_____

_____

_____

_____

_____

FIGURE 3.1. Schedule analysis form. Adapted from Paine, Radicchi, Rosellini, Deutchman, and Darch (1983, p. 81). Copyright 1983 by the authors. Adapted by permission.

Assessing Student Engagement Rates

Assessing Student Engagement Rates is designed for use with the *Classwide Engagement Rate Recording Form* (see Figure 3.2). Although this method is especially appropriate for evaluating the need for and effects of proactive interventions, it can be used with virtually all of the strategies in the book. Because of the long intervals between observations (10 to 15 minutes), it is ideal for use by classroom teachers as well as consultants. Moreover, when used by observers other than the teacher, it can be combined with narrative recording to yield a comprehensive picture of the classroom environment. *Narrative recording*, the qualitative description of classroom activities and student behavior, can provide helpful information about classroom environments as well as the performance of individual students. The following guidelines for using narrative recording to assess the classroom environment are based on Evertson (1985): (1) conduct an observation for 30 to 45 minutes; (2) plan the observation for the beginning of the lesson, if possible; (3) document the sequence of activities and include descriptions of student behaviors, teacher behaviors, and class activities; (4) document the length of activities and transitions; and (5) record as much of the teacher–student dialogue as possible.

ASSESSING STUDENT ENGAGEMENT RATES

Overview

High rates of student engagement are associated not only with an orderly classroom environment but also with improved academic achievement. This procedure provides a measure of classwide student engagement rates for use in planning and evaluating a variety of proactive, academic, and behavioral interventions.

Purpose

To obtain classwide measures of student engagement rates for evaluating classroom environments and intervention effectiveness.

Materials

1. *Classwide Engagement Rate Recording Form* (see Figure 3.2)
2. Watch, preferably with second hand

Procedure

1. Select a target period for observation.
2. Beginning at a randomly determined minute in the initial 10 minutes of the target period and at regular intervals thereafter (10 or 15 minutes), conduct a classwide observation as described below.

3. Using a *Classwide Engagement Rate Recording Form* and beginning at one side of the room and continuing until all students are rated, classify each student according to one of the five following categories:
   a. *Academic on-task:* student is engaged in the academic task at hand as defined by the teacher;
   b. *Procedural on-task:* student is engaged in the classroom procedure at hand as defined by the teacher;
   c. *Sanctioned off-task:* student is not engaged in a task but has teacher permission for nonengagement;
   d. *Unsanctioned off-task:* student is not engaged in the task that he or she is supposed to be doing;
   e. *Dead time:* student is waiting; no specified activity.
4. Sum the number of students in each category across all intervals. Then obtain a percentage for each category by dividing the total number of students in each category by the product of the number of intervals times the total number of students. For example, if there are 25 students in the classroom and a total of 6 were off-task without teacher permission across four intervals, the percentage of students with unsanctioned off-task behavior for the observational period is 6% ($6/[4 \times 25] = 6\%$).

Variations

1. Rate a small group of target students rather than the entire classroom group.
2. Rate students in only three categories: academic on-task, procedural on-task, and off-task/dead time.

Note

Because of the relatively long intervals between recording student engagement rates, this procedure can be combined with a classroom narrative recording—that is, a qualitative description of student and teacher activities.

Source

Evertson, C. M., & Emmer, E. T. (1982). Effective management at the beginning of the school year in junior high classes. *Journal of Educational Psychology, 74*, 485–498. Copyright 1982 by the American Psychological Association. Adapted by permission.

PROACTIVE CLASSROOM MANAGEMENT INTERVENTIONS

The interventions in this chapter have been organized according to six tasks identified by the effective teaching literature (e.g., Emmer, Evertson, Clements, & Worsham, 1997; Evertson, Emmer, Clements, & Worsham,

CLASSWIDE ENGAGEMENT RATE RECORDING FORM

Teacher _____ School _____
Description of class or group _____
Class activity _____
Date of observation _____ Time of observation _____ to _____
Observer _____ Length of observation interval _____

Directions: Scan the class or group at the designated interval (e.g., 10 or 15 minutes) and tally the number of students in each behavior category. Tally marks for each interval should sum to the number of students in the entire group.

Interval	Academic on-task	Procedural on-task	Sanctioned off-task	Unsanctioned off-task	Dead time
1					
2					
3					
4					
5					
6					
7					
8					
9					
10					
11					
12					
Totals					

Percentage of students per category $= \dfrac{\text{Total number of students per category}}{\text{Number of intervals} \times \text{Total number of students}}$

Percentage of academic on-task students $=$ _____

Percentage of procedural on-task students $=$ _____

Percentage of sanctioned off-task students $=$ _____

Percentage of unsanctioned off-task students $=$ _____

Percentage of dead-time students $=$ _____

FIGURE 3.2. Classwide engagement rate recording form.

1994) as critical to successful classroom management: (1) organizing a productive classroom environment, (2) establishing classroom rules and procedures, (3) managing transitions, (4) managing independent seatwork, (5) communicating competently with students, and (6) teaching prosocial behaviors. Taken together, the 14 interventions targeting these six tasks form the basis of a comprehensive classroom management system that can help teachers establish and maintain productive, disruption-free learning environments.

Organizing a Productive Classroom Environment

Although the impact of classroom environments on student achievement and behavior has long been recognized (Adams & Biddle, 1970; Axelrod, Hall, & Tams, 1979; Solomon & Kendall, 1976; Weinstein, 1977, 1979, 1996), relatively little research has examined the effects of specific seating arrangements on achievement or learning-related variables, such as attention and participation. Studies (Emmer et al., 1980; Evertson, 1985, 1989a) of elementary and secondary classrooms indicate that effective managers design classroom arrangements that enable all students to see instruction, provide ready access to frequently used materials and equipment, keep high-traffic areas free of congestion, and facilitate monitoring student work and behavior. Some authors (e.g., Paine et al., 1983) advocate arranging desks in rows facing the chalkboard to promote attention to teacher-directed instruction and reduce opportunities for inappropriate student interaction. Compared with table seating arrangements, row arrangements produce significantly lower rates of off-task behavior (Axelrod et al., 1979; Wheldall, Morris, Vaughan, & Ng, 1981) and significantly higher rates of academic productivity (Bennett & Blundell, 1983).

Field testing indicates that another effective seating arrangement consists of rows of paired desks facing the chalkboard, with a larger space between rows in the center of the room. Such an arrangement not only maximizes classroom space but also facilitates implementation of interventions involving student dyads (e.g., *Classwide Peer Tutoring*; *The Peer Tutor Spelling Game*) or intraclass teams (e.g., *The Good Behavior Game*; *Improving Social Studies Homework Compliance with the Tic–Tac–Toe Game*). Arranging desks in rows or pairs rather than clusters is strongly recommended at the beginning of the year when teachers are establishing classroom management routines and expectations for behavior. Seating arrangements that avoid placing students in very close proximity to each other are especially important for new teachers, whose classroom management skills are likely to be less well developed than those of more experienced teachers. During field testing, first-year teachers who had studied cooperative learning strategies in their college coursework or observed veteran teachers using such strategies often began the year by arranging their classrooms in desk clusters of four to six students, only to find that they had difficulty maintaining student attention and productivity.

The intervention in this section, *Promoting On-Task Behavior with a Circular Desk Arrangement*, is designed to facilitate on-task behavior and group discussion by means of a circular seating arrangement. Other useful seating arrangements are described in Emmer et al. (1997), Evertson et al. (1994), Weinstein (1996), and Wolfgang (1996).

PROMOTING ON-TASK BEHAVIOR
WITH A CIRCULAR DESK ARRANGEMENT

Overview

The manner in which desks are arranged in the classroom can have significant effects on student behavior and performance. The traditional arrangement of desks in rows may reduce unwanted peer interaction but may not be conducive to on-task behavior during instructional and independent work periods for students seated farther away from the teacher. Arranging desks in clusters may facilitate cooperative learning but may also reduce teacher control and encourage off-task behavior because of increased opportunities for unsanctioned peer interaction. Here students are seated in a circular desk arrangement to facilitate on-task behavior and participation during class discussions. Compared with rows, circular seating arrangements resulted in significantly higher rates of on-task behavior and on-task responses, regardless of student ability. Circular arrangements may be especially important for low-achieving students, who benefit from increased opportunities to respond to instructional material.

Purpose

To increase positive student participation during class discussions by arranging desks in a circle.

Materials

None

Observation (Select One or More)

Option 1
1. Select an instructional period during which you wish to increase student participation rates.
2. Using a *Classwide Scanning Form* with a 5-minute interval, tally the number of students in each of the categories below, beginning with the left side of the room and continuing for 20 to 30 minutes:

   a. *On-task behavior:* constructive contributions to the academic activity, includ-
      ing hand-raising, discussion comments, appropriate questions, and listen-
      ing;
   b. *Off-task behavior:* behavior that does not contribute to the lesson, including
      verbal or physical aggression, other disruptive behaviors, and detachment
      from the activity.
3. Conduct these observations for 4 to 7 days.

Option 2
1. Using a *Group Event Recording Form,* tally the number of student behaviors in the
   following five categories during class discussions in a selected instructional period as follows:
   a. *Discussion comments:* verbal responses relevant to the academic activity;
   b. *Questions:* questions regarding the academic activity directed to peers or the
      teacher;
   c. *Hand raises:* student raising a hand to make a contribution to the discussion;
   d. *Off-task behavior:* verbal or physical action not directed toward the academic
      activity;
   e. *Disruptive behavior:* conduct that disrupts the activities of the classroom or in-
      dividual students.
2. Conduct these observations for 4 to 7 days.

Option 3
1. Using a *Group Event Recording Form,* tally the frequency of discussion comments
   as defined above during a selected instructional period for 4 to 7 days.

Option 4
1. Select a small number of target students who participate the least frequently in
   class discussions.
2. Using a *Group Event Recording Form,* record the number of discussion comments,
   questions, and hand raises made by target students during class discussions in a
   selected instructional period for 4 to 7 days.

Procedure

1. Arrange student desks in a circle for one or more instructional periods during
   which you wish to promote class discussions, such as social studies, literature,
   or creative writing.
2. Place the teacher's chair at one end of the circle.
3. Conduct the lesson as usual.

Evaluation (Select One or More)

Option 1
1. Compare the percentages of students displaying on-task and off-task behavior
   during the selected instructional period before and after implementation.

Option 2

1. Compare the frequency of relevant student contributions, (including discussion comments, questions, and hand raises), off-task behavior, and disruptive behavior for the entire class during the selected instructional period before and after implementation.

Option 3

1. Compare the frequency of discussion comments for the entire class during the selected instructional period before and after implementation.

Option 4

1. Compare the frequency of discussion comments, questions, and hand raises for target students during the selected instructional period before and after implementation.

Variation

Arrange desks in a circle for the entire school day.

Notes

1. In the original study, out-of-order comments (call-outs relevant to the discussion) increased somewhat with the circular arrangement. To reduce call-outs, teach appropriate behavior during class discussions using *Say Show Check: Teaching Classroom Procedures* prior to implementation. During this training session, have students practice moving their desks quickly and quietly to form the circle.
2. If students sit at tables rather than at individual desks, have them push the tables against the wall and then arrange their chairs in a circle in the center of the classroom during the discussion period.

Source

Rosenfield, P., Lambert, N. M., & Black, A. (1985). Desk arrangement effects on pupil classroom behavior. *Journal of Educational Psychology, 77,* 101–108. Copyright 1985 by the American Psychological Association. Adapted by permission.

Establishing Classroom Rules and Procedures

Compared with ineffective teachers, effective teachers spend more time establishing classroom rules and procedures for student behavior and explicitly teaching them, especially at the beginning of the year (Emmer et al., 1980; Moskowitz & Hayman, 1976; Sanford & Evertson, 1981). They use specific, concrete rules, model and rehearse classroom routines and procedures, introduce more procedures as needed, and continue to review the rules throughout the first weeks of school. Explicit teaching of classroom rules early in the year not only facilitates a smoother school beginning but has positive long-term effects on student behavior and performance. In classes where teachers establish routines on the first day of school, students are more engaged in academic activities during the rest of the year (Emmer et al., 1980; Evertson & Emmer, 1982; Evertson et al., 1983). Direct instruction in rules and routines is especially important for prekindergarten and primary grade students, who are less familiar with classroom routines and require more socialization in the culture of the school (Brophy, 1988).

At the same time, however, rules alone are ineffective in modifying student behavior (e.g., Madsen, Becker, & Thomas, 1968; Medland & Stachnik, 1972). The use of rules must occur in the context of a comprehensive instructional and behavior management program that includes careful planning, learning activities that promote active student responding, and consistent consequences for rule infractions. This section includes two strategies designed to enhance the effectiveness of classroom rules. *Active Teaching of Classroom Rules* provides a systematic procedure for teaching and rehearsing rules that is ideal for implementation at the beginning of the school year. *Say Show Check: Teaching Classroom Procedures* is a keystone strategy with a model–lead–practice format that can be used not only to teach classroom rules and routines but also to introduce any of the interventions in this book.

ACTIVE TEACHING OF CLASSROOM RULES

Overview

Simply listing classroom rules on a chart or the chalkboard is not sufficient to develop and maintain appropriate student behavior. In contrast, actively teaching classroom rules not only communicates to students exactly what is expected but also provides teachers with opportunities to reinforce behavior consistent with the rules. This proactive intervention teaches classroom rules as a lesson with feedback and examples and includes a brief daily review and rehearsal. In the original study in a seventh-grade mathematics class, actively teaching classroom rules resulted in a reduction in disruptive behavior and an increase in appropriately engaged behavior.

Purpose

To help create and maintain an orderly, productive classroom through the explicit teaching of classroom rules.

Materials

1. Posterboard chart with a list of classroom rules, such as:
   a. Be prepared for class every day.
   b. Be considerate of others.

    c. Be on time to class.

    d. Do what you are asked to do, the first time you are asked.

    e. Follow directions.

2. 8½" × 11" sheets of paper listing the rules, one per student

Observation (Select One or Both)

Option 1

1. Using a *Classwide Scanning Form* with a 5-minute interval, scan the room begin-ning with the left side and tally the number of students displaying each of the three categories of behavior listed below:

    a. *Disruptive behavior:* behavior that produces physical changes in the classroom, including noise, and is unrelated to the assignment or interferes with the completion of the assignment by other students (e.g., talking without per-mission, throwing paper);

    b. *Inappropriately engaged behavior:* engaging in activities and/or directing atten-tion toward materials other than those assigned (e.g., writing notes, playing with materials);

    c. *Appropriately engaged behavior:* directing attention toward or engaging in the as-signment (e.g., raising hand, writing on worksheets).

2. Conduct these observations for 20 to 30 minutes during a selected instruction-al period for 4 to 7 days.

Option 2

1. Using a *Group Event Recording Form*, record the number of disruptive behaviors as defined above during a selected instructional period for 4 to 7 days.

Procedure

1. During a selected instructional period, display the classroom rules and give each student a handout listing the rules.

2. Tell students that you will be observing them at various times during the lesson to see if they are following the rules.

3. Spend about 10 minutes discussing the rules and their importance, providing specific examples, and having students provide examples.

4. During the lesson, provide behavior-specific praise and feedback at least three times for students following one or more of the rules. For example, say, "I ap-preciate how Row 3 students are following directions."

5. After the first day, spend about 3 minutes reteaching one or two rules at the be-ginning of each class.

Evaluation (Select One or Both)

Option 1

1. Compare the percentages of students displaying disruptive behavior, inappro-priately engaged behavior, and appropriately engaged behavior before and af-ter implementation.

Option 2
1. Compare the frequency of disruptive behaviors before and after implementation.

Variation

Have students take home the copies of the rules, discuss them with their parents, and return them signed.

Note

This intervention was originally used with an intact group of students who were taught by different teachers in different classrooms. For self-contained classroom groups, reteach the rules at the beginning of the school day.

Source

Johnson, T. C., Stoner, G., & Green, S. K. (1996). Demonstrating the experimenting society model with classwide behavior management interventions. *School Psychology Review, 25,* 199–214. Copyright 1996 by the National Association of School Psychologists. Adapted by permission.

SAY SHOW CHECK: TEACHING CLASSROOM PROCEDURES

Overview

Originally used with preschoolers, this keystone strategy helps to prevent disruptive behavior by providing direct instruction in how students are to behave during classroom routines and activities. Knowing motor and procedural rules builds students' sense of security in the classroom and prevents them from having to discover the rules by accidentally misbehaving and being reprimanded. This intervention can be adapted for any grade and any classroom procedure.

Purpose

To teach organizational and motor rules through explicit teaching, practice, and feedback.

Materials

None

Observation (Select One or Both)

1. Record the number of reprimands you deliver during certain classroom routines, such as class discussions, independent seatwork, or small-group work for 4 to 7 days.

2. Using a *Group Event Recording Form*, tally the number of inappropriate or disruptive behaviors during one or more classroom routines for 4 to 7 days. *Inappropriate or disruptive behaviors* are defined as any behaviors that interfere with the completion of classroom routines, such as verbal or physical aggression, dawdling, and failing to follow directions.

Procedure

Step 1: Say
1. Use words to verbally encode the motor or procedural rule.

> "We raise our hands when we want to participate in class discussions."

Step 2: Show
1. Show the rule visually by having a student model the correct behavior or do it yourself.

> "Serena, show the class how we raise our hands and wait to be called on to participate in discussions."

Step 3: Check
1. Check students' understanding by exhibiting the incorrect behavior while asking them to watch for a mistake.

> Call out, "*I know, I know!*" while wildly waving your hand. Then ask, "Class, did I ask to participate correctly?"

2. Demonstrate the correct behavior or ask a student to demonstrate it to the class and have students respond as to the correctness of the behavior.

> "Randy, show us how we raise our hands and wait to be called on to participate. Was that correct, class?"

3. Praise the student for the correct demonstration and the rest of the class for watching attentively.

Evaluation (Select One or Both)

1. Compare the number of reprimands delivered during selected classroom routines before and after implementation.
2. Compare the number of inappropriate or disruptive behaviors during selected routines before and after implementation.

Note

When using this strategy with upper elementary or middle school groups, demonstrate the incorrect behavior (see Step 3) cautiously, if at all. Field testing suggests that demonstrating the incorrect behavior or having a student demonstrate it can result in temporary increases in incorrect responding in an effort to attract peer attention.

Source

Managing Transitions

Changing from one activity or task to another occupies a significant portion of the school day. In fact, some studies (Durkin, 1978–1979; Ysseldyke et al., 1989) have found that students spend more time in transitions than instruction. Effective teachers are able to maximize active student engagement in learning activities while initiating fewer transitions and minimizing the time students spend making transitions between activities or waiting for lessons to begin (Brophy, 1988; Weade & Evertson, 1988). Smooth, rapid transitions protect learning time not only by reducing the time needed to change from one activity to another but also by minimizing the time needed to regain control lost after ineffective transitions. Moreover, because disruptive behavior is significantly more likely to occur in the context of transitions, establishing orderly transitional procedures decreases the likelihood that students will behave inappropriately (Arlin, 1979). Keeping transitions as rapid as possible is especially important for disabled and disadvantaged students, who are already at risk for lower engagement rates (Friedman et al., 1988; Stanley & Greenwood, 1983).

The interventions in this section use a variety of behavioral techniques to facilitate quick, disruption-free transitions. *Teaching Transition Time* provides students with direct instruction, guided practice, and feedback in making transitions. In *Speeding Up Transitions: Beat the Buzzer*, an intervention particularly well suited to prekindergarten and primary grade classrooms, making rapid transitions becomes an enjoyable classwide contest. *Peer-Monitored Transitions* combines peer-mediated and self-management procedures, with students monitoring and delivering rewards for quick changes between activities. Critical elements in all three interventions include preparing students for transitions, closely monitoring compliance, and providing positive feedback for successful transitions.

TEACHING TRANSITION TIME

Overview

The average elementary school classroom makes between 8 and 10 transitions of about 8 minutes each per day. As a result, one entire day per week of instructional time is lost to transitions. Reducing transition time between activities enhances learning opportunities because more time is available for instruction.

Purpose

To increase available instructional time by systematically teaching procedures for rapid and orderly transitions between tasks and activities.

Materials

1. Stopwatch or watch with second hand
2. Posterboard chart listing the following four rules for transition as follows:

> RULES FOR MAKING TRANSITIONS
> 1. Move quietly.
> 2. Put your books away and get what you need for the next activity.
> 3. Move your chair quietly.
> 4. Keep your hands and feet to yourself.

Observation (Select One or Both)

1. Select one or more times during the day when the class changes from one activity to another. Record the number of minutes required for students to complete one or more transitions for 4 to 7 days.
2. Count the number of disruptive behaviors that occur during one or more transitions for 4 to 7 days. *Disruptive behaviors* are defined as behaviors that interfere with the orderly completion of a transition, such as verbal or physical aggression, dawdling, and failing to follow directions.

Procedure

1. Display the chart with the four transition rules on it and teach the transition time lesson as described below.
2. "Transition time is the time it takes to change what you are doing. What is transition time?" [Have students respond as a group.]
3. "It is important that transition time be quick and quiet. What is important about transition time?" [Have students respond as a group.]
4. "That's right! I'm going to tell you four ways to make transition time quick and quiet. Move quietly during transition time. What is one way for transition time to be quick and quiet?" [Have students respond.] "Good. Now I'm going to tell you some more ways." [Repeat the procedure for all four rules.]
5. "Let's say all four ways to make transition time quick and quiet." [Point to the chart and have students respond.]
6. "I'm going to show you what I mean. Watch while I change activities at my desk." [Sit at your desk, put one book away, get out another book, have a pencil ready, and sit quietly.] "What did I do during this transition time?" [Call on individual students to review the first two rules.]
7. "Good, you're really watching! Now watch again as I show you a different kind of transition." [Put the book away, get out another book and pencil, stand up,

push your chair in quietly, walk to the reading table, sit down, open a book, and wait quietly.] "What did I do during this transition time?" [Call on individual students to review all four rules.]
8. "Great! Now I'm going to watch. I know you can change what you're doing by moving quietly, getting the proper materials ready, moving your chairs quietly, and keeping your hands and feet to yourself." [Have students practice while you monitor and give positive feedback.]

Evaluation (Select One or Both)

1. Compare the number of minutes required to complete one or more transitions before and after implementation.
2. Compare the frequency of disruptive behavior incidents during one or more transitions before and after implementation.

Variation

As an additional incentive for rapid transitions, time transitions with a stopwatch, as in *Speeding Up Transitions: Beat the Buzzer.*

Notes

1. The signal for transition time is: "It's transition time. Get ready for _____. You need _____."
2. For maximum benefit, the transition time lesson should be taught during the first week of school and retaught after school breaks or whenever transitions become lengthy or disruptive.

Source

Paine, S. C., Radicchi, J., Rosellini, L. C., Deutchman, L., & Darch, C. B. (1983). *Structuring your classroom for academic success* (pp. 84–88). Champaign, IL: Research Press. Copyright 1983 by the authors. Adapted by permission.

SPEEDING UP TRANSITIONS: BEAT THE BUZZER

Overview

First taught to parents to help habitually late children complete morning routines more promptly, this strategy has been applied to clean-up routines with preschoolers and transitions between activities with kindergartners to reduce dawdling and disruptive behavior. Although no backup contingencies are used in this adaptation, either positive or negative, reductions in time needed for transitions are often rapid and dramatic.

Purpose

To improve clean-up routines and reduce transition time by creating a game-like atmosphere.

Materials

1. Watch with second hand
2. Kitchen timer with a bell or stopwatch (see Variation 1)

Observation (Select One or Both)

1. Record the number of minutes required to complete one or more transitions or clean-up routines for 4 to 7 days.
2. Using a *Group Event Recording Form*, record the number of disruptive behaviors during one or more transitions for 4 to 7 days. *Disruptive behaviors* are defined as any behaviors that interfere with the orderly completion of a transition, such as verbal or physical aggression, dawdling, and failing to follow directions.

Procedure

1. At clean-up or transition time, give the following directions:

   > "Boys and girls, today we are going to play a game. I am going to set this timer to ring in _____ minutes, and I want to see if you can [move from first task or activity to second task or activity] before the buzzer rings. All your materials from _____ must be put away, and you must be ready for _____ when the buzzer goes off. Get ready to beat the buzzer! [Set the timer for slightly less than the average amount of time needed for clean-up or transition during the observation period.] . . . Go!"

2. If the buzzer rings before the transition is completed, continue timing but allow the children to finish.
3. Reduce the time allowed for transition gradually over the first few days of implementation until the desired criterion time is reached.

Evaluation (Select One or Both)

1. Compare the number of minutes required to complete one or more transitions or clean-up routines before and after implementation.
2. Compare the frequency of disruptive behaviors during one or more transitions before and after implementation.

Variations

1. Use a stopwatch or watch with a second hand to time clean-up routines or transitions. Modify the directions as follows:

"Boys and girls, today we are going to play a game. I am going to give you ____ minutes on this stopwatch [watch] and I want to see if you can [move from first task or activity to second task or activity] before the time is up. All your materials from ____ must be put away, and you must be ready for ____ when the time is up. Get ready to beat the stopwatch [watch]! . . . Go!"

2. To provide additional reinforcement, have the principal congratulate the students when they complete the transition within the criterion amount of time (see *Encouraging Academic Achievement with Principal Praise*).
3. Write the permitted amount of time for the transition on the chalkboard and take away 5 minutes of recess that day for each 1 minute over the criterion.
4. Use peer monitors to set the timer (or use the stopwatch or watch) and record the time needed for transitions.
5. Create a line graph on the chalkboard to record the number of minutes required to complete the target transitions each day for several weeks. Provide an activity reward, such as extra outdoor recess, when the time has been reduced to the desired criterion.

Notes

1. In the original study, children who completed morning routines on time were allowed to stay up an extra half hour at bedtime, whereas failing to beat the buzzer resulted in a half-hour loss of television time.
2. This intervention has been used successfully with elementary grade children as well as prekindergarten and kindergarten students in the field testing. Using a stopwatch or watch rather than a kitchen timer does not appear to reduce the effectiveness of the strategy and is more acceptable to upper elementary grade students.

Sources

Drabman, R. S., & Creedon, D. L. (1979). Beat the buzzer. *Child Behavior Therapy*, *1*, 295–296. Copyright 1979 by The Haworth Press. Adapted by permission.
Wurtele, S. K., & Drabman, R. S. (1984). "Beat the buzzer" for classroom dawdling: A one-year trial. *Behavior Therapy*, *15*, 403–409. Copyright 1984 by the Association for Advancement of Behavior Therapy. Adapted by permission.

PEER-MONITORED TRANSITIONS

Overview

Peer-mediated interventions can not only reduce teachers' classroom management duties but exert powerful positive influences on student behavior. In this strategy, students are trained to serve as peer monitors to award points for appropriate behavior during transitions. Originally used with behaviorally disordered kindergarten students, peer monitoring resulted in dramatic decreases in disruptive behavior and increases in positive participation during clean-up routines and transitions.

Purpose

To reduce transition time and increase positive participation during transitions by using a peer-monitored reward system.

Materials

1. Posterboard chart or section of the chalkboard with student names for recording points
2. Stopwatch or watch with second hand
3. 8½" × 11" sheets of paper for recording points, one for each team, with the names of the members for that team listed down the left side of the paper and three columns going across the paper, one for each of the target transition behaviors
4. Slips of paper with students' names written on them, placed in a box or jar

Observation (Select One or More)

Option 1
1. Using a sheet of paper listing student names and attached to a clipboard, award one point for each of the following behaviors during a selected transition (such as restroom break) for 4 to 7 days for the entire class or for a selected group of students:
   a. *Appropriate cleanup behavior:* helping to clean up without fighting, being disruptive, or leaving the room without permission;
   b. *Appropriate bathroom behavior:* walking to the restroom, using it within 3 minutes, and walking directly back to the classroom;
   c. *Appropriate waiting behavior:* returning to the assigned area or desk and waiting without disturbing others.

Option 2
1. Using a *Group Event Recording Form*, record the number of disruptive behaviors during one or more transitions for 4 to 7 days. *Disruptive behaviors* are defined as any behaviors that interfere with the orderly completion of a transition, such as verbal or physical aggression, dawdling, and failing to follow directions.

Option 3
1. Record the number of minutes required to complete one or more transitions for 4 to 7 days.

Procedure

1. Select a transition period, such as cleanup or bathroom time, during which dawdling and disruptive behavior are especially likely to occur.

2. Tell students that they are going to learn a new way to help each other make quick transitions between activities.
3. Divide the students into teams by tables, rows, or some other method and explain that they will be working in teams to earn points for quick and orderly transitions.
4. Select a peer monitor for each team. Explain that all students will have an opportunity to serve as peer monitors or "captains."
5. Explain that the captains' duties are to participate in the transition, watch their teammates, remind them of the appropriate behaviors, and award points for their participation at the end of the transition period.
6. Explain that each student can earn one point for each of the following behaviors (or other behaviors relevant to the target transition):
   a. *Appropriate cleanup behavior:* helping to clean up without fighting, being disruptive, or leaving the room without permission;
   b. *Appropriate bathroom behavior:* walking to the restroom, using it within 3 minutes, and walking directly back to the classroom;
   c. *Appropriate waiting behavior:* returning to the assigned area or desk and waiting without disturbing others.
7. Display the chart for awarding points or create a chart on a section of the chalkboard and explain the reward system as follows:
   a. Students earning three points are eligible to vote for and participate in a daily outdoor activity or a free-time activity.
   b. Students earning two points can participate in the activity but cannot vote on its selection.
   c. Students earning less than two points must remain inside during the outdoor activity and clean other areas of the classroom or may not participate in the free-time activity.
8. Explain that at the end of each transition period, the captains will meet with you and team members to award points. Display the sheets for recording points and demonstrate how to record points next to team members' names.
9. Conduct a training session that includes a rehearsal of the captains' duties and appropriate transition behaviors.
10. Explain that on all subsequent days, students will be eligible to serve as captains if they receive three points on the previous day. Place the names of all those with three points in a box or jar and draw one name for each team.
11. During the first several days of the intervention, remind the captains of the procedures and their duties. If captains award points incorrectly, provide corrective feedback.
12. As the intervention continues, reduce the frequency of reminders and corrective feedback provided to captains.

Evaluation (Select One or More)

Option 1
1. Compare the number of points awarded for appropriate cleanup, bathroom, and waiting behaviors (or other relevant transition behaviors) for the entire class or for the selected group of students before and after implementation.

Option 2
1. Compare the frequency of disruptive behaviors during one or more transitions before and after implementation.

Option 3
1. Compare the number of minutes required to complete one or more transitions before and after implementation.

Variation

Award points by teams rather than to individual students. That is, if every student on a team displays the appropriate transition behaviors in that category, award a point to the team. Provide privileges as described above. Rotate captain duties on a random basis.

Note

Although in the original study, peer monitors often failed to withhold points for undesirable behavior, this did not alter the overall effectiveness of the intervention.

Source

Smith, L. K., & Fowler, S. A. (1984). Positive peer pressure: The effects of peer monitoring on children's disruptive behavior. *Journal of Applied Behavior Analysis, 17*, 213–217. Copyright 1984 by the Society for the Experimental Analysis of Behavior. Adapted by permission.

Managing Independent Seatwork

Students in the elementary grades spend about 60 to 70% of their time doing seatwork (Filby & Cahen, 1985; Fisher et al., 1980; Good, 1983). Seatwork includes tasks that are performed without the teacher's direct supervision and typically consist of reading and writing activities. Although seatwork enables teachers to assist individuals or small groups, grade papers, plan, and deal with the myriad of daily classroom tasks, the use of seatwork is also associated with several instructional and behavior management problems. First, if seatwork occurs in conjunction with individual or small-group instruction, as is common practice in the elementary grades, the teacher must deliver that instruction while simultaneously ensuring that seatwork students perform their assigned tasks and do not disrupt teacher-directed instruction. Second, student engagement rates are considerably lower for seatwork compared with teacher-led instruction (Anderson, 1981; Kounin, 1970, Rosenshine, 1980), especially if students do not have regular contact with teachers to obtain feedback (Fisher et al.,

1980). In fact, as the length of the seatwork period increases, the engagement rate decreases (Filby & Cahen, 1985). Third, excessive use of seatwork activities is associated with lower student achievement compared with active teaching (Good, 1983). Learning is often compromised because students fail to understand their tasks or the teacher's goal in assigning the work. Teachers spend little time preparing students to complete written assignments (Durkin, 1978–1979), and many students view the primary purpose of seatwork as completing it and handing it in (Anderson, 1984a, 1984b; Anderson, Brubaker, Alleman-Brooks, & Duffy, 1985). Finally, behavior problems are especially prevalent in classrooms in which teachers rely excessively on seatwork (Moskowitz & Hayman, 1976).

The strategies in this section are designed to promote academic productivity and decrease disruptive behavior during seatwork. For maximum effectiveness, they should be implemented in the context of a seatwork structure characterized by clear explanations of the goals to be achieved by seatwork, specific instructions for completing assignments, and frequent monitoring of students for signs that they do not understand their seatwork tasks. In *Checking Stations*, students learn a self-managed error correction procedure that eliminates the need to wait for teacher assistance with seatwork. *The Coupon System: Decreasing Inappropriate Requests for Teacher Assistance* uses a peer-monitored response cost system to encourage independent effort during seatwork. In *The Study Game: Increasing Productivity during Seatwork*, a game-like format provides incentives for appropriate behavior during seatwork. Chapter 4 presents several interventions that are designed to replace seatwork with peer-supervised skills practice (*Classwide Peer Tutoring; Join the Team: Reciprocal Peer Tutoring; Peer Tutoring in Sight Words; Reciprocal Peer Tutoring to Improve Math Achievement;* and *The Peer Tutoring Spelling Game*).

CHECKING STATIONS

Overview

Providing students with immediate feedback about their performance not only enhances learning but prevents mistakes from being perpetuated. This intervention teaches students to correct some of their own papers at one or more checking stations in the classroom and thus reduces the burden of grading papers for teachers. Checking stations decrease "down time" and increase productivity because students do not need to wait to receive feedback on written work.

Purpose

To improve productivity and learning by providing immediate feedback to students on written assignments.

Materials

1. One or more checking stations, consisting of a small table or two adjacent desks, with a separate station for each subject area
2. Red pen or marker, one per checking station
3. Teacher-prepared answer keys
4. Box, tray, or folder for corrected work
5. Posterboard chart at the checking stations listing the following rules:
   a. Only one person at each checking station.
   b. Leave your pens and pencils at your desk.
   c. Check your work quietly.
   d. Place corrected work in the box.
6. Stickers, homework passes, and/or other small reinforcers

Observation (Select One or More)

1. Calculate the percentage of papers students complete during the independent seatwork period for 4 to 7 days.
2. Calculate average grades on seatwork for the entire class or for a selected group of students for 4 to 7 days.
3. Using a sheet of paper attached to a clipboard, record the number of student requests for help during independent seatwork for 4 to 7 days.

Procedure

1. Tell the students that they are going to be learning a new way of correcting their own papers.
2. Review the rules and model the checking procedure as follows:
   a. If someone is already at a checking station, use another station or stay at your desk until it is clear.
   b. Leave pencils and pens at your desk and take your paper to the checking station.
   c. Check each answer with the answer key.
   d. Circle wrong answers with the red pen or marker.
   e. Go back to your seat, cross out the wrong answers, and write in the correct answers.
   f. Check your paper again with the answer key.
   g. Put the corrected paper in the box.
3. Tell students that you expect them to be honest and that each day you will look at some of the papers to make sure they have been checked correctly. Tell them that if those students have found all their mistakes, they will earn a reward (such as a sticker, homework pass, or special classroom privilege).
4. Praise students for correct checking behavior at the stations.
5. Spot check some of the papers each day to review accuracy. Provide praise and a small reward if students have found all of their mistakes.
6. Phase out the rewards as students become accustomed to using the checking stations.

Evaluation (Select One or More)

1. Compare the classwide percentage of papers completed during independent seatwork before and after implementation.
2. Compare average grades on seatwork for the entire class or for the selected group of students before and after implementation.
3. Compare the frequency of student requests for help during independent seatwork before and after implementation.

Variation

For the primary grades, illustrating the rules chart with pictures and reviewing the procedures frequently are recommended to ensure smooth implementation.

Notes

1. Begin with a checking station in one subject only. Mathematics is recommended as the easiest subject for checking.
2. If cheating occurs, provide some kind of consequence, such as a writing time-out (see *Eliminating Disruptive Lunchroom Behavior with Mediation Essays*) or time lost from recess.

Source

Paine, S. C., Radicchi, J., Rosellini, L. C., Deutchman, L., & Darch, C. B. (1983). *Structuring your classroom for academic success* (pp. 123–127). Champaign, IL: Research Press. Copyright 1983 by the authors. Adapted by permission.

THE COUPON SYSTEM: DECREASING INAPPROPRIATE REQUESTS FOR TEACHER ASSISTANCE

Overview

Students' excessive or inappropriate requests for help can disrupt ongoing instruction and reduce opportunities for learning in both whole-class and small-group situations. This intervention uses a response cost token system to encourage independent effort and reduce unnecessary requests for help. Originally used with a single learning-disabled student, the strategy has been modified for a classwide format by using peer monitoring and a group contingency to reduce teacher supervision time. The individualized format is included as a variation. The strategy is especially useful when the teacher is engaged in small-group instruction while the rest of the class is performing independent seatwork.

Purpose

To decrease inappropriate requests for help with a peer-monitored response cost token system.

Materials

1. "Coupons," consisting of 1" × 2" construction paper strips, a set number per team or target student
2. Paper or plastic cups, one per team
3. Tape (see Variation 1)

Observation (Select One or Both)

1. Using a sheet of paper attached to a clipboard, record the frequency of requests for help made by the entire class or a small group of students during a selected instructional period, such as seatwork, for 4 to 7 days.
2. Using a sheet of paper attached to a clipboard, record the frequency of disruptive behaviors displayed by the entire class or a small group of students during a selected instructional period for 4 to 7 days. *Disruptive behaviors* are defined as any student behaviors that interfere with ongoing instruction or the on-task behavior of another student, such as calling out, being out of seat, or talking loudly.

Procedure

1. Explain to the students that they will be playing a game to help them learn to work more independently during the selected instructional period.
2. Divide the class into teams according to rows, tables, or desk clusters.
3. At the beginning of the target period, assign a student "captain" for each team and give each team a predetermined number of strips of construction paper placed in a paper or plastic cup on the captain's desk or in the center of the table. Using different colored strips for each team prevents students from supplementing their tokens with those taken from other teams.
4. Explain that the strips are coupons that can be redeemed for various privileges, such as lunch with the teacher, free time, a special art activity, extra recess time, etc.
5. Distribute to the teams one more coupon than the permitted number of requests for assistance (e.g., six coupons for five requests), and explain that team members will receive the reward if their team has at least one coupon left at the end of the period.
6. Each time a student requests help, assess the student's ability to understand and complete the task. If the student seeks assistance after you have informed him or her not to do so by saying, "I think you understand," instruct the captain of that team to remove one coupon and return it to you.
7. At the end of the period, have captains count the number of remaining coupons and indicate which teams will be receiving the reward.
8. As students successfully decrease the number of inappropriate requests for help, decrease the number of coupons distributed per team.

Evaluation (Select One or Both)

1. Compare the frequency of requests for help made by the entire class or the target students during the selected instructional period before and after implementation.

2. Compare the frequency of disruptive behaviors displayed by the entire class-room group or the target students during the selected instructional period before and after implementation.

Variations

1. For implementation with a single student or a small group of students, tape a predetermined number of coupons on the desk of each target student and remove them yourself for inappropriate requests for help.
2. This intervention can also be used to decrease inappropriate or disruptive behaviors during seatwork (e.g., calling out without permission, talking loudly, getting out of seat, etc.). Give a predetermined number of coupons to the teams and administer rewards to teams having at least one coupon left at the end of the seatwork period.
3. Instead of distributing coupons to teams, place a predetermined number of coupons in a plastic or paper cup on your desk or at the table where you are conducting small-group instruction, and remove one coupon for each call-out, out-of-seat, or other disruptive behavior during the seatwork period. Be sure the coupons are visible to the students. If at least one coupon remains at the end of the period, the entire class receives the reward.

Notes

1. If the intervention is targeted at only a few students, it is important to limit rewards to various forms of teacher attention (e.g., eating lunch with the teacher, helping the teacher prepare materials, etc.) or positive school–home notes so that other students are not deprived of the opportunity to earn tangible rewards.
2. Because asking for assistance is appropriate when students do not understand assignments or lack the skills necessary to complete them, assessing students' competence to complete assigned tasks prior to removing coupons is an important component of this strategy.

Source

Salend, S. J., & Henry, K. (1981). Response cost in mainstreamed settings. *Journal of School Psychology, 19*, 242–249. Copyright 1981 by Elsevier Science Ltd, Oxford, England. Adapted by permission.

THE STUDY GAME: IMPROVING PRODUCTIVITY DURING SEATWORK

Overview

Managing small-group instruction while simultaneously supervising the rest of the class in independent seatwork is one of the most difficult classroom management tasks for teachers. This intervention takes the form of a classroom game similar to "Seven-Up" to create incentives for productivity during seatwork periods so that the teacher can conduct small-group instruction without having to stop to deal with disruptions. It requires no backup reinforcers and a minimum of teacher time and has been shown to be highly effective in increasing study rates and decreasing disruptive behaviors.

Purpose

To increase on-task behavior and reduce disruptions during independent seatwork and small-group instructional time.

Materials

1. Stopwatch or watch with second hand
2. Sheet of paper for recording names of best studiers (optional)
3. Posterboard chart with a list of student names down the left side and a series of columns for awarding stars; gold stars or stickers (see variation)
4. "Best Studier" certificates (see variation)

Observation (Select One or Both)

Option 1
1. Select a period during which small-group instruction and independent seatwork occur and conduct the following observations for 4 to 7 days.
2. Using a *Group Interval Recording Form* with a 10-second interval, observe each student on a consecutive basis, beginning with the left side of the room. Continue until the observation period is over (between 20 minutes and the length of the target period).
3. Code students according to the following two categories:
   a. *Nonstudy:* student is out of seat, talks without permission, is not working, or is not attending to instruction or the task at hand;
   b. *Study:* student is looking at the appropriate materials, answering teacher's questions, working on the assignment, or otherwise responding appropriately to instruction.

Option 2
1. Using a *Group Event Recording Form*, count the number of disruptive behaviors during the selected small-group instructional and independent seatwork time. *Disruptive behaviors* are defined as student behaviors that interfere with the learning of others, such as calling out, being out of seat, and talking loudly.

Procedure

1. Tell the students you want them to learn to work harder on their seatwork while you are working with small groups and so you will be looking for the "best studiers" ("star studiers," etc.) during that time.

2. Tell them that after the seatwork period, you will select the seven best studiers to go to the front of the classroom. Explain that you will be looking up from the reading circle (or other small-group instruction) several times and noticing the students who are the best studiers.

3. Praise appropriate studying behaviors at regular intervals during the seatwork period. Make one positive comment about every 3 to 5 minutes, such as, "Tonya is being a good studier." If desired, use a sheet of paper to record the names of the best studiers.

4. At the conclusion of the seatwork period, call the seven best studiers to the front of the room and praise them for their efforts.

5. Have the rest of the students put their heads down on their desks and close their eyes, while the seven students tiptoe around, lightly tap one of the seated students on the head, and return to the front of the room.

6. Have the seated students open their eyes. Then have the seven who were touched stand up and try to guess who tapped them. If they guess correctly, they get to be "it" on the next round.

7. Conduct several rounds of the game. Praise the class for learning to be good studiers.

Evaluation (Select One or Both)

Option 1

1. Compare the percentage of students with study and nonstudy behaviors during the selected period before and after implementation.

Option 2

1. Compare the frequency of disruptive behaviors during the selected period before and after implementation.

Note

Demonstrate and have students practice the procedure before implementation. This increases motivation and helps to ensure that tapping and moving around the room go smoothly.

Variation

Instead of playing the Seven-Up game to reward the best studiers, display a posterboard chart with a list of student names. Place a gold star or sticker next to the names of the "best studiers" for the day or send home "best studier" certificates each day with the seven selected students.

Source

Hall, R. V., Panyan, M., Rabon, D., & Broden, M. (1968). Instructing beginning teachers in reinforcement procedures which improve classroom control. *Journal of Applied Behavior Analysis, 1*, 315–322. Copyright 1968 by the Society for the Experimental Analysis of Behavior. Adapted by permission.

Communicating Competently with Students

One of the most important dimensions of effective classroom management is the teacher's ability to communicate with students (Anderson, Evertson, & Brophy, 1979; Emmer et al., 1980, 1997). Effective teachers maintain more direct eye contact, use a businesslike tone of voice, and more frequently scan the entire group, all behaviors that communicate teacher competence from the very first day of school (Brooks, 1985). In addition, effective teachers display more behaviors that communicate their acceptance of students, such as dealing with students' feelings, using praise, giving encouraging feedback, and smiling, especially on the first day of school (Moskowitz & Hayman, 1976). Unfortunately, teachers' communications with students sometimes fail to achieve the desired result and may, at times, have the opposite effect to that intended (e.g., Madsen, Becker, Thomas, Koser, & Plager, 1968; Thomas, Becker, & Armstrong, 1968). In one study (Madsen, Becker, Thomas, Koser, & Plager, 1968), delivering high rates of reprimands in an effort to reduce standing-up behavior resulted in more stand-ups! This section presents strategies targeting three key communication competencies: (1) delivering effective praise, (2) delivering effective reprimands, and (3) communicating positive expectations.

Delivering Effective Praise

Numerous studies attest to the power of contingent teacher attention and praise in creating a positive classroom climate and enhancing student behavior (Becker, Madsen, Arnold, & Thomas, 1967; Broden, Bruce, Mitchell, Carter, & Hall, 1970; Brophy, 1981). Despite the effectiveness of praise and teachers' reported preference for positive interventions such as praise over negative strategies such as reprimands (Elliott et al., 1984; Witt, Martens, & Elliott, 1984; Witt & Robbins, 1985), teachers' natural rates of praise are quite low, especially after the early elementary grades (Abramowitz, O'Leary, & Rosén, 1987; Strain, Lambert, Kerr, Stagg, & Lenkner, 1983; Thomas, Presland, Grant, & Glynn, 1978; White, 1975). Moreover, teacher praise is almost exclusively for academic performance rather than appropriate social behavior, such as following classroom rules and procedures (Heller & White, 1975; Strain et al., 1983; White, 1975).

Characteristics of Effective Praise. Even when teachers do praise students, their praise often fails to shape behavior in the desired direction because it does not function as effective reinforcement. For praise to be effective as a reinforcer, it must have three characteristics: contingency, specificity, and sincerity. That is, praise should be contingent on the performance of the desired behavior, it should specify the characteristics of the behavior that is being praised, and it should sound credible to the student being praised. Unfortunately, most teacher praise fails to promote positive behavior change because it is not delivered contingent on the desired behavior, lacks specificity in identifying target behaviors, and/or lacks credibility and sincerity (Brophy, 1981).

A second problem associated with the use of praise as a classroom management strategy is that praise is not sufficient by itself to maintain high levels of on-task behavior. Although many teachers have been taught to praise positive behavior and ignore negative behavior, this praise-and-ignore strategy can lead to the spread of inappropriate behavior and does nothing to teach more positive alternative behaviors (Kounin, 1970). Moreover, ignoring student misbehavior, especially after the primary grades, can lead to an escalation of misbehavior because of the reinforcement provided by peer attention. In fact, using praise as a management strategy without including some form of negative consequences has been associated with dramatic declines in on-task behavior and in some cases, with chaotic classrooms (Acker & O'Leary, 1987; Pfiffner, Rosén, & O'Leary, 1985; Rosén, O'Leary, Joyce, Conway, & Pfiffner, 1984). Finally, even appropriately delivered praise will have little effect on student performance if existing academic skill deficiencies are not identified and addressed. In other words, social reinforcement in and of itself is not sufficient to sustain on-task behavior if students are unable to perform their assigned tasks (Becker et al., 1967; Hay, Hay, & Nelson, 1977).

The intervention in this section, *Improving Achievement and Behavior with Contingent Praise,* combines the three characteristics of effective praise with the incentives offered by a team competition. Public posting and visual cuing further enhance the effectiveness of the praise, which is delivered contingent upon academic productivity rather than social behavior.

IMPROVING ACHIEVEMENT AND BEHAVIOR WITH CONTINGENT PRAISE

Overview

Although praise is important for creating a positive classroom climate, it is frequently ineffective in improving achievement or behavior because it lacks contingency, specificity, or credibility. This strategy combines the ingredients of effective praise with visual cues and public recognition to improve academic productivity and behavior. Dramatic improvements in on-task behavior as well as in classwork accuracy and completion rates have been reported, even when praise is delivered only for academic performance. Applied in the original study to a small group of students, it is adapted here for total classroom use by using group-oriented praise and a group contingency.

Purpose

To improve academic achievement and on-task behavior during the independent seatwork period by using systematic praise and reinforcement.

Materials

1. "Good Work" cards, consisting of 3" × 5" index cards, one per team or target student per day; if desired, write "Good Work Card" at the top of each card or have the students do so
2. Posterboard chart listing the names of the teams down the left side and columns for affixing stars
3. Small gold stars for the "Good Work" cards
4. Large gold stars or stickers for the class chart

Observation (Select One or More)

Option 1
1. Using a *Group Event Recording Form*, record the number of target off-task behaviors exhibited by the entire class during an instructional period for 4 to 7 days. For example, tally out-of-seat and talk-out behaviors during this period.

Option 2
1. Calculate the class average percent correct for classwork in a selected academic subject for 5 to 10 days or for several weeks.

Option 3
1. Select a small group of students who frequently exhibit off-task behavior during a selected instructional period.
2. Using a *Group Interval Recording Form*, glance at a target student every 10 seconds and record the student's behavior at that instant as on-task or off-task. Record behavior for each target student in turn as follows for 20 to 30 minutes:
   a. *On-task behavior:* attending to the assigned task, including looking at the textbook, writing on worksheets, raising one's hand to ask task-related questions, and looking at the teacher during instruction;
   b. *Off-task behavior:* non-task-related behaviors such as being out of seat and talking to other students.
3. Conduct these observations for 4 to 7 days.

Option 4
1. Select a small group of students who are frequently unproductive or disruptive during classwork or independent seatwork.

2. Calculate the percent accuracy and completion rate for each student for one or more classwork assignments during the selected period by dividing the number of correct problems by the total number of problems assigned.
3. Record these observations for 5 to 10 days.

Procedure

1. Select an instructional period when students are especially off-task and unproductive.
2. Divide the class into teams by rows or tables or some other method.
3. Explain to the students that they will be working in teams to earn gold stars for accurate work. At the beginning of the selected period, distribute Good Work cards to each team. If students are seated at tables or in desk clusters, place a Good Work card on the table or on a desk in the cluster. If students are seated in rows, tape a Good Work card on the wall or chalkboard near the row.
4. During the instructional period, pick up a student paper from each team three times (three different students). If a problem is correctly completed, deliver a specific praise statement, using the team's name (e.g., "Good, Orioles, you're getting your addition problems right!"; "Table 3, you're doing a fine job on your spelling!") and put a star on the team's Good Work card.
5. If no problems are correct at that time, return the paper to the student with no comment.
6. At the end of the period, have each team report the number of stars received by all team members and praise the teams for working hard.
7. Place a large gold star or sticker on the class chart to indicate the team(s) with the largest number of stars on their Good Work cards.

Evaluation (Select One or More)

Option 1
1. Compare the frequency of off-task behaviors for the entire class during the selected instructional period before and after implementation.

Option 2
1. Compare the class average percent correct for classwork in the selected academic subject before and after implementation.

Option 3
1. Compare on- and off-task behavior rates for target students during the selected instructional period before and after implementation.

Option 4
1. Compare classwork percent accuracy and completion rates for target students for the selected instructional period before and after implementation.

Variation

To use this intervention with individuals or small groups of students, modify the procedures as follows:

1. Distribute Good Work cards to target students.
2. During the instructional period, pick up each student's paper five times and give a specific praise statement for correct problems, using the student's name (e.g., "Good, Sam, you got that reading question right!"; "Tywanda, you're doing a good job on those subtraction problems!").
3. Also put one star on the student's Good Work card if any problems are correctly completed.
4. If no problems are correct at that time, return the paper to the student with no comment.
5. If you wish, have students take the Good Work cards home daily for parents to review and return signed.

Note

Because this intervention requires teachers to move around the room to check papers and deliver praise during independent seatwork, it is not suitable for use during a period that also includes small-group instruction. To implement it during a period that includes both small-group instruction and independent seatwork, use the variation with a small group of students and teach them to bring their papers and Good Work cards to you for a quick review before returning to their seats.

Source

Hay, W. M., Hay, L. R., & Nelson, R. O. (1977). Direct and collateral changes in on-task and academic behavior resulting from on-task versus academic contingencies. *Behavior Therapy, 8,* 431–441. Copyright 1977 by the Association for Advancement of Behavior Therapy. Adapted by permission.

Delivering Effective Reprimands

Teachers use reprimands more frequently than any other behavior management strategy. Teachers deliver verbal reprimands much more often than praise (Brophy, 1981; Thomas et al., 1978), about once every 2 minutes in some studies (Heller & White, 1975; White, 1975). Teacher reliance on reprimands is related to the efficacy of reprimands in maintaining appropriate classroom behavior. Numerous studies (Abramowitz et al., 1987; Acker & O'Leary, 1987; O'Leary, Kaufman, Kass, & Drabman, 1970; Rosén et al., 1984) have documented the successful use of reprimands in reducing inappropriate behavior in regular and special education classes. Moreover, some researchers (Abramowitz, O'Leary, & Futtersak, 1988) have found that reprimands result in improvement not only in social behavior but also on measures of academic productivity, such as assignment completion.

Although reprimands can help maintain an orderly, productive classroom, there are several problems associated with the use, or rather, the overuse and misuse of reprimands. First, reprimands can be highly disruptive to ongoing instruction, especially when they are long, loud, and delivered at a distance from the misbehaving student. Second, although reprimands may temporarily suppress inappropriate behavior, they quickly lose their effectiveness if they are used excessively. Students habituate rapidly to frequent reprimands, so that teachers must increase the frequency and volume of their reprimands to obtain the same results. Third, attention from peers can sustain negative student behavior, even in the context of teacher reprimands. Similarly, by providing teacher attention for misbehavior, frequent reprimands can actually reinforce the very behaviors they are designed to reduce (Hall et al., 1968; Madsen, Becker, Thomas, Koser, & Plager, 1968; Thomas et al., 1968).

Components of Effective Reprimands. Research on teacher–student communications has identified four dimensions that enhance reprimand effectiveness: (1) brevity, (2) softness, (3) proximity, and (4) physical contact. First, short reprimands consisting of the student's name and no more than two other words are more effective than long reprimands, probably because short reprimands deliver less attention for misbehavior and are less likely to prompt arguments from misbehaving students (Abramowitz et al., 1988). Second, soft reprimands audible only to the student being reprimanded can have pronounced positive effects on behavior, whereas loud reprimands are ineffective and can lead to a vicious cycle of more frequent reprimands followed by more disruptive behavior (O'Leary et al., 1970). Third, reprimands have little effect when delivered from a distance but produce a marked reduction in disruptive behavior when delivered within 1 meter of the misbehaving student (Van Houten, Nau, MacKenzie-Keating, Sameoto, & Colavecchia, 1982). Proximity may also be responsible for the "spillover" effects observed in some studies (Van Houten et al., 1982), in which misbehavior decreases for nontarget students when pupils seated nearby are reprimanded. Fourth, physical contact enhances the effectiveness of verbal reprimands. Van Houten et al. (1982) found that reprimands combined with eye contact and a firm grasp of the student's shoulder were more effective than verbal reprimands alone. In *Short, Soft, and Close: Delivering Effective Reprimands* these four dimensions are combined to maximize the effectiveness of verbal reprimands. Because of the possibility that students may misinterpret or respond negatively to any form of physical teacher–student contact, however, the addition of physical contact is included only as a variation.

SHORT, SOFT, AND CLOSE: DELIVERING EFFECTIVE REPRIMANDS

Overview

Although teachers use reprimands more often than any other strategy to control problem behavior, reprimands are often ineffective in improving on-task behavior or academic productivity. This intervention combines three elements that have been demonstrated to enhance reprimand effectiveness: brevity, softness, and proximity. Short, soft reprimands delivered in close proximity to misbehaving or unproductive students are less embarrassing and thus less likely to provoke a confrontation. Moreover, they interfere less with ongoing instruction, reduce adult attention for inappropriate behavior, and elicit less peer attention. The addition of touch has also been found to enhance the effectiveness of reprimands. Because many teachers are reluctant to use even positive touch for fear that it may be misinterpreted by students or parents and because touching a disruptive student can provoke a confrontation, using touch is included only as a variation.

Purpose

To reduce off-task and disruptive behavior by using short, soft, and close reprimands.

Observation (Select One or More)

Option 1
1. Select an instructional period in which students are most disruptive and unproductive.
2. Using a *Classwide Scanning Form*, scan the room every 3 to 5 minutes from left to right and tally the number of students in each of the following behavior categories:
    a. *On-task behavior:* answering or asking lesson-oriented questions, participating in class discussions, looking at the teacher during instruction, sitting quietly and waiting for directions, or any other behavior consistent with the ongoing lesson or activity;
    b. *Off-task behavior:* sitting without appropriate materials, looking at nonlesson materials, or looking around the room after assignments have been made;
    c. *Disruptive behavior:* any behavior that disrupts the academic performance of another student, including making noises, calling out, and physical aggression.
3. Record these behaviors for 20 to 30 minutes for 4 to 7 days.

Option 2
1. Select a small group of students who frequently exhibit off-task or disruptive behavior during a selected instructional period, such as independent seatwork.
2. Using a *Group Interval Recording Form*, glance at a target student every 10 seconds and record the student's behavior at that instant as on-task, off-task, or disruptive as defined above.

3. Record behavior for each target student in turn for 20 to 30 minutes for 4 to 7 days.

Option 3
1. Calculate the class average percent correct for daily work during the selected instructional period for 5 to 10 days.

Option 4
1. Using a sheet of paper attached to a clipboard, record the number of reprimands you deliver to the entire class or a small group of students during a selected instructional period for 4 to 7 days.

Procedure

1. If this intervention is primarily directed at a small group of students, move them near the front of the classroom or to an area of the classroom that you can reach rapidly.
2. When a student exhibits an undesired behavior, move to within touching distance, obtain eye contact, and deliver a short, soft, and close reprimand as follows:
   a. *Short:* no more than two words in addition to the student's name (e.g., "Sam, stop talking!");
   b. *Soft:* audible only to the student being reprimanded;
   c. *Close:* near enough to the student to touch him or her and obtain eye contact.
3. Try to catch the reprimanded student being good within the next few minutes so you can reinforce positive academic or social behavior.

Evaluation (Select One or More)

Option 1
1. Compare the percentages of on-task, off-task, and disruptive students before and after implementation.

Option 2
1. Compare on-task, off-task, and disruptive behavior rates for the small group of students before and after implementation.

Option 3
1. Compare the class average percent correct for daily work during the selected period before and after implementation.

Option 4
1. Compare the number of reprimands you deliver to the entire class or the small group of students during the selected period before and after implementation.

Variation

If the student is off-task, gently lay a hand on the student's upper arm or shoulder for the duration of the reprimand (3 to 4 seconds). Do not use this variation if the student is exhibiting disruptive behavior or has a history of negative responses to physical touch, or if school district policy discourages physical teacher–student contact.

Notes

1. Even if this intervention is directed primarily at a small group of unproductive or disruptive students, short, soft, and close reprimands should be used with all the students in the class during implementation because of evidence of positive "spillover" effects. That is, peers seated near target students also show improvement in on-task behavior and productivity.
2. Attempt to obtain eye contact when delivering reprimands, but do not force the student to look at you. Forcing eye contact may be shaming for some students and may provoke a confrontation. Moreover, if obtaining eye contact prolongs the length of the reprimand, the reprimand will be less effective.

Sources

Abramowitz, A. J., O'Leary, S. G., & Futtersak, M. W. (1988). The relative impact of long and short reprimands on children's off-task behavior in the classroom. *Behavior Therapy*, *19*, 243–247. Copyright 1988 by the Association for Advancement of Behavior Therapy. Adapted by permission.

O'Leary, K. D., Kaufman, K. F., Kass, R. E., & Drabman, R. S. (1970).The effects of loud and soft reprimands on the behavior of disruptive students. *Exceptional Children*, *37*, 145–155. Copyright by The Council for Exceptional Children. Adapted by permission.

Van Houten, R., Nau, P. A., MacKenzie-Keating, S. E., Sameoto, D., & Colavecchia, B. (1982). An analysis of some variables influencing the effectiveness of reprimands. *Journal of Applied Behavior Analysis*, *15*, 65–83. Copyright 1982 by the Society for the Experimental Analysis of Behavior. Adapted by permission.

Communicating Positive Expectations

A key element in creating a productive classroom environment is communicating positive expectations for academic and social behavior (Brophy, 1988). Although teachers often spend considerable time exhorting students to behave appropriately, there is no evidence that this strategy is effective in shaping positive social behavior (Miller, Brickman, & Bolen, 1975). Similarly, holding high academic expectations without simultaneously designing an instructional program that permits students to be successful is likely to increase frustration rather than achievement. In contrast, when teachers consistently treat students as if they respect themselves and others, are capable of succeeding, and wish to act responsibly, and then reward behaviors directed toward those outcomes, students are more likely to attribute the same desirable qualities to themselves and behave accordingly (Brophy, 1988).

The first intervention in this section, *Promoting Positive Behavior through Attribution*, makes explicit teachers' positive expectations for an entire classroom of students and can be used to target a wide variety of academic and social behaviors. The second intervention, *Problem-Solving Student Conferences*, provides a structure for conferencing with students with persistent problems. Although proactive, group-focused interventions can prevent most behavior problems, the growing number of difficult-to-teach students makes it imperative that teachers acquire strategies for effectively communicating with individual students or small groups of students who are chronically disruptive, defiant, or unproductive. Like the other intervention in this section, it communicates positive expectations by conveying to students the belief that they can collaborate with teachers in solving their own classroom problems. A sample conference with two inattentive and disruptive students is included for practice purposes.

PROMOTING POSITIVE BEHAVIOR THROUGH ATTRIBUTION

Overview

Although teachers often use *persuasion* in an effort to change student behavior ("You should work harder"; "You should be more polite"), there is little empirical evidence that this strategy is effective. In contrast, this intervention uses *attribution* ("You are working hard"; "You are being polite") to shape student behavior in positive directions. Positive attributions are made both verbally and in written form to individual students and to the entire classroom group. Attribution has an important advantage over strategies that use reinforcement because it has the potential to elicit desired behaviors as well as maintain them. Communicating expectancies in the form of attributions has been demonstrated to produce significant improvement not only in behavior but also academic performance and self-esteem. Interestingly, in the original study, differences in the effects of attribution versus persuasion were larger for low-ability than for high-ability students when the target behaviors were academic.

Purpose

To improve student behavior and/or academic performance by creating positive expectancies in the form of attributions.

Materials

None

Observation (Select One or Both)

Option 1
1. Select an academic or social behavior you wish to modify, such as failure to complete classwork on time or unkind or impolite language.
2. Using a sheet of paper attached to a clipboard, record the frequency of the target behavior for the entire class or a small group of students during a selected instructional period for 4 to 7 days.

Option 2
1. If academic productivity is the target behavior, record the average percent correct for classwork or homework in a selected subject for the entire class or a small group of the least productive students for 5 to 10 days.

Procedure

1. Make positive verbal comments attributing the desired behavior to the students as individuals and as a group. Deliver one positive comment per student per day for 3 days.
    a. To encourage academic productivity, say:

    "You really work hard in _____!" (math, reading, etc.)
    "You're working harder in _____!"
    "You're getting lots of work done in _____!"

    b. To encourage positive social behaviors, such as using kind and polite language, say:

    "You're really a kind and polite class."
    "You're really working at showing each other respect."
    "You're trying harder to be especially thoughtful."

2. If academic productivity is the target, also write positive comments on classwork, quiz, and test papers attributing the desired behavior to the students for 3 days. Write one comment per target student per day, such as:

    "You're working harder, good!"
    "You're trying more, keep at it!"
    "I can tell you're trying harder!"

3. Point out part of the class (e.g., the first row, one of the tables) as being exceptional in exemplifying the target behavior, with comments such as: "The students at Table 3 are really working well together today!"
4. Make opportunities to praise the class publicly for the target behavior. For example, comment in students' hearing to another staff member that your class is the most hard-working, well-mannered, and so forth, in the school. If students happen to observe other groups that are not hard-working, polite, and so forth, comment, "Our class is (hard-working, polite, and so forth) and would not do that."

Evaluation (Select One or Both)

Option 1

1. Compare the frequency of the target behavior for the entire class or the small group of students during the selected period before and after implementation.

Option 2

1. Compare the average percent correct for classwork or homework in the selected subject for the entire class or the small group of students before and after implementation.

Variations

1. Have the principal, assistant principal, or counselor send a note to the class indicating that the students' positive behavior has been observed and making comments such as, "It is evident that each of you is (exhibiting the target behavior, e.g., working hard, being polite and kind, etc.)." Or use principal attention (see *Encouraging Academic Achievement with Principal Praise*) as an unexpected reward.
2. Send a brief note to parents praising the class or the target group for exemplifying the desired behavior for each of 3 days or for an entire week.

Note

Teachers in the field testing often ask why attribution appears to be more successful than persuasion in changing behavior. According to the authors of the original study, appealing to someone to change a particular behavior (persuasion) may have a negative implication, namely that the person is not currently the kind of individual who possesses that desirable behavior. In contrast, attribution implies something positive by suggesting that the individual already embodies the desired behavior.

Source

Miller, R. L., Brickman, P., & Bolen, D. (1975). Attribution versus persuasion as a means for modifying behavior. *Journal of Personality and Social Psychology, 31,* 430–441. Copyright 1975 by the American Psychological Association. Adapted by permission.

PROBLEM-SOLVING STUDENT CONFERENCES

Overview

Resolving conflicts with students who are chronically unproductive or disruptive is critical to maintaining a positive classroom climate and preventing the escalation of problem behaviors. In this strategy, the teacher works with an individual student or a small group of students to develop a plan to reduce or eliminate a continuing classroom problem. Problem-solving conferences are designed to be used when previous group-oriented or other routine interventions have been unsuccessful in changing student behaviors. This intervention can not only increase student commitment to making positive changes but also improve teacher–student relationships.

Purpose

To solve persistent problems of low student productivity or misbehavior with individual or small-group student conferences.

Materials

None

Observation (Select One or More)

1. Using a *Group Event Recording Form*, record the frequency of one or more target behaviors for one student or a small group of students during a selected instructional period. For example, tally the number of call-outs and out of seats for 4 to 7 days.
2. On a sheet of paper attached to a clipboard, record the number of reprimands you deliver to a target student or a small group of students during a selected instructional period for 4 to 7 days.
3. Calculate classwork or homework completion rates for a target student or a small group of students in one or more academic subjects for 5 to 10 days.

Procedure

Step 1: Identify the problem
1. Schedule a meeting with the student (or the small group of students) at a time when the rest of the class is occupied elsewhere.
2. State the purpose of the meeting.
3. Ask the student to express his or her view of the situation.
4. If the student is unable or unwilling to do so, describe the problem yourself and ask for a reaction.
5. Discuss your concerns about the problem behavior and the problems it is causing.
6. Stress that something must be done to solve the problem and that the problem will not be allowed to continue.
7. Ask the student what will happen if the behavior continues.
8. Listen to the student's concerns but do not get sidetracked.

Step 2: Select a solution
1. Invite the student to suggest a solution. If the student is unable to do so, offer two or more alternatives. Try to have a plan for increasing desirable behavior rather than just reducing negative behavior.

2. Ask for the student's reaction to check whether the plan is understood and accepted.
3. If the student proposes a solution that shifts blame to others, listen but continue to focus on the student's contribution.

Step 3: Obtain a commitment to try one of the solutions
1. Ask the student to accept the solution and try it for a specified period.
2. Arrange to meet again to evaluate the effectiveness of the plan. The student's commitment can be given orally or in written form, as in a contract.
3. If the student is not making reasonable efforts to follow the agreed-upon plan, spell out the consequences to underscore the seriousness of the situation: "You will need to choose between following our agreement or discussing your behavior with the principal and your parents."
4. If the plan is not successful, follow through with the consequences and work with the student to alter the plan. Consulting with the principal, counselor, and/or other teachers in developing an alternative plan is also helpful.

Evaluation (Select One or More)

1. Compare the frequency of the target behavior(s) for the target student(s) during the selected instructional period before and after implementation.
2. Compare the frequency of reprimands delivered to the target student(s) during the selected instructional period before and after implementation.
3. Compare classwork or homework completion rates for the target student(s) in one or more academic subjects before and after implementation.

Notes

1. Using this intervention successfully requires the ability to communicate a willingness to listen to the student's perspective while keeping the focus on solving the problem. Field testing indicates that role playing with colleagues prior to implementation is helpful in developing an appropriate balance of empathy and assertiveness. A sample conference is included in Figure 3.3.
2. Although groups of students often display a pattern of socializing and distracting behaviors, conducting problem-solving conferences with groups larger than three or four is not recommended.
3. Conferencing with parents of chronically unproductive or disruptive students is strongly recommended if classroom-based strategies are unsuccessful in solving the problem.

Source

Evertson, C. M., Emmer, E. T., Clements, B. S., & Worsham, M. E. (1994). *Classroom management for elementary teachers* (3rd ed., pp. 152–155). Boston: Allyn & Bacon. Copyright 1994 by Allyn & Bacon. Adapted by permission.

SAMPLE STUDENT CONFERENCE

TEACHER: Trevor and Alan, I've asked you to stay for a conference with me because of a problem we've been having during social studies. I have to take more and more of our instructional time to remind you two to listen quietly and pay attention. I wonder what you think about this problem?

TREVOR: I don't know.

ALAN: (*shrugs shoulders*)

TEACHER: I am very frustrated about this situation. Do you remember that I had to tell you both several times today to stop talking?

ALAN: I guess so.

TREVOR: Yeah.

TEACHER: Can you tell me why your talking and joking together creates a problem in our class?

TREVOR: I guess it bothers the other kids.

TEACHER: Alan, what do you think?

ALAN: We don't get our work done.

TEACHER: That's right. It makes it hard for other students to listen and learn what we are studying, and it makes it hard for the two of you to get your work done.

TREVOR: Brian and Carlos talk all the time, too.

TEACHER: Yes, it would help if they talked less, but what can we do about *your* behavior to solve the problem?

ALAN: Social studies is boring.

TEACHER: It's hard to listen quietly sometimes. But I have to be able to teach the whole class so that everybody will be prepared for seventh-grade social studies next year. Can you think of a way we could handle this?

TREVOR: I guess we could stop messing around so much.

ALAN: Maybe we could talk at lunch instead of in class.

TEACHER: That would be a big help. I would really appreciate that, and I bet the other students would, too. I also think you have good ideas and could share them more in our class discussions. How about raising your hand more often, and I'll make sure to call on you several times during the period?

TREVOR: Okay.

ALAN: That's all right with me.

TEACHER: How about if we try this for the rest of the week and then talk again and see if it solves our problem?

BOYS: Okay.

TEACHER: Great! I know you both want to make this a great sixth-grade year.

FIGURE 3.3. Sample conference for *Problem-Solving Student Conferences.* Adapted from Evertson, Emmer, Clements, and Worsham (1994, pp. 152–155). Copyright 1994 by Allyn & Bacon. Adapted by permission.

Teaching Prosocial Behaviors

Especially in the preschool and early elementary years, student misbehavior may occur because children have not been taught the appropriate behavior for the situation. If children do not know the appropriate behavior, they can only learn it by misbehaving and being reprimanded, which can create a negative classroom climate and is highly disruptive to instruction. Ignoring misbehavior is not only often ineffective (Kounin, 1970) but fails to help children acquire behaviors that are more appropriate for that situation. At the same time, however, teachers cannot interrupt instruction to conduct a lesson in appropriate social behavior every time a rule infraction occurs.

The intervention in this section serves as a keystone proactive strategy in a comprehensive classroom management system because it simultaneously teaches critical social competencies while it prevents misbehavior from escalating into a major disturbance. Moreover, it minimizes interruptions in teacher-directed instruction, especially if the variation with a self-management component is implemented. *Sit and Watch: Teaching Prosocial Behaviors* removes misbehaving students for a brief timeout to the classroom periphery so that they may observe their peers behaving appropriately. A variation of this intervention designed for use at recess or in physical education classes is presented in Chapter 5.

SIT AND WATCH: TEACHING PROSOCIAL BEHAVIORS

Overview

Children often misbehave because they have not learned the appropriate skills in social situations or have not been held accountable for their behavior. This intervention uses contingent observation, which combines instruction with a brief timeout, to teach students prosocial behaviors they are not presently displaying. As a proactive classroom management strategy, it not only increases instructional opportunities by minimizing the time needed for behavior sanctioning but also helps to prevent inappropriate behavior from escalating by avoiding punitive strategies that can provoke arguments and confrontations. Originally used with preschool children in a day care setting, this procedure is easily adapted for elementary grade students in a wide variety of school situations.

Purpose

To teach appropriate social behaviors in a naturalistic context.

Materials

1. Designated "Sit and Watch" chair on the edge of classroom activities (with or without a "Sit and Watch Chair" label attached to it)

2. "Quiet Place" in the classroom, consisting of a comfortable chair or pillow on a rug as far away as possible from the center of classroom activity
3. Posterboard chart with a list of classroom rules, such as:
   a. Follow the teacher's directions.
   b. Be polite and kind to others.
   c. Finish all your work.
   d. Respect others and their property.

Observation (Select One or Both)

1. Using a *Group Event Recording Form,* tally the number of disruptive behaviors for the entire class or for one or more target students during a selected period for 4 to 7 days. *Disruptive behaviors* are defined as aggression, crying and fussing, having tantrums, destructive use of toys or classroom materials, and interfering with the learning of other students.
2. Using a sheet of paper attached to a clipboard, record the number of reprimands you deliver to the entire class or one or more target students during a selected period for 4 to 7 days.

Procedure

1. Place a chair away from the center of classroom activity but in a place where students can continue to observe the ongoing lesson (e.g., in a corner but facing the class rather than the wall).
2. Tell the students that they will be learning a new way to get the most out of their lessons by using a Sit and Watch chair.
3. Point out the Sit and Watch chair and explain you will be telling students who break classroom rules to sit in the chair for a short time and watch the other students behaving appropriately.
4. Teach the Sit and Watch procedure using *Say Show Check: Teaching Classroom Procedures.*
5. When inappropriate behavior occurs, first describe it to the misbehaving student:

   "Don't hit other children at your table."

6. Then describe what would have been appropriate behavior in the situation:

   "Keep your hands to yourself when you are doing your work."

7. Tell the student to sit in the Sit and Watch chair and observe the appropriate social behavior of the other children:

   "Sit here and watch how the other children work without hitting."
   (For preschoolers, escort them to the chair.)

8. When the student has been watching quietly for a brief period (about 1 minute for preschoolers, 3 minutes for older children), ask if he or she is ready to rejoin the activity and display the appropriate behavior:

   "Do you know how to work without hitting now?"

9. If the student indicates by nodding or verbalizing readiness to return, allow him or her to do so. If the child does not respond or responds negatively, tell him or her to sit and watch until ready to perform the appropriate behavior:

> "Sit here and watch the children until you think you can do your work without hitting others."

10. When the student sits quietly for another brief period, return and repeat Steps 8 and 9.
11. When the student returns to the group, give positive attention for appropriate behavior as soon as possible:

> "Good, you're doing your work without hitting others."

12. If the student cries for more than a few minutes or refuses to sit quietly so that other children's activities are disturbed, take him or her to the Quiet Place in the classroom. Explain the reason for the removal by saying:

> "Since you can't sit quietly here, you need to go to the Quiet Place and practice sitting quietly."

13. When the student is calm or sitting quietly in the Quiet Place, ask if he or she is ready to sit quietly and watch. Return the student to the Sit and Watch chair after a positive response and continue from Step 7.

Evaluation (Select One or Both)

1. Compare the frequency of disruptive behaviors for the entire class or for one or more target students during the selected period before and after implementation.
2. Compare the frequency of reprimands delivered to the entire class or one or more target students during the selected period before and after implementation.

Variations

1. For a variation suitable for recess or physical education periods, see *Reducing Disruptive Behavior in Physical Education Classes with Sit and Watch.*
2. Instead of approaching students in the Sit and Watch chair and asking them if they are ready to return to the group, teach them to raise their hands to indicate readiness to return. With this variation, the teacher does not need to interrupt instruction to interact with the child. (Thanks to Margaret Opalski, first-grade teacher at St. Anthony's School, for this variation.)

Notes

1. This intervention works best when the activity is highly reinforcing so that even a brief timeout is undesired.
2. For very defiant or undercontrolled students, providing a backup Quiet Place in another location, such as a nearby classroom or the principal's office, is es-

sential to the success of this strategy. In these cases, arrange for the student to be escorted to the other classroom or the principal's office by a teacher's aide, if available, or other staff member. Using *Say Show Check: Teaching Classroom Procedures*, practice the entire procedure with the child and the participating staff members and discuss it with the child's parents. Ask staff members to interact with the child as little as possible during the Quiet Place time. These out-of-class timeouts should last no longer than about 20 minutes and should be followed in the classroom by returning the child to the Quiet Place and continuing from Step 13.

Source

Porterfield, J. K., Herbert-Jackson, E., & Risley, T. R. (1976). Contingent observation: An effective and acceptable procedure for reducing disruptive behavior of young children in a group setting. *Journal of Applied Behavior Analysis, 9,* 55–64. Copyright 1976 by the Society for the Experimental Analysis of Behavior. Adapted by permission.

SUPPLEMENTARY READINGS

Emmer, E. T., Evertson, C. M., Clements, B. S., & Worsham, M. E. (1997). *Classroom management for secondary teachers* (4th ed.). Boston: Allyn & Bacon.
Evertson, C. M., Emmer, E. T., Clements, B. S., & Worsham, M. E. (1994). *Classroom management for elementary teachers* (3rd ed.). Boston: Allyn & Bacon.

These companion volumes describe classroom management principles and procedures based on more than 20 years of observational studies and field experiments in over 500 elementary and secondary classrooms. The focus is on preventing problems by developing rules and procedures for instructional and behavior management systems at the beginning of the year. Chapters present guidelines for organizing the classroom, selecting and establishing rules, managing student work, and managing special groups, such as low-ability classes. Numerous case examples and practice activities are included.

Gettinger, M. (1988). Methods of proactive classroom management. *School Psychology Review, 17,* 227–242.

This article presents an overview of theoretical and empirical advances in proactive classroom management. The author reviews research on classroom management, including studies evaluating the effectiveness of training teachers in proactive management methods. Also addressed are the implications of this research for consultants seeking to help teachers apply proactive management techniques in their classrooms.

Kauffman, J. M., Hallahan, D. P., Mostert, M. P., Trent, S. C., & Nuttycombe, D. G. (1993). *Managing classroom behavior: A reflective case-based approach.* Boston: Allyn & Bacon.

Ideal for preservice or inservice training, this book takes a case-based approach to classroom management. The first section reviews basic concepts in classroom management, including identifying, analyzing, and changing behavior; communicating with students; collaborating with other educators; and working with parents. The second section consists of 15 factual (not hypothetical) cases presented from the teacher's point of view for analysis and discussion. No solutions are presented to these challenging cases, which include examples from elementary, secondary, and special education classrooms.

Kounin, J. (1970). *Discipline and group management in classrooms*. New York: Holt, Rinehart & Winston.

This classic set of observational studies of 80 elementary school classrooms is considered to be the foundation of proactive classroom management. Kounin and his colleagues analyzed videotapes of activities in well-managed and ineffectively managed classrooms and identified the key behaviors of successful versus unsuccessful teachers.

Paine, S. C., Radicchi, J., Rosellini, L. C., Deutchman, L., & Darch, C. B. (1983). *Structuring your classroom for academic success*. Champaign, IL: Research Press.

This often quoted book describes a comprehensive classroom system originally designed to promote achievement and positive behavior for disadvantaged primary grade students. The authors emphasize the use of efficient instructional and management strategies as a means of preventing discipline problems. Included are explicit instructions and scripts for introducing each procedure, including creating a classroom point system, establishing classroom rules, dealing with transition time, and handling student requests for assistance.

Weinstein, C. S. (1996). *Secondary classroom management: Lessons from research and practice*. New York: McGraw-Hill.

Weinstein, C. S., & Mignano, A. J., Jr. (1992). *Elementary classroom management: Lessons from research and practice*. New York: McGraw-Hill.

Each of these companion volumes integrates research-based classroom management strategies with the thinking and practices of four actual teachers working in a variety of school settings. The focus is on creating a learning environment that prevents misbehavior and on managing classroom subsettings, such as seatwork, group work, and recitations and discussions. The principles and strategies are illustrated with real-life examples from the teachers' classrooms.

CHAPTER 4

♦♦♦

Interventions to Improve Academic Performance

♦

OVERVIEW

The majority of referrals to school psychologists involve students with academic problems (Ownby, Wallbrown, D'Atri, & Armstrong, 1985; Shinn, Nolet, & Knutson, 1990). With the increasing heterogeneity of students, including children of poverty, children for whom English is a second language, and other diverse learners, school psychologists will need to expand their services from assessing and classifying students to helping teachers develop instructional strategies that can enhance students' academic performance in the regular classroom (Berliner, 1988). In particular, consultants need information about effective, practical interventions that help students develop and practice critical academic skills and that can be implemented using regular curricular materials. An increasing body of research (e.g., Berliner, 1988; Brophy, 1986; Greenwood, Carta, & Hall, 1988; Greenwood, Delquadri, et al., 1984; Greenwood, Dinwiddie, et al., 1984; Rosenshine, 1980) demonstrates that interventions that promote high rates of accurate student responding have positive effects on academic performance. Such strategies are especially important for diverse learners, such as pupils in poor urban environments, who receive fewer opportunities to respond to academic material (Greenwood, 1991; Greenwood et al., 1989; Stanley & Greenwood, 1983). Moreover, academic enhancement interventions are critical in combating the development of a failure identity among children, especially those who may already be displaying aggressive and noncompliant behavior (Forehand & Wierson, 1993). Given the well-documented relationship between aggression and academic failure (e.g., Dishion, Patterson, Stoolmiller, & Skinner, 1991; Kupersmidt

& Coie, 1990; Loeber, 1990), interventions that focus only on reducing inappropriate behavior are insufficient to assist at-risk children (Coie & Krehbiel, 1984).

TARGETS OF ACADEMIC INTERVENTIONS

Although many interventions designed to enhance academic achievement have targeted on-task behavior, improvement in on-task behavior does not necessarily lead to increases in academic performance (e.g., Broughton & Lahey, 1978; Hay et al., 1977; Kohler, Schwartz, Cross, & Fowler, 1989). Rather, interventions that increase on-task behavior only make students more available for learning. If students have skill deficits, direct remediation will also be necessary to improve performance. Improvements in on-task behavior will in all likelihood be short-lived if students do not simultaneously receive help in mastering instructional material. In contrast, targeting accurate and/or rapid academic responding has been associated with improvement in both achievement and on-task behavior (Aaron & Bostow, 1978; Ayllon & Roberts, 1974; Broughton & Lahey, 1978; Greenwood et al., 1989; Hay et al., 1977; Van Houten, Hill, & Parsons, 1975).

Academically focused interventions also have the potential to reduce disruptive behavior by creating a classroom structure in which students are productively engaged (Lentz, 1988). The less "down time," the fewer the opportunities for unproductive behavior to escalate into disruption. In fact, reductions of nontargeted disruptive behavior were observed in several of the original studies for the interventions included in this chapter (e.g., Fantuzzo, King, & Heller, 1992; Greenwood, Carta, & Maheady, 1991; Gardner, Heward, & Grossi, 1994; Witt, Hannafin, & Martens, 1983).

Types of Academic Problems

Academic problems may be characterized as skill deficiencies, fluency problems, performance problems, or some combination of these (Lentz & Shapiro, 1986). *Skill deficits* refer to inadequate mastery of academic skills that have been previously taught. *Fluency problems* refer to deficiencies in the rate at which skills are accurately performed. That is, the student possesses the requisite skills but cannot perform them at an adequate rate of speed. *Performance problems* refer to academic problems in which the student possesses adequate skills and fluency but does not produce work of satisfactory quantity, quality, or both for some reason. Many of the strategies in this chapter are designed to enhance skill acquisition and fluency by increasing opportunities to respond to academic material. Others target performance problems by using contingency-based systems, especially group-oriented contingencies that capitalize on peer influence to encourage academic productivity.

The interventions in this chapter are organized into three categories: (1) strategies designed to enhance academic productivity, including classwork and independent seatwork; (2) interventions focusing on homework performance; and (3) interventions targeting specific academic subjects, including reading, mathematics, written language, and the content areas of science and social studies. Reading interventions are subdivided into strategies targeting fluency, vocabulary, and comprehension, whereas written language interventions are subdivided into spelling and written expression strategies.

EVALUATING THE EFFECTIVENESS
OF ACADEMIC INTERVENTIONS

The evaluation methods for the interventions in this chapter rely primarily on assessments used in typical regular education classroom accountability systems, such as grades on classwork, quizzes, and tests; homework completion rates; and homework grades. Other evaluation methods assess learning-related variables such as participation in class discussions or the number of different strategies students use while reading. Because all of the interventions are designed for classwide application, a variety of group-oriented academic measures are also included, such as class percentages of students with poor or failing grades, class average test scores, and class average correct responses to teacher questions. Moreover, because interventions targeting academic performance also have the potential to improve social behavior by increasing academic engagement and reducing opportunities for disruption, several interventions include measures for assessing behavioral outcomes.

Curriculum-Based Measurement

In addition to the evaluation methods built into each intervention, procedures for conducting curriculum-based measurements (CBMs) in reading, mathematics computation, spelling, and written expression are presented in the introductions to the strategies in each of these subject areas, using the same intervention format. CBM is one of several models of curriculum-based assessment (CBA), a testing methodology that uses the curriculum in which students are being instructed as the basis for decision making.

Originally developed by Deno, Mirkin, and their colleagues at the

University of Minnesota Institute for Learning Disabilities (Deno, 1985, 1986; Deno & Mirkin, 1977), CBM is a generic measurement system that uses a set of brief, standardized measures of basic skills in reading, mathematics, spelling, and written expression for assessing academic performance. Among the key features of CBM are the brevity of the assessments (1 to 3 minutes), its emphasis on fluency (a metric combining rate plus accuracy) as the primary behavior of interest, and the frequent administration of "skill probes" to monitor student progress. Information from CBMs can be used to identify academic problems and assess whether instructional programs and interventions addressing those problems are effective (Shinn, 1989; Shinn et al., 1990). CBM is ideally suited to evaluating the effects of school-based interventions because measures can be administered repeatedly, are based on students' actual instructional materials, and, despite their brevity, have been shown to be reliable and valid methods of identifying academic problems and determining whether interventions targeting those problems are successful in improving student performance (e.g., Deno, Marston, & Mirkin, 1982; Deno, Mirkin, & Chiang, 1982; Deno, Mirkin, & Wesson, 1984; Germann & Tindal, 1985; Marston & Magnusson, 1985).

Additional Measures for Evaluating Academic Interventions

In addition to CBMs and the evaluation methods built into the interventions, several useful measures for assessing teacher perceptions of academic performance and the efficacy of academic interventions have recently been published. Shapiro (1996a, 1996b) has developed a structured teacher interview for assessing reading, mathematics, spelling, and writing performance based on the behavioral consultation process presented by Bergan and his colleagues (Bergan, 1977; Bergan & Kratochwill, 1990; Kratochwill & Bergan, 1990). The seven-page form assesses the curriculum, instructional procedures, and student achievement and includes a brief rating scale of behavior problems that commonly interfere with successful academic performance during various reading and math activities, including small-group instruction, independent seatwork, and homework.

Another measure with potential usefulness for assessing teacher perceptions of the effectiveness of academic interventions is the Academic Performance Rating Scale (APRS; DuPaul, Rapport, & Perriello, 1991). Originally designed to measure teacher judgments of academic skill deficits in students with disruptive behavior disorders and to be sensitive to small changes in academic performance as a result of treatment, this 19-item scale assesses a variety of academic behaviors in reading, mathematics, and language arts, including the amount and accuracy of work completion, attentiveness, and persistence with written work. It yields four scores: Academic Success, Impulse Control, Academic Productivity, and a Total score. The complete APRS, directions for scoring, and norms for grades 1 through 6 by gender are included in Shapiro (1996b).

Anesko, Schoiock, Ramirez, and Levine (1987) have developed the Homework Problems Checklist (HPC) for use in designing and monitoring the effectiveness of strategies targeting homework compliance. The HPC consists of 20 items taken from literature reviews and interviews with parents and professionals working with elementary school students and assesses the frequency and degree of homework problems from the perspective of the child's parents. The parent responds on a 4-point scale to yield a total checklist score ranging from 0 to 60 points. The HPC has a Cronbach's alpha of .91 and has been demonstrated to be sensitive to changes produced by a behavioral intervention program (Anesko & O'Leary, 1982).

INTERVENTIONS TO IMPROVE
ACADEMIC PRODUCTIVITY

This section includes strategies that target academic productivity in the classroom. The first intervention in this section, *The Daily Assignment,* as well as several other interventions in subsequent sections, uses home-based reinforcement to improve academic performance. Teachers have long used school–home notes to communicate with parents about students' academic and social behavior. School–home notes encourage parental involvement in their children's classroom performance, permit a broader range of reinforcers than are generally available to teachers, and have demonstrated efficacy for behavior and academic performance problems (Budd et al., 1981; Kelley, 1990). Home–school notes can be arrayed along a continuum of parental involvement, ranging from notes that merely provide information to notes that ask parents to deliver predetermined consequences contingent upon the reported school behaviors. Demands on teacher time in terms of the quantity and complexity of academic and behavior ratings also vary considerably.

Although strategies that include home consequences for academic achievement can have powerful effects on student behavior, establishing and maintaining an effective school–home communication system for even a single student can be difficult, much less for an entire classroom of students with productivity problems. Students with poor academic performance may be unwilling to convey notes home if they perceive that those communications are documenting their problems. In addition, parents may have difficulty consistently providing the agreed-upon contingencies, or teachers may forget or be reluctant to record student performance on a daily or weekly basis (e.g., Smith et al., 1988). Not surprisingly, the vast majority of published school–home note interventions have targeted individual students or small groups of students, usually in special education settings. In contrast, the school–home notes included in this book were originally designed or have been adapted for classwide application. To facilitate implementation, detailed guidelines for all intervention components, including introductory letters to parents, have been provided for all school–home strategies.

Two interventions in this section (*Classwide Peer Tutoring* and *Join the Team: Reciprocal Peer Tutoring to Raise Achievement*) use peer tutoring formats to increase academic engagement rates and consolidate skills. Unlike traditional peer tutoring, which is designed to remediate the deficiencies of individual pupils by pairing them with high-achieving students, often from a higher grade level, the peer tutoring interventions included here were originally designed or have been adapted for use in a single classroom and on a classwide basis. Because peers supervise academic responding, every student can engage in direct practice of a specific academic skill during instructional periods, leaving teachers free to supervise the tutoring process, give help as needed, and prompt appropriate behavior. Moreover, because peer tutors are provided with the correct answers for tutoring tasks, the strategy permits immediate error correction and additional drill on errors.

Classwide peer tutoring (CWPT) was developed by Greenwood and his colleagues at the University of Kansas (e.g., Delquadri, Greenwood, Whorton, Carta, & Hall, 1986; Greenwood, Delquadri, et al., 1984; Greenwood, Dinwiddie, et al., 1984; Greenwood et al., 1988, 1991) to improve the achievement of low-SES urban students at risk for academic failure. CWPT has been successful in improving student performance in a wide variety of settings, including regular classrooms, resource rooms, and self-contained classes for learning-disabled, educable mentally retarded, and behavior-disordered students. Longitudinal studies indicate that CWPT can help prevent school failure as measured by special education placement, type of special services provided, and achievement on standardized tests (Greenwood, Terry, Utley, Montagna, & Walker, 1993). Another version of CWPT appears in the section on interventions for written language (*The Peer Tutoring Spelling Game*).

Reciprocal peer tutoring (RPT) was developed by Fantuzzo and his associates at the University of Pennsylvania (Fantuzzo, Davis, & Ginsburg, 1995; Fantuzzo et al., 1992; Fantuzzo & Rohrbeck, 1992; Pigott, Fantuzzo, & Clement, 1986) to improve the mathematics performance of small groups of underachieving students. Studies indicate that RPT not only has significant positive effects on mathematics achievement but is also associated with improved classroom behavior (Fantuzzo et al., 1992). Two variations of RPT are included in the section on mathematics interventions.

Although both CWPT and RPT involve peer tutoring formats, they differ in several respects. RPT includes self-management and subgroup contingencies, with groups of students selecting and working to obtain their own group rewards. In contrast, CWPT does not include backup contingencies, relying instead on the game-like atmosphere to provide motivation. Moreover, CWPT has been applied in a variety of basic skills areas, including oral reading, spelling, and mathematics computation, whereas RPT has been used primarily to enhance mathematics skills. Here RPT has been adapted for use in any academic subject in which skills practice is desirable.

The remainder of the interventions in this section are designed to enhance academic productivity by providing systematic performance feedback, often in the context of group contingencies or self-management procedures. In *Increasing Academic Performance by Reinforcing Correct Answers,* students earn access to free-time activities by accumulating points for accurate classwork assignments. *Winning the Recess Game: Raising Class Averages with a Free-Time Contingency* combines contracting and public posting with an interdependent group contingency. *Stop the Clock: Improving Productivity during Small-Group Instruction,* which targets on-task behavior during seatwork, uses a stopwatch to enhance the salience of teacher feedback. *Improving Academic Productivity with Performance Feedback* combines a variety of strategies known to improve academic productivity: timing of work periods, feedback, public posting of student scores, and praise. In *Self-Monitoring to Improve Work Completion,* students learn to maintain work completion charts as a way of monitoring their own academic productivity. *Encouraging Academic Achievement with Principal Praise* uses the most influential individual in the school to provide positive feedback for academic excellence or improvement in academic performance. Several other interventions in this book (e.g., *Speeding Up Transitions: Beat the Buzzer; Promoting Positive Behavior through Attribution; Red Light/Green Light*) include variations in which principal attention is used as a reinforcer for positive academic or social behavior.

THE DAILY ASSIGNMENT

Overview

School–home notes focusing on academic performance rather than behavior have several advantages. First, teachers are more likely systematically to record academic behaviors, such as percent correct on classwork, than social behaviors, such as call-outs. Second, parents may be able to help students improve their academic achievement by intervening with them at home. Third, reducing disruptive behavior does not necessarily result in a corresponding improvement in academic achievement. This intervention differs from most school-note strategies in that the actual classroom assignment, rather than a specially created note summarizing student performance, serves as the home communication. This has the advantage of providing parents with more detailed information about students' school work as well as encouraging academic support at home. Use of the daily assignment note in conjunction with a home-based reinforcement program produced not only marked increases in academic performance but also large decreases in disruptive behavior. Originally used with a small group of students in a regular classroom, it is adapted here for classwide application, with the small-group format included as a variation.

Purpose

To improve academic performance with a school–home note and home-based reinforcement program.

Materials

1. Copies of introductory parent letter (see Figure 4.1), one per student
2. Daily student assignments, graded, one per student

Observation (Select One or Both)

Option 1
1. Record percent correct on daily classwork in a selected academic subject for a small group of students or the entire class for 5 to 10 days.

Option 2
1. Using a *Classwide Scanning Form,* scan the room every 5 minutes from left to right during a selected instructional period and tally the number of students in each of the following behavior categories:
   a. *Appropriate behavior:* following classroom rules and procedures and complying with teacher directions;
   b. *Inappropriate behavior:* being out of seat, running, making noises, talking out, failing to follow teacher instructions, or interfering with the appropriate behavior of others.
2. Conduct these observations for 30 to 45 minutes for 4 to 7 days.

Procedure

1. Select an instructional period in which students are especially unproductive and/or disruptive.
2. Explain to the students that you will be sending home one of their classwork assignments each day to their parents and asking their parents to support their efforts to be successful learners.
3. Distribute the introductory parent letters, review them with the class, and send them home.

4. After parents have received the letters, grade one classwork assignment each day for each student and have students take the assignments home to review with their parents.

Evaluation (Select One or Both)

Option 1
1. Compare percent correct on daily classwork in the selected subject for the small group of students or the entire class before and after implementation.

Option 2
1. Compare percentages of students with appropriate and inappropriate behavior during the selected instructional period before and after implementation.

School Letterhead

Date:

Dear parent:

To help your child get more out of (selected academic subject), I will be providing you with more information about your child's classwork. Beginning on (date of implementation), your child will be bringing home a graded Daily Assignment that indicates the percentage of correct answers. Please use the Daily Assignment as follows:

During the first week of the Daily Assignment, give your child praise and privileges for remembering to bring home the assignment. Privileges effective with children include watching television, playing a video game, going to a friend's home, and having a special dessert or treat. Review the assignment with your child and praise him or her for correct answers. If no questions were answered correctly, please praise your child only for bringing home the assignment. If your child fails to bring home the assignment, please do not provide praise or privileges.

During the second week, please continue to praise your child for correct answers but give privileges only for improvement or for a certain level of performance, such as 85% correct or more. Discuss with your child the amount of improvement or performance level required to earn privileges so that he or she understands these goals. Again, if your child fails to bring home the assignment, do not give praise or privileges.

Please feel free to call me if you have any questions. Thank you for your support as we work together to help your child achieve excellence in school.

Sincerely yours,

Name of teacher

FIGURE 4.1. Introductory parent letter for *The Daily Assignment.* Adapted from Witt, Hannafin, and Martens (1983). Copyright 1983 by Elsevier Science, Ltd, Oxford, England. Adapted by permission.

Variation

Select a small group of academically unproductive students. Conduct individual conferences with their parents to review the intervention procedures and provide information on how to praise their children and how to select privileges. Make weekly telephone calls to parents to help ensure that they are distributing privileges consistently, to monitor the amount of progress parents are expecting from their children, and to assist with any implementation problems.

Note

In the original study, an aide was available to grade student papers. If grading student papers the same day students complete them is not possible, return graded papers the following day and use those as the home notes. Modify the parent letter accordingly.

Source

Witt, J. C., Hannafin, M. J., & Martens, B. K. (1983). Home-based reinforcement: Behavioral covariation between academic performance and inappropriate behavior. *Journal of School Psychology, 21,* 337–348. Copyright 1983 by Elsevier Science, Ltd, Oxford, England. Adapted by permission.

CLASSWIDE PEER TUTORING

Overview

Classwide peer tutoring (CWPT) is a low-cost, efficient strategy that enhances student achievement by increasing opportunities for active responding and immediate feedback. It has been successfully used with students of diverse ability levels in elementary and middle school settings, as well as with students with learning disabilities, attentional problems, and behavior disorders. Rather than supplanting the regular curriculum, CWPT relies on the same materials and has been successfully applied in a wide variety of academic areas, including oral reading, vocabulary, mathematics, and spelling. CWPT is associated not only with gains in standardized test scores and classroom measures of academic performance but also with reductions in disruptive and off-task behavior.

Purpose

To increase academic achievement and reduce "down time" by providing additional opportunities for students to practice tasks in various subjects.

Materials

1. Slips of paper with student names for assigning partners and hat or box for name drawing

2. Worksheets or reading materials for tutoring pairs (see Figure 4.2)
3. Kitchen timer, stopwatch, or watch
4. Posterboard chart for posting team totals and daily and weekly winning teams
5. Large stars or stickers

Observation (Select One or Both)

1. Collect measures of achievement for the entire class or for selected students in the subject area(s) in which tutoring will be used, such as percent correct on daily classwork for 5 to 10 days or percent correct on weekly quizzes or end-of-unit tests for several weeks.
2. Administer *Curriculum-Based Oral Reading Probes* to a group of selected students.

Procedure

1. Explain to the students that they will be learning an exciting new way of working together to get more out of their lessons.
2. Conduct an initial training session in which you act as tutor while a student serves as tutee. Then select two more students to tutor each other for 1 minute while the others watch and you give corrective feedback. After conducting a few more demonstrations, have the entire class practice the procedure.
3. Review the rules for CWPT before each session until students are successfully following the procedures, and then provide periodic rule reviews as needed. To avoid increased noise levels, teach students to talk only during tutoring sessions, speak only to their tutoring partners, and use "inside" voices.
4. The entire CWPT procedure requires 30 minutes, with each student tutoring for 10 minutes and receiving tutoring for 10 minutes. An additional 5 to 10 minutes is needed to sum and post individual and team points. The steps in the procedure are described below.
5. On Mondays of each week, have students draw names from a hat or box for assignment to partners and partners to one of two teams. Students remain on the team for the entire week. Use random pairings in areas such as spelling and mathematics, where tutors can use answer sheets against which to check tutees' responses for accuracy. For tutoring in oral reading and vocabulary, pair students according to their reading group placement.
6. Designate one partner in each pair as the first tutor and give the tutor a set of academic materials relevant to current instruction. Examples of items from several subject areas are presented in Figure 4.2. (Note that items from only one subject area are used during one tutoring session, however.) The tutor dictates the items one at a time, and the tutor responds orally, as in oral reading, or, for other subjects, writes the responses. For oral reading, give the tutor and tutee copies of the same reading selection. Use a timer or write the time on the chalkboard to signal the beginning of the first 10-minute period.
7. Tutors award 2 points to tutees for each correct first-time response and 1 point for practicing the correct response three times after an error. For oral reading, tutors award 2 points for every line read correctly and 1 point for practicing the correct response three times after an error. Tutors present the

    set of problems, word list, or reading passage as many times as possible during the 10-minute period.

8. After 10 minutes, have students switch roles for another 10 minutes. Use the timer or write the time on the board to signal this 10-minute period.
9. During CWPT time, move around the classroom monitoring tutoring, giving corrective feedback, and awarding bonus points to tutoring pairs who are displaying correct and positive tutoring behaviors.
10. At the end of the CWPT session, have each pair of students report total points earned. Sum the individual points for each team, and determine the winning team. Post the total score for each team on a chart displayed at the front of the room.
11. Lead the class in applauding the winning team for the day. The weekly winner is recognized with a "Team of the Week" star on the chart. The losing team is also praised for effort and challenged to work harder.

Evaluation (Select One or Both)

1. Compare percent correct scores on classwork, quizzes, or end-of-unit tests in the selected subject area(s) for the entire class or selected students before and after implementation.
2. Compare scores on *Curriculum-Based Oral Reading Probes* for selected students before and after implementation.

Variation

Use principal attention as described in *Encouraging Academic Achievement with Principal Praise* to recognize the weekly team winner.

Notes

1. Field testing suggests that beginning with a highly structured subject, such as spelling or mathematics computation, facilitates implementation. When students have mastered the procedures, introduce CWPT in another area, such as reading vocabulary or oral reading. Maximum benefits are obtained when students engage in CWPT three or four times a week.
2. Although CWPT has been used most frequently in reading, mathematics, and spelling, field testing indicates that it is also helpful in increasing academic engagement and achievement in other subjects, including English, social studies, and science. Workbook pages or the reproducible skill sheets that accompany many textbooks can be used by giving tutors copies of a correctly completed page. CWPT can also be used as a format for checking homework assignments. (Thanks to John McCaul, junior high teacher at St. Anthony's School, for this variation.)
3. Teachers are often concerned that CWPT will lead to increased noise levels and diminish their control over student behavior. An orderly environment can be maintained by continually monitoring during CWPT (vs. grading papers or performing other administrative functions), awarding bonus points for follow-

ing the rules, and administering brief timeouts from the opportunity to earn points by having students put their pencils down for 15 to 30 seconds if classroom noise becomes excessive.

Sources

Delquadri, J., Greenwood, C. R., Whorton, R., Carta, J. J., & Hall, R. V. (1986). Classwide peer tutoring. *Exceptional Children, 52,* 535–542. Copyright 1986 by The Council for Exceptional Children. Adapted by permission.

Greenwood, C. R., Carta, J. J., & Maheady, L. (1991). Peer tutoring programs in the regular education classroom. In G. Stoner, M. R. Shinn, & H. M. Walker (Eds.), *Interventions for achievement and behavior problems* (pp. 179–200). Silver Spring, MD: National Association of School Psychologists. Copyright 1991 by the National Association of School Psychologists. Adapted by permission.

CLASSWIDE PEER TUTORING WORKSHEET

Points awarded

Match the following states and capitals:

1. Utah	a. Richmond	_____
2. Virginia	b. Olympia	_____
3. Washington	c. Salt Lake City	_____

Spell the following words:

1. teacher	_____
2. patience	_____
3. infinite	_____

Find the error in these sentences:

1. Tom said, I can't go now.	_____
2. When Kay discusses politics.	_____
3. Jamal and me walked to the store.	_____

Solve the following problems:

1. $3 \times 5 =$	_____
2. $6 \times 12 =$	_____
3. $7 \times 2 =$ ___	

Points earned: _____
Bonus points: _____
Total points: _____

Names of tutoring pair: _____

Team: 1   2   (circle)

FIGURE 4.2. Samples of items and worksheet format for *Classwide Peer Tutoring.* Adapted from Delquadri, Greenwood, Whorton, Carta, and Hall (1986). Copyright 1986 by The Council for Exceptional Children. Adapted by permission. Also adapted from Greenwood, Carta, and Maheady (1991). Copyright 1991 by the National Association of School Psychologists. Adapted by permission.

JOIN THE TEAM: RECIPROCAL PEER TUTORING
TO RAISE ACHIEVEMENT

Overview

Reciprocal peer tutoring and group contingencies have both been found to be effective methods of improving academic achievement. This intervention combines an interdependent group contingency with peer tutoring in a game-like format, with peer tutoring operations converted into roles on four-person teams. Originally applied to small groups of underachieving students in regular classrooms, the strategy was successful in increasing the rate and accuracy of arithmetic problem completion to a level equivalent to the average student performance. It is adapted here for total classroom use and can be used with any subject that includes fact drills.

Purpose

To increase academic performance and productivity through a peer-mediated group contingency strategy.

Materials

1. *Reinforcement Menus,* one per team
2. Posterboard chart listing the tasks for each team role
3. Worksheets or other instructional materials for teams
4. "Team Score Cards," consisting of $3'' \times 5''$ index cards with the names of team members listed and space to record scores, one per team per week
5. Backup reinforcers, such as video game tokens, homework passes, stickers, wrapped candy, and inexpensive school supplies
6. Posterboard chart listing team names with space to affix stars; small and large gold stars (see variation)

Observation (Select One or More)

1. Calculate percent correct scores on daily classwork assignments in a selected academic subject for a small group of students or the entire class for 5 to 10 days.
2. Calculate the class average percent correct score for daily classwork assignments in a selected subject for 5 to 10 days or on weekly quizzes in that subject for several weeks.
3. If the subject selected is mathematics, administer *Curriculum-Based Mathematics Probes* to a small group of students, with probes based on one or more of the skills that are currently being taught. Administer three probes and calculate the average score for each student.

Procedure

1. Explain to the students that they will be playing a game to get the most out of the selected subject.

2. Divide the class into groups of four. Explain that the game is like a sport and that each group includes a coach, scorekeeper, referee, and manager.
3. Conduct a training session that includes the following:
   a. Using modeling and demonstrations to teach students the tasks required for each role;
   b. Practicing the coordination of the roles during simulated fact drill sessions;
   c. Assessing team members' ability to perform their roles competently.
4. After training, have each team select a team name, devise a "pep talk" for the coach, consisting of the team's strategies for increasing academic performance (e.g., "work hard," "work carefully," "don't talk"), and select backup reinforcers from a *Reinforcement Menu.*
5. At the beginning of each week, have students select the roles they will be performing for that week.
6. At the beginning of each peer tutoring session, have each team select a daily goal for the number of problems or items it must answer correctly to count the day as a win from a list of three possible goals. These goal choices should represent a narrow range of numbers close to the total of the individual goals that would be appropriate for each team member.
7. Distribute the worksheets or skill exercises and tell students the amount of time they have to complete them.
8. Teams proceed as follows:
   a. The coach (peer instructor) orients team members to their task, records the team's daily goal on the team score card, reminds members of their strategies for increasing their performance, and encourages them to use those strategies to increase their performance.
   b. At the end of the drill period, the scorekeeper (peer observer) counts the number of problems completed correctly by each team member and writes the number down on each member's worksheet.
   c. The referee (peer evaluator) independently counts the number of correctly completed problems and records the number by each individual's name on the team score card.
   d. The manager (peer reinforcer) determines the team's total score and compares it with the team's goal for the day. If the goal is met, the manager declares that the team has won.
   e. At least three group members must be present to conduct the intervention. If one team member is absent, the roles of scorekeeper and referee are combined.
9. Teams are eligible to obtain the group-determined reinforcers after four wins.

Evaluation (Select One or More)

1. Compare percent correct scores on daily classwork assignments in the selected academic subject for the small group of students or the entire class before and after implementation.
2. Compare the class average percent correct score for daily classwork assignments in the selected subject or on weekly quizzes in that subject before and after implementation.

3. If the subject selected was mathematics, compare average scores on three additional *Curriculum-Based Mathematics Probes* for the target students before and after implementation.

Variation

Display a chart listing the names of the teams. Each day, place a small gold star next to the names of teams that meet their daily goal (or have a team member do so). After four wins, place a large gold star on the chart for that team.

Notes

1. In the original study, 1-hour training sessions were conducted separately with each of three treatment groups. For classwide implementation, two or three training sessions of 30 minutes each are recommended, with a review of procedures at the beginning of each week.
2. Team members should be matched as closely as possible on skills in the selected academic subject.

Source

Pigott, H. E., Fantuzzo, J. W., & Clement, P. W. (1986). The effects of reciprocal peer tutoring and group contingencies on the academic performance of elementary school children. *Journal of Applied Behavior Analysis, 19,* 93–98. Copyright 1986 by the Society for the Experimental Analysis of Behavior. Adapted by permission.

INCREASING ACADEMIC PERFORMANCE BY REINFORCING CORRECT ANSWERS

Overview

Although many interventions attempt to improve academic performance by targeting on-task behavior, this strategy targets academic behavior directly by providing reinforcement for accuracy of classwork assignments. In the original study, students earned rewards based on their individual performance, with positive effects obtained for both academic achievement and on-task behavior. Because delivering individual reinforcers to a large number of students can be time-consuming, this adaptation includes several variations designed to facilitate classwide implementation.

Purpose

To improve academic performance by applying group contingencies to correct academic responses.

Materials

1. *Reinforcement Menus,* one per student
2. Posterboard chart or section of the chalkboard with a list of student names for recording daily points
3. Posterboard chart displaying a list of free-time activities along with the point values required to earn them, such as:
   a. Drawing or coloring at seat = 8 points
   b. Drawing on chalkboard = 10 points
   c. Listening to tapes = 15 points
   d. Playing board games with a classmate = 18 points
   e. Playing educational games on the computer = 20 points

Observation (Select One or Both)

Option 1
1. Select an instructional period in which you wish to improve academic productivity. Calculate percent correct scores on daily classwork for the entire class or a small group of students for 5 to 10 days.

Option 2
1. Using a *Group Interval Recording Form* and beginning at the left side of the room, glance at a different student every 5 seconds and record that student's behavior as either on-task or off-task as defined below at the moment of observation.
   a. *On-task behavior* is defined as being seated, looking at or working on the assignment, or talking with the teacher on a task-related topic.
   b. *Off-task behavior* is defined as being out of seat, talking to peers, calling out, working on nonassignment materials, looking at another student's work, sitting without working, or interfering with the work of another student.
2. Conduct these observations for 20 to 30 minutes for 4 to 7 days during the selected instructional period.

Procedure

1. Tell the students that they will be playing a game to help them learn more during the selected subject and have a chance to earn points toward free-time activities. Display the chart listing students' names for recording points.
2. Using the *Reinforcement Menus,* help students develop a rank-ordered list of free-time activities.
3. Explain that they will earn one point for each check mark signifying a correct answer on their worksheets. Also explain that activities available to them at free time will depend on the number of points they earn during the work period.
4. Create and display the chart specifying point values for the selected activities.
5. During independent seatwork time in the target subject, circulate around the room, placing check marks under all correctly worked problems and × marks under all incorrect responses. Give praise for correctly worked problems and make no comment regarding incorrect responses.

6. At the end of the work period, record each student's point score on the chart and provide access to free-time activities according to the number of points earned.
7. As academic productivity improves, record points for an entire week and provide access to free-time activities as the final Friday activity.

Evaluation (Select One or Both)

Option 1
1. Compare percent correct scores on daily classwork in the selected subject for the entire class or the small group of students before and after implementation.

Option 2
1. Compare classwide rates of on-task and off-task behavior before and after implementation.

Variations

Variation 1
1. At the beginning of each work period, tell students that they each have 20 points (the number of points should correspond to the number of problems on that day's worksheet[s]) and will lose 1 point for each × mark.
2. Record point scores and allow access to free-time activities for which students have sufficient points remaining.

Variation 2
1. Divide the class into teams according to rows, tables, or some other grouping.
2. List team names on the points chart and provide access to free-time activities contingent on each team member earning the required number of points for that activity. For example, every student on the team must earn at least 15 points in order to listen to tapes.

Variation 3
1. Tell the students that they will be working together as a team to earn points toward free-time classwide activities.
2. Help students develop a rank-ordered list of classwide free-time activities, and require each student in the class to earn the required number of points for the reward to be delivered.

Notes

1. In the original study, positive reinforcement, response cost, and a mixed contingency all increased academic performance, with no significant difference among the treatments, although the first two systems produced more immediate changes. Moreover, increases in academic performance and on-task behavior persisted following the withdrawal of treatment in all three contingency groups.

2. In the original study, students worked on sets of 20 math problems during the intervention session. The point system should be adjusted according to the number of problems or items on student worksheets.

Source

Broughton, S. F., & Lahey, B. B. (1978). Direct and collateral effects of positive reinforcement, response cost, and mixed contingencies for academic performance. *Journal of School Psychology, 16,* 126–136. Copyright 1978 by Elsevier Science, Ltd, Oxford, England. Adapted by permission.

WINNING THE RECESS GAME: RAISING CLASS AVERAGES WITH A FREE-TIME CONTINGENCY

Overview

Interdependent group contingency systems, which provide a common set of consequences depending on the performance of the group as a whole, have been demonstrated to be effective in increasing on-task behavior and timely assignment completion and reducing disruptive behavior. This intervention combines an interdependent free-time group contingency with public posting of individual grades to target academic achievement in several subject areas. In the original study, academic performance improved for both target and nontarget students and under both daily and weekly reward conditions.

Materials

1. Copies of a contract describing the intervention procedures, one per student (see Figure 4.3)
2. Posterboard chart or section of the chalkboard for recording individual grades and weekly class averages
3. *Reinforcement Menus,* one per student (see Note)

Observation (Select One or Both)

1. Record daily percent correct on classwork assignments for each student for 5 to 10 days or for several weeks in one or more subjects in which improvement is desired. Then calculate the class average for daily percent correct in the target subject(s). Note that these observation measures are used in the intervention procedures.
2. If reading, mathematics, spelling, and/or written expression are among the target subjects, administer *Curriculum-Based Measurements* in those areas to a small group of students.

Procedure

1. Tell the students that they will be playing a new game to encourage them to do their best in the target subject(s).

2. Distribute copies of the contract to each student and review the "Recess Game" procedures and reward system as described below.

3. Post individual grades (without names) for the selected academic subject(s) collected during the observation period on the chart or chalkboard. Calculate and post the class average grade in the target subject(s).

4. Explain that 1 minute of extra recess time will be awarded to everyone for each 1-point improvement of the weekly class average(s) over the observation period.

5. Explain that the amount of extra recess time will be based on the preceding weekly average and will be awarded every day of the week. For example, if the class improves 4 points during the first week of the intervention, 4 minutes of extra recess time will be awarded every day during the second week. Explain that performing below the observation level will not result in the loss of recess time.

6. Grade and return papers in the selected academic subject(s) on the same day if possible or the day after they are completed. Post individual grades in random order (without student names) on the chart or chalkboard.

7. Every Monday morning, update the new weekly average in front of the class, praise the students for any improvement, and announce the amount of extra recess time that will be awarded that week, if any.

Evaluation (Select One or Both)

1. Compare daily percent correct on classwork assignments for each student and the class average daily percent correct in the target subject(s) before and after implementation.

2. Compare scores on *Curriculum-Based Measurements* for the small group of students in the target subject(s) before and after implementation.

CLASS CONTRACT FOR THE RECESS GAME

To help our class achieve our best performance in (name of subject[s]), we will be playing The Recess Game, as follows:

Our class will be able to earn 1 minute of extra recess time for a whole week for each 1-point improvement of our weekly class average. For example, if the class improves 4 points during the first week of the game, we will earn 4 minutes of extra recess every day during the second week. If our average falls below the previous average, however, we will not lose any recess time.

I agree to participate in The Recess Game and to try my best in (name of subject[s]).

Signed: _____
                    (name of student)

Date: _____

FIGURE 4.3. Sample contract for *Winning the Recess Game: Raising Class Averages with a Free-Time Contingency.* Adapted from Bear and Richards (1980). Copyright 1980 by the National Association of School Psychologists. Adapted by permission.

Variations

1. Write the contract on a chart and post it rather than giving students individual copies.
2. Instead of posting individual grades, create teams based on rows, tables, or some other classroom groupings and post averages under team names or numbers. Calculate a classwide average derived from team scores and use that average to determine the amount of extra recess time.
3. Award extra recess time based on daily rather than weekly class averages. That is, calculate class averages each day after school and deliver the appropriate reward on the following school day. Modify the contract accordingly.
4. Deduct 1 minute of recess time for every 1-point decrease in the daily or weekly class average for the selected academic subject(s) and modify the contract accordingly.
5. Send home copies of the class contract and have parents sign and return them.

Note

Prior to implementation in the original study, students were asked to write down what they would most like to earn as a reward for improving their academic performance. If desired, *Reinforcement Menus* may be used to survey student preferences for use in reinforcement selection. Rewards that can be provided in small increments, such as minutes of recess time, are easiest to deliver in this intervention, however.

Source

Bear, G. G., & Richards, H. C. (1980). An interdependent group-oriented contingency system for improving academic performance. *School Psychology Review, 9,* 190–193. Copyright 1980 by the National Association of School Psychologists. Adapted by permission.

STOP THE CLOCK: IMPROVING PRODUCTIVITY DURING SMALL-GROUP INSTRUCTION

Overview

Maintaining an orderly classroom environment during small-group instruction, such as reading circles, is a perennial classroom management problem in the elementary school grades. Although behavior among children in the teacher-directed group is usually appropriate, students who are left to work independently are much more likely to be off-task or disruptive. Teacher efforts to manage the large group can interfere with small-group instruction, with the result that academic productivity decreases for students in both instructional formats. This intervention combines teacher feedback using a stopwatch as a signaling device with a group free-time incentive to improve on-task behavior and decrease disruptions during seatwork time. In the original study, there was no difference in effectiveness between two different signaling procedures: a stopwatch and a 9-inch stop-clock that provided continuous visual feedback on the amount of time earned or lost.

Purpose

To increase on-task behavior and reduce disruptive behavior during small-group instruction and seatwork using a group free-time contingency.

Materials

1. Stopwatch, preferably with an audible click
2. Posterboard chart listing classroom rules, such as:
   a. Stay in your seat unless you have permission to get up.
   b. Talk only when you are called on.
   c. Work quietly on your assignments during seatwork time.
3. Paper or plastic bag containing slips of paper with descriptions of free-time activities written on them (see Variation 2)

Observation (Select One or More)

Option 1
1. Calculate percent correct scores on seatwork assignments during a small-group instructional period for the entire class or a small group of students for 5 to 10 days.

Option 2
1. Using a *Group Event Recording Form,* record the frequencies of the following behaviors during a small-group instructional period for a small group of students or the entire class:
   a. *Out of seat:* not sitting firmly in a seat unless talking with the teacher or aide;
   b. *Talk-out:* talking to a classmate or making an audible vocalization, such as laughing or humming.
2. Conduct these observations for 4 to 7 days.

Option 3
1. Using a sheet of paper attached to a clipboard, record the number of reprimands you deliver to the entire class during a small-group instructional period for 4 to 7 days.

Procedure

1. Tell the students that the class will be doing something new to help them get more out of their school work.

2. Display the stopwatch and explain that students who are not in the reading circle (or small group) are expected to follow the classroom rules and do 15 minutes (or some appropriate number of minutes) of good work during the period.
3. Review the classroom rules and help students provide examples of appropriate and inappropriate behaviors during the work period.
4. Explain that prior to the start of each work period, you will tell students the total amount of time available for that period and the amount of work time necessary (generally 15 minutes less than the total). Whatever time remains at the end will be free time.
5. Explain that you will be keeping track of the amount of good work with a stopwatch that you will stop whenever any student breaks a rule.
6. Explain that you will let the class know when 15 minutes of good work has been completed.
7. At the beginning of small-group instruction each day, allow students to vote for a classwide rewarding activity, such as alphabet bingo, eraser tag, musical chairs, drawing, listening to music, free time, etc.
8. Hold up the stopwatch and inform the class that the watch is being started. Whenever a student breaks a rule, follow these procedures:
   a. Hold up the stopwatch and stop it.
   b. Speaking so that the entire class can hear, tell the misbehaving student(s) what to do (e.g., "Sam, stop talking and get back to your work").
   c. If a student does not comply at once, give a reminder such as "Sam, the watch is stopped!" or "Sam, you're killing time!"
   d. When students are again following the rules and working, hold up the stopwatch and restart it.
9. At the end of 15 minutes of good work, announce that reading circle time (or other small-group instruction) is over and state how much free time the class has earned that day.
10. Praise students for working hard and deliver the agreed-upon free-time activity at the end of the morning period or at the end of the day.

Evaluation (Select One or More)

Option 1
1. Compare percent correct scores on seatwork assignments during the small-group instructional period for the entire class or the small group of students before and after implementation.

Option 2
1. Compare the frequency of out of seats and talk-outs during the small-group instructional period for the small group of students or the entire class before and after implementation.

Option 3
1. Compare the frequency of reprimands delivered to the entire class during the small-group instructional period before and after implementation.

Variations

1. Implement the intervention during a whole-group instructional period during which students are especially off-task and unproductive.
2. Instead of having students vote for a classwide activity each day, use a "grab bag" containing slips of paper with descriptions of free-time activities written on them. At the end of the work period, select a student to draw a slip from the grab bag and permit students to engage in that activity for the amount of time they have earned.

Note

To avoid disrupting instruction, make reminders to students that the watch has been stopped as brief as possible.

Source

Cowen, R. J., Jones, F. H., & Bellack, A. S. (1979). Grandma's rule with group contingencies: A cost-efficient means of classroom management. *Behavior Modification, 3*(3), 397–418. Copyright 1979 by Sage Publications, Inc. Adapted by permission.

IMPROVING ACADEMIC PRODUCTIVITY WITH PERFORMANCE FEEDBACK

Overview

This intervention combines a variety of strategies known to improve academic productivity: timing of work periods, feedback, public posting of student scores, and praise. Dramatic improvement in story writing, reading comprehension, and vocabulary have been obtained using this combination of strategies. Although the intervention requires the teacher to calculate student averages daily and class averages weekly in the target academic areas, no backup reinforcers are necessary.

Purpose

To improve academic productivity by increasing the amount of feedback provided to students.

Materials

1. Prepare a posterboard chart as follows:
   a. Down the left-hand side, write each student's name.
   b. Across the top, make eight columns to record the following scores in the selected subject(s):
      1. Each student's daily score
      2. Each student's weekly average score

3. Each student's cumulative number of perfect papers
4. Weekly class average score
   c. To target two academic areas, divide each column in half.
   d. Laminate the chart so that it can be reused.
2. Water-based pens for marking the chart, with different colors for different academic areas
3. Stopwatch
4. Red pen, one per student

Observation (Select One or Both)

1. If reading is one of the target subjects, administer *Curriculum-Based Oral Reading Probes* with comprehension questions to a small group of students.
2. Record daily scores on skills exercises in the target academic subject(s) for the entire class for 5 to 10 days or for several weeks.

Procedure

1. Introduce the intervention as follows:

   "Starting today, we are going to do something different. While you are doing your [selected academic subject], I am going to time you with this stopwatch, and you are going to have exactly 25 minutes [or the time needed to complete the assignment] to do your work. At the end of this time, you'll have a chance to score your work and to see how many problems you have done correctly. You will then put your pencils in your desk and pick up your red pens and draw a line under the last problem you have completed. You will then grade your work as we go along and count the number of problems answered correctly and put this score at the top of your paper."

2. Display the chart and explain that its purposes are to encourage the class as a whole to beat its highest total weekly score and encourage individual students to beat their daily and weekly scores. Keeping a running total of the number of perfect papers for each student prevents ceiling effects because the number of problems a student can work correctly is fixed by the number of problems in each assignment.
3. Change the scores at the beginning of each target instructional period. Praise students who exceed their highest daily and weekly scores, and praise the class when it exceeds its highest weekly score. Also point out perfect scores and praise those students.

Evaluation (Select One or Both)

1. If reading is one of the target subjects, compare scores on *Curriculum-Based Oral Reading Probes* for the small group of students before and after implementation.

2. Compare daily scores on skills exercises in the target academic subject(s) for the entire class before and after implementation.

Variations

1. Divide the class into teams according to rows, tables, or some other arrangement. Have students select team names and post team daily and weekly averages and classwide weekly averages rather than individual student scores.
2. Post only class average scores for the target academic subjects.

Notes

1. Evaluation and public recognition for improvement are integral aspects of this intervention. If teachers are reluctant to post individual grades because they find individual charting too cumbersome or are concerned that students may be embarrassed by having their grades displayed, one of the group variations may be used (see Note 2, however).
2. In the original study, students were often observed to praise their classmates who exceeded their highest score and low-achieving students who demonstrated improvement.

Source

Van Houten, R., Hill, S., & Parsons, M. (1975). An analysis of a performance feedback system: The effects of timing and feedback, public posting, and praise upon academic performance and peer interaction. *Journal of Applied Behavior Analysis, 8,* 449–457. Copyright 1975 by the Society for the Experimental Analysis of Behavior. Adapted by permission.

SELF-MONITORING TO IMPROVE WORK COMPLETION

Overview

Self-observation is an important component in the process of helping students become self-directed learners. Moreover, self-monitoring has the potential of being sufficiently reinforcing in and of itself so that no backup reinforcers are needed to maintain appropriate behavior once the technique has been acquired. This intervention is designed to increase academic productivity by raising students' awareness of their own rates of assignment completion. Originally applied to a single disruptive and unproductive third grader, it is adapted here for classwide implementation.

Purpose

To increase academic productivity with self-monitoring of assignment completion.

Materials

1. 8½" × 11" paper labeled "My Work Completion Chart," with a list of the target academic subjects down the left-hand side of the page and five columns going across the page, one for each day of the week, one copy per student per week
2. Box or tray labeled "Work Completion Box"
3. Box or tray labeled "Chart Box"
4. Red pen and posterboard chart entitled "We're in the Red," with student names listed down the left side and five columns going across for each day of the week (see Variation 1)

Observation (Select One or Both)

1. Record the number of daily assignments completed at 80% accuracy or greater during one or more instructional periods for the entire class or a small group of students for 5 to 10 days.
2. Calculate the class average for daily work during one or more instructional periods for 5 to 10 days.

Procedure

1. Explain to students that they will be learning a new way of improving their grades in the selected academic subject(s) by managing their own classwork.
2. Explain that daily assignments must be at least 80% correct to be accepted as complete.
3. Display the work completion box and the chart box, distribute the work completion charts, and explain the procedures for recording assignment completion as follows:
   a. Place completed assignments in the work completion box.
   b. Put a check in the column for that day of the week and that subject on the work completion charts.
   c. If there is more than one assignment that day in the subject, put additional checks in that column, corresponding to the number of assignments completed.
   d. Keep work completion charts in an easily accessible work folder.
   e. Place your work completion charts in the chart box at the end of the week.
4. Review work completion charts with individual students or as a classwide activity periodically to provide additional feedback and ensure that students are following the procedures correctly.

Evaluation (Select One or Both)

1. Compare the number of daily assignments completed at 80% accuracy or greater in the selected academic subject(s) for the entire class or the small group of students before and after implementation.
2. Compare the class average for daily work in the selected academic subject(s) before and after implementation.

Variations

1. After grading assignments, use a red pen to circle checks on students' work completion charts corresponding to assignments that are 80% correct or better. Return the charts to students on Mondays, have them review the number of red circles on their charts, and praise them for working hard. If desired, use a posterboard chart entitled "We're in the Red" to record the number of red circles students earn each week.

2. This intervention is designed for students in self-contained classes. If teachers have students for only one or two subjects, list only those subjects on the work completion charts. Alternatively, collaborate with other teachers who share the same group to have students carry a common chart with them from class to class. Have students return completed charts to their last period teacher at the end of the week to be copied and returned to the appropriate subject area teacher for review. Have homeroom or first period teachers distribute new charts each week.

Notes

1. In the original study, index cards taped to the student's desk were used to record work completion. To facilitate whole-class implementation, $8\frac{1}{2}'' \times 11''$ sheets of paper that can be easily photocopied have been substituted.

2. In one variation of the original study, self-monitoring was combined with twice-weekly meetings with a psychologist who reviewed the work completion chart with the student. Without the self-monitoring intervention, however, these meetings had little effect on academic productivity.

Source

Piersel, W. C. (1985). Self-observation and completion of school assignments: The influence of a physical recording device and expectancy characteristics. *Psychology in the Schools, 22,* 331–336. Copyright 1985 by John Wiley & Sons, Inc. Adapted by permission.

ENCOURAGING ACADEMIC ACHIEVEMENT WITH PRINCIPAL PRAISE

Overview

All too often principals' attention is delivered contingent upon student misbehavior or lack of academic productivity rather than positive behavior. Because of their special status in the school, however, principals can serve as powerful reinforcing agents for academic achievement. This intervention uses principal attention to recognize not only high-achieving students for their superior work but also low achievers for their efforts to improve. In the original study, brief principal attention delivered twice weekly resulted in improved academic achievement for a majority of students in two third-grade classrooms.

Purpose

To improve productivity and reduce off-task behavior by providing positive principal attention for appropriate academic performance.

Materials

1. Chart paper or a section of the chalkboard for listing student names, two sheets per day
2. Timer, stopwatch, or watch with second hand (see Variation 1)
3. Red pens (see Variation 1)
4. Posterboard chart with student names listed down the left side and five columns going across (see Variation 2)
5. Gold stars or stickers (see Variation 2)

Observation (Select One or Both)

1. Record percent correct scores for classwork in a selected academic subject for the entire class for 5 to 10 days or several weeks.
2. Calculate the class average percent correct score on weekly quizzes in a selected academic subject for several weeks.

Procedure

1. Explain the purpose and procedures of the intervention to the principal and arrange for an appropriate time for him or her to visit the classroom to deliver the praise.
2. Tell students that you will be sharing the results of their hard work in the selected academic subject with the school principal.
3. Grade classwork papers each day and create two lists on chart paper or on the chalkboard as follows:
   a. A list entitled "Moving Up" with the names of students who have improved their scores over the previous day;
   b. A list entitled "Top Scorers" with the names of the five students obtaining the highest scores that day.
4. Display these lists in a prominent place in the classroom or on the chalkboard.
5. At an agreed-upon time, the principal enters, asks the students on the first list to stand, and announces that those students improved their scores on the assignment.
6. The principal praises them for their improvement and announces that he or she hopes to recognize everyone for improvement on a return visit.
7. The principal then asks the five highest scoring students to stand and praises them for their achievement.

8. The principal's visit should last less than 3 minutes and should be repeated at least twice a week during the intervention.

Evaluation (Select One or Both)

1. Compare percent correct scores for classwork in the selected academic subject for the entire class before and after implementation.
2. Compare class average percent correct scores on weekly quizzes in the selected academic subject before and after implementation.

Variations

Variation 1
1. Give brief, timed classwork assignments (such as sets of math problems to be completed in 5 minutes) each day.
2. Using a timer, stopwatch, or watch with second hand, signal the class to begin.
3. After the set time has elapsed, have students score their own papers with red pens or exchange papers for scoring.
4. Collect papers, verify student scoring, and prepare and post the two lists of student names as described above.
5. Continue with the intervention procedures, beginning with Step 5.

Variation 2
1. Instead of preparing daily lists, make a chart listing all the students' names, with columns for affixing stars.
2. Each day, place gold stars or stickers next to the names of students whose scores have improved and next to the names of the five highest scorers.
3. During the principal's classroom visit, he or she uses the chart to identify students for praise.

Notes

1. In the original study, principal attention lasted less than 3 minutes per session.
2. This form of brief, positive principal attention can be used as a reinforcer for many of the interventions in the book, especially those involving intraclass competitions.

Sources

Copeland, R. E., Brown, R. E., & Hall, R. V. (1974). The effects of principal-implemented techniques on the behavior of pupils. *Journal of Applied Behavior Analysis, 7,* 77–86. Copyright 1974 by the Society for the Experimental Analysis of Behavior. Adapted by permission.

Darch, C. B., & Thorpe, H. W. (1977). The principal game: A group consequence procedure to increase classroom on-task behavior. *Psychology in the Schools, 14,* 341–347. Copyright 1977 by John Wiley & Sons, Inc. Adapted by permission.

INTERVENTIONS TO IMPROVE
HOMEWORK COMPLETION

After years of debate over the efficacy of homework, recent reviews of homework research (Keith, 1982; Paschal, Weinstein, & Walberg, 1984) have concluded that time spent on homework enhances achievement for both elementary and secondary school students. Keith (1982) found that the amount of time students spent on homework was second only to intellectual ability as a predictor of grades. Homework shows larger effects on reading and social studies performance than on other subject areas and has equally beneficial effects for students in low- and middle-SES groups and of varying achievement levels (Walberg, Paschal, & Weinstein, 1985). Effects are especially large when feedback is provided in the form of teacher comments or grades (Paschal et al., 1984; Walberg et al., 1985). In addition to enhancing student achievement, homework can also facilitate parent–child communication about school and increase home–school collaboration (Olympia, Sheridan, & Jenson, 1994).

Despite the documented benefits of homework, many students lack the self-discipline, academic skills, or both necessary to complete their homework. Motivating students to complete homework consistently and accurately has been a perennial problem for teachers and parents alike (Lieberman, 1983). Although books for parents on managing children's homework abound (e.g., Clark & Clark, 1989; Levine & Anesko, 1987; Rosemond, 1990), parents may have difficulty following the prescribed procedures, and the programs often have little or no empirical validation.

Interventions in this section are drawn from three general categories of strategies targeting homework compliance: (1) school–home programs, (2) teacher-based interventions, and (3) student-mediated programs (Olympia, Sheridan, & Jenson, 1994). Because homework is assigned at school but completed at home, interventions that increase collaboration between teachers and parents have the potential to enhance homework quality and completion rates. Unfortunately, many homework interventions require substantial investments of time to implement and monitor effectively, and parents may fail to participate consistently despite extensive school-based efforts to promote their involvement. In contrast, the two school–home strategies for enhancing homework completion included here were either originally designed or have been adapted to be as simple and efficient as possible without sacrificing treatment efficacy. *Improving Homework Submission with School–Home Notes* provides parents with specific information about students' homework performance without requiring any response other than returning a signed note once each grading period. *Increasing Homework Completion with a Daily Report Card* asks parents to talk with their children about their homework each day but does not require the school–home notes to be returned.

The teacher-based intervention in this section, *Improving Homework Compliance with Public Posting and Group Contingencies,* was developed during field testing. It combines the intraclass competition and group contingency system of *The Good Behavior Game Plus Merit* with the public posting component of *Improving Science Test Grades with Public Posting* to target homework completion rates, accuracy, or both.

Because students must do their homework outside of the classroom and away from direct teacher supervision, self-management strategies are ideally suited to interventions targeting homework completion. *Self-Managed Teams to Monitor Homework* combines self-management with group-oriented contingencies to prompt, monitor, and reinforce homework completion. *Self-Instruction to Improve Homework Completion,* which is based on Meichenbaum and Goodman's (1971) self-instructional methodology, provides classwide training in covert verbalizations designed to motivate homework performance.

IMPROVING HOMEWORK SUBMISSION
WITH SCHOOL–HOME NOTES

Overview

Although teachers have frequently sent notes home or called parents to inform them of children's failure to complete homework satisfactorily, there is little empirical evidence that these contacts result in improved homework performance. This intervention uses a single note that provides specific information to parents about their child's rate of homework submission, the class's homework schedule, and the importance of homework. In the original study, middle school students with low homework submission rates showed substantial gains in homework performance, with the effectiveness of the school–home note lasting for about one grading period.

Purpose

To increase the rate of homework submission by using an informative school–home note.

Materials

School–home notes, one per student per grading period (see Figure 4.4)

Observation (Select One or Both)

1. Calculate the percentage of homework submission in one or more subjects for each student for the current grading period or the previous period (e.g., 15/20

assignments or 75%). Note that these data are used in the intervention procedures.

2. Calculate the percentage of homework submission with an 80% or better accuracy rate for each student or a small group of students for 5 to 10 days or several weeks.

Procedure

1. Tell students that you will be sending a note home to their parents about their rate of homework submission to encourage them to do their best in the selected subject(s).
2. Explain to students that the note includes the following information:
   a. Their homework submission rate for the first set of assignments for that grading period or, if the intervention is being implemented at the beginning of the grading period, for the previous period;
   b. An evaluative statement as follows:
      90% submission rate and over = excellent
      80% and over = good
      less than 80% = unsatisfactory;
   c. The homework schedule for the target subject(s);
   d. The importance of homework for skill development;
   e. A request to parents that they sign the bottom part of the note indicating that they understand the homework schedule and then return the note with their child.
3. Fill out the notes and send them home with the students. Remind them that the notes must be signed by their parents and returned.
4. Praise students for returning the signed notes. If any students do not return the notes, deliver a consequence (e.g., students must write an essay during recess on the importance of homework or complete an essay about complying with classroom procedures using the form presented in *Eliminating Disruptive Lunchroom Behavior with Mediation Essays*. Then send the notes home again.
5. At the beginning of each grading period, revise the notes to reflect changes in students' homework submission rates and in the homework schedule and send home the new version.

Evaluation (Select One or Both)

1. Compare the percentage of homework submission in one or more subjects for each student or the small group of students before and after implementation.
2. Calculate the percentage of homework submission with an 80% or better accuracy rate for each student or the small group of students before and after implementation.

Variation

Use the school–home note system but target absenteeism or tardiness instead of homework submission rate. Modify the note accordingly, and compare rates of absenteeism or tardiness before and after implementation.

Notes

In the original study, a call-in service for parents that provided a tape-recorded message of homework assignments and class rates of homework submission did not increase the effectiveness of the school–home note.

Source

Lordeman, A. M., & Winett, R. A. (1980). The effects of written feedback to parents and a call-in service on student homework submission. *Education and Treatment of Children, 3,* 33–44. Copyright 1980 by Pressley Ridge School. Adapted by permission.

School Letterhead

Date:

Dear parent:

    I am writing to provide you with information about your child's rate of submitting homework in _____ (subject or subjects) for the past grading period (or the grading period so far). Your child, _____, has completed _____ out of _____ assignments during this period for a homework submission rate of _____. (Use a separate sentence for each subject being targeted.) To evaluate this rate (these rates), please use the following guide:

    90% submission rate and over = excellent
    80% submission rate and over = good
    less than 80% submission rate = unsatisfactory

    You should expect that your child will have homework in _____ (subject or subjects) according to this schedule: _____ (e.g., "every day except Friday"). Completing homework consistently and carefully is very important in the development of academic skills. Please encourage your child to do his or her best on all homework and to turn in homework each time that it is assigned.

    Please sign the bottom part of this note indicating that you understand the homework schedule for _____ (subject or subjects) and return it with your child. Please feel free to call me if you have any questions. Thank you for your support as we work together to help your child achieve his or her maximum potential in school.

Sincerely yours,

Name of teacher _____
****

I understand my child's homework schedule for _____ (subject or subjects).

_____
       Name of child

_____   _____
       Parent signature   Date

FIGURE 4.4. School–home note for *Improving Homework Submission with School–Home Notes.* Adapted from Lordeman and Winett (1980). Copyright 1980 by Pressley Ridge School. Adapted by permission.

INCREASING HOMEWORK COMPLETION
WITH A DAILY REPORT CARD

Overview

The daily report card is a school–home note designed to improve student performance by providing feedback to parents regarding their children's academic or social behavior. This version is unusual in that it was originally applied to an entire fourth-grade class characterized by poor homework compliance and a high frequency of talk-outs during instructional periods. Improvements in homework and behavior were obtained regardless of whether report cards were sent home on a daily or a weekly basis. Two adaptations are included here: one for self-contained classes and one for classes that have several different teachers. Because of the large number of ratings (21) required for each student if homework, classwork, and behavior are simultaneously evaluated, daily report cards with classwork and behavior ratings are presented as variations.

Purpose

To improve homework assignment completion rates by using a daily report card.

Materials

1. "Daily Report Cards," consisting of 3″ × 5″ index cards or 8½″ × 11″ papers photocopied and then cut into 3″ × 5″ rectangles, one per student per day (see Figure 4.5)
2. Tape for attaching cards to student desks
3. Introductory parent letter, one per student (see Figure 4.6)
4. Posterboard chart listing definitions for the report card ratings

Observation (Select One or More)

1. Calculate the percent completion and/or accuracy of homework assignments for the entire class or a group of selected students for 5 to 10 days or longer.
2. Calculate the percent completion and/or accuracy of classwork assignments for the entire class or a group of selected students for 5 to 10 days or longer.
3. Using a sheet of paper attached to a clipboard, record the frequency of one or more inappropriate behaviors (e.g., talk-outs and out of seats) during a selected instructional period for the entire class for 4 to 7 days.

Procedure

1. One week prior to the first intervention day, send the introductory letter to each student's parents describing the Daily Report Card.

For self-contained classes
2. On the first intervention day, tape a report card to each student's desk. Tell students that their homework will be scored on a scale of 1 to 4 in each subject as follows:

a. 4 = all homework is complete and totally correct;

b. 3 = all homework is complete and mostly correct;

c. 2 = all homework is complete but is mostly incorrect;

d. 1 = incomplete assignments.

3. Remind them that a missing card will be regarded as a card with all "1" or incomplete ratings.

4. During each instructional period in which homework has been assigned, check for homework completion and mark each student's card as described above. Do not interact with the students in any particular way other than to mark the cards.

5. After rating homework completion, sign or initial the cards and tell students to take them home.

6. Send the report cards home daily for the first month. After that, continue to mark the cards on a daily basis, but have students keep them in their work folders and take them home on Fridays. Send a brief letter to parents informing them of this change when it occurs.

For students who change classes

2. On the first intervention day, distribute the cards and have students write their name, date, and subjects (in order of their daily occurrence) on the cards. Tell them that their homework will be scored on a scale of 1 to 4 during each period as follows:

a. 4 = all homework is complete and totally correct;

b. 3 = all homework is complete and mostly correct;

c. 2 = all homework is complete but is largely incorrect;

d. 1 = incomplete assignments.

3. Remind them that a missing card will be regarded as a card with all "1" or incomplete ratings.

4. Check for homework completion, and mark each student's card as described above.

5. After rating homework completion, sign or initial each card, and tell students to take the cards to their next class.

6. Have the last period teacher send the report cards home daily for the first month. After that, continue to score the cards on a daily basis, but have students keep them in their work folders and take them home on Fridays. Send a brief letter to parents informing them of this change when it occurs.

Evaluation (Select One or More)

1. Compare the percent completion and/or accuracy of homework assignments for the entire class or the group of selected students before and after implementation.

2. Calculate the percent completion and/or accuracy of classwork assignments for the entire class or the group of selected students before and after implementation.

3. Compare the frequency of the target inappropriate behaviors during the selected instructional period before and after implementation.

DAILY REPORT CARD

Name of student _____ Date _____

Period/Subject	Homework	Teacher
1. _____	1 2 3 4	
2. _____	1 2 3 4	
3. _____	1 2 3 4	
4. _____	1 2 3 4	
5. _____	1 2 3 4	
6. _____	1 2 3 4	
7. _____	1 2 3 4	

Note: Homework ratings are as follows:

4 = All homework is complete and totally correct
3 = All homework is complete and mostly correct
2 = All homework is complete but is mostly incorrect
1 = Incomplete assignments

FIGURE 4.5. School–home note for *Increasing Homework Completion with a Daily Report Card*. Adapted from Dougherty and Dougherty (1977, p. 193). Copyright 1977 by John Wiley & Sons, Inc. Adapted by permission.

School Letterhead

Date:

Dear parent:

Beginning this week, I (we) will be sending home a Daily Report Card to inform you about your child's rate of completing homework assignments. Please review your child's Daily Report Card every evening. Review the positive ratings first, no matter how few they are, and encourage your child to keep up the good work in that subject. Then discuss with your child ways that he or she can do better in other areas.

The cards will be sent home with your child each day. Please treat any missing cards or missing ratings as "incomplete."

Please save these cards to monitor your child's progress and feel free to use them when you communicate with me (us). I (We) are looking forward to working with you to help your child have a very successful school year! If you have any questions about the Daily Report Card, please do not hesitate to call.

Sincerely yours,

Name of teacher(s)

FIGURE 4.6. Introductory parent letter for *Increasing Homework Completion with a Daily Report Card*. Adapted from Dougherty and Dougherty (1977). Copyright 1977 by John Wiley & Sons, Inc. Adapted by permission.

Variations

Variation 1
1. Include classwork ratings on the report card, with scoring as follows:
   a. 4 = excellent
   b. 3 = good
   c. 2 = fair
   d. 1 = poor
2. Amend the parent letter to reflect this addition.

Variation 2
1. Include behavior ratings on the report card, with scoring as follows:
   a. 4 = no talk-outs (or other target behavior)
   b. 3 = 1 talk-out
   c. 2 = 2 talk-outs
   d. 1 = more than 2 talk-outs
2. Amend the parent letter to reflect this addition.

Note

This intervention is most effective when teachers grade or at least review homework on the day it is due. If it is not possible to grade homework on the same day it is due, explain to students and parents that homework ratings are based on the previous day's assignments.

Source

Dougherty, E. H., & Dougherty, A. (1977). The daily report card: A simplified and flexible package for classroom behavior management. *Psychology in the Schools, 14,* 191–195. Copyright 1977 by John Wiley & Sons, Inc. Adapted by permission.

IMPROVING HOMEWORK COMPLIANCE WITH PUBLIC POSTING AND GROUP CONTINGENCIES

Overview

This strategy targets homework completion by combining the public posting component of an academic intervention (*Improving Science Test Grades with Public Posting*) with the group contingency system and game-like format of an intervention originally designed to reduce disruptive behavior (*The Good Behavior Game Plus Merit*). A variation targeting homework accuracy as well as completion rates is included in this adaptation. Either the original version or the response cost variation of *The Good Behavior Game Plus Merit* may be used.

Purpose

To improve homework performance by providing public recognition and group-oriented rewards for homework completion in a game-like atmosphere.

Materials

1. Posterboard chart entitled "Homework Stars," with student names listed by teams down the left-hand side and a series of columns going across the chart; color coding student names facilitates team identification
2. Stickers or stars

Observation (Select One or More)

1. Calculate homework completion rates in one or more academic subjects for each student or a small group of students for 5 to 10 days or several weeks.
2. Calculate the percentage of students completing all homework assignments in one or more academic subjects for 5 to 10 days or several weeks.
3. Calculate grades in one or more selected academic subjects, such as those in which achievement is poorest, for 5 to 10 days or several weeks for the entire class or a small group of students.

Procedure

1. Divide the students into teams by rows, tables, or some other grouping and implement *The Good Behavior Game Plus Merit* for at least one instructional period.
2. Each day, check each student's homework completion rate. Place a gold star or sticker on the "Homework Stars" chart for students who have completed every assignment and praise the students in front of the entire class.
3. Award five merit points to the team with the largest number of "homework stars" to add to its score for the Good Behavior Game Plus Merit for the day.
4. Acknowledge the daily team winner of the Good Behavior Game Plus Merit, and deliver a reward as described in that intervention.
5. At the end of the week, sum the points from the Good Behavior Game Plus Merit, and declare a weekly team winner.
6. Also sum the homework stars for each team, and declare a weekly Homework Stars team winner.

Evaluation (Select One or More)

1. Compare homework completion rates in one or more academic subjects for each student or for the small group of students before and after implementation.
2. Compare the percentage of students completing all homework assignments in one or more academic subjects before and after implementation.

3. Compare grades in the selected academic subjects for the entire class or the small group of students before and after implementation.

Variations

1. Provide rewards on a weekly basis rather than a daily basis.
2. Use principal attention as described in *Encouraging Academic Achievement with Principal Praise* to reward the weekly team winner(s).
3. Add a homework accuracy criterion (e.g., 80% accuracy or better) for homework to be considered complete.

Note

Field testing indicates that this intervention is easy to implement and highly acceptable to teachers, in part because many teachers use some form of public posting for homework completion. Some teachers prefer to post the "Homework Stars" chart in the hall outside their classrooms to enhance the public recognition aspect.

Sources

Darveaux, D. X. (1984). The Good Behavior Game Plus Merit: Controlling disruptive behavior and improving student motivation. *School Psychology Review, 13*, 510–514. Copyright 1984 by the National Association of School Psychologists. Adapted by permission.

Van Houten, R., & Lai Fatt, D. (1981). The effects of public posting on high school biology test performance. *Education and Treatment of Children, 4*, 217–226. Copyright 1981 by Pressley Ridge School. Adapted by permission.

SELF-MANAGED TEAMS TO MONITOR HOMEWORK

Overview

Although homework interventions with teacher-delivered contingencies can be effective, drawbacks include loss of teaching time and difficulty monitoring an activity that does not occur at school. This intervention combines self-management strategies with group contingencies and cooperative learning to help students monitor their own homework completion and accuracy. Teams of four students meet in structured sessions to review homework goals, monitor assignments, and complete team score cards. Substantial gains in homework completion rates and scores on standardized tests and curriculum-based measures have been obtained, along with parent reports of significantly fewer problems associated with homework completion. In the original study with sixth graders, training was conducted in small groups and intervention sessions occurred outside of the regular classroom. Here the procedures have been adapted for classwide training and implementation.

Purpose

To improve the completion and accuracy rates of daily homework assignments through self-management procedures.

Materials

1. Daily homework assignment in selected academic area
2. Answer sheets corresponding to homework assignments, one per team
3. "Team Score Cards," consisting of 3″ × 5″ index cards, one per team per week; score cards should list team members' names down the left-hand side, with a series of columns for team members' daily scores, weekly homework accuracy goal, and goal completion rating
4. Posterboard chart listing the duties for each team role
5. "League Score Card," consisting of a posterboard chart with team names and columns for posting "win" stickers
6. "Win" stickers or stars
7. Raffle tickets for twice weekly drawings, consisting of slips of paper with students' names on them, with box
8. Backup reinforcers, such as fast food certificates, video game tokens, school supplies, or wrapped candy

Observation (Select One or More)

1. Calculate homework completion rates in one or more academic subjects for each student or for a small group of students for 1 to 3 weeks by counting the number of days that homework is returned and expressing this number as a percentage. For example, if a student returns homework papers on 9 out of 15 days, the homework completion rate for that student is 60%.
2. Use the procedure described above to calculate the percentage of students in the entire class whose homework submission rate is below 80%.
3. Calculate daily homework accuracy for the entire class or a small group of students in one or more academic subjects for 5 to 10 days by counting the number of correct problems completed, dividing by the number of problems assigned, and multiplying that number by 100%. For example, if a student answers 10 of 20 problems correctly, his or her homework accuracy rate is 50%.
4. Conduct *Curriculum-Based Measurements* for a small group of students in the selected academic subject(s).

Procedure

1. Explain to students that they will be playing a game to help them get more out of their homework assignments in the selected academic subject(s). Tell them that the game is like baseball (football, etc.) in that they will be divided into teams and each player on the team will be assigned a special role.

2. Explain that teams consist of four members, including a "coach," "scorekeeper," "manager," and "pinch hitter." The pinch hitter's role is to attend team meetings and take the role of other team members when they are absent or unavailable.

3. Explain the steps for each team meeting as follows:

Step 1: The coach:
a. Prompts and directs team functions;
b. Assembles the team and reviews the daily team goal;
c. Reviews homework completion strategies as needed.

Step 2: The scorekeeper:
a. Counts the number of assignments turned in and grades them according to a sheet supplied by the teacher;
b. Determines each team member's homework accuracy score;
c. Completes a team score card.

Step 3: The manager:
a. Totals the daily team score and declares a win or loss depending on whether the team matches or exceeds its daily goal;
b. Posts a win sticker on the league score card if appropriate;
c. Distributes raffle tickets to team members who meet or exceed their daily individual goals.

Step 4: The coach:
a. Prompts team members to select a goal or reads the teacher-selected goal for the next homework assignment.

4. Conduct a demonstration of a team meeting, using four students to play the roles.

5. After the demonstration, assign students to teams and roles to students on a random basis. Have teams select a team name and discuss strategies for increasing homework accuracy and completion. Each student performs the assigned role for 3 days, after which roles are reassigned so that each student eventually has an opportunity to perform all team functions.

6. Conduct team meetings daily at the beginning of the selected academic period(s). Meetings should last 10 to 15 minutes, after which students hand in their corrected homework to the teacher. If homework scores are incorrectly calculated, correct them and remind teams to score accurately.

7. Give raffle tickets to the managers of teams that have met their weekly goal for distribution to team members. Have students place their raffle tickets in a box.

8. Each week, set a homework completion and accuracy criterion necessary to receive team reinforcement (e.g., homework must be returned with an accuracy rate of at least 80%). Each team member must average at least that score to receive team reinforcement. Raise the criterion as students become more successful in submitting homework.

9. Conduct a raffle twice weekly and deliver rewards to the students whose names are drawn.

Evaluation (Select One or More)

1. Compare homework completion rates in one or more academic subjects for each student or for the small group of students before and after implementation.
2. Compare the percentage of students in the entire class whose homework submission rate is below 80% before and after implementation.
3. Compare daily homework accuracy rates for the entire class or the small group of students in the selected academic subject(s) before and after implementation.
4. Compare scores on *Curriculum-Based Measurements* for the small group of students in the selected academic subject(s) before and after implementation.

Variations

1. Have students select a homework accuracy rate goal each week from a list of three possible goals determined by the teacher.
2. Instead of holding a twice-weekly raffle, give rewards to members of the team(s) with the most win stickers at the end of the week.

Notes

1. In the original study, groups of eight students participated in 2 days of training, and each student received a seven-page handbook of procedures. For classwide use, conducting three 30-minute training sessions, with a brief review of procedures at the beginning of each intervention session, is recommended for smooth implementation.
2. Despite positive gains in homework completion rates, the authors reported that there were only negligible differences in accuracy rates between treatment and control groups. As with any academic intervention, carefully assessing students for the presence of academic skills deficits versus performance deficits is critical to success.

Source

Olympia, D. E., Sheridan, S. M., Jenson, W. R., & Andrews, D. (1994). Using student-managed interventions to increase homework completion and accuracy. *Journal of Applied Behavior Analysis, 27,* 85–99. Copyright 1994 by the Society for the Experimental Analysis of Behavior. Adapted by permission.

SELF-INSTRUCTION TO IMPROVE HOMEWORK COMPLETION

Overview

Self-management interventions are designed to teach students to engage in a set of prescribed activities in an effort to improve their performance on other target behaviors. One form of self-management is self-instruction training, which teaches students to use covert verbalizations to direct their overt behavior. Self-instruction can be especially useful as a component in homework interventions because students complete homework outside of the school environment and beyond the control of teacher-administered contingencies. In the original study with three emotionally disturbed special education students, training was provided on an individual basis outside of the classroom. In this adaptation, training is conducted on a classwide basis, with students practicing self-instruction procedures in pairs to improve their homework completion rates.

Purpose

To improve homework completion rates with self-instruction training.

Materials

1. Sample homework task, such as a set of math problems, one per student
2. Introductory parent latter (Figure 4.7, see Variation 2)
3. Posterboard chart and stars or stickers (see Variation 3)

Observation (Select One or Both)

1. Calculate the percentage of completed homework assignments for a small group of students or the entire class in one or more academic subjects for 5 to 10 days or several weeks.
2. Calculate the percentage of homework assignments that are completed with 80% or above accuracy for a small group of students or the entire class in one or more academic subjects for 5 to 10 days or several weeks.

Procedure

1. Tell the students that they are going to learn a new way of helping themselves to complete all of their homework and earn higher grades as a result.
2. Tell them that learning to say the following set of instructions to themselves will help them remember to do their homework assignments.

> "Now, what time is it? Oh! Time for me to do my homework. Where am I going to do it? I know, I'll do it in the _____ [in whatever room the student usually does homework]. Now, what homework do I have for tonight? Okay, first I'll do _____, then _____, and then _____. Good! It looks like I have a lot to do, but I'll do the best I can. If my mind wanders, I'll tell myself, 'Back to work!' After I'm finished I can play [talk on the telephone, have fun, etc.]."

3. Distribute the sample homework tasks and demonstrate the self-instruction procedure as follows:
   a. Model performance on the sample homework task by saying the self-instructions out loud to yourself.
   b. Have one student perform the sample task while instructing himself or herself out loud.
   c. Have the student perform the task but this time whisper the instructions to himself or herself.

d. Have the student silently speak the words to himself or herself as he or she performs the task.

e. Have students practice the self-instruction procedure in pairs. Move around the class to praise students for practicing the self-instructions correctly and provide feedback as needed.

4. Remind students that saying these things will help them to remember to do their homework assignments. Provide daily practice in the self-instruction procedure, preferably at the end of the school day.

Evaluation (Select One or Both)

1. Compare the percentage of completed homework assignments for the small group of students or the entire class in one or more academic subjects before and after implementation.

2. Compare the percentage of homework assignments that are completed with 80% or above accuracy for the small group of students or the entire class in one or more academic subjects before and after implementation.

Variations

1. Add instructions that target homework accuracy as well as completion as follows:

   "I'll do the very best I can and check my work over carefully after I'm done."

2. Send a letter to parents that describes the self-instruction training and includes the instructions students are to use at home.

3. Make a posterboard chart entitled "Homework Stars" with student names down the left-hand side and a series of columns to the right for charting homework completion. Place stars or stickers beside the names of students who hand in all assigned homework each day.

Notes

1. The self-instruction training in this intervention is based on Meichenbaum and Goodman's (1971) procedure.

2. Because this intervention is aimed at prompting students to approach homework assignments rather than solving the problems, assessing students' ability to perform the assigned homework is an important prerequisite to implementation.

Sources

Fish, M. C., & Mendola, L. R. (1986). The effect of self-instruction training on homework completion in an elementary special education class. *School Psychology Review, 15,* 268–276. Copyright 1986 by the National Association of School Psychologists. Adapted by permission.

Meichenbaum, D. H., & Goodman, J. (1971). Training impulsive children to talk to themselves: A means of developing self-control. *Journal of Abnormal Psychology, 77,* 115–126. Copyright 1971 by the American Psychological Association. Adapted by permission.

School Letterhead

Date:

Dear parent:

Beginning this week, our class will be learning a new way to improve homework completion (and accuracy). These self-management procedures are designed to improve students' ability to take responsibility for their own homework assignments. We will be practicing the following self-instructions regularly in class just before dismissal:

"Now, what time is it? Oh! Time for me to do my homework. Where am I going to do it? I know, I'll do it in the _____ [in whatever room the student usually does homework]. Now, what homework do I have for tonight? Okay, first I'll do _____, then _____, and then _____. Good! It looks like I have a lot to do, but I'll do the best I can. If my mind wanders, I'll tell myself, 'Back to work!' After I'm finished I can play [talk on the telephone, have fun, etc.]." [If desired, add accuracy statements.]

Please remind your child to practice these self-instructions at the beginning of the homework period. Please also help your child to choose a regular time and place for completing homework and encourage your child to try hard on all assignments.

If you have any questions, please do not hesitate to call me. Thank you for your assistance in helping our students do their best on their homework assignments.

Sincerely yours,

Name of teacher

FIGURE 4.7. Introductory parent letter for *Self-Instruction to Improve Homework Completion.* Adapted from Fish and Mendola (1986). Copyright 1986 by the National Association of School Psychologists. Adapted by permission. Also adapted from Meichenbaum and Goodman (1971). Copyright 1971 by the American Psychological Association. Adapted by permission.

INTERVENTIONS TO IMPROVE
READING PERFORMANCE

Learning to read at an early age is fundamental to long-term school success in every academic area (Juel, 1988, 1996; Stanovich, 1986, 1993–1994). Although the relative effectiveness of various methods of reading instruction continues to be hotly debated (e.g., Foorman, 1995; Stahl & Kuhn, 1995), there is a growing consensus that reading acquisition is significantly related to the development of phonological awareness, the conscious understanding that words are composed of individual phonemes or sounds (Adams, 1990; Felton & Pepper, 1995; Stanovich, 1986; Wagner & Torgesen, 1987). Failing to acquire these critical early reading skills has profound and long-lasting consequences for subsequent reading development. In a longitudinal study of 54 children from first through fourth grades, Juel (1988) found that the probability that a poor reader at the end of first grade would remain a poor reader at the end of fourth grade was .88. In addition, reading failure is associated with an increased risk for a host of negative developmental outcomes, including dropping out of school, teen pregnancy, substance abuse, unemployment, and antisocial behavior (McGill-Franzen & Allington, 1991; Sturge, 1982).

Despite the documented importance of reading to school and life success, instructional practices often fail to provide adequate opportunities for students, especially diverse learners, to become proficient readers. First, the amount of time allocated for reading instruction varies tremendously across classrooms (Berliner, 1981). In a fifth-grade sample, Fisher and his colleagues (Fisher et al., 1980) found that reading and reading-related instructional time ranged from a low of 60 minutes per day in some classes to 140 minutes per day in others. Moreover, there were dramatic differences in the time teachers spent teaching different skills. Some fifth-grade classes received less than 10 minutes per day of instruction in reading comprehension, whereas others received about 50 minutes per day.

In addition, although poor readers might be expected to receive extra reading instruction in the classroom in order to catch up with more proficient readers, this is unfortunately not the case (Baker, Kameenui, Simmons, & Stahl, 1994). On the contrary, less proficient readers are likely to receive less exposure to print in the classroom and less adequate instruction than skilled readers (Allington, 1983b, 1984). In a first-grade sample, Allington (1984) found that skilled readers read approximately three times as many words per week during group reading instruction as did less skilled readers. Total number of words read per week ranged from a low of 16 for one child in an unskilled reading group to a high of 1,933 for a child in a skilled reading group. At the end of first grade, poor readers have read less than half the words in running text compared to good readers (Juel, 1988).

As children progress through school, the differences between poor and proficient readers in terms of print experiences and opportunities to learn new words increase and set into motion a self-perpetuating cycle. Good readers read more and acquire larger vocabularies, which enhances their language skills, fund of general knowledge, and overall cognitive development, which in turn facilitates the development of higher-order thinking and problem-solving skills in other academic areas (Baker et al., 1994; Stanovich, 1986, 1993–1994). In contrast, poor readers read less often and acquire less adequate vocabularies and language skills, which further limits their comprehension and ability to broaden their knowledge base and profit from instruction in the content areas. Stanovich (1986) has termed this phenomenon "Matthew effects" from the passage in the Gospel according to St. Matthew: "For unto every one that hath shall be given, and he shall have abundance: but from him that hath not shall be taken away even that which he hath" (XXV: 29).

Although reading assessment has been a frequent topic in the school psychology literature, descriptions of reading interventions are much less common. This relative neglect is surprising in view of the fact that most students referred for special education evaluations are referred because of poor progress in reading (Lentz, 1988). Unfortunately, reading problems are prevalent not merely among handicapped students but among regular education students as well. The most recent National Assessment of Educational Progress (NAEP) in reading achievement indicates that many students are failing to acquire critical reading skills, with 41% of fourth graders, 31% of eighth graders, and 25% of 12th graders reading below the most basic level of proficiency (Mullis, Campbell, & Farstrup, 1993). Given the persistence of early reading problems and their debilitating effects on academic and social development, implementing interventions that help entire classes of students become proficient, motivated readers should be a priority for consultants and teachers at every grade level.

Evaluating the Effectiveness of Reading Interventions

Methods for assessing the effectiveness of the reading interventions in this section include analyses of data that are naturally collected in classrooms, such as percent correct on skills exercises and end-of-unit tests. Also included are guidelines for constructing, administering, and scoring CBMs to evaluate reading fluency and comprehension. These *Curriculum-Based Oral Reading Probes* provide a quick, reliable, and valid method of assessing the need for and the effects of reading interventions and have been demonstrated to be highly correlated with standardized measures of comprehension (Deno, Mirkin, & Chiang, 1982; Marston, 1989; Shinn, Good, Knutson, Tilly, & Collins, 1992). Moreover, although schools are shifting from basal to literature-based reading series and whole-language instruction, oral reading probes derived from basal readers can be used to assess student progress regardless of the actual type of curriculum used in the classroom (Shapiro, 1996a). Norms for evaluating student performance on reading CBMs are provided below. Local norms can also be developed for a classroom, school, or district by administering oral reading probes to a randomly selected group of students in each grade and obtaining the median level of performance. Procedures for developing local norms are presented in Marston and Magnusson (1988) and Shinn (1989).

CURRICULUM-BASED ORAL READING PROBES

Overview

Norm-referenced reading tests are time consuming to administer and score and often have little relationship to the materials students are reading in the classroom. Oral reading probes, a form of curriculum-based measurement (CBM), provide a reliable and valid method of assessing reading skills and evaluating the effectiveness of reading interventions because measures are derived from the actual curriculum. Oral reading probes can reliably differentiate among regular education students, Chapter 1 students, and learning-disabled students. Moreover, when oral reading probes are conducted frequently and the results graphed, they can enhance reading achievement. In addition to monitoring individual student progress, oral reading probes can be used to develop classroom, school, and district performance norms.

Purpose

1. To determine whether a student is appropriately placed in the curriculum materials.
2. To provide information for identifying reading goals.
3. To establish baseline reading levels that can serve as comparison points for charting student progress through the reading curriculum.
4. To provide a reliable and efficient method for assessing the effectiveness of reading interventions.

Materials

1. Three reading passages should be selected for each book in a basal reading series. Two copies of each reading passage selected are required: one for the student to read and the other to score the student's oral reading. The student's textbook and teacher's guide, a photocopy of the passage, or a copy covered with a transparency may be used for this purpose. For preprimers and primers, select brief passages (less than 50 words). For grades 1–3, select 50–100 word passages. For grades 4–8, select 150–200 word passages. Passages should be text rather than poetry or plays, should not have too much dialogue, and need not be limited to the beginning of stories.
2. If you wish to assess comprehension, prepare five to eight comprehension questions for each passage. Questions should include at least one "who," "what," "where," "why," and inferential question.
3. Stopwatch or watch with second hand

Procedure

Administration (reading fluency only)
1. Using the book in which the student is currently placed, administer the passage (probe) from the beginning of the book, then the one from the middle, and then the one from the end.

2. Give the following directions:

> "When I say 'Start,' begin reading aloud at the top of this page. Read across the page. Try to read each word. If you come to a word you don't know, I'll tell it to you. You will have 1 minute. Be sure to do your best reading. Are there any questions? Start."

3. At the end of one minute, say, "Stop!" and place a vertical line on your copy of the passage after the last word read.

Administration (reading fluency and comprehension)

1. Randomly select one of the three passages for that level for the comprehension screening. Administer two probes as described above but give these directions for the third:

> "When I say 'Start,' begin reading aloud at the top of this page. Read across the page. Try to read each word. If you come to a word you don't know, I'll tell it to you. I will be asking you a few questions after each passage."

2. Allow the student to finish reading the entire passage, but mark where he or she is at the end of each minute.
3. Permit the student to look at the probe while you are asking the comprehension questions.

Scoring reading fluency

1. Mark errors as follows:
   a. *Error of omission*: student leaves out an entire word.
   b. *Error of substitution*: student says the wrong word.
   c. *Error of addition*: student adds a word or words.
   d. Repetition of words and self-correction are not counted as errors.
   e. If the student pauses for 3 seconds, supply the word and count it as an error.
   f. If the student mispronounces a proper noun, count it as an error the first time but not subsequently.
   g. If the student deletes suffixes such as *ed* or *s*, do not count the deletion as an error.
   h. If the student mispronounces a word, provide the correct pronunciation and tell the student to continue if he or she hesitates.
2. To determine reading rate, count the number of words read correctly in 1 minute and the number incorrect. If the student reads for 1 minute, the number of words read correctly is the rate per minute. If the student reads for more than 1 minute, as when comprehension questions are administered, divide the number of words read correctly by the number of minutes read.
3. Score each of the three probes by summing the words read correctly, the words read incorrectly, and calculating the percentage of questions answered correctly, if comprehension questions were administered. The student's scores on that book are the *median* correct, *median* incorrect, and *median* comprehension scores (if used). The median score is the middle of the three scores on the

passages and is used rather than the mean score to control for the effects of difficulty.

4. Consult the criteria for frustration, instruction, and mastery levels in Table 4.1. Median comprehension scores are 80% correct for all levels. If the student is within the criteria for instructional level, move up the series and give the next set of three probes. If not, move down.

5. Continue to give probes until the median scores for at least two sets of probes are instructional and the one above them is frustrational. The student's placement is at the highest instructional level.

6. Local norms or the scores in Table 4.2 may also be used for evaluating student performance.

Scoring comprehension

1. The comprehension score equals the percentage of questions answered correctly for that passage.

Notes

1. Because correlations between measures of comprehension and oral reading rate are consistently higher than .70, evaluating comprehension is usually redundant to assessing reading fluency. Students referred for reading problems whose assessed oral reading rates are consistent with expectations for their grade level should receive a full evaluation of their comprehension skills.

2. Criteria for evaluating student performance may also be obtained by collecting local norms within a classroom, school, or district. Detailed descriptions of the procedures are included in Marston and Magnusson (1988) and Shinn (1989).

3. To evaluate the effectiveness of reading interventions, administer three probes from the materials the student is currently using, preferably once or twice weekly, and compare preintervention to postintervention scores. Having students graph their own progress is strongly recommended.

Sources

Marston, D., & Magnusson, D. (1988). Curriculum-based measurement: District level implementation. In J. L. Graden, J. E. Zins, & M. J. Curtis (Eds.), *Alternative educational delivery systems: Enhancing instructional options for all students* (pp. 137–172). Washington, DC: National Association of School Psychologists. Copyright 1988 by the National Association of School Psychologists. Adapted by permission.

Shapiro, E. S. (1996). *Academic skills problems: Direct assessment and intervention* (2nd ed.). New York: Guilford Press. Copyright 1996 by The Guilford Press. Adapted by permission.

Shinn, M. R. (Ed.). (1989). *Curriculum-based measurement: Assessing special children.* New York: Guilford Press. Copyright 1989 by The Guilford Press. Adapted by permission.

TABLE 4.1. Revised Placement Criteria for Direct Reading Assessment

Grade level of materials	Level	Words correct per minute	Errors per minute
1–2	Frustration	<40	>4
	Instructional	40–60	4 or fewer
	Mastery	>60	4 or fewer
3–6	Frustration	<70	>6
	Instructional	70–100	6 or fewer
	Mastery	>100	6 or fewer

Note. The data are from Fuchs and Deno (1982). The table is reprinted from Shapiro (1996a, p. 116). Copyright 1996 by The Guilford Press. Reprinted by permission.

TABLE 4.2. Means and Standard Deviations for Curriculum-Based Measures in the Fall, Winter, and Spring

Curriculum measures	Grade	Fall Mean	*SD*	Winter Mean	*SD*	Spring Mean	*SD*
Reading	1	18.93	36.06	51.69	49.82	71.34	39.37
Spelling		8.78	10.28	25.44	18.31	41.75	19.56
Math		5.07	5.11	16.71	8.94	25.04	11.44
Reading	2	51.30	41.23	72.78	43.85	82.06	38.72
Spelling		33.08	18.68	55.65	23.13	66.39	21.66
Math		23.37	10.59	27.31	12.69	33.38	15.02
Written expression		7.88	6.40	16.72	9.98	24.61	11.53
Reading	3	87.66	40.06	106.91	40.55	114.61	38.41
Spelling		60.35	23.29	81.41	24.75	81.80	14.32
Math		13.73	7.04	20.95	10.23	25.32	12.19
Written expression		19.26	9.92	27.83	11.94	31.22	12.37
Reading	4	105.49	42.50	114.59	40.67	118.31	42.78
Spelling		77.32	26.08	88.78	21.27	93.78	15.29
Math		23.47	9.65	28.78	12.30	34.06	13.31
Written expression		29.07	12.96	36.44	12.36	38.82	13.08
Reading	5	117.65	40.17	129.16	42.63	134.39	40.10
Spelling		90.55	24.31	100.96	20.26	100.73	20.11
Math		31.47	16.15	47.04	19.74	55.26	23.28
Written expression		37.08	14.72	44.61	13.65	44.20	13.73
Reading	6	115.16	39.38	120.15	37.35	131.25	39.07
Spelling		100.75	30.78	116.01	22.05	111.84	19.65
Math		58.35	27.70	72.97	29.05	84.14	32.71
Written expression		44.95	13.98	47.61	14.17	50.94	15.55

Note. These scores were obtained from a 1983–1984 CBM standardization sample of 2,720 elementary grade students in the Minneapolis Public Schools (total $N = 8,160$). Scores represent words read correctly per 1 minute for reading, correct letter sequences per 2 minutes for spelling, digits correct per 2 minutes for mathematics, and words written correctly per 3 minutes for writing with 1-minute planning. The table is reprinted from Marston and Magnusson (1988, p. 149). Copyright 1988 by the National Association of School Psychologists. Reprinted by permission.

Overview of Reading Interventions

Two major skills are required for fluent reading: (1) decoding, the process leading to word recognition, and (2) comprehension, the process in which word meanings are integrated into sentences and text structures (Juel, 1988, 1996). Research indicates that poor readers fall into three categories: (1) those with deficient decoding skills but adequate comprehension; (2) those with adequate decoding skills but deficient comprehension, and (3) children with deficits in both areas, with the vast majority of poor readers suffering from a combination of poor decoding and comprehension skills (Aaron & Joshi, 1992). Here reading interventions are grouped according to their primary target: fluency, sight word vocabulary, or comprehension. Because of the interrelated nature of the reading process, however, interventions targeting one type of skill also have the potential to improve other competencies.

Improving Reading Fluency

Fluency—the ability to read quickly and accurately—is an essential feature of competent reading (Allington, 1983a). If students are to be free to attend to comprehension, they must be able to identify words quickly and automatically. Students who misidentify more than 5% of the words in textual material or read at a rate of less than 100 words per minute (for students at or above the second grade) have decoding problems severe enough to impair their ability to comprehend what they read (Grossen & Carnine, 1991). Despite the critical role of fluency in the comprehension of textual material, until recently little attention has focused on reading for fluency in either assessment or instruction. The two interventions in this section are designed to enhance students' ability to read rapidly and accurately. By increasing fluency, they also improve readers' ability to focus more attention on the meaning of what they are reading. Thus, strategies that promote automatic decoding also facilitate text comprehension. *Repeated Readings* is a simple but highly effective intervention that builds fluency by providing multiple practice opportunities with the same text. *Listening Previewing*, an intervention that has been used extensively with both regular and special education students, enhances fluency and comprehension by using teachers, parents, or peers as reading models prior to independent reading.

REPEATED READINGS

Overview

Repeated practice in oral reading has been demonstrated to improve reading rate, reading accuracy, and comprehension. In this simple intervention, which is especially useful for slow and hesitant readers, students engage in repeated practice by reading short passages from their regular textbooks or curricular materials several times until a satisfactory fluency level is achieved. Although designed primarily to improve reading fluency and word recognition skills, this strategy also improves comprehension because as students expend less attention on decoding, they have more attention available for comprehension. Moreover, verbal cues can be used to direct students' attention to different purposes: reading for fluency or reading for comprehension. The optimal number of repetitions for improving both rate and comprehension appears to be four.

Purpose

To improve reading rate and comprehension by providing additional opportunities to practice.

Materials

1. Stopwatch or watch with second hand
2. Stickers (optional)
3. Sheets of paper or copies of students' reading passages for marking errors (optional)

Observation (Select One or More)

Option 1
1. To evaluate reading fluency, have a group of selected students, such as a reading group, read a short passage from regular curricular materials.
2. Calculate reading rate (words per minute) for each student by dividing the number of words read correctly by the number of seconds read and multiplying by 60.

Option 2
1. To evaluate comprehension, calculate scores on comprehension skill sheets or end-of-unit reading tests for a group of selected students or the entire class for several weeks.

Option 3
1. Administer *Curriculum-Based Oral Reading Probes* to a group of selected students, using both the fluency and comprehension options.

Procedure

1. During reading circle time, explain to students that they will be learning a way of improving their reading skills similar to the type of practice that helps athletes develop skill at their sports.
2. Give the first student the assigned reading passage.
3. To enhance reading fluency, give the following directions:

"I want you to read this story out loud as quickly and correctly as you can. I am going to time you with this stopwatch. If you read quickly and accurately, you will get a sticker." (This last direction may be omitted.)

4. To enhance comprehension, give the following directions:

"I want you to read this story out loud. I want you to remember as much about the story as you can. The important thing is to find out as much about the story as you can. When you are done, I am going to ask you to retell the story to me [or answer some questions about the story]."

5. Use a stopwatch to record the amount of time for each reading. Keep the stopwatch in view to underscore the verbal directions.
6. If desired, record the number of errors (mispronunciations, substitutions, and omissions) on your copy of the passage or on a separate sheet of paper.
7. When the student finishes reading the passage, tell him or her to read it again. A shortened version of the directions can be used:

"Remember, read as quickly and correctly as you can."

8. Time the reading again. Have the student read the passage three or four times. If comprehension is being targeted, have the student retell the story or answer a few different questions about the story after each reading. After the student finishes the final reading, give praise for reading accurately and quickly (and/or for understanding the story).
9. Proceed through the reading material for the day's lesson, following the same procedure with the other students in the reading group.

Evaluation (Select One or More)

Option 1
1. Compare reading rate for the selected group of students before and after implementation. Use only the *final* measure of reading rate on each assessment for comparative purposes.

Option 2
1. Compare scores on comprehension skill sheets or end-of-unit reading tests for the selected group of students or the entire class before and after implementation.

Option 3
1. Compare scores on *Curriculum-Based Oral Reading Probes* for the selected group of students before and after implementation.

Variations

1. Use *Classwide Peer Tutoring* rather than reading circles as a format for the intervention. Pair students from the same reading group.

2. Use parent volunteers or classroom aides to provide extra practice in repeated readings for low-performing students.

Notes

1. To build comprehension skills, ask a different comprehension question or set of questions after each rereading.
2. Field testing indicates that this intervention can easily be implemented by parents to help children improve their reading skills at home. Students may read to their parents or read into a tape recorder. Upper elementary and middle school students often prefer the second option.

Sources

O'Shea, L. J., Sindelar, P. T., & O'Shea, D. J. (1985). The effects of repeated readings and attentional cues on reading fluency and comprehension. *Journal of Reading Behavior, 17*, 129–142. Copyright 1985 by the National Reading Conference, Inc. Adapted by permission.

Samuels, S. J. (1979). The method of repeated readings. *The Reading Teacher, 32*, 403–408. Copyright 1979 by the International Reading Association. All rights reserved. Adapted by permission.

LISTENING PREVIEWING

Overview

Having students preview what they read has been shown to improve oral reading performance. In this intervention, the teacher reads the assigned passage aloud while students follow along silently prior to independent reading. Higher reading rates have been obtained with learning-disabled elementary and middle school students as well as with regular education students. Listening previewing has also been shown to be superior in improving oral reading performance to previewing by the traditional method of silent reading.

Purpose

To enhance oral reading skills by providing an opportunity for students to hear what they will read prior to reading it themselves.

Materials

1. Stopwatch or watch with second hand
2. Sheets of paper or copies of students' reading passages for marking errors (optional)
3. Notebooks or folders with loose-leaf paper for graphing words-read-correctly rates, one per student (optional)

Observation (Select One or Both)

Option 1

1. Administer *Curriculum-Based Oral Reading Probes* to the students in a reading group or a group of selected students by having each student read a 2-minute timed sample from the previous day's reading passage.
2. Calculate each student's words-read-correctly rate by subtracting the number of errors from the total number of words read and then dividing that figure by 2 (minutes).
3. Record and graph (or have students graph) the words-read-correctly rates.

Option 2

1. Calculate scores on reading skill sheets, quizzes, or end-of-unit tests for all the students in a reading group or for selected students for 5 to 10 days or for several weeks.

Procedure

1. Divide the reading lesson into passages according to the number of students in the reading group.
2. Tell the students to follow along as you read the first passage aloud.
3. After completing the first listening preview, have the first student read that passage aloud.
4. Repeat this process until you have previewed the entire reading lesson and each student in the reading group has read aloud. If desired, record the number of errors (mispronunciations, substitutions, and omissions) on your copy of the passage or on a separate sheet of paper.
5. Calculate and graph words-read-correctly rates for students in the reading group as often as possible (at least once a week for several weeks) or teach students to chart their own progress on line graphs in their work folders.

Evaluation (Select One or Both)

Option 1

1. Compare words-read-correctly rates for the target students before and after implementation.

Option 2

1. Compare scores on reading skill sheets, quizzes, or end-of-unit tests for the target students before and after implementation.

Variations

1. Have parent volunteers, aides, or peer tutors conduct the listening previews.
2. Using a *Classwide Peer Tutoring* format, divide the class into pairs, with a higher performing student paired with a lower performing student. Have the higher performing students read first to serve as models for the lower performing stu-

dents. This variation is used in the Peabody Reintegration Project at Vanderbilt University (see Fuchs, Dempsey, Roberts, & Kintsch, 1995).
3. Have parents or older siblings conduct listening previews at home.
4. Prerecord or have aides, parent volunteers, or high-performing students prerecord selected reading passages for independent listening previews at listening stations in the classroom.

Note

Having students record and graph their words-read-correctly reading rate enhances the effectiveness of this intervention.

Sources

Fuchs, D., Dempsey, S., Roberts, H., & Kintsch, A. (1995). Best practices in school reintegration. In A. Thomas & J. Grimes (Eds.), *Best practices in school psychology—III* (pp. 879–891). Washington, DC: National Association of School Psychologists. Copyright 1995 by the National Association of School Psychologists. Adapted by permission.
Rose, T. L. (1984). The effects of two prepractice procedures on oral reading. *Journal of Learning Disabilities, 17,* 544–548. Copyright 1984 by PRO-ED, Inc. Adapted by permission.
Rose, T. L., & Sherry, L. (1984). Relative effects of two previewing procedures on LD adolescents' oral reading performance. *Learning Disability Quarterly, 7,* 39–44. Copyright 1984 by the Council for Learning Disabilities. Adapted by permission.

Improving Reading Vocabulary

Given the large and cumulative differences in word knowledge between proficient and poor readers (Juel, 1988; Stanovich, 1986), building vocabulary is an important goal for classroom reading interventions. Although vocabulary instruction has been demonstrated to improve students' word knowledge and reading comprehension (Beck, Perfetti, & McKeown, 1982; Stahl & Fairbanks, 1986), teachers spend little time helping students learn or practice new vocabulary during reading lessons. Durkin (1978–1979) found that only 19 minutes of 4,469 total minutes of reading instruction (less than 0.5%) was devoted to vocabulary instruction. Similarly, in a sample of first- through fifth-grade teachers who were observed over a 3-month period, Roser and Juel (1982) reported that teachers spent an average of only 1.67 minutes on vocabulary during each reading lesson. In fact, the modal amount of time spent on instruction in word meaning was zero! Moreover, the usual basal reading series method of briefly introducing new words prior to having students read stories provides insufficient practice to master vocabulary, especially for diverse learners and disabled readers (Sindelar & Stoddard, 1991). *Peer Tutoring in Sight Words* creates additional opportunities for classwide supervised practice of new vocabulary by training higher performing readers to tutor their less proficient classmates.

PEER TUTORING IN SIGHT WORDS

Overview

Although peer tutoring is frequently used by teachers as a supplemental instructional strategy, the common procedure is to have students who have mastered a given concept or skill tutor other pupils who have not achieved mastery. In contrast, this intervention provides training for both tutors and tutees in the acquisition of new sight word vocabulary. In the original study, first graders were able to perform the appropriate tutoring and testing behaviors accurately, with both tutors and tutees increasing their knowledge of sight words. In this adaptation, the procedures have been simplified to reduce teacher preparation time. The entire intervention takes approximately 30 minutes, including tutor training, tutor–tutee practice and testing, and graphing test results.

Purpose

To build sight word vocabulary through a peer tutoring procedure.

Materials

1. Tutor folders, consisting of 9″ × 14″ manila folders, one for each tutor–tutee pair, containing three 3½″ × 3¾″ paper pockets, stapled to the right-hand side of the folder as follows:
   a. The "GO" pocket contains the word cards tutors are to present to tutees, up to 10 cards at a time.
   b. The "STOP" pocket receives the word cards when the tutee reaches criterion on that word during tutoring.
   c. The "STAR CARD" pocket holds a 3″ × 5″ "Star Card" with tutor and tutee names printed on it and a grid with spaces for up to 10 stickers or red ink-stamped stars. It also holds two different colored crayons for marking word cards and completing the bar graph.
   d. A bar graph is stapled to the left-hand side of the folder.
   e. On the back of the folder are a picture of a "smiley face" and a large **X**.
2. Sets of word cards for each tutoring session, one set per tutor–tutee pair, consisting of 3″ × 5″ index cards with words printed in ½″ to 1″ lowercase letters with a black marker; sets may be individualized, based on missed words on pretests or prior skill exercises, or they may consist of the weekly list of vocabulary words from the basal reader or other materials for that reading group.
3. Stickers or red-ink stamp depicting stars
4. Kitchen timer with bell (optional)

Observation (Select One or Both)

1. Calculate scores on a pretest of 30 to 100 words selected from the basal reader or regular curricular materials for a selected group of students or the entire class. Words should be presented on flash cards, with credit given for correctly identifying a word three out of three times it is presented.
2. Calculate scores on daily or weekly sight vocabulary exercises for a selected group of students or the entire class for several weeks.

Procedure

1. Tell the students that they are going to play an exciting game to help them learn new words.
2. On the basis of reading group placement or a reading pretest, divide the students into tutors and tutees, with the half of the class in the highest reading groups or scoring highest on the pretest as tutors. Pair the highest performing tutor with the highest performing tutee, the next highest performing tutor with the second highest performing tutee, and so on.
3. Divide the tutors into "Tutor Huddles," consisting of groups of three or four students. Include one of the highest performing tutors in each of the huddles.
4. Conduct a 30-minute classwide session orienting students to the procedures described below. Follow up with two 30-minute sessions of supervised practice for each Tutor Huddle as part of the reading instructional period, and then conduct periodic classwide reviews as needed.
5. When you give a signal (using the timer if desired), each tutor gets his or her tutee's folder and moves to a designated area in the classroom for Tutor Huddle while the tutees remain at their desks and work on seatwork or look at books.
6. During the 5-minute Tutor Huddle, each tutor holds up to the group and reads orally each of the words he or she will be teaching the tutee that session.
7. If the tutor correctly identifies the word, the other huddle members say, "Yes." If the tutor is incorrect, they try to say the correct word. If other huddle members cannot identify the word, they raise their hands to obtain teacher help.
8. Circulate from huddle to huddle to provide assistance and reinforce appropriate tutoring behavior.
9. After 5 minutes, signal the end of the Tutor Huddle and the beginning of peer tutoring.
10. Have the tutors join the tutees in pairs to practice their GO pocket words for 5 minutes. Have tutors present the word cards as many times as possible during this period. Train tutors to prompt a first error by saying, "Try again." If the tutee still does not respond correctly, the tutor prompts him or her to say the word (e.g., "Say 'dog' ").
11. Signal the end of the practice period and the beginning of the test period. Tutors again present the GO words. Each word card is shown only once during the test period, and tutors do not prompt or give feedback. If a tutee says the word correctly, the tutor places it on the "smiley face" located on the back

of the folder. If the tutee misses the word, the tutor places it on the X located next to the smiley face on the back of the folder.

12. Have tutors mark the back of each word card with a "smile" if the card was in the "smile" stack and an X if it was in the X pile.
13. When the tutee correctly identifies a word during testing on three testing sessions, the tutor moves it to the STOP pocket and colors a square on the bar graph. Teach tutors to use the different crayons to alternate colors for each session and to draw a line on the graph if no cards were moved.
14. Have tutors return the folders to their proper place.

Evaluation (Select One or Both)

1. Compare scores on the same test of 30 to 100 words selected from the basal reader or regular curricular materials for the selected group of students or the entire class before and after implementation.
2. Compare scores on daily or weekly sight vocabulary drills for the selected group of students or the entire class before and after implementation.

Variations

1. Switch the roles of tutor and tutee every week so that all students have the opportunity to take both roles and have the additional 5 minutes of sight word practice in the Tutor Huddle.
2. Implement the intervention in stages. First, teach students procedures for the Tutor Huddles and peer tutoring practice periods. After huddling and tutoring procedures are well established, teach students how to test tutees, move cards to the STOP pocket, and color squares on the bar graph.
3. Use the Tutor Huddles and peer tutoring procedure for practicing vocabulary words, but omit the test period. With this variation, the only materials needed are multiple sets of word cards for each reading group.

Notes

1. Small-group follow-up training sessions may be conducted during reading circle time, if desired.
2. Teaching the tutors a brief standardized prompting procedure not only provides them with a functional prompt to use when tutees make errors but also prevents time-consuming individualized prompting, which reduces tutees' opportunities to respond.

Source

Heron, T. E., Heward, W. L., Cooke, N. L., & Hill, D. S. (1983). Evaluation of a classwide peer tutoring system: First graders teach each other sight words. *Education and Treatment of Children, 6,* 137–152. Copyright 1983 by Pressley Ridge School. Adapted by permission.

Improving Reading Comprehension

Despite the importance of reading comprehension in helping students increase background knowledge and learn from their textbooks, classroom observational studies reveal that teachers often fail to provide explicit instruction in reading comprehension. In a sample of teachers in grades 3 through 6, Durkin (1978–1979) found that although teachers often *assessed* comprehension by asking questions, they did not *teach* students how to comprehend what they were reading. If students, especially diverse learners, are to be able to gain meaning from their texts, teachers must provide direct instruction in comprehension strategies, including explanations, modeling, and guided practice, rather than merely testing comprehension (Pressley & Wharton-McDonald, 1997). Improving comprehension is even more challenging than improving word recognition, however, because of the complex, multidimensional nature of comprehension and its relationship to general cognitive ability (Aaron, 1995).

This section includes two basic types of interventions designed to improve comprehension skills. The first category focuses on *prereading activities,* such as setting a purpose for reading, developing background knowledge of the material to be read, and teaching vocabulary (Grossen & Carnine, 1991). Helping students acquire essential background knowledge and vocabulary is especially important for low-achieving and learning-disabled readers, whose deficiencies in these areas often prevent them from obtaining meaning from textual material. *Reconciled Reading* reverses the order in which teachers normally conduct reading lessons by presenting enrichment and extension activities before stories are read. By activating concepts and providing practice with vocabulary prior to reading, this strategy enhances students' contextual knowledge and thus improves their ability to understand and profit from the subsequent lesson.

The second group of interventions is designed for use during the *reading process.* Because a major factor contributing to poor readers' difficulty comprehending text is their failure to use efficient cognitive strategies (Idol, 1987; Short & Ryan, 1984), these interventions provide explicit instruction and guided practice in the metacognitive skills used by proficient readers. Several are based on the schema theory of reading comprehension, which proposes that comprehension results from the correspondence between readers' existing knowledge structures (schemata) and the text. In *Group Story Mapping,* students complete a pictorial map that focuses their attention on important elements common to narrative text while they are reading. Because the map is generic, it can be applied to many kinds of reading material. An adaptation of story mapping for enhancing comprehension of content area textbooks is included in a later section of this chapter (*Improving Understanding of Textual Material in Social Studies with a Critical Thinking Map*). *Using Story Grammar to Aid Comprehension* helps students monitor their own comprehension and integrate information into a coherent story by completing a set of five generic questions. *Story Retelling* is a peer-mediated intervention that provides practice in verbal rehearsal of story material to improve comprehension and recall of information. This systematic form of retelling, which is often used for comprehension assessment, permits students to practice comprehension skills without direct teacher supervision.

RECONCILED READING

Overview

Most basal reading lessons emphasize evaluating students' comprehension of materials after reading rather than teaching comprehension strategies before reading. This intervention, which is based on schema theory, reverses the basal reading sequence so that students participate in enrichment activities prior to reading the story. This is an effective strategy for improving comprehension because it gives students additional opportunities to activate and enhance existing knowledge structures (schemata) and acquire new knowledge and concepts before reading. Preteaching vocabulary words that will help students understand the concepts presented in basal stories appears to be especially important in promoting comprehension.

Purpose

To improve reading comprehension by reversing the traditional basal reading sequence and providing enrichment activities prior to reading.

Observation (Select One or Both)

1. Calculate scores on daily vocabulary or comprehension skill sheets, weekly quizzes, and/or end-of-unit tests for a selected group of students or the entire class for 5 to 10 days or several weeks.
2. Administer *Curriculum-Based Oral Reading Probes* with comprehension questions to a selected group of students.

Procedure

Step 1: Enrichment activities to build background knowledge and introduce vocabulary
1. Begin by turning to the last section in the reading lesson in the teacher's manual, often called "Enrichment Activities."

2. Conduct several of the suggested activities to build background information and vocabulary.

Step 2: Skill lessons explicitly related to the story
1. Use the activities for skill instruction in the teacher's manual, such as comprehension or word attack skill lessons. Teach these skills in the context of the story rather than with isolated sentences or paragraphs.

Step 3: Questions to alert selective attention
1. Review questions taken from those listed after the story. Ask questions that reflect relevant information to be obtained from reading. For example, help students make predictions about the content or outcome of the story.
2. Be sure to select questions that assess both higher and lower level thinking skills (e.g., inferential and literal thinking).

Step 4: Guided silent reading
1. Have students read the story silently to apply background knowledge and skills on their own.

Step 5: Assessment of vocabulary, story comprehension, and skills learning
1. Conduct a brief question and discussion period following reading to evaluate the lesson's four instructional goals:
   a. Building story background to aid comprehension;
   b. Teaching specific vocabulary;
   c. Teaching reading subskills, such as predicting outcomes;
   d. Focusing attention on relevant story information.

Evaluation (Select One or Both)

1. Compare scores on daily vocabulary or comprehension skill sheets, weekly quizzes, and/or end-of-unit tests for the selected group of students or the entire class before and after implementation.
2. Compare reading comprehension scores on *Curriculum-Based Oral Reading Probes* for the selected group of students before and after implementation.

Variations

1. In Step 4, implement *Listening Previewing* prior to having students read silently.
2. After silent reading in Step 4, pair students and have them take turns reading the story aloud to each other before returning to the reading group.

Note

Because this intervention requires teachers to reverse their usual practice in reading instruction, demonstrating the steps in the strategy and providing guided practice are especially important.

Sources

Reutzel, D. R. (1985). Reconciling schema theory and the basal reading lesson. *The Reading Teacher, 39,* 194–197. Copyright 1986 by the International Reading Association. All rights reserved. Adapted by permission.

Thames, D. G., & Readence, J. E. (1988). Effects of differential vocabulary instruction and lesson frameworks on the reading comprehension of primary children. *Reading Research and Instruction, 27*(2), 1–12. Copyright 1988 by the College Reading Association. Adapted by permission.

GROUP STORY MAPPING

Overview

Story mapping is based on the schema theory of reading comprehension, which emphasizes linking previous knowledge structures (schemata) with textual material. A prereading pictorial technique provides a framework that directs the reader's attention to important interrelated elements in narrative stories, such as setting, characters, problem, goal, action, and outcome. The intervention is delivered in three phases, which are designed to increase students' independent use of story mapping over time and can be implemented in a small-group or class-wide format. Studies have documented the effectiveness of the strategy in improving not only reading comprehension but also listening comprehension, spontaneous story writing (journaling), and performance on standardized and criterion-referenced tests for low-achieving, learning-disabled, and nondisabled students.

Purpose

To improve reading comprehension by developing a greater correspondence between prior knowledge and present reading material.

Materials

1. Overhead projector
2. Story map transparency and individual student paper copies (see Figure 4.8), one per student per story
3. List of 10 comprehension questions for each student, one list per story (see Figure 4.9)

Observation (Select One or More)

1. Calculate percent correct scores on the 10 comprehension questions or comprehension skill sheets for the entire class, selected reading groups, or selected students for 5 to 10 days or for several weeks.

2. Administer *Curriculum-Based Oral Reading Probes* evaluating both reading rate and comprehension to selected students.
3. Calculate percent correct scores on daily, weekly, or end-of-unit reading quizzes and tests for the entire class, selected reading groups, or selected students for 5 to 10 days or for several weeks.

Procedure

Phase 1: Modeling the use of story mapping
1. After silent reading, display an overhead transparency of the story map to the entire class or a reading group. Using the transparency and paper copies of the story map, have students complete their own copies as you call on individual students for responses. Be sure to give all students equal opportunities to respond.
2. Have students hand in their story maps, put away their books or reading materials, and answer the 10 written comprehension questions (or complete comprehension skill sheets) independently.

Phase 2: Checking student use of story mapping
1. Have the students independently fill in the story map. Tell them that they can fill in the maps as they read the story, after they read it silently, or a combination of both.
2. After silent reading and story map completion, bring students to the reading group (if you are using a small-group rather than a whole-class format) and call upon students to identify story map contents as before. Record responses on the story map transparency, and have students make any necessary corrections on their individual maps.
3. Have students hand in their maps and books or reading materials and answer the comprehension questions as before.

Phase 3: Independent use of story mapping
1. Have students silently read stories and complete their story maps. Do not have them respond as a group to story map elements.
2. Test comprehension as described above.

Phase 4: Maintenance
1. Have students read silently and answer comprehension questions without the story maps. If scores fall below 80% accuracy for 2 consecutive days, reinstate the maps.

Evaluation (Select One or More)

1. Compare percent correct scores on comprehension questions or skill sheets for the entire class, selected reading groups, or selected students before and after implementation.

2. Compare reading rate and comprehension scores on *Curriculum-Based Oral Reading Probes* for selected students before and after implementation.
3. Compare percent correct scores on daily, weekly, or end-of-unit reading quizzes and tests for the entire class, selected reading groups, or selected students before and after implementation.

Variation

After Phase 1, have students work in pairs to complete their story maps and answer comprehension questions before proceeding to Phase 2.

Notes

1. If story mapping will be used in all reading groups, conducting Phase 1 as a classwide presentation is recommended.
2. In the original study, story mapping was taught in groups of 11 students that included learning-disabled and low-achieving students along with nondisabled pupils, indicating that ability grouping is not necessary to achieve positive results.

Source

Idol, L. (1987). Group story mapping: A comprehension strategy for both skilled and unskilled readers. *Journal of Learning Disabilities, 20,* 196–205. Copyright 1987 by PRO-ED, Inc. Adapted by permission.

Name: _____

Date: _____

1. Where did this story take place?
2. When did this story take place?
3. Who were the main characters in the story?
4. Were there any other important characters in the story? Who?
5. What was the problem in the story?
6. How did _____ try to solve the problem?
7. Was it hard to solve the problem? Explain.
8. Was the problem solved? Explain.
9. What did you learn from reading this story? Explain.
10. Can you think of a different ending?

FIGURE 4.8. Comprehension questions for *Group Story Mapping.* From Idol (1987, p. 197). Copyright 1987 by PRO-ED, Inc. Reprinted by permission.

MY STORY MAP

NAME _____ DATE _____

```
┌─────────────────────────────────────────────────────────────────┐
│ The Setting                                                       │
│    Characters:            Time:            Place:                 │
│                                                                   │
│                                                                   │
└─────────────────────────────────────────────────────────────────┘
              │
              ▼
┌─────────────────────────────────────────────────────────────────┐
│ The Problem                                                       │
│                                                                   │
│                                                                   │
└─────────────────────────────────────────────────────────────────┘
              │
              ▼
┌─────────────────────────────────────────────────────────────────┐
│ The Goal                                                          │
│                                                                   │
│                                                                   │
└─────────────────────────────────────────────────────────────────┘
              │
              │        ┌──────────────────────────────────────────┐
              │        │ Action                                   │
              │        │                                          │
              ◄────►   │                                          │
              │        │                                          │
              │        │                                          │
              │        └──────────────────────────────────────────┘
              ▼
┌─────────────────────────────────────────────────────────────────┐
│ The Outcome                                                       │
│                                                                   │
└─────────────────────────────────────────────────────────────────┘
```

FIGURE 4.9. Story map components for *Group Story Mapping.* From Idol (1987, p. 199). Copyright 1987 by PRO-ED, Inc. Reprinted by permission.

USING STORY GRAMMAR TO AID COMPREHENSION

Overview

One of the chief characteristics distinguishing poor readers from skilled readers is their failure to apply metacognitive or active reading strategies to aid their comprehension. Story grammar training is designed to assist students in encoding, integrating, and retrieving story information by focusing their attention on story structure. Students learn to ask five "wh" questions about the settings and episodes of a story that guide them in attending to and remembering important information. By providing learners with an organizational framework within which to integrate new story information and structure it for retrieval, story grammar training can have a powerful positive impact on the reading comprehension of poor and skilled readers alike. Training may be delivered in small-group or classwide formats.

Purpose

To improve reading comprehension by providing an organizational framework for learning and remembering story information.

Materials

1. Three or four narrative passages similar to students' regular curricular materials (may be taped)
2. Overhead projector
3. Transparency of the five "wh" questions
4. Paper copies of the five "wh" questions, one per student per story (see Figure 4.10)
5. Posterboard chart listing the five "wh" questions (optional)

Observation (Select One or Both)

1. Administer *Curriculum-Based Oral Reading Probes* with comprehension questions to selected students or selected reading groups.
2. Calculate percent correct scores on reading comprehension skill exercises, end-of-story tests, and/or end-of-unit tests for 5 to 10 days or for several weeks for selected students, selected reading groups, or the entire class.

Procedure

1. Tell the students that they are going to play a game to help them become better readers. The game is called "Reading Mysteries," and "Storyteller" and "Detective Reader" are the main characters.
2. Tell them that the job of Storyteller (the person who wrote the story) is to provide specific clues to enable readers to make predictions about the story based on past experiences.
3. Tell them that their job as Detective Reader is to search for clues in the story,

ask questions when they don't understand, and make predictions about upcoming story events based on background knowledge.

4. Read a narrative passage or play a taped example of a story.
5. Using an overhead transparency, introduce the five "wh" story grammar questions and give students paper copies of the questions. If desired, display a posterboard chart listing the five questions.
6. Model the use of the story grammar questions for the example, calling on students to supply the answers. Have them fill in the answers on their papers as you do so on the transparency.
7. Tell the students that to be good Detective Readers, they should recite the five questions to themselves during silent reading. (If writing on their reading materials is permitted, they should also underline and label the answers to the five questions during study time.)
8. Review the strategies and have students practice applying them for at least two more sessions as a classwide activity or in reading groups.
9. As students become proficient in using the strategies, gradually eliminate the use of paper copies for the five questions.

Evaluation (Select One or Both)

1. Compare scores on *Curriculum-Based Oral Reading Probes* with comprehension questions for selected students or selected reading groups before and after implementation.
2. Compare percent correct scores on reading comprehension skill exercises, end-of-story tests, and/or end-of-unit tests for selected students, selected reading groups, or the entire class before and after implementation.

Variation

Using a *Classwide Peer Tutoring* format and matching students from the same reading group, have students work in pairs to answer the five questions before coming to the reading circle.

Notes

1. Conducting an initial whole-class presentation is recommended if all reading groups will be using the story grammar strategy.
2. In the original study, attribution training, consisting of self-statements stressing the importance of effort in reading, did not enhance the effectiveness of story grammar training.

Source

Short, E. J., & Ryan, E. B. (1984). Metacognitive differences between skilled and less skilled readers: Remediating deficits through story grammar and attribution training. *Journal of Educational Psychology, 76,* 225–235. Copyright 1984 by the American Psychological Association. Adapted by permission.

BE A DETECTIVE READER AND SOLVE THE READING MYSTERY

Name: _____ Date: _____

1. Who is the main character?

_____

2. Where and when did the story take place?

_____

_____

_____

3. What did the main character do?

_____

_____

_____

4. How did the story end?

_____

_____

_____

5. How did the main character feel?

_____

_____

_____

FIGURE 4.10. Questions for *Using Story Grammar to Aid Comprehension*. Adapted from Short and Ryan (1984, p. 228). Copyright 1984 by the American Psychological Association. Adapted by permission.

STORY RETELLING

Overview

Although verbal rehearsal improves memory and recall of what has been read, students are often provided with few opportunities to practice organizing and retelling information. In this strategy, students verbally rehearse important story information by retelling a story to partners, using outlines. By requiring readers to relate the parts of the story to each other and to their own experiential backgrounds, retelling improves reading comprehension and recall of story information. Moreover, the benefits of story retelling transfer to subsequent reading material. This intervention requires four training sessions to teach students how to use the outlines and can be delivered in a classwide or small-group format.

Purpose

To improve reading comprehension and recall of information by providing practice in verbal rehearsal of story material.

Materials

1. Paper copies of story outline, one per student (see Figure 4.11)
2. Overhead projector (optional)
3. Transparency of story outline (optional)

Observation (Select One or Both)

1. Administer *Curriculum-Based Oral Reading Probes* with comprehension questions to selected students or selected reading groups.
2. Calculate percent correct scores on reading comprehension skill exercises, end-of-story tests, and/or end-of-unit tests for 5 to 10 days or for several weeks for selected students, selected reading groups, or the entire class.

Procedure

1. During a classwide orientation or reading circle time, tell the students that they will be learning a new and exciting way to understand and remember more about what they read. For the four training sessions, assign students to pairs, matching students with similar levels of reading performance.
2. Tell them that they will be reading a passage and picking out the important ideas in that passage.
3. Have the students read the assigned passage silently.
4. Give them copies of the story outline, review it with them, and have them complete it. If desired, use an overhead projector and transparency of the outline to demonstrate completion. Accept all student ideas, and do not make any corrections.
5. After students complete the outline, have them work in pairs to retell "all the important ideas in the story" to their partners, as if their partners had never read the story. Give each member of the pair a turn at retelling the story.
6. For the first two training sessions, guide students in completing the outline. Provide help if needed for the third session but have the students complete the outline alone for the fourth session. Then have them work in pairs to retell the story as described above.
7. Reverse the order of retelling for the partners over the four training sessions.

Evaluation (Select One or Both)

1. Compare scores on *Curriculum-Based Oral Reading Probes* with comprehension questions for selected students or selected reading groups before and after implementation.
2. Compare percent correct scores on reading comprehension skill exercises, end-of-story tests, and/or end-of-unit tests for selected students, selected reading groups, or the entire class before and after implementation.

Variation

Use the outlines and paired retelling format to improve comprehension in content areas, such as social studies and science. Substitute the word "passage" for "story" in the outlines.

Notes

1. Note that unlike other reading interventions that provide an organizational framework for encoding and retrieving information, the teacher neither provides explicit instructions concerning what constitutes an important idea or relevant detail nor formally evaluates student responses.
2. In the original study, students receiving story retelling training performed significantly better in reading comprehension and recall compared with students trained to illustrate the important ideas in the story.

MY STORY RETELLING OUTLINE

Directions: Write down what you think are the most important ideas and supporting details in the story you have just read. Be prepared to retell all the important ideas from the story to your partner as if your partner has never read the story.

First Important Idea: _____

_____

   Supporting Detail: _____

   Supporting Detail: _____

Second Important Idea: _____

_____

   Supporting Detail: _____

   Supporting Detail: _____

Third Important Idea: _____

_____

   Supporting Detail: _____

   Supporting Detail: _____

Fourth Important Idea: _____

_____

   Supporting Detail: _____

   Supporting Detail: _____

FIGURE 4.11. Outline for *Story Retelling.* Adapted from Gambrell, Pfeiffer, and Wilson (1985, p. 218). Adapted with permission of The Helen Dwight Reid Educational Foundation. Published by Heldref Publications, 1319 18th Street, N.W., Washington, DC 20036-1802. Copyright 1985.

Source

Gambrell, L. B., Pfeiffer, W. R., & Wilson, R. M. (1985). The effects of retelling upon reading comprehension and recall of text information. *Journal of Educational Research, 78*(4), 216–220. Adapted with permission of The Helen Dwight Reid Educational Foundation. Published by Heldref Publications, 1319 18th Street, N.W., Washington, DC 20036-1802. Copyright 1985.

INTERVENTIONS TO IMPROVE MATHEMATICS PERFORMANCE

The most recent National Assessment of Educational Progress (NAEP) in mathematics (Mullis, Dossey, Owen, & Phillips, 1993) reveals serious deficiencies in math achievement among the general student population. More than one-third of students at the three grades assessed (4, 8, and 12) failed to reach even the Basic level of proficiency (partial mastery). Among fourth graders, nearly 40% scored at the Below Basic level. Moreover, ethnic groups show marked disparities in achievement, with some minority groups especially at risk. Although 30 to 44% of the Asian/Pacific Islander students and 19 to 32% of White students performed at or above the Proficient level, 10% or fewer of American Indian, Black, or Hispanic students achieved that level of performance. Learning-disabled students also exhibit significant mathematics deficits, with skills plateauing at a fourth- or fifth-grade level for secondary school pupils (Algozzine, O'Shea, Crews, & Stoddard, 1987; Cawley & Miller, 1989; McLeod & Armstrong, 1982).

Students who are referred for problems in mathematics generally exhibit two types of deficits (Shapiro, 1996a). The first type of deficit consists of problems in mastering computational skills, including the basic operations of addition, subtraction, multiplication, and division. A related problem is lack of fluency with math facts. In addition to knowing math facts, students must be able to solve computational problems rapidly enough to keep up with the pace of the classroom curriculum. The majority (61%) of secondary school students with learning disabilities in mathematics still rely on counting on their fingers to perform computational tasks, indicating that they have failed to develop the kinds of automatic skills that permit mastery of more difficult problems (McLeod & Armstrong, 1982).

The second category of math deficits involves problems with mathematics applications, including areas such as money, measurement, time, and word problems (Shapiro, 1996a). Just as students who fail to master decoding are unlikely to succeed in comprehending what they read, so students with computational skill deficits will have trouble applying and reasoning with those skills. Moreover, because of the sequential nature of the mathematics curriculum, skill deficits become cumulative, so that students fall farther behind their peers with each passing grade. Most students with learning disabilities in mathematics make only minimal progress from one year to the next in math achievement (Cawley & Miller, 1989).

Research on mathematics instruction suggests that for many students, poor mathematics achievement may be more related to "curriculum disabilities" arising from the shortcomings of current textbooks and instructional practices rather than to learning disabilities internal to students (Carnine, 1994; Carnine, Jones, & Dixon, 1994). Studies have reported wide variations in the amount of time allocated for mathematics instruction from one classroom to another and in the amount of time allocated to different skill areas, with the most time spent teaching computational skills rather than helping students develop conceptual understanding and providing opportunities to apply concepts and skills (Fisher et al., 1980; Porter, 1989). In a second-grade sample, the average student in one classroom received 9 minutes of instruction over the course of the year in computations with money, whereas in another classroom, the average student received 315 minutes of instruction on that topic during the year (Fisher et al., 1980). In many elementary school classrooms, mathematics instruction consists of brief teacher presentations followed by extended periods of seatwork (Good, 1983). Moreover, mathematics textbooks include insufficient amounts of review and practice for the topics they cover, so that students are exposed to many concepts and skills without having the opportunity to master them (Carnine et al., 1994). Instead, the spiral curriculum, which is intended to deepen understanding by revisiting the same concepts year after year, results in superficial coverage of many topics during the school year (Englemann, Carnine, & Steely, 1991). Given the increasing diversity of student abilities in the regular classroom and the lack of opportunities provided by mathematics textbooks to practice concepts and skills, interventions that enhance students' opportunities to respond to math material are needed for many, if not most students, if they are to become proficient in this critical academic area.

The interventions in this section are designed to enhance mathematics skills acquisition and fluency using a variety of strategies, including self-management, performance feedback, peer tutoring, and contingent reinforcement. In *Cover, Copy, and Compare: Increasing Math Fluency,* students learn a five-step procedure that allows for self-correction and increased opportunities to respond to mathematics material. *Improving Math Performance with Explicit Timing* uses timing and performance feedback to improve fluency with math facts. Two interventions rely on peer tutoring formats to increase opportunities to respond and motivation for academic productivity. In *Reciprocal Peer Tutoring to Improve Math Achievement,* which combines self-management procedures with group contingencies, tutoring pairs select and work toward their own math performance goals. *Improving*

Math Performance with Reciprocal Peer Tutoring and Parental Involvement adds a home-based component to peer tutoring to provide additional reinforcement for math achievement. *Improving Math Completion Rates and Accuracy with Free Time* is a simple strategy requiring no material resources that makes access to free time contingent on classwide productivity in mathematics.

Evaluating the Effectiveness of Mathematics Interventions

Measures for assessing the effectiveness of the math strategies in this section range from classwide percent correct rates on daily work to conduct grades for interventions that target student attitudes during mathematics instruction as well as math productivity. In addition to the evaluation procedures provided for each intervention, directions for constructing and administering CBMs in mathematics are provided below. In developing *Curriculum-Based Mathematics Probes,* Shapiro (1996a) recommends that teachers use the school district's scope-and-sequence list of computation skills to rate students' mastery, instructional, and frustration levels. Items can then be developed to assess computational skills that fall between teachers' ratings of mastery and frustration levels. Reproducible forms listing expected whole-number computation skill competencies for grades 1 through 5 and teacher interview forms using this procedure are included in Shapiro (1996b). Table 4.3 presents placement criteria for evaluating performance on math probes.

CURRICULUM-BASED MATHEMATICS PROBES

Overview

Curriculum-based measurement (CBM) in mathematics provides useful information for making decisions regarding the computational skills students have or have not mastered. Math probes can be constructed to assess a single skill, such as two-digit subtraction with borrowing, or multiple skills, such as addition and subtraction facts with results less than 20. Because math probes yield information on fluency as well as accuracy, they are especially helpful for identifying students who have learned basic concepts but cannot perform computations fast enough to be at mastery levels. Information from math probes can be used to develop short- and long-term goals for individual students and classroom groups and, with repeated administration, to assess progress toward these goals. Math probes can be administered to individuals or groups of students.

Purpose

1. To assess math fluency and accuracy for selected computational skills.
2. To provide information for designing math interventions.
3. To monitor the acquisition of newly taught math skills.

4. To assess the effectiveness of math interventions.
5. To provide information for program evaluation.

Materials

1. Stopwatch or watch with second hand
2. Pencils with erasers, two per student

Single-skill probes
1. Two or three sheets of written or typed math problems assessing the same skill, with enough room left for computation, about 30–35 problems per sheet for single-digit problems and fewer for more complex problems, one set of sheets per student

Multiple-skill probes
1. Two or three sheets of written or typed math problems, with two or three types of computational skills on each sheet, about 30–35 problems per sheet for simpler problems and fewer for more complex problems, one set of sheets per student

Procedure

Administration
1. Obtain the sequence of instruction for computational skills for the school district.
2. Define the specific type(s) of math problems to be assessed. These should be skills that fall between students' mastery and frustrational levels.
3. Prepare the probes as described above.
4. For *single-skill probes*, give the following directions:

> "The sheets on your desk are math facts. All the problems are [addition or subtraction or multiplication or division] facts. When I say 'Start,' turn the sheets over and begin answering the problems. Start with the first problem on the left on the top row [point]. Work across and then go to the next row. If you can't answer the problem, make an × on it and go on to the next one. If you finish one sheet, go on to the next. Are there any questions? Start!"

For *multiple-skill probes*, give the following directions:

> "The sheets on your desk are math facts. There are several types of problems on the sheets. Some are [addition, subtraction, multiplication, and/or division]. Look at each problem carefully before you answer it. When I say 'Start,' turn the sheets over and begin answering the problems. Start with the first problem on the left on the top row [point]. Work across and then go to the next row. If you can't answer the problem, make an × on it and go on to the next one. If you finish one sheet, go on to the next. Are there any questions? Start!"

5. Monitor students to make sure that they work the problems in rows and do not skip around or answer only the easy problems.
6. For addition and subtraction probes, say "Stop!" after 2 minutes. For multiplication and division probes, say "Stop!" after 5 minutes.

Scoring

Option 1: Digits-correct scoring method
1. Count the separate correct digits in an answer. For all skills except long division, count only digits below the line. For long division, count all digits above and below the line.
2. When scoring multiplication problems, score digits as correct if the addition operations are performed correctly, even if the answer is incorrect. That is, do not penalize students twice for a single error.
3. When scoring division problems, count digits as incorrect if the incorrect operation is performed or if incorrect place values are used.
4. If the student completes the worksheet before the time is up, divide the number of correctly written digits by the total number of seconds and multiply by 60 to obtain the digits correct per minute.
5. Count omitted problems as errors. Because this will inflate the number of incorrect digits and deflate the number of correct digits, report two scores: one with omitted items counted as incorrect and one without counting omitted items as incorrect.
6. Consult Table 4.3 to evaluate the student's level. If the student's score is significantly below instructional level, move downward to a less challenging probe. If the student's score is close to or within the instructional or mastery level, administer one additional probe of those same skills. The median or middle score for all probes of the same skill is the score for that skill or cluster.

Option 2: Percent-correct scoring method
1. Count any omitted problems as errors.
2. Divide the number of problems completed correctly by the total number of problems to obtain the percent correct score.

Notes

1. Although placement criteria are available only for the digits-correct scoring method, many teachers and consultants are unfamiliar with this procedure. The traditional percent-correct method is therefore included as an option. Local norms for either scoring method may be obtained by administering probes to the entire class or to 5 to 10 children in the same classroom or grade who are considered to be achieving at expected levels in mathematics. Descriptions of local norming procedures are included in Marston and Magnusson (1988) and Shinn (1989).
2. The scores in Table 4.2 may be used for comparison purposes. Additional norms (median digits correct and median errors) from a rural midwestern school district for 2-minute timings of math probes are presented in Shapiro (1996a).

TABLE 4.3. Placement Criteria for Direct Assessment of Math

Grade		Criterion	
		Median digits correct per minute	Median digits incorrect per minute
1–3	Frustration	0–9	8+
	Instructional	10–19	3–7
	Mastery	20+	≤2
4+	Frustration	0–19	8+
	Instructional	20–39	3–7
	Mastery	40+	≤2

Note. The data are from Deno and Mirkin (1977). The table is reprinted from Shapiro and Lentz (1986, p. 124). Copyright 1986 by Lawrence Erlbaum Associates, Inc. Reprinted by permission.

Sources

Marston, D., & Magnusson, D. (1988). Curriculum-based measurement: District level implementation. In J. L. Graden, J. E. Zins, & M. J. Curtis (Eds.), *Alternative educational delivery systems: Enhancing instructional options for all students* (pp. 137–172). Washington, DC: National Association of School Psychologists. Copyright 1988 by the National Association of School Psychologists. Adapted by permission.

Shapiro, E. S. (1996). *Academic skills problems: Direct assessment and intervention* (2nd ed.). New York: Guilford Press. Copyright 1996 by The Guilford Press. Adapted by permission.

Shinn, M. R. (Ed.). (1989). *Curriculum-based measurement: Assessing special children.* New York: Guilford Press. Copyright 1989 by The Guilford Press. Adapted by permission.

COVER, COPY, AND COMPARE: INCREASING MATH FLUENCY

Overview

Although most children with learning problems can use counting strategies to solve basic addition and subtraction problems, they often require large amounts of time to complete math problems. Their slow rate of speed places them at a severe disadvantage in the classroom and can lead to failure in their mathematics curriculum. In this intervention, students learn a five-step procedure that provides for increased opportunities to respond to mathematics material and self-evaluation of responses. Cover, Copy, and Compare is an efficient strategy for increasing fluency in basic math facts that requires little student training or teacher time. Originally used with individuals and small groups of students, it is adapted here for classwide implementation.

Purpose

To improve accuracy and speed with basic mathematics facts.

Materials

1. Training sheets of 10 math problems, with problems listed down the left side and the answer provided for each problem, one per student, one to three sets per session
2. Assessment sheets with the same math problems listed down the left side but with blanks next to each problem for written responses
3. 3″ × 5″ index cards, one per student
4. Stopwatch or watch with second hand for teacher (optional)
5. Overhead projector and transparency example of a training sheet (optional)
6. Stopwatches or watches with second hands for students (Variation 2)
7. Posterboard chart for displaying the class average number of correctly completed problems during timed tests (Variation 4)

Observation (Select One or More)

1. Calculate percent correct scores on math worksheets for 5 to 10 days for the entire class or a selected group of students.
2. Count the number of correct digits on problems on math worksheets. For example, for a worksheet with 10 2-digit division problems, in which each quotient consists of 1 digit, there are 10 possible correct digits for that worksheet. Record the number of correct digits for 5 to 10 days for the entire class or a selected group of students.
3. To determine rate as well as accuracy, give a selected group of students or the entire class a fixed amount of time to complete math worksheets. Count the number of correct digits as described above, multiply by 60, and divide by the number of seconds allotted to the task. This yields the number of digits correct per minute.
4. Administer *Curriculum-Based Mathematics Probes* to a selected group of students.

Procedure

1. Tell the students that they will be learning a new method of improving their mathematics performance called Cover, Copy, and Compare.
2. Give training sheets to the students. If desired, use an overhead projector displaying a transparency of a training sheet during the introductory session.
3. Conduct a training session in which you teach students to follow the Cover, Copy, and Compare procedure:
   a. Silently read the first problem and the answer on the left side of the paper.
   b. Cover that problem and answer with an index card.
   c. Write the problem and answer from memory on the right side of the page.
   d. Uncover the problem and answer on the left side to check the written response.
   e. Evaluate the response.

   f. If the problem and answer are written incorrectly, repeat the procedure with that item before proceeding to the next item.

   g. Repeat this procedure with the rest of the problems on the sheet.

4. After demonstrating these steps on the chalkboard or with the overhead projector, have students complete one or more training sheets and provide corrective feedback as needed.

5. Daily or several times a week, provide students with sets of training sheets (one to three sets) and have them follow the Cover, Copy, and Compare procedure.

6. Once or twice a week, administer the assessment sheets that correspond to the training sheets. If desired, time these assessment sessions.

7. When students reach mastery level on one set of problems, provide them with another set of problems. Mastery level is defined as 90% or better accuracy and/or 40 digits correct per minute.

Evaluation (Select One or More)

1. Compare percent correct scores on math worksheets for the entire class or the selected group of students before and after implementation.

2. Compare the number of correct digits on problems on math worksheets for the entire class or the selected group of students before and after implementation.

3. Compare the digits-correct-per-minute rate on problems on math worksheets for the entire class or the selected group of students before and after implementation.

4. Compare scores on *Curriculum-Based Mathematics Probes* for the selected group of students before and after implementation.

Variations

1. Prepare training and assessment sheets with a larger number of problems (20 to 30). This variation eliminates the need for several sets of sheets per session.

2. Give students stopwatches or watches with second hands and teach them to record the number of seconds needed to complete math worksheets.

3. Have students chart their progress in terms of number of problems completed correctly and/or number of correct digits per minute on individual record sheets kept in their mathematics folders.

4. Prepare a posterboard chart displaying the class average number of problems completed correctly on the timed assessments or on other timed math tests.

Note

This strategy works best for basic math facts in addition, subtraction, multiplication, and division.

Sources

Lee, M. J., & Tingstrom, D. H. (1994). A group math intervention: The modification of cover, copy, and compare for group application. *Psychology in the Schools, 31,* 133–145. Copyright 1994 by John Wiley & Sons, Inc. Adapted by permission.

Skinner, C. H., Turco, T. L., Beatty, K. L., & Rasavage, C. (1989). Cover, copy, and compare: A method for increasing multiplication performance. *School Psychology Review, 18,* 412–420. Copyright 1989 by the National Association of School Psychologists. Adapted by permission.

IMPROVING MATH PERFORMANCE WITH EXPLICIT TIMING

Overview

Developing fluency with math facts is an important competency for students. In this simple intervention, timing mathematics seatwork in 30-minute trials is used to help students become more automatic in math facts and thus become more proficient in solving math problems. The use of explicit timing has been demonstrated to increase the rate of problems worked correctly while simultaneously maintaining very high levels of accuracy.

Purpose

To enhance fluency with basic math facts by timing mathematics performance.

Materials

1. Stopwatch or watch with second hand
2. Kitchen timer with bell
3. Sets of math worksheets with 100 basic problems (addition, subtraction, etc.), with problems on one side only and sheets stapled together, one set per student per session

Observation (Select One or Both)

1. Calculate the correct-problems-per-minute rate on math worksheets for a selected group of students or the entire class for 5 to 10 days by dividing the number of problems worked correctly by the number of minutes students are given to work. For example, if students have 30 minutes available to work and a student completes 45 problems correctly, the correct-problems-per-minute rate for that student is 1.5.
2. Calculate accuracy scores on math worksheets for a selected group of students or the entire class for 5 to 10 days by dividing the number of problems worked correctly by the number of correct problems plus the number of incorrect problems. For example, if a student works 30 problems correctly and 10 problems incorrectly, that student's accuracy score is 75%.

Procedure

1. At the beginning of the mathematics seatwork period, tell students that the work period is 30 minutes long (or the available number of minutes) and that

you will be timing the period as a way of helping them improve their performance.

2. Tell students that you will set the timer for the amount of the time in the period. Inform them that you will also be timing them with a stopwatch in 1-minute timings.
3. At the beginning of each timing, say: "Pencils up, ready, begin!" to signal students to begin working.
4. At the end of the 1-minute interval, say "Stop!" and have students draw a line after the last problem answered. Repeat this procedure throughout the 30-minute period until the last timing is completed.
5. When the timer rings, announce that the work period is over. Teach students to stop when the timer rings, even if they are in the middle of a timed period.

Evaluation (Select One or Both)

1. Compare correct-problems-per-minute rates on math worksheets for the selected group of students or the entire class before and after implementation.
2. Compare accuracy scores on math worksheets for the selected group of students or the entire class before and after implementation.

Variation

Use a stopwatch for all timing instead of a kitchen timer. Write the start and stop times for the work period on the chalkboard.

Notes

1. In the original study, a spring-wound interval timer with a bell was used. A kitchen timer has been substituted in this adaptation.
2. Because it is not possible to have 30 1-minute timings within a 30-minute period, the actual time available for students to work is always less than 30 minutes.

Source

Van Houten, R., & Thompson, C. (1976). The effects of explicit timing on math performance. *Journal of Applied Behavior Analysis, 9,* 227–230. Copyright 1976 by the Society for the Experimental Analysis of Behavior. Adapted by permission.

RECIPROCAL PEER TUTORING TO IMPROVE MATH ACHIEVEMENT

Overview

Reciprocal peer tutoring (RPT) is an intervention that combines self-management techniques and group contingencies within a peer tutoring format. Unlike many self-management strategies that focus on individual students, RPT is designed to help students manage their academic progress in a group context. Students are taught to act as instructional partners for each other, select team goals for academic performance, and manage their own group reward contingencies. RPT has been demonstrated to enhance not only math performance but also students' perceptions of their own scholastic competence and self-control and earns high satisfaction ratings from both teachers and students. In the original study, student pairs selected and received their own team rewards. For ease of implementation, two classwide systems of reward selection and delivery are included here as variations. The intervention takes approximately 30 minutes—20 minutes for peer tutoring and 10 minutes for individual drills and checking.

Purpose

To improve mathematics performance and behavior during math instruction by means of peer tutoring, group rewards, and self-management procedures.

Materials

1. *Reinforcement Menus* with activity rewards, one per student pair
2. "Team Score Cards," consisting of $3'' \times 5''$ index cards or $8\frac{1}{2}'' \times 11''$ sheets of paper, one per student pair per week
3. "Happy face" or other kinds of stickers for team score cards
4. Flash cards with mathematics problems printed on the front and the problems plus computational steps and the answers printed on the back, one problem per card, one set of cards per student pair
5. $8\frac{1}{2}'' \times 11''$ sheets of paper, divided into four sections: "try 1," "try 2," "help," and "try 3"
6. Instructional prompt cards or sheets with specific instructions related to common mistakes in solving math problems, one prompt card or sheet per student pair
7. Problem drill sheets with 16 problems (or some appropriate number), one per student per session
8. Answer sheets for problem drill sheets, one per student per session (optional)
9. Posterboard chart or section of the chalkboard to record team wins (see Variation 1)

Observation (Select One or More)

Option 1
1. Calculate percent correct scores on daily math drill sheets or weekly math quizzes for a selected group of students or the entire class for several weeks.

Option 2
1. Administer *Curriculum-Based Mathematics Probes* to a selected group of students.

Option 3

1. Based on students' current behavior, calculate conduct grades for the entire class as follows:
   a. A = excellent classroom behavior in terms of on-task behavior and ability to complete work independently;
   b. B = above average classroom behavior in these areas;
   c. C = average classroom behavior in these areas;
   d. D = below average classroom behavior, characterized by high rates of off-task behavior and difficulty following rules and completing work independently;
   e. F = poor classroom behavior, characterized by high rates of off-task and disruptive behavior and low rates of independent work completion.
2. Convert these letter grades to numerical equivalents ranging from 5 (A) to 1 (F) and then calculate the class average conduct grade.

Procedure

1. Tell the students that they will be learning to work in teams to help each other do well in mathematics.
2. Divide the class into pairs. Provide each pair with a *Reinforcement Menu* listing activity rewards, such as serving as teacher's helper, working on special projects, using classroom computers, and working in centers. Help each pair select a reward for the day.
3. Meet weekly with each team to help the students select their team goal (the number of problems they believe they can answer correctly as a team). Teams select goals from a list of recommended choices, based on your estimates of realistic academic objectives for that team.
4. After each pair has chosen a team goal, have the pairs record their expected individual contribution to the team (each student's individual goal), the sum of the individual goals (each pair's team goal), and their choice of a reward on the team score card.
5. At the beginning of each tutoring session, give a set of flash cards to each pair, and tell the students to choose who will act as "teacher" first.
6. Have the teachers hold up flash cards for the students and tell the students to work the problem on their worksheets in the section marked "try 1" while their teachers observe their work.
7. If the problem is solved correctly, the teachers praise the students and present the next problem. If the solution is incorrect, the teachers give students instructional prompts read from a prompt card and tell them to try again in the worksheet section marked "try 2."
8. If the students do not solve the problem correctly on the second try, teachers help them by computing the problem in the "help" section. As teachers work the problem, they explain what they are doing at each step and answer students' questions. Then the teachers tell the students to work the problem again in the "try 3" section. If teachers have trouble answering students' questions, they ask the classroom teacher for help.

9. After 10 minutes, signal the pairs to switch roles for a second 10-minute tutor-ing session.
10. During tutoring sessions, walk around the room supervising and identifying strategies teachers can use to help their students.
11. After the second tutoring session, give each student a problem drill sheet and have students work on their own for a fixed period of time, such as 7 to 10 minutes.
12. Then have students switch papers with their team partner. Have them use an answer sheet to correct their partner's work or provide the correct answers yourself as students check papers.
13. Have the pairs first determine their team's total score by counting the num-ber of problems each team member completed correctly and then compare their team score with their team goal to see if they have "won" (met their goal).
14. If a team wins, give the students a sticker to put on their score card for that day. After five wins, schedule a time when the team can engage in the previ-ously selected rewarding activity.

Evaluation (Select One or More)

Option 1
1. Compare percent correct scores on daily math drill sheets or weekly math quizzes for the selected group of students or the entire class before and after implementation.

Option 2
1. Compare scores on *Curriculum-Based Mathematics Probes* for selected students be-fore and after implementation.

Option 3
1. Compare class average conduct grades before and after implementation.

Variations

1. Provide rewards on a weekly classwide basis rather than on a daily team basis as follows:
   a. In addition to having teams record their wins on team score cards, record daily team wins on a posterboard chart or a section of the chalkboard.
   b. Set a criterion for weekly classwide rewards, such as 80% of the teams achieving their goals on 4 of 5 days.
   c. Deliver rewards, if earned, to the entire class on Friday.
   d. Gradually increase the criterion as students become more successful.
2. Have the class vote to select one reward for the week and deliver it on Friday to winning team members. Nonwinning teams must read quietly at their seats, continue working on academic tasks, or go to another room to be supervised

by another staff member. Arranging for nonwinning teams to leave the classroom facilitates delivery of group activity rewards, such as watching videos.

Note

If two teachers are using this intervention with Friday afternoon group activity rewards, as in Variation 2, one teacher can deliver the reward to winning teams in his or her classroom while the other teacher supervises teams who did not earn the reward in the other room.

Sources

Fantuzzo, J. W., King, J. A., & Heller, L. R. (1992). Effects of reciprocal peer tutoring on mathematics and school adjustment: A component analysis. *Journal of Educational Psychology, 84,* 331–339. Copyright 1992 by the American Psychological Association. Adapted by permission.

Fantuzzo, J. W., & Rohrbeck, C. A. (1992). Self-managed groups: Fitting self-management approaches into classroom systems. *School Psychology Review, 21,* 255–263. Copyright 1992 by the National Association of School Psychologists. Adapted by permission.

IMPROVING MATH PERFORMANCE WITH RECIPROCAL PEER TUTORING AND PARENTAL INVOLVEMENT

Overview

This intervention combines reciprocal peer tutoring (RPT) with a parent involvement component. Unlike many school–home strategies that simply provide information to parents, this intervention invites parents to develop a system of home rewards to support their child's academic performance. Compared with control groups, students participating in RPT with parental involvement as well as RPT alone showed significantly greater gains on curriculum-based math measures and standardized math achievement tests and on teacher and student self-report measures of adjustment. In the original study, several school meetings were held with parents to provide information about the RPT intervention and discuss how they could contribute to its effectiveness, with follow-up telephone calls to monitor home-based reward systems and other forms of parental participation. In this adaptation, a parent informational letter has been substituted for the series of meetings and telephone calls. This intervention can be modified for implementation in any academic subject that includes fact drills, such as spelling, reading vocabulary, history, and geography.

Purpose

To improve mathematics performance and classroom behavior by combining reciprocal peer tutoring with home-based rewards.

Materials

1. *Reinforcement Menus* with activity rewards, one per student pair
2. Introductory parent letter (see Figure 4.12), one per student
3. "Team Score Cards," consisting of 3" × 5" index cards or 8½" × 11" sheets of paper, one per student pair per week
4. "Happy face" or other kinds of stickers for team score cards
5. Flash cards with mathematics problems printed on the front and the problems plus computational steps and the answers printed on the back, one problem per card, one set of cards per student pair
6. 8½" × 11" sheets of paper, divided into four sections: "try 1," "try 2," "help," and "try 3"
7. Instructional prompt cards or sheets with specific instructions related to common mistakes in solving math problems, one prompt card or sheet per student pair
8. Problem drill sheets with 16 problems (or some appropriate number), one per student per session
9. Answer sheets for problem drill sheets, one per student per session (optional)
10. Reward certificates (see Figure 4.13)

Observation (Select One or More)

1. Administer *Curriculum-Based Mathematics Probes* to a selected group of students.
2. Calculate the problems-worked-correctly rate per minute on math skills sheets for the entire class or a selected group of students during a 20- to 30-minute period by dividing the number of problems worked correctly by the number of minutes in the period.
3. Using a sheet of paper attached to a clipboard, tally the number of disruptive behaviors exhibited by the entire class or a small group of students during the math instructional period. *Disruptive behaviors* are defined as any behaviors that interfere with the learning of another student, such as calling out, getting out of seat, or verbal or physical aggression.

Procedure

1. Tell the students that they will be learning to work in teams to help each other do well in mathematics and that their parents will be invited to provide support and rewards in that effort.
2. Send a letter to parents that provides information about the RPT intervention and invites them to consider several options for involvement (see Figure 4.12).
3. Divide the class into pairs. Provide each team with a *Reinforcement Menu* listing activity rewards, such as serving as teacher's helper, working on special projects, using classroom computers, and working in centers. Help each pair select a reward.
4. Meet weekly with each team to help the students select their team goal (the number of problems they believe they can answer correctly as a team). Teams select goals from a list of recommended choices, based on your estimates of realistic academic objectives for that team.

5. After each pair has chosen a team goal, have the pairs record their expected individual contribution to the team (each student's individual goal), the sum of the individual goals (each pair's team goal), and their choice of a reward on the team score card.

6. At the beginning of each tutoring session, give a set of flash cards to each pair and tell the students to choose who will act as "teacher" first.

7. Have the teachers hold up flash cards for the students and tell the students to work the problem on their worksheets in the section marked "try 1" while their teachers observe their work.

8. If the problem is solved correctly, the teachers praise the students and present the next problem. If the solution is incorrect, the teachers give students instructional prompts read from a prompt card and tell them to try again in the worksheet section marked "try 2."

9. If the students do not solve the problem correctly on the second try, teachers help them by computing the problem in the "help" section. As teachers work the problem, they explain what they are doing at each step and answer students' questions. Then the teachers tell the students to work the problem again in the "try 3" section. If teachers have trouble answering students' questions, they ask the classroom teacher for help.

10. After 10 minutes, signal the pairs to switch roles for a second 10-minute tutoring segment.

11. During tutoring sessions, walk around the room supervising and identifying useful strategies teachers can use to help their students.

12. After the second tutoring segment, distribute a problem drill sheet to each student and have students work on their own for a fixed period of time, such as 7 to 10 minutes.

13. Then have students switch papers with their team partner. Have them use an answer sheet to correct their partner's work or provide the correct answers yourself as students check papers.

14. Have the pairs first determine their team's total score by counting the number of problems each team member completed correctly and then compare their team score with their team goal to determine if they have "won" (met their goal).

15. If a team wins, give the students a sticker to put on their score card for that day. After three wins, deliver the reward and give them reward certificates to take home to their parents. Parents are to sign the certificates and indicate the type of reward provided (if any) and any additional comments.

16. Remind students to return the reward certificates to you so that you can monitor the home-based rewards.

Evaluation (Select One or More)

1. Compare scores on *Curriculum-Based Mathematics Probes* for the selected group of students before and after implementation.

2. Compare problems-worked-correctly-per-minute rates for the entire class or the selected group of students before and after implementation.

3. Compare the frequency of disruptive behaviors exhibited by the entire class or

School Letterhead

Date:

Dear parent:

I am delighted to inform you that our class will be participating in a reciprocal peer tutoring (RPT) program designed to improve children's skills in mathematics. RPT is a collaborative learning strategy in which students work in pairs to set goals for improving their math skills, practice math problems, and provide each other with helpful feedback. Students who meet their goals three times in a row will earn a classroom reward and will receive a reward certificate to take home to let you know they have achieved their goals. RPT will take place (number of times a week) at (time of day) for about 30 minutes per session.

A key component of RPT is parental involvement. Research shows that when parents participate in the program, children not only improve their math skills substantially but also develop more positive attitudes toward school. You can be involved in several ways:

1. By providing rewards and privileges to your child when he or she brings home a reward certificate;
2. By attending classroom sessions to observe your child participating in RPT;
3. By serving as helpers in the classroom during RPT sessions.

If you would like to participate by providing home rewards to your child, suggested rewards and incentives include:

1. Special time with parents (shopping; eating out; going to the movies, video arcade, park, or zoo)
2. Money ($1, $2, or $3 per reward certificate)
3. Food treats (candy, baking a cake, choice of meal or dessert at home)
4. Toys (baseball cards, doll clothes, Nintendo cartridge)
5. Having friends spend the night on the weekend
6. Home privileges (chore-free day, getting first pick among the children for chores that week)
7. Awards (award banner made by the parent and given to the child)

Please indicate below how you would like to participate and have your child return the bottom half of this letter. Please feel free to call me if you have any questions about RPT or ways in which you can participate. Your participation is completely voluntary and very welcome! I am looking forward to working with you to help your child become the best mathematics student he or she can be!

Sincerely yours,

Name of teacher
===
Reciprocal Peer Tutoring (RPT) in Mathematics Program

_____ I would like to participate by providing my child with home rewards.
_____ I would like to participate by attending classroom sessions to observe my child participating in RPT.
_____ I would like to participate by helping in the classroom during RPT sessions.
_____ I do not wish to participate at this time.

Name of parent: _____

Name of student: _____

FIGURE 4.12. Introductory parent letter for *Improving Math Performance with Reciprocal Peer Tutoring and Parental Involvement.* Adapted from Heller and Fantuzzo (1993). Copyright 1993 by the National Association of School Psychologists. Adapted by permission.

School Letterhead

Date:

Dear parent:

I am delighted to inform you that your child _____, has achieved his or her team goal in reciprocal peer tutoring (RPT) in mathematics three times. Please praise your child for this excellent achievement. Because of his or her hard work, your child has earned a reward at school. If you would like to provide a reward or privilege to your child at home for this achievement, please do so.

Please sign your name below, indicate what reward you provided (if any), add any comments you like, and have your child return this certificate to me. Thank you very much for your participation in our Reciprocal Peer Tutoring program!

Sincerely yours,

Name of teacher

****

Name of parent: _____

Type of reward provided: _____

Comments: _____

_____

_____

FIGURE 4.13. Reward certificate for *Improving Math Performance with Reciprocal Peer Tutoring and Parental Involvement.* Adapted from Heller and Fantuzzo (1993). Copyright 1993 by the National Association of School Psychologists. Adapted by permission.

the small group of students during the math instructional period before and after implementation.

Variation

Send home the reward certificates, but do not require parents to sign and return them.

Note

In the original study, teacher aides conducted the classroom peer tutoring sessions and contacted parents to monitor the home-based rewards and other forms of parental involvement.

Source

Heller, L. R., & Fantuzzo, J. W. (1993). Reciprocal peer tutoring and parent partnership: Does parent involvement make a difference? *School Psychology Review,* *22,* 517–534. Copyright 1993 by the National Association of School Psychologists. Adapted by permission.

IMPROVING MATH COMPLETION RATES AND ACCURACY WITH FREE TIME

Overview

Free time has often been used as a reward for appropriate student social behavior. In this simple intervention, which requires no material resources or student training, free time is made contingent on productivity in mathematics. Originally implemented with a single student in a self-contained second-grade classroom, it is adapted here for classwide use, with variations for individual and team rewards.

Purpose

To increase the accuracy and completion rates of mathematics classwork with a group-oriented free-time contingency.

Materials

None

Observation (Select One or Both)

1. Calculate the percent correct rate for math classwork assignments by dividing the number of problems worked correctly by the number of problems assigned for 5 to 10 days for each student. Then calculate the class average percent correct rate by adding the percent correct rates for all students and dividing by the total number of students. Note that this score is used in the intervention procedures.
2. Administer *Curriculum-Based Mathematics Probes* to a selected group of students.

Procedure

1. Tell the students that they will be able to earn free time if the class correctly completes a specified average number of problems during each mathematics classwork session.
2. Set the free-time period from 5 to 15 minutes, depending on the length of the entire mathematics period.

3. Using the class average percent correct rate from the observation period, select a criterion for assignment completion that is 5% higher. For example, if the average percent correct rate was 70%, set the criterion at 75%.
4. During the mathematics instructional period, set a fixed amount of time for classwork completion. At the end of that time, have students exchange papers for checking and report the number of problems completed correctly (without names) to you.
5. Record these scores on the chalkboard and obtain a class average. Collect papers for spot checking and recording of individual grades.
6. If the class average meets the criterion, praise the students for their hard work and award the free time. If not, encourage students to try harder next time and continue with the mathematics lesson.
7. When the class has met the criterion for 5 consecutive days, increase it by several more percentage points. Continue to increase it gradually until students are performing at a 90% or better accuracy rate.

Evaluation (Select One or Both)

1. Compare the class average percent correct rate for math classwork assignments before and after implementation.
2. Compare scores on *Curriculum-Based Mathematics Probes* for the selected group of students before and after implementation.

Variations

1. Check papers yourself instead of having students check them. Award the free time earned (if any) on the following day.
2. Require the class to meet the criterion for 4 out of 5 consecutive days and award free time on Fridays. For this variation, provide a longer free-time period.
3. Divide the class into teams and award free time to teams whose average meets the criterion. Require teams not meeting the criterion to continue working on skill sheets.

Note

As with any intervention that targets academic productivity, assessing students' ability to perform the assignments at the selected criterion level prior to implementation is essential.

Source

Johnston, R. J., & McLaughlin, T. F. (1982). The effects of free time on assignment completion and accuracy in arithmetic: A case study. *Education and Treatment of Children, 5,* 33–40. Copyright 1982 by Pressley Ridge School. Adapted by permission.

INTERVENTIONS TO IMPROVE
WRITTEN LANGUAGE PERFORMANCE

Although writing is a complex and challenging task, it is a crucial skill for school success because it is a fundamental way of communicating ideas and demonstrating knowledge in the content areas (Hillocks, 1987; Hooper et al., 1993). Outside the school setting, writing is a necessary part of many jobs and serves as a critical means for sharing thoughts and feelings with others (Bradley-Johnson & Lesiak, 1989). Unfortunately, writing problems are not only characteristic of most students with identified disabilities, they are also pervasive in the general student population (Hooper et al., 1993; Stein, Dixon, & Isaacson, 1994). According to the results of the 1990 National Assessment of Educational Progress in writing (Gentile, 1992), the majority of today's students cannot write with proficiency. Only 1% of fourth graders and 8% of eighth graders were able to write a well-developed narrative. No student of either grade level was able to produce an informative paper with a fully developed discussion.

The prevalence of writing problems among both learning-disabled and general education students suggests that poor writing achievement is related less to internal student disabilities than to inadequate writing instruction. Studies (Bridge & Hiebert, 1985; Petty & Finn, 1981) have documented pronounced differences from classroom to classroom in the amount of time devoted to direct writing instruction and to student writing. In general, students spend very little time writing and receive little specific feedback on their efforts. At the elementary level, writing activities consist largely of copying words, sentences, or paragraphs to demonstrate knowledge of grammar, punctuation, or spelling. Few writing assignments involve writing more than a single sentence (Bridge & Hiebert, 1985). Thus many writing problems may be due to a combination of the complexity of the task and the lack of time allotted to teaching it (Stein et al., 1994).

Until very recently, there has been much less interest in designing interventions to improve written expression skills compared with interventions targeting reading and mathematics, perhaps because writing requires many interrelated skills and competencies, including handwriting, capitalization and punctuation, vocabulary and word usage, spelling, and expressiveness (Bradley-Johnson & Lesiak, 1989; Shapiro, 1996a). Since the inclusion of written expression as a category of learning disabilities in Public Law 94-142, however, researchers and practitioners alike have focused more attention on this critical academic and occupational skill. Helping regular education teachers implement classroom strategies that enhance the writing skills of all students as well as developing strategies to assist children with identified writing disabilities are important roles for school consultants. Despite increased interest in writing interventions, however, school psychologists still receive little training in understanding the nature, prevalence, assessment, and remediation of writing disabilities (Kulberg, 1993).

This section includes interventions targeting two aspects of writing: spelling and written expression. Helping students to develop an adequate level of competence in the mechanics of writing so that these difficulties do not significantly interfere with higher-order writing processes is an important goal of writing instruction (Graham, Harris, & MacArthur, 1993). Students also need carefully designed composition instruction focusing on the important ideas of writing, such as the writing process, text structures, and writing for an audience (Stein et al., 1994).

Improving Spelling Performance

Spelling is a critical ingredient of writing. Without adequate spelling skills, students are severely limited in their ability to communicate with others through written language (Graham & Miller, 1979). Spelling problems are especially characteristic of learning-disabled students (Deshler, Schumaker, Alley, Warner, & Clark, 1982). Spelling deficits severely impede composition efforts for poor spellers, such as learning-disabled students and other diverse learners, because these students must devote so much attention to writing mechanics that they have little remaining for higher-order writing processes (Graham, 1990; Stein et al., 1994). The traditional instructional format, in which new words are introduced on Mondays, spelling activities are conducted during the week, and the words are tested on Fridays, continues to be the most popular method for teaching spelling. Unfortunately, this approach, which fails to accommodate the wide range of spelling abilities and spelling problems within most classrooms, fails to help many students become proficient spellers (Okyere & Heron, 1991). Moreover, for most students, spelling is not an intrinsically motivating activity (Graham, 1983). To be maximally effective, strategies targeting spelling performance should not only provide additional opportunities for skills practice but also enhance motivation to improve achievement in this area.

This section includes two interventions designed to improve spelling achievement. *The Peer Tutoring Spelling Game* creates a classwide peer tutoring format within which even very young children can acquire and practice spelling skills without direct teacher supervision. *Increasing Spelling Performance with Group Contingencies* uses an interdependent group contingency to motivate students to improve their performance on weekly spelling tests.

Evaluating the Effectiveness of Spelling Interventions

Methods for evaluating the effectiveness of the spelling interventions in this section include naturally collected data, such as individual student scores on weekly spelling tests, and classwide assignments, such as the percentage of students meeting a certain criterion on spelling tests. Procedures for conducting CBMs in spelling (*Curriculum-Based Spelling Probes*) are also presented. Recently, spelling instruction based on published spelling texts has declined in favor of spelling instruction that is integrated within language arts and other content areas (Shapiro, 1996a). Because words for weekly spelling tests would be drawn from a number of nonstandardized sources in the case of integrated instructional methods, using previously prepared graded word lists is recommended for progress monitoring. Sets of word lists for grades 1 through 6 are presented in Harris and Jacobson (1972).

Two options are included for scoring CBMs in spelling: correct letter sequences and number of words spelled correctly. Although correct letter sequences appears to be somewhat more sensitive to changes in student progress, many teachers and consultants lack experience using this scoring method. Studies indicate that both the number of correct letter sequences and the number of words spelled correctly are highly correlated with standardized measures of spelling (Deno, Mirkin, Lowry, & Kuehnle, 1980) and that CBMs can reliably distinguish among mildly disabled, Chapter 1, and regular education students regardless of which of the two scoring methods is used (Deno et al., 1980; Shinn & Marston, 1985; Shinn, Ysseldyke, Deno, & Tindal, 1986).

CURRICULUM-BASED SPELLING PROBES

Overview

In spelling, all students in a classroom are usually placed in the same level of the curriculum regardless of their skill development. For that reason, the results of curriculum-based measurements (CBMs) in spelling are not generally used to make recommendations for moving students to a different level of the spelling curriculum. Instead, spelling probes are conducted to indicate the degree to which students need additional practice with words that have been previously taught but not mastered. Spelling probes can also reveal the types of errors typically made by students, such as missing medial vowels or spelling all words phonetically. Analyzing these types of errors yields information for specific instructional recommendations. Spelling probes may be administered to students individually or in groups.

Purpose

1. To provide information regarding a student's level of spelling skill development compared with that of peers.

2. To set short- and long-term goals for spelling instruction and remediation.
3. To evaluate the effectiveness of spelling interventions.
4. To provide information for program evaluation.

Materials

1. Three sets of 20 to 25 words taken randomly from the spelling textbook or basal reader series, depending on which is used for spelling instruction; if spelling is integrated into other subject areas, lists can be generated by writing grade-level words on cards and randomly selecting sets of cards
2. Pencils, two per student
3. Sheets of lined paper, one per student
4. Stopwatch or watch with second hand

Procedure

Administration
1. Give the following directions:

> "I am going to read some words to you. I want you to write the words on the sheet in front of you. Write the first word on the first line, the second word on the second line, and so on. I'll give you 7 seconds to spell each word. When I say the next word, try to write it, even if you haven't finished the last one. Are there any questions?"

2. Say each word twice. Use homonyms in a sentence.
3. Dictate words for 2 minutes. Do not dictate a new word in the last 3 seconds and allow the student to finish the last word.

Scoring

Option 1: Correct letter sequences method
1. Score the probes as follows:
   a. Each word has an extra character placed before and after it. For example, the word BUTTER has seven possible letter sequences.
   b. Count the number of correct letter sequences. For example:

   BUTTER has seven letter sequences correct.
   BUTTAR has five letter sequences correct.
   BUTER has five letter sequences correct.
   BATTAR has three letter sequences correct.

2. Divide the number of correct letter sequences by the total seconds dictated and multiply by 60 seconds to obtain the letter-sequences-correct-per-minute rate. For example, if words are dictated for 2 minutes, the formula is

$$\frac{\text{Correct letter sequences}}{120 \text{ seconds}} \times 60 \text{ seconds} = \text{Letter sequences correct per minute}$$

3. Compare the correct-letter-sequences rate to Table 4.2, the student's individual norms, or local norms.

Option 2: Number of words spelled correctly method
1. Count the number of words spelled correctly in 2 minutes to obtain a words-spelled-correctly rate for the probe.
2. Compare the words-spelled-correctly rate to the student's individual norms or local norms.

Notes

1. Shinn (1989) recommends a 10-second dictation rate for grades 1–3 rather than a 7-second interval. Teachers and consultants making this modification should be aware that the spelling scores in Table 4.2 are based on a 7-second interval.
2. Many teachers and consultants are unfamiliar with the letter-sequences-correct scoring method and prefer a words-spelled-correctly method. To evaluate spelling probes results using this metric, classroom, school, or district norms can be developed for spelling performance based on guidelines described in Marston and Magnusson (1988) and Shinn (1989).

Sources

Marston, D., & Magnusson, D. (1988). Curriculum-based measurement: District level implementation. In J. L. Graden, J. E. Zins, & M. J. Curtis (Eds.), *Alternative educational delivery systems: Enhancing instructional options for all students* (pp. 137–172). Washington, DC: National Association of School Psychologists. Copyright 1988 by the National Association of School Psychologists. Adapted by permission.

Shapiro, E. S. (1996). *Academic skills problems: Direct assessment and intervention* (2nd ed.). New York: Guilford Press. Copyright 1996 by The Guilford Press. Adapted by permission.

Shinn, M. R. (Ed.). (1989). *Curriculum-based measurement: Assessing special children.* New York: Guilford Press. Copyright 1989 by The Guilford Press. Adapted by permission.

THE PEER TUTORING SPELLING GAME

Overview

Maximizing the amount of active academic responding in the classroom has been demonstrated to be an effective method of increasing student achievement. This strategy targets spelling accuracy by combining classwide peer tutoring with public posting in a game-like format. In addition to providing increased opportunities for each student to practice spelling without increasing the total amount of time set aside for spelling instruction, it prevents reinforcement of errors because peer tutors provide immediate feedback for responses. Moreover, because the peer tutoring game takes only 15 minutes to complete, it can be easily implemented within the spelling instructional period regardless of whether all students are placed in the same set of materials or are grouped for instruction.

Purpose

To improve spelling accuracy by increasing opportunities to respond without increasing the amount of time set aside for spelling instruction.

Materials

1. List of spelling words or regular spelling materials, one per student pair
2. Spelling form (see Figure 4.14) or lined paper for writing spelling words, one form or paper per student
3. Red and blue slips of construction paper in a box, with an equal number of each color and summing to the total number of students in the class
4. Posterboard chart or section of the chalkboard listing names of each student, with columns for posting individual spelling scores
5. Posterboard chart or section of the chalkboard listing the team names, with columns for posting Red and Blue team point totals and weekly team winners
6. Kitchen timer with bell (optional)
7. Notebooks or folders with loose-leaf paper, one per student (see Variation 2)

Observation (Select One or Both)

1. Calculate percent correct scores on weekly spelling tests for the entire class or a selected group of students for several weeks.
2. Administer *Curriculum-Based Spelling Probes* to a selected group of students.

Procedure

1. Tell the students that they will be playing an exciting new game to help them get the most out of their spelling lesson. Allow about 30 minutes for the first day of training.
2. Tell the students that the game is like basketball. In this game, they will make "baskets" (2 points) and "foul shots" (1 point). Select one student to demonstrate tutoring to the class, using the procedures described below. Then select two more students and guide them through the procedures in front of the class. Conduct two more demonstrations with other student pairs. Then have the entire class practice the procedures while you walk around the room giving corrective feedback and praise for appropriate tutoring.
3. On Monday of each week, teach the list(s) of new words to the entire class or to the spelling groups.
4. Also on Monday, have each student draw a red or blue slip of paper from a box for assignment to one of two teams. Then create tutor pairs within each team. Teams and pairs remain the same during the entire week. If students are grouped for spelling instruction, pair members of the same group for tutoring.
5. Begin the tutoring game by asking students to move to their tutoring stations (paired desks or some other arrangement where they can work in pairs). Designate one student to serve as tutor first. Distribute the new word list(s) and spelling forms or sheets of paper.

6. Signal the students to begin and, if desired, set a timer for 5 minutes. Tutors present tutees with the list of words as many times as possible during this period. The tutor says a word while the tutee writes it on his or her paper. The tutee then orally spells out to the tutor the word he or she has written.

7. If the word is correct, the tutor says, "Correct, give yourself 2 points!" ("basket"), and the tutee marks a "2" on his or her list. If the word is incorrect, the tutor points to, pronounces, and spells the missed word orally to the tutee. The tutee must write it correctly three times before receiving the next word. After the word has been corrected, the tutee receives 1 point ("foul shot").

8. After 5 minutes, give a signal indicating that the pair should reverse roles.

9. During tutoring, walk around the room, supervising and awarding bonus points ("referee points") to tutors for examples of positive tutoring, up to 5 additional points per student.

10. After another 5 minutes, give a signal to stop. Have tutoring pairs add up their points, including any bonus points. Have students report their individual point totals and record them on the individual point chart. Then add up the points for each team and enter the totals on the team chart.

11. On Friday, give a spelling test on the words tutors have practiced. Have team pairs exchange papers, correct each other's answers, and award 3 points (or some appropriate number of points) for each correctly spelled word.

12. Have each student report his or her individual points and enter them on the individual score chart.

13. Add individual points into the team totals for the week, announce the winning team for the week, and post the winner on the team chart. The winning team is applauded, and the losing team is also praised for its efforts.

14. Randomly spot check students' scoring and point additions for tutoring sessions and check all Friday test papers. Provide feedback to the class for scoring errors and adjust team scores accordingly.

Evaluation (Select One or Both)

1. Compare percent correct scores on weekly spelling tests for the entire class or the selected group of students before and after implementation.

2. Compare scores on *Curriculum-Based Spelling Probes* for the selected group of students before and after implementation.

Variations

1. Keep teams constant during the week but change tutor pairs within teams each day.

2. Instead of posting individual student scores on a chart or on the chalkboard, have students record their individual point totals in their spelling or language arts notebooks.

Notes

1. Creating a permanent classroom arrangement of paired desks facilitates implementation, especially if peer tutoring is used on a daily basis.

2. Selecting new teams each week increases the probability that each student will have an opportunity to participate on a winning team.
3. In the original study, 18 new words were introduced each Monday and practiced in the peer tutoring game during the week.

Source

Delquadri, J. C., Greenwood, C. R., Stretton, K., & Hall, R. V. (1983). The peer tutoring spelling game: A classroom procedure for increasing opportunity to respond and spelling performance. *Education and Treatment of Children, 6,* 225–239. Copyright 1983 by Pressley Ridge School. Adapted by permission.

THE PEER TUTORING SPELLING GAME

Correct first time = 2 points
Write 3 times = 1 point

POINTS

_____	1. _____
_____	2. _____
_____	3. _____
_____	4. _____
_____	5. _____
_____	6. _____
_____	7. _____
_____	8. _____
_____	9. _____
_____	10. _____
_____	11. _____
_____	12. _____
_____	13. _____
_____	14. _____
_____	15. _____
_____	16. _____
_____	17. _____
_____	18. _____

_____ **Points earned**
_____ **Bonus points**
_____ **TOTAL POINTS**

Names of tutoring pair: _____   _____

Name of team: _____ Red _____ Blue

FIGURE 4.14. Tutee form for *The Peer Tutoring Spelling Game.* Adapted from Delquadri, Greenwood, Stretton, and Hall (1983). Copyright 1983 by Pressley Ridge School. Adapted by permission.

INCREASING SPELLING PERFORMANCE
WITH GROUP CONTINGENCIES

Overview

This strategy uses a group-oriented contingency system to motivate student performance on weekly spelling tests. In the original study, three types of group contingencies (independent, interdependent, and dependent) were presented on alternate days in the context of a token economy system, with substantial improvement in spelling performance on daily tests under all conditions. This adaptation presents the interdependent group contingency version, with the other two group contingencies included as variations. This simple intervention fits readily into typical classroom instructional and management routines and can be adapted to target student performance in any subject.

Purpose

To increase spelling accuracy by using group performance contingencies.

Materials

1. Posterboard chart titled "We Have Spelling Class" (optional)
2. Gold stars (optional)
3. Slips of paper with students' names and box (see Variation 2)

Observation (Select One or More)

1. Calculate percent correct scores on weekly spelling tests for the entire class or a group of selected students for several weeks.
2. Calculate the percentage of students in the entire class who score 90% or better on weekly spelling tests for several weeks.
3. Administer *Curriculum-Based Spelling Probes* to a group of selected students.

Procedure

1. On Monday of the week of implementation, tell students that they will be learning a new way of working together to do their best in spelling.
2. Tell them that all students will have an opportunity to participate in a special Friday activity (listening to tapes, having a popcorn party, watching a video, etc.) if the average score for the class is 90% or better on the Friday spelling test. Tell students that the better each one of them scores on the test, the better the chances that the class will average 90% and receive the reward.
3. Teach the week's spelling words as usual during the week.
4. Administer the weekly spelling test on Friday. At the completion of the test, have the students exchange their papers and mark them as you read the correct spellings for the words.
5. Collect the tests, check for grading errors, and calculate students' scores and the class average.

6. Praise the class and provide the rewarding activity if the criterion of 90% has been met. Encourage the students to try harder if the criterion is not met.
7. If desired, place a gold star on the chart if the criterion has been met.

Evaluation (Select One or More)

1. Compare percent correct scores on weekly spelling tests for the entire class or the group of selected students before and after implementation.
2. Compare the percentage of students in the entire class who score 90% or better on weekly spelling tests before and after implementation.
3. Compare scores on *Curriculum-Based Spelling Probes* for the group of selected students before and after implementation.

Variations

1. Permit each student scoring 90% or better on the spelling test to participate in the Friday activity. This variation is most easily implemented if students who are not eligible to participate can be supervised by another staff member in another room.
2. After the test papers have been graded, place the names of all the students (or the tests, face down) in a box and have a student randomly select one name (or test). If the score on that test is 90% or better, all students may participate in the Friday activity. Do not identify the name of the individual student whose test is selected to the class.

Notes

1. In the original study, students earned points for positive behaviors and for scoring 90% or better on spelling tests that could be exchanged for money at the end of the year (1 point = 1¢). Because many teachers prefer not to use money as a reinforcer, an end-of-the-week activity has been substituted in this adaptation.
2. Although all three contingencies were effective in improving spelling performance on daily tests in the original study, students preferred the independent (Variation 1) over the interdependent or dependent contingency.

Source

Shapiro, E. S., & Goldberg, R. (1986). A comparison of group contingencies for increasing spelling performance among sixth-grade students. *School Psychology Review, 15,* 546–557. Copyright 1986 by the National Association of School Psychologists. Adapted by permission.

Improving Written Language

In the past decade, research on the cognitive processes underlying writing has led to a shift in writing instruction from an emphasis on product (e.g., grammar, mechanics, and content) to the processes used to generate that product, such as brainstorming, writing multiple drafts, developing a sense of audience, and incorporating feedback from others. As a result, writing interventions are increasingly designed to enhance student performance of various aspects of the writing process, including planning, sentence generation, and revising (Hayes & Flower, 1986). Such interventions are especially important for learning-disabled and diverse learners, whose compositions are typically brief, poorly organized, and impoverished in both content and development (Graham et al., 1993).

The interventions in this section focus on several writing process components, including fluency and compositional elements such as planning, revising, and editing. *Increasing Writing Productivity with Self-Monitoring* is designed to increase writing fluency by using self-recorded word counts of freewriting. All of the other interventions use some form of strategy instruction to enhance written expression skills. Strategy instruction guides students through a series of steps associated with successful planning, writing, and revising text and has been demonstrated to be effective in improving the writing of both regular and special education students (Graham et al., 1993; Stein et al., 1994).

Two interventions focus on teaching revision strategies. Less skilled writers often fail to revise their compositions, and when they do, their revisions generally fail to improve the quality of their work (Beal, Garrod, & Bonitatibus, 1990; Stoddard & MacArthur, 1993). In keeping with the increasing availability of computers in the classroom, both interventions make use of processing programs to facilitate making revisions. Paper and pencil variations are included for teachers who have limited access to computers or who prefer not to use them as part of writing instruction. In *Peer Editing*, pairs of students work together to learn systematic collaboration techniques as well as a four-question editing strategy. *Improving Writing Revision Skills by Monitoring Comprehension* combines strategy instruction, peer collaboration, and word processing to improve revising skills. The final intervention in this section, *Composition Strategy Development in Writing*, provides training in a self-questioning text-evaluation strategy to enhance story writing performance and motivation to write.

Evaluating the Effectiveness of Written Language Interventions

Evaluating the effectiveness of interventions targeting written expression can be difficult because of the complexity of the writing process. In fact, deciding how to rate students' written language samples is perhaps the greatest problem in evaluating writing instruction (Howell, Fox, & Morehead, 1993). Moreover, obtaining frequent measures of progress in writing for individual students, much less for entire classes, can be very time consuming. The evaluation strategies in this section have been designed to be as brief and practical as possible and still provide meaningful information about progress toward intervention goals. Measures include ratings on simple holistic scales, number of mechanical errors, word counts, and number and quality of revisions. This section also presents procedures for conducting *Curriculum-Based Written Expression Probes*. The total number of words written and the total number of words spelled correctly in 3 minutes in response to a story starter correlate highly with scores on standardized writing measures (Deno, Marston, & Mirkin, 1982).

In addition to these CBM procedures, several published scales with CBM features have utility for assessing writing skills and the effects of writing interventions. Tindal and Hasbrouck (1991) have developed a rating system that focuses on three specific dimensions of the writing process: story–idea, organization–cohesion, and conventions–mechanics, with each dimension scaled along a 5-point continuum. Assessment results can be used to diagnose problems, develop instructional interventions, and evaluate program outcomes. Howell et al. (1993) describe procedures for developing local written expression norms that can then be used to evaluate future writing samples. Based on an analysis of story starters, with 2 minutes to plan and 3 minutes to write, the assessment includes measures of total words written, total words spelled correctly and incorrectly, total words in correct sequence, and a sorting into five groups based on a holistic standard that balances writing quality and mechanics. Samples of several papers at the five levels illustrate each rank for use in rating students' subsequent productions. Shapiro (1996b) has developed the Quality Evaluation Measure for Written Products, a 4-point rating scale for assessing written language skills based on 3-minute story starters. This one-page checklist evaluates capitalization, punctuation, sentence construction, paragraph construction, and appearance of written product for elementary grade writing. Samples of scoring exercises are included for practice.

CURRICULUM-BASED WRITTEN EXPRESSION PROBES

Overview

With the increased focus on writing across the curriculum, assessing students' writing skills has become an important competency for teachers. In curriculum-based measurement (CBM) of written expression, students are provided with story starters or writing prompts and asked to write for 3 minutes as rapidly as possible. Studies indicate that the number of words written and the number of words spelled correctly during these writing probes are highly correlated with standardized measures of written expression and that CBMs in writing can reliably differentiate between learning-disabled and regular education students. Written expression probes may be administered to students individually or in groups.

Purpose

1. To determine students' level and type of skills in writing, relative to their peers.
2. To provide specific information for developing written expression goals in the classroom.
3. To assess the effectiveness of writing interventions.
4. To provide data for program evaluation.

Materials

1. Topic sentences or story starters to provide ideas for students' writing, such as:
   a. When Latoya woke up that morning, she knew that something in her life was about to change.
   b. I will never forget the first time I met my best friend.
   c. The best thing about Saturday is . . .
   d. I would like to be a _____ when I grow up because . . .
2. Pencils or pens, two per student
3. Sheets of lined paper, two or three per student
4. Stopwatch or watch with second hand

Procedure

Administration

1. Give students copies of the story starter or topic sentence and give the following directions:

   > "I want you to write a story. I am going to read a sentence to you first, and then I want you to write a short story about what happens. You will have 1 minute to think about the story you will write and then have 3 minutes to write it. Do your best work. If you don't know how to spell a word, you should guess. Use the sentence I read as your first sentence. Are there any questions? For the next minute, think about . . . [read story starter]."

2. After 1 minute, say, "Start writing."
3. After 3 minutes, say, "Stop and put your pencil down."

Scoring

Option 1: Words written correctly

1. Count the number of words that are correctly written. A word is counted as correct if it can be recognized, even if it is misspelled. If the student stops writing before the 3 minutes are up, divide the number of correctly written words by the number of seconds spent writing and multiply by 180 to obtain the words-written-correctly rate per 3 minutes.
2. Do not count numerals (e.g., *1997*, *3*) as words.
3. If students write the story starter as part of the story, as directed, include the words in the starter as part of the total word count.
4. Compare the words-written-correctly rate to Table 4.2, the student's individual norms, or local norms.

Option 2: Words spelled correctly
1. Count the number of words spelled correctly. A word is counted as correctly spelled if it is a recognizable word and is correctly spelled.
2. Compare the words-spelled-correctly score to the student's individual norms or local norms.

Option 3: Quality evaluation of writing mechanics
1. Assess writing mechanics such as capitalization, punctuation, sentence construction, paragraph construction, and appearance of the written product by using quality evaluation measures (see Notes below).

Notes

1. Developing local norms to evaluate writing probes is strongly recommended. Select 5 to 10 students in the same grade who are not experiencing difficulty in written expression. Administer the story starters as described above. To obtain classwide norms, administer story starters to all the students in a class. Detailed descriptions of local norming procedures are presented in Marston and Magnusson (1988) and Shinn (1989).
2. Quality evaluation measures for assessing written expression are included in Shapiro (1996b) and Tindal and Hasbrouck (1991).
3. Lists of story starters are provided in Shapiro (1996a) and Heward, Heron, Gardner, and Prayzer (1991).

Sources

Marston, D., & Magnusson, D. (1988). Curriculum-based measurement: District level implementation. In J. L. Graden, J. E. Zins, & M. J. Curtis (Eds.), *Alternative educational delivery systems: Enhancing instructional options for all students* (pp. 137–172). Washington, DC: National Association of School Psychologists. Copyright 1988 by the National Association of School Psychologists. Adapted by permission.

Shapiro, E. S. (1996). *Academic skills problems: Direct assessment and intervention* (2nd ed.). New York: Guilford Press. Copyright 1996 by The Guilford Press. Adapted by permission.

Shinn, M. R. (Ed.). (1989). *Curriculum-based measurement: Assessing special children.* New York: Guilford Press. Copyright 1989 by The Guilford Press. Adapted by permission.

INCREASING WRITING PRODUCTIVITY WITH SELF-MONITORING

Overview

Providing students with writing opportunities is an important instructional responsibility for teachers. Because children may write much more slowly and awkwardly than they speak, however, this limits the extent and effectiveness of their writing experiences. This intervention uses self-recorded word counts of freewriting to increase writing performance rates. Self-recording provides students with opportunities for positively evaluating their own progress in writing more words and yields important program evaluation data by showing teachers when changes in instruction are followed by increases in writing. Originally implemented in first-, second-, and fourth-grade classrooms, self-recording of word counts produced increases in the number of words written and improvements in freewriting expressiveness. Moreover, writing mechanics showed little deterioration for timed 3- and 5-minute writing compared with untimed 15- to 20-minute writing periods. Several variations that provide individual or group rewards in addition to public recognition for improvements in spelling performance are included.

Purpose

To increase freewriting rates with self-recorded word counts.

Materials

1. Journals or notebooks for student writing, with student-made line graphs for recording word counts, one journal per student (additional journals are optional for Variation 3)
2. Posterboard chart with bar graph for recording class word counts
3. Red felt-tip marker
4. Set of writing prompts (optional)
5. Watch with second hand and kitchen timer or stopwatch (see Variation 1)
6. Colored posterboard charts with bar graphs for recording class word counts in additional subject areas (see Variation 3)
7. Colored markers, with a different color for each additional subject area, one marker per student (see Variation 3)

Observation (Select One or Both)

1. Count the number of words in freewriting samples for a group of selected students or the entire class for several weeks. Count each word whether it is a conventional standard spelling or an unconventional invented spelling.
2. Administer *Curriculum-Based Written Expression Probes* to a small group of students whose level of writing productivity is about average for the class. Count the number of correctly written words for each student and then calculate a group average by summing individual student scores and dividing by the number of students in the small group.

Procedure

1. Select a time for freewriting in individual journals, such as at the beginning of the day, after lunch, or during the language arts period. Freewriting should be conducted daily or several times a week.
2. Explain to students that they will be learning to evaluate their progress in writing by counting and recording the number of words they write during each session.
3. Display the class chart and explain that you will be graphing the total number

of words written by the class for each writing session. Using the group average number of words written correctly calculated during the observation period or some other criterion, set a weekly goal of total words to be written by the class. Draw a red line on the class chart to indicate that goal. Raise the goal by about 5% each week.

4. Discuss specific topics that students may select, provide a writing prompt, or permit students to select their own topics. Provide approximately 15 minutes for writing.

5. After students finish writing, demonstrate how to create a simple line graph in their journals and have them record the number of words they wrote during that session on their graphs. Tell them to count all the words, regardless of whether they believe the words are correctly spelled.

6. Provide an opportunity for students voluntarily to share their writing with the rest of the class.

7. Each week, review journals to monitor student self-recording and to obtain the class word count total for recording on the class chart. Discuss progress in achieving the weekly goal and praise the students if they meet or exceed it.

Evaluation (Select One or Both)

1. Using individual student graphs or the class chart, compare the number of words in freewriting samples for the group of selected students or the entire class before and after implementation.

2. Compare the average number of correctly written words for the group of selected students on *Curriculum-Based Written Expression Probes* before and after implementation.

Variations

1. Instead of giving students 15 minutes to write, use timed 3- to 5-minute writing periods as follows:
   a. Provide a topic for writing and lead a brief brainstorming discussion.
   b. Set the timer or stopwatch or write the times to begin and stop on the chalkboard and have students write as quickly as they can for that period.
   c. Signal when 1 minute, 30 seconds, and 10 seconds remain.
   d. When the time is up, have students record their number of words written on their graphs as described above.
   e. Provide the following consequences:
      1. After writing a total of 550 words, the student receives a homework pass in a selected subject.
      2. After writing a total of 1,000 words, the student receives a pencil sharpener (or other school supply item) from the principal.
      3. After every student has written 1,700 words, the class earns a popcorn and video party.

2. Provide classwide rewards or privileges, such as additional recess time, if the class achieves the weekly goal.

3. For self-recorded progress in writing across the curriculum, have students use

self-recording of word counts in other subjects, such as science and social studies. Have them use colored markers to create bar graphs for each target subject in their writing journal or use separate journals for each subject. Post color-coded class charts to record total word counts for each of the target subjects.

Notes

1. In the original study, freewriting increased in both loose (15- to 20-minute) and tight (3- or 5-minute) writing periods, but student satisfaction appeared to be greater with timed writing.
2. Teachers in the field testing report that conducting freewriting at transition times during the day, such as after lunch or after recess, helps students to refocus and reduces off-task and disruptive behavior.
3. If students attempt to increase their word counts by writing "very, very," introduce a rule that prohibits counting immediately repeated words.

Source

Moxley, R. A., Lutz, P. A., Ahlborn, P., Boley, N., & Armstrong, L. (1995). Self-recorded word counts of freewriting in grades 1–4. *Education and Treatment of Children, 18*, 138–157. Copyright 1995 by Pressley Ridge School. Adapted by permission.

PEER EDITING

Overview

Learning to revise is an important element of the composition process. To revise successfully, students must reflect on what they have written and develop criteria for evaluating their work. Less skilled writers tend to make few revisions and those they make are usually attempts to correct mechanical errors and have little impact on overall quality. In this intervention, students learn a systematic strategy for working in pairs to help each other revise written productions. Peer editing not only increases the number of substantive revisions and the quality of those revisions but also enhances the overall quality of student writing. Moreover, gains made during instruction using word processors for composition and revision generalize to handwritten compositions. Originally implemented with a small group of learning-disabled middle schoolers, the intervention is adapted here for classwide use.

Purpose

To improve writing performance by combining strategy instruction with peer collaboration.

Materials

1. Computers and word processing programs
2. Printed copies of the peer-editing strategy instructions, one per student
3. 10 writing prompts on computer disks; prompts should be designed to elicit personal narratives, such as:

> "Think about a time when you were surprised by something. What happened and why were you so surprised? Write a story for your friends to read about this time when you were surprised."

4. Printed copies of sample personal narratives with revisions for training, three per student
5. Pencils for making notes on first drafts, two per student
6. Overhead projector and transparency of a sample personal narrative with revisions (optional)
7. Pencils or pens and composition paper for each student (see Variation 1)
8. Paper copies of writing prompts, one prompt per student (see Variation 1)

Observation (Select One or More)

Option 1
1. Have a group of selected students or the entire class write and revise three stories as follows:
   a. In an initial writing session using computers, have students call up the file on the disk that has a writing prompt printed at the top.
   b. Tell them to take a minute to read the prompt and plan.
   c. Tell them that they will have a chance to make revisions later.
   d. Have students compose their stories at the computers, save them, and print copies.
   e. In a second writing session, give students printed copies of their stories and tell them to think about changes they can make to improve them and to make notes on the draft using a pencil.
   f. Then have them make revisions on the computer and print final drafts.
2. Analyze student compositions for one or more of the following measures:
   a. Number of words
   b. Proportions of spelling, capitalization, and punctuation errors, defined as follows:
      1. *Proportion of spelling errors:* the number of misspelled words divided by total words
      2. *Proportion of capitalization errors:* the number of beginning-of-sentence capitalization errors divided by the number of sentences
      3. *Proportion of punctuation errors:* the number of end-of-sentence punctuation errors divided by the number of sentences
   c. Number of revisions, including changes in spelling, capitalization, punctuation, format, or morphological changes (e.g., tense, number), and additions
   d. Overall quality of the final draft on a scale from 1 to 7 (unsatisfactory, poor, fair, average, good, very good, excellent)

    e. Quality change from first to second draft on a 5-point scale from −2 (second draft much worse than first) to +2 (second draft much better than first)

Option 2
1. Rate student revisions on a scale of 1 to 3 (worse, no change, or better) for each of the three compositions.

Option 3
1. Administer *Curriculum-Based Written Expression Probes* to a group of selected students.

Procedure

1. Tell students that they are going to learn to work in pairs to improve their written compositions.
2. If necessary, conduct training sessions on the operation of the computers and the word processing program that will be used for the intervention.
3. Discuss with students the characteristics of a personal narrative; for example, "A personal narrative is a true story about you that describes something that happened to you so clearly that the reader feels as if he or she had been there."
4. Give each student a sample personal narrative and conduct a training session that includes an introduction to the peer editing procedures and a discussion of the importance of revision and positive peer support during the revision process. Use one pair of students to demonstrate the peer editing procedures first and then have the class practice in pairs. If desired, use an overhead projector with a transparency of a sample narrative to demonstrate the revision procedures.
5. Give the students copies of the peer editing strategy instructions (see below) and review each of the nine steps in the revision process, using the sample personal narrative. Explain that both students complete the first two steps. Then each student works independently on the other student's paper, after which they discuss the two papers in turn.
   a. Listen carefully and follow along as the author reads aloud.
   b. Tell the author what you liked best.
   c. Reread the paper to yourself.
   d. Ask yourself the four revision questions:
      1. *Parts?* Does it have a good beginning, middle, and ending?
      2. *Order?* Does it follow a logical sequence?
      3. *Details?* Where could more details be added?
      4. *Clarity?* Is there any part that is hard to understand?
   e. Make notes on the draft based on the revision questions.
   f. Discuss your suggestions with the author.
   g. Work independently at the computer to revise your own paper.
   h. Then meet again with your peer editor to discuss the revisions you each made and to check each other's papers for mechanical errors.
   i. Work independently at the computer to make final revisions and print out your compositions.

6. Have students practice the strategy with two prepared stories and one from the observation period (if available). Move around the room encouraging the peer editing pairs and prompting when necessary.
7. Conduct at least one other practice session using another sample story or stories from the observation period.
8. Using the prepared prompts or other story starters, have students compose stories at the computer and apply the peer editing strategy. Encourage them to share their finished stories with their classmates and parents and help them select some of their final drafts to display in the classroom or on a writing bulletin board in the hallway.

Evaluation (Select One or More)

Option 1
1. Have the group of selected students or the entire class compose three more stories and compare their performance on one or more of the following measures before and after implementation:
   a. Number of words
   b. Proportions of spelling, capitalization, and punctuation errors
   c. Number of revisions
   d. Overall quality of the final draft
   e. Quality change from first to second draft

Option 2
1. Have the entire class or the group of selected students compose three more stories and compare the quality of revisions before and after implementation.

Option 3
1. Compare scores on *Curriculum-Based Written Expression Probes* for the group of selected students before and after implementation.

Variations

1. Have students use paper and pencil rather than computers for composing and revising. Provide printed copies of writing prompts. After the peer editor pairs make notes about suggested changes on each other's first drafts, have students recopy their own stories with the revisions.
2. Have students use only two revision questions:
   a. *Clarity?* Is there anything that is not clear?
   b. *Details?* Where could more information be added?

Notes

1. In the original study, students signed a contract stating that they would work hard to learn the strategy and to improve their writing revisions.
2. Students in the original study made more revisions with handwriting than with word processing, both before and after implementation. The authors suggest

that this increase was due to incidental revisions made during recopying, whereas revisions made with the word processor were intentional.

Source

Stoddard, B., & MacArthur, C. A. (1993). A peer editor strategy: Guiding learning-disabled students in response and revision. *Research in the Teaching of English, 27,* 76–103. Copyright 1993 by PRO-ED, Inc. Adapted by permission.

IMPROVING WRITING REVISION SKILLS BY MONITORING COMPREHENSION

Overview

Elementary school students generally do not revise their writing frequently or skillfully, in part because they overestimate the communicative quality of their writing. Students also fail to revise appropriately because of insufficient instruction and practice in specific strategies for evaluating the comprehensibility of their written compositions. Here, students are taught a self-questioning text-evaluation strategy to notice and repair textual problems. Learning and practicing the strategy has been associated with increases in revisions that improve the overall communicative quality of writing. In the original study, students reviewed and revised prepared stories rather than their own compositions and were trained in individual sessions outside the classroom. In this adaptation, revision strategies are taught in the context of a classroom writing instructional program, and alternative procedures are provided for making handwritten versus computer-assisted revisions.

Purpose

To help students detect and revise problems in written compositions using a self-questioning strategy.

Materials

1. Computers with word processing programs (optional)
2. 3" × 5" index cards or 8½" × 11" sheets of papers listing the revision questions, one per student
3. Sets of 15 stories, each with clear and problematic versions, typed in large font on separate sheets of paper or on computer disks, and prepared as follows:
   a. The clear stories should not present any obvious comprehension problems.
   b. For 11 stories, remove a key sentence so that it is not clear what happened in the story or how the problem in the story was resolved ("missing-sentence" stories).
   c. For four additional stories, include contradictory information ("contradictory" stories). For example, include a sentence or phrase that conflicts with prior statements.

d. Stories typed on paper should be double-spaced and have wide margins for facilitating writing revisions.

e. One set of stories is needed per student.

4. Posterboard chart listing revision questions (optional)

5. An additional set of six missing-sentence and six contradictory stories on computer disk or typed on paper for the observation/evaluation component, one set per student

Observation (Select One or Both)

Option 1: Computer version

1. Present three missing-sentence and three contradictory stories to a selected group of students or the entire class on a computer.

2. Tell students to detect the target problem in each story and have them dictate their revisions to you as you type them into the computer or have them type the revisions themselves.

3. Obtain a problem detection rate across both story categories for each student by summing the number of detected missing-sentence story problems and the number of detected contradictory story problems.

4. Obtain a revision rating for each student by rating the revision of the target problem as adequate or inadequate for each story.

Option 2: Handwritten version

1. Present three missing-sentence and three contradictory stories typed on paper to the entire class.

2. Tell students to detect the target problem in each story and have them write their revisions by hand.

3. Obtain one or more of the following measures:

   a. Obtain a problem detection rate across both story categories for each student by summing the number of detected missing-sentence story problems and the number of detected contradictory story problems.

   b. Obtain a revision rating for each student by rating the revision of the target problem as adequate or inadequate for each story.

   c. Obtain a problem detection and revision rate for each student by summing the number of target problems that are detected and revised adequately.

   d. Obtain the class average problem detection and revision rate by adding individual student problem detection and revision scores and dividing by the total number of students.

Procedure

1. Tell students that they will be learning a way of asking themselves questions about stories that will help them make their own writing more understandable and enjoyable to others.

2. If computers will be used, conduct training sessions as needed on the operation of the computers and the word processing program that will be used for the intervention.

3. Using stories from the missing-sentence category, present the first story on computer or provide students with printed copies. Read the story aloud while the students follow along.
4. Explain that the story is difficult to understand and that the students will learn a way to find the parts of the story that are not clear.
5. Give each student an index card or sheet of paper listing the following revision questions:
   a. Who are the people in the story, and what are they like?
   b. What is happening in the story?
   c. Why are the people doing what they do?
   d. Where does the story take place?
   e. When does the story take place?
6. Review the questions with the class and model the process of detecting story problems. If desired, post a chart listing the revision questions at the front of the classroom.
7. Present the second story and model the use of the revision questions again.
8. For the third story, encourage the students to ask and answer the questions themselves. If desired, have them write the answers to the questions on the index card or sheet of paper.
9. Have students practice independently with another three stories. If most students do not successfully detect the target problem on the sixth story, model the procedures again and present a seventh story.
10. The following week, conduct the same procedures, using the four remaining stories in the missing-sentence story category and the four stories in the contradictory story category.
11. Using samples of student compositions, provide additional practice in using the revision questions until students are successfully detecting problems in their compositions.

Evaluation (Select One or More)

Option 1
1. Present a second set of three missing-sentence and three contradictory stories on the computer to the selected group of students or the entire class.
2. Compare problem detection rates and revision ratings before and after implementation.

Option 2
1. Present a second set of three missing-sentence and three contradictory stories typed on paper to the entire class.
2. Compare one or more of the following measures before and after implementation:
   a. Problem detection rates across both story categories for each student;
   b. Revision ratings for each student;
   c. Problem detection and revision rates for each student;
   d. The class average problem detection and revision rate.

\Variations

1. Conduct training in small groups rather than on a classwide basis.
2. Have students work in pairs to detect and revise text problems. Demonstrate positive peer tutoring practices during training sessions. This variation can be implemented with stories presented on paper or on computer.

Notes

1. The text evaluation questions are taken from the following source: Capelli, C. A., & Markman, E. M. (1985, April). *Improving comprehension monitoring through training in hypothesis testing.* Paper presented at the biennial meeting of the Society for Research in Child Development, Toronto, Ontario, Canada.
2. For classwide training, two sessions of about 45 minutes each are suggested.

Source

Beal, C. R., Garrod, A. C., & Bonitatibus, G. J. (1990). Fostering children's revision skills through training in comprehension monitoring. *Journal of Educational Psychology, 82,* 275–280. Copyright 1990 by the American Psychological Association. Adapted by permission.

COMPOSITION STRATEGY DEVELOPMENT IN WRITING

Overview

Self-regulated strategy development (SRSD) is an instructional approach designed to assist students with written language problems by teaching specific strategies for planning and revising text in the context of a set of self-regulation procedures. Here a series of minilessons based on the SRSD model is used to teach a story grammar strategy and to promote positive attitudes toward writing. SRSD has been successful in improving the quality of writing performance for both learning-disabled and normally achieving students. In this adaptation, paired and small-group learning activities are included at several steps in the training process to provide additional opportunities for feedback and collaboration without direct teacher supervision.

Purpose

To improve writing performance with a self-regulated story grammar strategy.

Materials

1. 8½″ × 11″ sheets of paper listing the five steps and the mnemonic in the story composition strategy, one per student
2. Previously written stories or typed sets of sample stories, two or three per student

3. Overhead projector and transparencies of sample stories and the five steps and mnemonic (optional)
4. Writing portfolios or folders, one per student
5. Story starters or writing prompts (e.g., "One day Tony noticed that there was something very different about the toy chest.")

Observation (Select One or Both)

1. Count the number of story parts contained in two or three stories for a group of selected students or the entire class.
2. Evaluate two or three stories for a group of selected students or the entire class according to the following 4-point holistic rating scale: 1 = unacceptable; 2 = poor; 3 = satisfactory; 4 = excellent.

Procedure

Stage 1: Initial conference
1. Tell the students that they will be learning a strategy to help them write better stories.
2. Lead a discussion that includes the following:
    a. The seven common parts of a story (see mnemonic in Stage 3);
    b. The goal for learning the composition strategy (to write stories that are more fun to write and more fun for others to read);
    c. The role of story parts in improving story quality;
    d. The procedures for learning the strategy, stressing students' roles as collaborators;
    e. The importance of effort in mastering the strategy.

Stage 2: Preskill development
1. Lead a discussion that includes the following:
    a. The parts or elements commonly included in the two major components of a story (setting and episode);
    b. Examples of these elements in literature the class is currently reading;
    c. The use of knowledge of story parts to understand the author's meaning;
    d. The ways in which authors develop or use story parts.
2. Have the class generate ideas for story parts, using sample story starters or writing prompts.
3. Have each student select two or three previously written stories from his or her writing portfolio or provide two or three sample stories. Divide the class into small groups or pairs to work together to determine which story parts are present in each story.
4. Using an overhead projector or the chalkboard, demonstrate how to create a bar graph recording the number of story parts in a story. Explain that graphing is a way students can monitor their own use of story parts and their progress in learning the strategy.

Stage 3: Discussion of the composition strategy

1. Give each student a copy of the five steps and the mnemonic for remembering the questions for story parts:

The composition strategy

   a. Think of a story you would like to share with others.
   b. Let your mind be free.
   c. Write down the story part reminder (mnemonic):
      W–W–W
      What = 2
      How = 2
   d. Make notes of your ideas for each part.
   e. Write your story, using good parts. Add, elaborate, or revise as you go. Make sense!

The mnemonic

   a. *Who* is the main character; who else is in the story?
   b. *When* does the story take place?
   c. *Where* does the story take place?
   d. *What* does the main character do or want to do; what do other characters do?
   e. *What* happens when the main character does it or tries to do it? What happens with other characters?
   f. *How* does the story end?
   g. *How* does the main character feel; how do other characters feel?

2. Lead a discussion that includes:
   a. The reason for each step;
   b. How and when to use the strategy, including linking it to writing book reports, biographies, and other compositions and to reading;
   c. The importance of student effort in mastering the strategy.

3. Provide models of self-statements that help free the mind and generate good ideas and story parts when writing and discuss how these self-statements can be useful.

4. Have students determine their own preferred self-statements, record them in their writing portfolios, and practice using them.

Stage 4: Modeling

1. Share a story idea with the class and model while "thinking out loud" how to use the strategy to develop the idea further.

2. Have students help as you plan and make notes for each story part on the chalkboard and write a first draft of the story.

3. While composing the story, model positive self-statements about the writing process.

4. When the story is completed, lead a discussion of the importance of what we say to ourselves and have students provide examples of self-statements they use when writing.

5. Have students review their previously recorded self-statements and add to or revise them as desired.

Stage 5: Memorization of the strategy and mnemonic
1. Divide the class into pairs and have students work together to memorize the five-step strategy, the mnemonic, and several positive self-statements.
2. Have student pairs review the story parts in one or more of their previously written stories or sample stories and graph the number of parts in their writing portfolios.

Stage 6: Collaborative practice
1. Remind students that the goal is to include all of the story parts in each of their stories. For students who typically use all or nearly all of the story parts, discuss how they can improve their parts with more detail, elaboration, and action.
2. Have students work in pairs to plan stories collaboratively. Move around the room to make sure students are using the strategy steps and mnemonic appropriately. Encourage students to use their self-statements covertly, if they are not already doing so.
3. When students complete a story, have them work with their partners to identify the story parts, compare counts of the parts, fill in their graphs, and then compare the numbers to the goal of seven parts per story.
4. Then lead a class discussion of ways students can maintain the strategy and generalize it to other experiences (e.g., use the strategy when reading stories in English class or when writing outlines).

Stage 7: Independent performance
1. Permit students who wish to continue to refer to their strategy prompts and set of self-statements to do so but encourage them to try writing without them.
2. Encourage students to continue using the graphing process for two more stories and then tell them that future use is up to them.

Evaluation (Select One or Both)

1. Compare the number of story parts in two or three stories for the group of selected students or the entire class before and after implementation.
2. Compare holistic ratings on two or three stories for the group of selected students or the entire class before and after implementation.

Variation

Divide the class into pairs and use a peer tutoring format throughout the entire intervention.

Note

Between one and three collaborative writing experiences (see Stage 6) are needed before students are ready to use the strategy independently.

Sources

Graham, S., Harris, K. R., & MacArthur, C. A. (1993). Improving the writing of students with learning problems: Self-regulated strategy development. *School Psychology Review, 22,* 656–670. Copyright 1993 by the National Association of School Psychologists. Adapted by permission.

Harris, K. R., & Graham, S. (1993). Cognitive strategy instruction and whole language: A case study. *Remedial and Special Education, 14,* 30–34. Copyright 1993 by PRO-ED, Inc. Adapted by permission.

INTERVENTIONS TO IMPROVE SOCIAL STUDIES AND SCIENCE PERFORMANCE

Recent national assessments indicate that diverse learners and general education students alike are performing poorly in social studies and science. The 1994 National Assessment of Educational Progress (NAEP) in geography found that although about 70% of students in grades 4, 8, and 12 had achieved a Basic level of performance (partial mastery), only about 25% of students in each grade had reached a Proficient level (solid academic performance), and only 2% to 4% had achieved an Advanced level (superior performance) (Williams, Reese, Lazer, & Shakrani, 1995). Students demonstrated even poorer achievement on the 1994 NAEP U.S. history assessment. On that assessment, 64% of fourth graders, 61% of eighth graders, and 43% of 12th graders attained at least the Basic level, whereas only 17% of fourth graders, 14% of eighth graders, and 11% of 12th graders reached the Proficient level. Across the three grades, only 1% to 2% reached the Advanced level in history proficiency (Williams, Lazer, Reese, & Carr, 1995).

Student performance in science has also long been viewed with concern. Trends for 9-, 13-, and 17-year-olds from NAEP science assessments conducted from 1969 to 1986 reveal that student achievement has either remained at the level of the first assessment or declined. More than half of 17-year-olds have such a poor understanding of science that they are inadequately prepared to enter jobs requiring technical skills or to benefit from on-the-job training for those positions. African-American and Hispanic students are even less well prepared, with an average level of proficiency at least 4 years below that of White students (Mullis & Jenkins, 1988).

Despite recent efforts to reform the science curriculum, current instructional practices provide insufficient opportunities to master scientific skills and concepts, especially for elementary grade students. Although about half of the third-grade teachers surveyed on the 1994 NAEP assessment reported providing science instruction for 1 to 2 hours a week, approximately 10% of the teachers spend much more time (7 or more hours per week) maintaining order and disciplining students. When third-grade students were surveyed about the nature of their science instruction, 11% reported *never* having a science lesson (Mullis & Jenkins, 1988).

Opportunities for successful performance in the content areas of social studies and science are also significantly affected by students' reading skills. Most learning-disabled and low-achieving students have reading deficits that prevent them from reading their textbooks with sufficient proficiency to acquire information from them and integrate that information with previously acquired knowledge (Lovitt & Horton, 1991). Moreover, despite the importance of helping students, especially diverse learners, to acquire and retain information from their texts, studies of social studies classrooms indicate that teachers spend very little time preparing students to read chapters in their textbooks. Teachers also provide virtually no direct instruction in study skills (1 to 3% of instructional time), such as outlining and scanning, that help students learn and remember textual material. Instead, teachers spend most of their time covering the curriculum and having students master facts (Durkin, 1978–1979; Neilsen, Rennie, & Connell, 1982).

Diverse learners' problems in reading and understanding their content-area textbooks are compounded by the fact that texts are often poorly written and "inconsiderate" of their readers (Armbruster, 1984). Social studies student textbooks and teacher editions include little reading comprehension or study skills instruction, and what little instruction is provided is often inadequate (Anderson & Smith, 1984; Armbruster & Gudbrandsen, 1986). Instead, textbooks require students to acquire and apply skills and concepts without providing help for teachers in teaching those skills and concepts or students in learning them. Science textbooks have been especially criticized for presenting excessive numbers of concepts and vocabulary words with insufficient opportunities for critical reading and thinking or practice and application (Anderson & Smith, 1984; Roth, Smith, & Anderson, 1984). In addition, although many textbooks currently provide guidelines for accommodating diverse learners in the classroom, these guidelines are seldom sufficient to meet the needs of these students (Parmar & Cawley, 1993).

Assisting students in becoming competent readers of their content-area texts is critically important, especially for learning-disabled, low-achieving, and other difficult-to-teach students. The basic reading skills of learning-disabled students plateau at about a fourth- or fifth-grade level during the high school years (Schumaker, Deshler, Alley, & Warner, 1983). These students also demonstrate deficiencies in the study skills and higher-order thinking skills that would enable them to gain meaning from their textbooks (Deshler et al., 1982). As they progress through the grades, the gap between their skill level and the reading level of their textbooks widens, reducing their ability to profit from social studies and science instruction. Already at risk for academic failure, these difficult-to-teach students may become so frustrated that they fail even to attempt to read their texts in these subjects.

Although university-sponsored program models (see Schumaker, Deshler, & McKnight, 1991) have been developed to improve content-area instruction for at-risk students in the mainstream, surprisingly few "stand alone" interventions targeting social studies or science performance have appeared in the literature, perhaps because achievement in the content areas is affected by a wide range of interrelated skills and competencies, including cognitive ability, background knowledge, and reading proficiency. The interventions in this section focus on two general targets: (1) improving students' ability and/or motivation to gain meaning from textual material and (2) enhancing students' opportunities to respond to academic material. Although these interventions were originally designed for implementation in social studies, science, or both, they can easily be adapted for use in other academic areas in which increasing textual comprehension or student response rates is desirable.

Two interventions focus on improving reading performance in the content areas, although they manipulate different learning-related variables. *Improving Social Studies Homework Compliance with the Tic–Tac–Toe Game* encourages students to read their social studies textbooks by creating a game in which successful performance is contingent upon accurate homework. *Improving Understanding of Textual Material in Social Studies with a Critical Thinking Map* directly targets comprehension skills by providing a framework for understanding and remembering expository textual material. This text structure strategy can be used to promote comprehension in any subject in which reading is designed to gather information.

Increasing active responding to academic material is especially important in social studies and science, where whole-class instruction is a common format and diverse learners can easily become passive observers. Two interventions encourage student responding by providing contingencies for appropriate participation in class discussions. *Improving Participation in Social Studies Classes* uses a peer-mediated strategy to provide immediate feedback and reinforcement for participation in discussions. *Using Response Cards to Improve Participation and Achievement in Science* increases responding during whole-class instruction by teaching students to write answers to teacher questions on individual laminated boards. *Using Cover, Copy, and Compare to Improve Geography Accuracy* permits all students to be engaged in high rates of academic responding by applying the Cover, Copy, and Compare (CCC) strategy to learning geography facts. In the CCC self-instructional procedure, students learn to deliver their own instructional prompts, evaluate their responses, and correct their own errors. The last intervention in this section, *Improving Science Test Grades with Public Posting*, is a simple strategy that uses feedback in the form of public posting to enhance student motivation for science performance. Variations for posting group averages as well as individual test scores are included.

Evaluating the Effectiveness of Social Studies and Science Interventions

Methods for assessing the effectiveness of the strategies in this section are quite diverse, including homework completion and accuracy rates, quiz and test grades, amount and quality of student participation in class discussions, classwide percentages of students with low grades, and attitudes toward the interventions. Evaluation measures for the intervention designed to promote reading comprehension for content-area textbooks include holistic rating scales assessing the quality of answers to comprehension questions and student self-reports of the number of comprehension and memory strategies used during reading.

IMPROVING SOCIAL STUDIES HOMEWORK COMPLIANCE WITH THE TIC–TAC–TOE GAME

Overview

Students with poor reading skills or low motivation to read often neglect homework assignments in social studies, science, or other subjects that involve reading their textbooks. As a result, they have difficulty participating in class discussions based on homework completion and miss valuable opportunities for additional skill practice. This intervention, which applies a group contingency in a game-like format to encourage students to complete textbook reading assignments, has been demonstrated to have positive effects on homework completion rates and academic performance. Originally applied to social studies homework, it can be implemented in any subject area that includes reading homework assignments.

Purpose

To increase homework completion rates in social studies and provide additional opportunities for active participation in social studies lessons.

Materials

1. 15 sentence-completion items (or a set of questions or exercises) from that day's assignment, one set per day; or 15 questions on worksheets, one worksheet per student (see Variation 1)

2. Notebook paper and pens or pencils for each student
3. Red pens, one per student
4. Backup reinforcers, such as wrapped miniature candy or inexpensive school supplies (optional)
5. Posterboard chart and stickers to record winning teams (see Variation 2)

Observation (Select One or More)

1. Calculate social studies homework completion rates for the entire class or a group of selected students for 5 to 10 days or several weeks.
2. Calculate percent correct scores for social studies homework assignments for the entire class or a group of selected students for 5 to 10 days or several weeks.
3. Calculate social studies quiz and test grades for the entire class or a group of selected students for several weeks.

Procedure

1. Tell students that they will be playing a tic–tac–toe game based on their homework to help them get more out of their social studies assignments.
2. Each day, give a reading assignment in the social studies textbook or other curricular materials as homework. Tell students to read the assignment and be prepared to answer questions about it the next day.
3. Divide the class into two teams on the basis of seating arrangements. If teams are not equal in number on a given day, ask a student volunteer to keep score at the chalkboard or shift students from one team to the other.
4. Present in random order 15 sentence-completion questions (or a set of questions assessing content knowledge) from the previous day's reading homework assignment. Tell the students to write the answers to each question as quickly as possible on their papers, turn over their papers, and raise their hands when they are finished.
5. Read each question aloud twice to the class. Say "stop" (indicating that the answer period for each question is over) when all members of one or both teams have their hands raised.
6. After all questions have been read, have the students use red pens to grade their papers as you read the correct answers. For each question, have students raise their hands to report whether they have answered it correctly and to determine which team has the greater number of correct answers for that question.
7. Create a tic–tac–toe grid on the chalkboard and have a student from the team winning that question put an X or O in one of the squares for that question.
8. Ask the next question and continue as before. If both teams have the same number of correct answers, no symbol is placed on the grid, and the next question is asked.
9. A team is declared the winner when it acquires three Xs or three Os in a straight line.
10. If students appear to be cheating, remove their answer sheets and tell them they are out of the game.

11. If the game is incomplete at the end of the 15 questions or the set of exercises, the team with the most Xs or Os wins.
12. Follow the game with a discussion of the assigned material. Collect student papers to review for accuracy of checking.
13. If desired, deliver a reward to the winning team, such as extra recess, lining up for lunch first, or drawing from a "surprise sack" containing assorted wrapped candy or school supplies.

Evaluation (Select One or More)

1. Compare percent correct scores for social studies homework assignments for the entire class or the group of selected students before and after implementation.
2. Compare percent correct scores for social studies homework assignments for the entire class or the group of selected students before and after implementation.
3. Compare social studies quiz and test grades for the entire class or the group of selected students before and after implementation.

Variations

1. Instead of reading the questions, present the questions on worksheets and have students complete them on their own. Score responses and play the game as described above.
2. Instead of giving daily rewards, post a "Team of the Day" sticker on a chart. At the end of the week, deliver the reward to the team with the most stickers.

Note

To avoid arguments over whether student answers are correct, emphasize that students are to score their papers according to the answers you give and model appropriate student behavior during the game. If a student argues excessively over the correctness of an answer, erase the most recent X or O for that team.

Source

Harris, V. W., & Sherman, J. A. (1974). Homework assignments, consequences, and classroom performance in social studies and mathematics. *Journal of Applied Behavior Analysis, 7*, 505–519. Copyright 1974 by the Society for the Experimental Analysis of Behavior. Adapted by permission.

IMPROVING UNDERSTANDING OF TEXTUAL MATERIAL IN SOCIAL STUDIES WITH A CRITICAL THINKING MAP

Overview

Students often make poor grades in content areas because they have difficulty comprehending their textbooks. Although they may have adequate word recognition skills, they have trouble learning and retaining the information in their texts because they lack strategies for thinking critically about what they are reading. In this intervention, students are taught to impose on the text a structure in the form of a map that provides a framework for guiding their thinking processes as they read. Use of critical thinking maps has been associated with significant increases in reading comprehension and vocabulary, with improvement generalizing to similar content. Originally used on an individualized basis with remedial reading and mildly retarded high school students, it is adapted here for classwide implementation.

Purpose

To improve reading comprehension in social studies by teaching students to use a five-component critical thinking map.

Materials

1. Copies of critical thinking maps, one per student (see Figure 4.15)
2. Copies of generic comprehension questions, one per student (see Figure 4.16)
3. Overhead projector and a transparency of the map (optional)
4. Red pens for checking papers, one per student (optional)
5. Notebook paper for graphing scores on comprehension questions (see variation)

Observation (Select One or More)

Option 1
1. Have the entire class answer the five generic comprehension questions (see Figure 4.16) after reading the social studies lesson for the day.
2. Score the questions using the following rating scale:
   a. 0 = no response or completely wrong
   b. 1 = poor response
   c. 2 = partially correct but incomplete response
   d. 3 = satisfactory response
   e. 4 = excellent response
3. Record comprehension scores for 5 to 10 days.

Option 2
1. Record grades on weekly or end-of-unit social studies quizzes and tests for the entire class for several weeks.

Option 3
1. Have a group of selected students or the entire class respond in writing to the following two questions:
   a. What do you do to help yourself *understand* what you read?
   b. How do you help yourself *remember* what you read?

2. Count the number of strategies students report using to understand (comprehension strategies) and remember (memory strategies) what they read as defined below:
   a. *Comprehension strategies* include paying attention to the text, reading slower, skimming for main ideas, and thinking about the lesson.
   b. *Memory strategies* include self-questioning, inferring meaning of unfamiliar words, and slowing down the reading process.
3. For each type of strategy, calculate the average number used by the group of selected students or the entire class by dividing the total number of strategies per category by the total number of students.

Procedure

Stage 1: Modeling phase
1. Using an overhead projector, display a transparency of the critical thinking map or reproduce it on the chalkboard. Explain to the students that they will be learning to use the map to get more out of reading their social studies textbooks.
2. Explain each of the map components as follows:
   a. *Important events:* important events, points, or steps that lead to the main intent or idea of the lesson, such as the positive and negative attributes of an issue or causal and/or temporal points;
   b. *Main idea/lesson:* the most important message conveyed by the author, whether explicit or implicit, reflecting the author's overall attitudes toward the information presented in the text;
   c. *Other viewpoints/opinions:* the reader's own viewpoints and opinions about what has been read, that is, background information and knowledge;
   d. *Reader's conclusions:* the reader's final conclusions about the passage, with reasons to support them based on combined knowledge from all of the preceding map components;
   e. *Relevance to today:* the reader's comparisons between the historical lesson and present day events so that modern people can make better choices by their understanding of past events.
3. Note the number of pages in the lesson to be read.
4. Read the passage aloud, interrupting yourself as you encounter answers to map components in the text.
5. Fill in the map components on the transparency or chalkboard as you identify answers to them in the lesson.
6. Read the map components aloud, checking for accuracy and adding more information as necessary.
7. Distribute copies of the generic comprehension questions and have students silently read the questions and write down their responses without referring back to the lesson.
8. Review the answers to the questions and have students correct their responses using red pens.
9. Continue this modeling phase for two lessons or until most students are achieving ratings of "3" (satisfactory) on four of the five questions.

Stage 2: Lead phase

1. Distribute copies of the map and instruct the students to read the social studies lesson silently.
2. Demonstrating with the overhead projector or on the chalkboard, help students reexamine the lesson for answers to map components and complete their maps.
3. Have students take turns orally rereading the contents of the map components, checking for accuracy, and adding more information if necessary.
4. Collect the maps, distribute the comprehension questions, and have students complete them.
5. Have students correct their own papers with red pens while you review answers to the questions and discuss any discrepancies between incorrect comprehension answers and correct map information. Have students rewrite incorrect comprehension answers.

Stage 3: Test phase

1. As students become successful in completing the map components, discontinue classwide demonstrations and provide individual help as needed.
2. When the majority of students are obtaining satisfactory ratings on all five of the comprehension questions with little or no assistance, discontinue use of the map.
3. If desired, discontinue the use of the comprehension questions. Instead, have students read the passage silently and then write a paragraph pertaining to each of the map components during class time or as a homework assignment.

Evaluation (Select One or More)

Option 1

1. Compare scores on the five generic comprehension questions after reading social studies lessons for the entire class before and after implementation.

Option 2

1. Compare grades on weekly or end-of-unit social studies quizzes and tests for the entire class before and after implementation.

Option 3

1. Compare the average number of comprehension and memory strategies reported by the group of selected students or the entire class on the two reading questions before and after implementation.

Option 4

1. Administer the two reading questions to the group of selected students or the entire class and rate student responses as improved or not improved. *Improved responses* are defined as responses indicating that students are more aware of the need to think about reading and/or to ask themselves questions about reading.
2. Calculate the percentage of students with improved responses for each category and across both categories.

Variations

1. Have students chart their scores on the generic comprehension questions on graphs in their social studies folders.
2. Periodically assign the generic comprehension questions as homework rather than classwork.

Note

In the original study, answers to the generic comprehension questions were scored on a 0- to 4-point rating scale that was individualized for each of the five questions.

Source

Idol, L. (1987). A critical thinking map to improve content area comprehension of poor readers. *Remedial and Special Education, 8*(4), 28–40. Copyright 1987 by PRO-ED, Inc. Adapted by permission.

Name _____   Chap. _____   Part _____
Date _____   Phase _____

A Map for Critical Thinking

Important Events, Points, or Steps

Main Idea/Lesson

Other Viewpoints/Opinions

Reader's Conclusion

Relevance to Today

FIGURE 4.15. Map for *Improving Understanding of Textual Material in Social Studies with a Critical Thinking Map.* From Idol (1987, p. 30). Copyright 1987 by PRO-ED, Inc. Reprinted by permission.

Generic Comprehension Questions

Chapter _____   Phase _____

Lesson _____   Day _____

Page _____

1. What is the main idea in this passage?
2. What were the important steps that led to the main idea?
3. What are some other points of view or missing information about this topic?
4. What is your own conclusion?
5. How is this passage relevant to a modern problem or issue?

FIGURE 4.16. Generic comprehension questions for *Improving Understanding of Textual Material in Social Studies with a Critical Thinking Map.* From Idol (1987, p. 32). Copyright 1987 by PRO-ED, Inc. Reprinted by permission.

IMPROVING PARTICIPATION IN SOCIAL STUDIES CLASSES

Overview

Class discussions are an integral activity in subjects such as social studies and science. All too often, however, discussions are not effective group learning experiences. Instead, only a few students participate actively, while the rest sit passively or become disruptive. Even when students participate in discussions, their contributions may fail to enhance learning because they lack quality in terms of content and relevancy. By providing immediate feedback and reinforcement for participation, this intervention encourages students to be active, responsible learners during lessons. Originally implemented in a seventh-grade social studies class, it can be easily adapted to any subject that includes discussion as a regular activity.

Purpose

To increase the quality and quantity of participation in classroom discussions by increasing student accountability.

Materials

1. Posterboard chart or sheet of paper listing student names for recording weekly average discussion grades
2. Posterboard chart listing the rules for class discussion (optional)
3. Slips of paper with students' names written on them, in a hat or basket (see Note)

Observation (Select One or More)

1. Using a sheet of paper attached to a clipboard, record the number of students who voluntarily participate in social studies discussions for 5 to 10 days. Calculate the percentage of classwide participation by dividing the number of students participating by the number of students in the class.
2. Using a sheet of paper with a list of student names attached to a clipboard, record the number of times each student or each member of a selected group of students voluntarily participates in social studies discussions for 5 to 10 days.
3. Using a sheet of paper attached to a clipboard, record the number of irrelevant statements made during class discussions. An *irrelevant statement* is defined as a statement that has no relationship to the topic being discussed or is intended to disrupt rather than facilitate the discussion.
4. Using a sheet of paper attached to a clipboard, record the number of disruptive behaviors displayed during class discussions. *Disruptive behaviors* are defined as any behaviors that interfere with ongoing discussion and instruction, such as being out of seat, not facing forward, and talking when not called upon.
5. Calculate percent correct scores on social studies classwork, quizzes, or end-of-unit tests for the entire class for several weeks.

Procedure

1. Explain to the students that you want to help them get more out of social studies by giving everyone a chance to participate in classroom discussions. Explain that participating in class is important because it is a good way of learning the material.
2. Review the following rules for class discussions and, if desired, post a chart listing them:
   a. Raise your hand and wait quietly when you have something to say.
   b. Speak only when the teacher calls on you.
   c. If someone else is called on, put your hand down and listen quietly. If you have more to add after the person is finished talking, raise your hand again.
   d. Respect everyone's contributions.
3. Tell the students that one of them will be designated each day to record a mark that you will give every time a student contributes a relevant question, answer, or comment to a discussion. Each mark stands for 1 point earned. Display a portion of the chalkboard with student names listed and space for recording points.
4. Explain that if any student makes an irrelevant statement or exhibits any disruptive behavior during a class discussion, that student will lose 1 point per disruption. Give examples of irrelevant statements and disruptive behaviors and lead a discussion of why these behaviors interfere with learning.
5. Explain that students who lose 3 points during one discussion must put their heads down on their desks (or lose 5 minutes of recess, have silent lunch that day, etc.) and will not have an opportunity to earn points for the rest of the period.
6. Explain that the total number of points earned or lost during each discussion will determine each student's daily social studies grade. Students who make no

contribution but pay attention to the discussion (i.e., display no disruptive behaviors) earn a C. Other grades are determined by the difference between the number of points earned and the number lost as follows:

a. Difference = −3, grade = F
b. Difference = −2, grade = D
c. Difference = −1, grade = C−
d. Difference = +1, grade = C+
e. Difference = +2, grade = B−
f. Difference = +3, grade = B
g. Difference = +4, grade = B+
h. Difference = +5, grade = A−
i. Difference = +6 or more, grade = A

7. At the beginning of each discussion, designate a student to record points on the chalkboard. For all relevant student contributions, say in a voice loud enough for all students to hear, "Please give [name of student] a point for that answer [question or comment]." Also praise students for positive contributions. For irrelevant statements or disruptive behaviors, instruct the recorder to deduct a point but do not make further comments. If students lose 3 points in one discussion, have them put their heads down on their desks or deliver some other consequence.

8. At the end of the week, average daily discussion grades and post them on a sheet of paper on the bulletin board or on a posterboard chart displayed at the front of the class.

Evaluation (Select One or More)

1. Compare the percentage of classwide participation in social studies discussions before and after implementation.

2. Compare individual rates of participation in social studies class discussions for each student in the class or in the target group before and after implementation.

3. Compare the frequency of irrelevant statements made during social studies class discussions before and after implementation.

4. Compare the frequency of disruptive behaviors during social studies class discussions before and after implementation.

5. Compare percent correct scores on social studies classwork, quizzes, or end-of-unit tests for the entire class before and after implementation.

Variations

1. Have students who persistently lose 3 points during a single class discussion complete a "Solving My Own Problems" essay from *Eliminating Disruptive Lunchroom Behavior with Mediation Essays.*

2. Instead of using a student recorder, record the points yourself.

3. Divide the class into teams according to rows or tables and award each team member a bonus point for each discussion in which every student on that team makes at least one positive contribution.

Note

To give everyone an equal chance to earn high marks, it is important to call on students in a systematic manner. This can be done by writing students' names on slips of paper, placing them in a hat or basket, and drawing without replacement.

Source

Smith, B. M., Schumaker, J. B., Schaeffer, J., & Sherman, J. A. (1982). Increasing participation and improving the quality of discussions in seventh-grade social studies classes. *Journal of Applied Behavior Analysis, 15,* 97–110. Copyright 1982 by the Society for the Experimental Analysis of Behavior. Adapted by permission.

USING COVER, COPY, AND COMPARE
TO IMPROVE GEOGRAPHY ACCURACY

Overview

Although geography instruction is offered or required in the majority of American elementary, middle, and high schools, numerous surveys demonstrate that many students are not learning basic concepts, such as place names. Moreover, place naming is among the prerequisite skills needed for college courses in geography and related fields. In this intervention, a Cover, Copy, and Compare (CCC) strategy is used to help students learn to identify states on a map of the United States. The CCC intervention consists of a set of self-instructional strategies designed to increase student responding to academic material and provide immediate reinforcement for correct responses. Originally implemented in a self-contained classroom with behavior-disordered students, the CCC intervention was successful in improving place-naming performance and was rated as highly acceptable by students.

Purpose

To increase geography place-naming accuracy by using self-instructional techniques.

Materials

1. Maps of the United States including all 50 states with their names, photocopied on yellow 8½" × 11" sheets of paper and stapled to the outside of manila file folders, one per student
2. Maps identical to the above but with the states' names deleted and horizontal lines provided for writing postal abbreviations of the states, photocopied on white 8½" × 11" sheets of paper, one per student, one for each intervention session and for each assessment

3. 50 3″ × 5″ index cards with state names and postal abbreviations printed on them in large black letters, divided into 5 sets (A, B, C, D, and E) of 10 states each, grouped so that they move from the west coast to the east coast of the United States, with Hawaii and Alaska included on the west coast
4. 3″ × 5″ blank index cards, 50 per student
5. Rubber bands, five per student
6. Pennies, one per student
7. Yellow labeled maps of the Canadian provinces stapled to the outside of manila file folders, one per student
8. White unlabeled maps of the Canadian provinces, with horizontal lines provided for labeling the provinces, one per student
9. Ten 3″ × 5″ index cards listing the names of the Canadian provinces, one set per student
10. Stopwatch or watch with second hand
11. Overhead projector and transparencies listing the names and abbreviations for the 50 states (see Variation 1)

Observation (Select One or Both)

Option 1
1. Distribute copies of a map of the United States with the states' names deleted and horizontal lines provided for writing the U.S. postal abbreviations of the states to the entire class. Have students label as many states as they can during a timed period (approximately 10 minutes).
2. Calculate the number of correctly labeled states for each student.
3. Then calculate the class average for correctly labeling states by summing individual student scores and dividing by the total number of students.

Option 2
1. Using a rating scale of 1 to 5 (1 = strongly disagree; 2 = disagree; 3 = neutral; 4 = agree; 5 = strongly agree), have students respond in writing to the following statements:
   a. I enjoy studying geography.
   b. The activities in geography class are interesting.
   c. The activities in geography class help me learn the material.
2. Calculate a class average rating for each statement by summing individual student ratings and dividing by the total number of students.

Procedure

Step 1: Preparing student materials
1. Distribute the blank index cards to students and tell them that they will be using them to learn to identify the names of the states.
2. Display and read the index cards from Set A and instruct students to copy each state on one of their index cards. To facilitate accuracy, spell each state aloud and have students work in pairs to check each other's cards after the set is com-

pleted. If students make errors, give them another card and the example to copy.
3. After Set A cards are completed, give students rubber bands to place around the cards. Follow a similar procedure for the remaining sets.
4. After all the index cards are completed, give each student a folder containing a yellow labeled map of the United States and a white unlabeled map. Have students place the cards from Set A in the folder and hand in the cards from Sets B through E.

Step 2: Cover, Copy, and Compare (CCC) training
1. Give each student a set of index cards with the names of the Canadian provinces, a penny, a file folder, and the yellow and white maps of the Canadian provinces. Teach students to use the five-step CCC procedure as follows:
   a. Shuffle the index cards and place them face down in a pile on your desk.
   b. Lift the top index card and look at the name of that province.
   c. Find the province on the yellow map.
   d. Turn the yellow map over by opening the file folder and place a penny on the appropriate spot on the white map for that province.
   e. Turn over the yellow map again and compare your answer with the labeled map. If you have placed the penny on the appropriate province, proceed to the next index card and repeat the procedure. If you have made an error, repeat the CCC procedure with that province until you mark the appropriate province with the penny.
2. Demonstrate the procedure at a work table and then have the students perform the procedure independently with five index cards.
3. Tell students to make an error on purpose with the third card to show that they can follow the procedure when they make mistakes.
4. Continue training until students can perform the procedure three consecutive times with five provinces.

Step 3: Using the CCC intervention
1. Immediately after training (or during the next geography lesson), have students shuffle their index cards from Set A and perform the CCC procedure with them five separate times. Move around the room to assist and encourage students as needed.
2. When students have finished, have them return their cards, pennies, and folders to an assigned area of the classroom.
3. Daily or at some appropriate interval, distribute the white U.S. maps and give the following instructions:

> "These index cards contain the names and initials [postal abbreviations] of some of the states. I will show you the cards and read the cards to you one at a time. After you see the card, write the initials of the state in the appropriate state on the map. I will present each card for only 10 seconds, so pay attention and work quickly. Ready, begin!"

4. Present the cards for the set(s) of states that students have practiced.

5. Collect the maps and reshuffle the cards so that the states are presented in random order each time.
6. Have students perform the CCC procedure with a set of cards until the majority of students achieve 85% accuracy or better for two consecutive assessments.

Evaluation (Select One or Both)

Option 1
1. Distribute copies of a map of the United States with the states' names deleted and horizontal lines provided for writing the U.S. postal abbreviations of the states to the entire class. Have students label as many states as they can during a timed period (approximately 10 minutes). Compare the class average for correctly labeled states before and after implementation.

Option 2
1. Compare class average ratings for statements assessing student attitudes toward geography class before and after implementation.

Variations

1. Use an overhead projector and transparencies instead of index cards (one transparency per set) to display the state names and abbreviations while students create their own sets of cards.
2. Instead of assessing mastery by reading the state names from index cards, provide students with blank maps and have them fill in the state names without prompting.

Note

A training session of about 30 to 45 minutes is required to teach the CCC procedure.

Source

Skinner, C. H., Belfiore, P. J., & Pierce, N. (1992). Cover, copy, and compare: Increasing geography accuracy in students with behavior disorders. *School Psychology Review, 21,* 73–81. Copyright 1992 by the National Association of School Psychologists. Adapted by permission.

IMPROVING SCIENCE TEST GRADES WITH PUBLIC POSTING

Overview

This strategy uses a combination of public posting of weekly test grades, teacher praise, and immediate feedback to motivate academic performance in science. It has been shown to produce dramatic improvement in test scores, especially for the lower third of a class, even when public posting alone is used and test scores are posted every other week. Although teachers sometimes worry that publicly displaying grades may embarrass students or invite negative peer remarks, public posting was associated in the original study with an increase in the number of positive peer comments concerning student performance. First used in high school biology classes, it can be implemented in any subject to enhance student motivation to improve test grades.

Purpose

To improve academic performance on science tests by providing public recognition for effort and achievement.

Materials

1. Posterboard chart listing student names, with columns for recording individual test scores and the weekly average class score; letters and numbers should be about 3 cm in height so that they are clearly visible to all students
2. Black and red felt-tip markers

Observation (Select One or Both)

1. Record student weekly test scores in science (or another subject) on a posterboard chart for several weeks but do not display it. (This measure is included in the intervention procedures.)
2. Calculate the percentage of students with grades of D or F for the current marking period or the school year thus far in science (or another subject).

Procedure

1. Display the chart with baseline scores where students can see it. Explain that you will be using the chart to record individual weekly test scores and class average test scores to provide students with information about their performance in science (or another subject) and to encourage them to try their best.
2. Explain that you will use a black felt-tip marker to record weekly individual test scores and weekly average class scores if those scores do not exceed the highest score obtained previously.
3. Explain that you will enter a score in red whenever students as individuals or as a class exceed their highest previous test score, regardless of whether it is a passing or failing score. Perfect scores will also be entered in red.
4. Encourage students to beat their highest previous score and to work together as a class to beat their highest previous average score.
5. Grade and return weekly test papers immediately or as soon as possible. Post scores and give praise whenever a student or the class beats a highest previous score.
6. Continue the intervention until the class test score average is at least 85% or better for the remainder of the school year.

Evaluation (Select One or Both)

1. Compare individual student weekly test scores and class average test scores for the target subject before and after implementation.
2. Compare the percentage of students with grades of D or F in the target subject before and after implementation.

Variation

Divide the class into teams based on seating arrangements and post average team scores rather than individual student scores (see Note).

Note

During field testing, teachers in the upper elementary and middle school grades often expressed concern that students with poor grades would be embarrassed by public posting of individual test scores. As a result, the intervention was modified for those grades to post team averages rather than individual student scores, and teachers held conferences with individual students to review their test scores. Posting individual student scores appears to be less of a concern for primary grade teachers, perhaps because many already use some form of public charting for a variety of academic and social behaviors.

Source

Van Houten, R., & Lai Fatt, D. (1981). The effects of public posting on high school biology test performance. *Education and Treatment of Children, 4,* 217–226. Copyright 1981 by Pressley Ridge School. Adapted by permission.

USING RESPONSE CARDS TO IMPROVE PARTICIPATION AND ACHIEVEMENT IN SCIENCE

Overview

Students learn and retain more when they actively respond during instruction. All too often, however, the organization of lessons does not provide for sufficient participation, and students become passive observers of instruction. For students already experiencing academic difficulties, this passivity compounds their problems because they miss opportunities to receive teacher feedback and improve their skills and understanding. In this intervention, students use laminated boards on which to write short answers in response to teacher questions. Using response cards is associated not only with increased responding rates but also with improved grades on quizzes and tests. Moreover, students enjoy the novelty of the strategy and prefer using response cards to raising their hands. Although this intervention does not directly target off-task or disruptive behavior, improvement in social behavior has also been observed. Originally used in social studies and science classes, this intervention can be implemented in any subject.

Purpose

To improve student participation and achievement in science by providing additional opportunities for active responding and feedback.

Materials

1. White laminated particle boards ($9'' \times 12''$), one per student
2. Dry-erase black markers, one per student
3. Stopwatch or watch with second hand
4. 10-question quiz consisting of 5 multiple-choice and 5 short-answer questions, one quiz per science lesson (optional)
5. Overhead projector and transparencies of science lesson material (see Variations 1 and 2)

Observation (Select One or More)

Option 1

1. Using a sheet of paper with a list of student names or a copy of a seating chart attached to a clipboard, record the number of times each student accurately answers a teacher-directed question during the science instructional period for 5 to 10 days.
2. Calculate the class average number of correct student responses to teacher questions by dividing the sum of the frequencies of individual student responses by the total number of students.

Option 2

1. Calculate grades on weekly quizzes or chapter tests in science for several weeks or longer for the entire class.

Option 3

1. Calculate the percentage of students with grades of D or F in science for the current grading period or the school year thus far.

Procedure

1. Explain to the students that they will be learning a new and better way to participate in science class.
2. Distribute the response cards and markers and conduct a 10- to 15-minute training session as follows:
   a. Tell students to answer questions by printing their answers in one or two words on their response cards.
   b. Pose a question and say, "Write," to cue the students to begin writing.
   c. After 5 seconds, say, "Hold up your cards." Remind students to hold their cards above their heads so that you can see all responses.
   d. Quickly scan all student responses and provide feedback as described below.
   e. To prevent doodling, tell students that they will be given 2 minutes (or some

other amount of time) at the end of each class period for drawing on the cards, provided that they write only answers to teacher questions on their cards during instruction.
3. During the lesson, present information for the first 10 or 15 minutes and orally question students after each fact or concept is taught.
4. During the rest of the instructional period, ask a series of questions reviewing the facts or concepts just presented. Have students respond to questions by writing one- or two-word answers on the cards and holding them up so they are visible.
5. After visually scanning all of the response cards, provide praise for correct answers or corrective feedback for incorrect answers as follows:
   a. If everyone has the right answer, give the feedback to the whole class (e.g., "Good, class, water vapor is a *gas*").
   b. If some students show incorrect answers, acknowledge that some have answered correctly and also provide the correct answer (e.g., "I see that many of you have *gas* as the answer. That is correct, water vapor is a *gas*.").
   c. If no students have the correct answer, indicate this and provide the correct answer (e.g., "I don't see any correct answers. The correct answer is *gas*. Water vapor in the atmosphere is a *gas*.").
   d. Note that in the feedback, students write and/or hear the correct answer to each question twice.
6. If desired, administer a 10-question quiz consisting of 5 multiple-choice and 5 short-answer questions at the end of each session.

Evaluation (Select One or More)

Option 1
1. Compare the class average number of correct responses to teacher questions during science instruction before and after implementation.

Option 2
1. Compare weekly quiz or chapter test grades in science for the entire class before and after implementation.

Option 3
1. Compare the percentage of students with grades of D or F in science before and after implementation.

Variations

1. Use an overhead projector and transparencies to present facts and concepts.
2. Use the overhead projector to display the 10 quiz questions.

Notes

For self-contained classes, have students keep response cards and markers at their desks. For classes that move from room to room for different subjects, collect the response cards and markers at the end of each period and distribute them prior to instruction.

Sources

Gardner, R. III, Heward, W. L., & Grossi, T. A. (1994). Effects of response cards on student participation and academic achievement: A systematic replication with inner-city students during whole-class science instruction. *Journal of Applied Behavior Analysis, 27,* 63–71. Copyright 1994 by the Society for the Experimental Analysis of Behavior. Adapted by permission.

Narayan, J. S., Heward, W. L., Gardner, R. III, Courson, F. H., & Omness, C. K. (1990). Using response cards to increase student participation in an elementary classroom. *Journal of Applied Behavior Analysis, 23,* 483–490. Copyright 1990 by the Society for the Experimental Analysis of Behavior. Adapted by permission.

SUPPLEMENTARY READINGS

Aaron, P. G. (Ed.). (1995). Mini-series: Recent advances in reading instruction and remediation. *School Psychology Review, 24*(3).

This mini-series consists of a state-of-the-art collection of articles reviewing recent research, issues, and controversies in reading assessment and intervention. Articles include overviews on the diagnosis and etiology of reading disabilities and debates between code-oriented and whole-language approaches to reading instruction. An extensive annotated bibliography is provided to direct readers to other useful reading resources.

Aaron, P. G., & Joshi, R. M. (1992). *Reading problems: Consultation and remediation.* New York: Guilford Press.

This book presents an overview of reading problems, assessment, and intervention in the context of an instructional consultation model. Two chapters describe intervention strategies, one focusing on word recognition and spelling and another on vocabulary and comprehension. Also included is a brief survey of software designed to assist reading instruction.

Adams, M. J. (1990). *Beginning to read: Thinking and learning about print.* Cambridge, MA: MIT Press.

This landmark synthesis of research in basic reading processes and reading instruction draws upon the rapidly growing fund of knowledge about phonological awareness to inform discussions of current controversies and issues. The author provides a comprehensive review of the merits and demerits of teaching phonics prior to reading and marshals research to answer the questions of what children need to learn in order to become good readers and what educators can do to prevent reading failure.

Beringer, V. W., & Hooper, S. R. (Eds.). (1993). Mini-series: Preventing and remediating writing disabilities: Interdisciplinary frameworks for assessment, consultation, and intervention. *School Psychology Review, 22*(4).

This mini-series is designed to provide an introduction to the writing process
and writing disabilities for school psychologists with no formal training in the field.
Two articles review writing interventions, including self-regulated strategy development and computer-assisted process-oriented approaches to writing instruction.

Carnine, D. (Ed.). (1984). Mini-series: Educational tools for diverse learners. *School
Psychology Review, 23*(3).

In this mini-series, the focus is on characteristics of effective and ineffective
instructional materials and methodology in the areas of reading, writing, mathematics, social studies, and science. Each article synthesizes research findings
around four curriculum design features that are critical to the success of diverse
learners and serve as guidelines for developing effective instructional tools: big
ideas, explicit strategies, scaffolding, and review.

Kelley, M. L. (1990). *School–home notes: Promoting children's classroom success.* New York:
Guilford Press.

This book reviews the literature on parent- and teacher-managed contingency systems and includes practical guidance on designing and implementing
school–home notes to promote positive classroom adjustment. Several case examples with elementary grade students are included. The book contains a variety of
reproducible handouts for parents and teachers and samples of school–home
notes.

Shapiro, E. S. (1996). *Academic skills problems: Direct assessment and intervention* (2nd
ed.). New York: Guilford Press.
Shapiro, E. S. (1996). *Academic skills problems workbook.* New York: Guilford Press.

The author presents a four-step model of direct academic assessment: (1) assessing the academic environment, (2) determining placement in the curriculum,
(3) designing and implementing instructional modifications, and (4) monitoring
progress. Case examples applying the assessment and intervention strategies are
provided. The companion workbook includes the complete manual for the Behavioral Observation of Students in Schools (BOSS), a classroom observational coding system, and a wealth of reproducible forms and practice exercises.

Shinn, M. R. (Ed.). (1989). *Curriculum-based measurement: Assessing special children.*
New York: Guilford Press.

This guide to curriculum-based measurement (CBM) consists of articles by
the core group of researchers and practitioners who originally developed CBM.
Chapters review procedures for implementing CBM in school settings for a variety of purposes, including identifying academic problems, writing Individualized
Education Plan (IEP) objectives, and evaluating intervention and program effectiveness. One chapter presents a case study illustrating how CBM is used in the
special education decision-making process, from referral to annual review.

CHAPTER 5

♦♦♦

Interventions to Modify Behavior and Enhance Social Competence

♦

OVERVIEW

Dealing with students who display problem behavior is one of the most frequent concerns of teachers (Chalfant & Pysh, 1989; Gallup, 1984; Veenman, 1984). Inappropriate or disruptive behaviors such as getting out of seat, calling out, and failing to comply with teacher directions not only interfere with the ability of the misbehaving student to benefit from instruction but also with the teacher's ability to maintain a productive, orderly environment. In extreme cases, a single behaviorally disordered child can become a "terrorist" who disrupts the learning of all the students in the classroom and wreaks psychological havoc on teachers, peers, and the school community (Rader, 1975). Managing student behavior can be especially difficult for beginning teachers, who have less experience establishing classroom behavior norms and responding to discipline problems. Although consistent use of proactive classroom management strategies helps to minimize opportunities for inappropriate behavior, teachers also need a repertoire of practical techniques for dealing effectively with problem behaviors when they arise. Strategies that enhance on-task behavior and reduce disruptive behavior are especially critical for promoting the academic development of disadvantaged students and other diverse learners, who are already at risk for lower academic engagement rates (Greenwood et al., 1989; Stanley & Greenwood, 1983).

This chapter is divided into three sections: (1) interventions designed to increase on-task behavior and reduce inappropriate behavior in the classroom; (2) interventions for improving behavior in less structured situations, such as the lunchroom, physical education, and the library; and (3) interventions to decrease verbal and physical aggression and increase prosocial behavior. The interventions encompass a broad spectrum of behavioral techniques, including group contingencies, self-management, public posting, response cost, school–home communications, and differential reinforcement of low rates of behavior (DRL). As with the proactive and academic interventions in this book, emphasis is placed on group-oriented strategies that utilize peer influence to encourage appropriate behavior. Many interventions rely on game-like formats in which intraclass teams compete for rewards or privileges delivered for compliance with classroom rules or other positive behaviors. Team-based rather than individually based contingencies are especially helpful for behavior-problem students, who are likely to receive lower rates of reinforcement from teachers and peers under typical classroom reward systems (Forehand & Wierson, 1993). Several interventions train peers to monitor behavior and deliver rewards or include peer-mediated variations that capitalize on the power of peer influence to shape behavior. Using peer-mediated strategies may also increase intervention effectiveness with behavior-problem students, who are often more responsive to peer pressure than to inducements offered by their teachers for behavior improvement.

EVALUATING THE EFFECTIVENESS OF BEHAVIORAL INTERVENTIONS

Many of the evaluation measures for the interventions in this chapter rely on direct observational recording of positive and negative social behaviors, such as the percentages of students displaying on-task, off-task, and disruptive behavior; classwide cooperative play rates; and frequencies of aggressive incidents or rule infractions. Other assessments involve monitoring teacher responses to disruptive or noncompliant behavior, such as number of timeouts or number of reprimands delivered. Because inappropriate and disruptive behavior can severely interfere with learning, methods of measuring academic productivity are also presented for many of the interventions. As in the other chapters, the emphasis is on classwide evaluation methods, although options for monitoring the behavior of individual students or small groups are provided for most strategies.

Gresham and Elliott (1990) have recently developed the Social Skills Rating System (SSRS), a nationally standardized social skills scale with several features that make it useful for designing and evaluating interventions for children with social behavior problems. The SSRS includes teacher, parent, and self-report scales for children and adolescents between 3 and 18 years of age, with norms stratified into three levels: preschool (ages 3–5), elementary (ages 5–12), and secondary (ages 13–18). The SSRS assesses three domains: Social Skills, Problem Behaviors, and Academic Competence. The Social Skills Scale includes five subscales (Cooperation, Assertion, Responsibility, Empathy, and Self-Control), with ratings based on frequency and importance. The Problem Behaviors Scale, which is included only in the teacher and parent forms, measures Externalizing Problems, Internalizing Problems, and Hyperactivity. The Academic Competence Scale includes items assessing reading and math performance, motivation, parental support, and cognitive functioning on a 5-point scale. An innovative feature of the SSRS is an Assessment-Intervention Record (AIR) that provides a method for integrating multirater assessment data, analyzing social skills strengths and weaknesses, and classifying social skills deficits linked to a model for developing intervention plans. A computer-assisted scoring program, which provides behavioral objectives and suggestions for planning interventions, is also available. The SSRS has been demonstrated to be useful in discriminating between mildly disabled and nondisabled students (Gresham & Elliott, 1990), predicting grade promotion and retention (Agostin & Bain, 1997), and evaluating the effectiveness of behavioral consultation for withdrawn children (Sheridan et al., 1990).

INTERVENTIONS TO INCREASE ON-TASK BEHAVIOR AND REDUCE INAPPROPRIATE BEHAVIOR IN THE CLASSROOM

The interventions in this section are designed to increase on-task behavior, such as listening and paying attention, and to reduce off-task behavior, whether passive (e.g., gazing at peers or playing quietly with nonlesson materials) or active (e.g., getting out of seat or calling out). The first three interventions rely on group contingencies in the context of team competitions that enlist peer influence as support for appropriate behavior. By far the most popular interventions in the field testing, they can have rapid and dramatic positive effects on classroom behavior. In *The Good Behavior Game*, probably the best known behavioral intervention in the literature, teams compete to earn rewards or privileges delivered for low levels of rule infractions. *Red Light/Green Light* is a variation of *The Good Behavior Game* that was developed during field testing. Especially useful for prekindergarten and primary grade classes, this strategy provides continuous visual feedback in the form of a "stoplight" that signals the level of student compliance with classroom rules and access to rewards. *The Good Behavior Game Plus Merit* is another variation that permits teams to earn bonus points for designated positive behaviors, a strategy that reduces the likelihood of misbehavior escalating after students realize that they have lost the opportunity to earn reinforcement.

Three interventions target misbehavior with response cost, which involves removing a specific amount of positive reinforcement following the occurrence of the undesired behavior. In *The Response Cost Raffle*, response cost is implemented in the context of a classwide lottery system, whereas in *Countdown to Free Time*, response cost is combined with an innovative visual cuing device to signal access to reinforcers.

Four interventions use public posting to motivate appropriate student behavior. Public posting involves displaying some kind of record, such as a chart or note, that documents student productivity or behavior. Although traditional public posting strategies often record incidents of negative behavior, such as when teachers write the names of misbehaving students on the chalkboard, the interventions included here record positive behavior. *Public Posting to Decrease Disruptive Behavior* is an all-positive intervention that monitors compliance with classroom rules rather than rule infractions. *The Star Chart* enhances on-task behavior by recording and displaying evidence of work completion. Although, like most public posting strategies, it was originally designed to monitor individual student performance, a group-oriented variation that encourages classwide academic productivity has been included. In *Using Peer Monitors to Improve On-Task Behavior*, students work in pairs to monitor their own productivity during independent seatwork while the teacher records positive performance on a classroom chart. Classwide and small-group variations are included for this strategy.

Self-management techniques involve teaching students to engage in some form of behavior, such as self-monitoring or self-evaluation, in an effort to alter a target behavior. Self-management procedures are especially appropriate for interventions targeting inappropriate behavior because self-monitoring not only increases students' sense of control over their own behavior but also increases the likelihood that they will be able to generalize their newly learned competencies to other situations (Shapiro & Cole, 1994). *Reducing Disruptive Behavior with Self-Managed Response Cost* is a contingency-based approach that focuses student attention on the consequences of appropriate and inappropriate behavior. *Self-Managed Behavior Ratings* includes both self-management and self-evaluation techniques, with students matching their own ratings with those of the teacher.

Although parents sometimes protest that they have no control over their children's behavior at school, carefully designed and implemented school–home interventions can exert powerful positive effects on classroom behavior and performance. Moreover, students consistently rate home-based interventions more highly than any other kind of intervention to address classroom behavior problems (Turco & Elliott, 1990). *Reducing Rule Violations with Good Day Awards* uses both school and home contingencies to improve compliance by combining public posting of rule violations in the classroom with an all-positive school–home note for appropriately behaving students. In contrast, *Enhancing the Effectiveness of School–Home Notes with Response Cost* adds a response cost component to enhance the effectiveness of a home–based reinforcement system targeting appropriate classroom behavior.

Theft in the classroom is unfortunately a common problem and can be stressful for teachers and students alike. Surprisingly, there are very few well-controlled studies of interventions that directly target stealing, perhaps because of the difficulties involved in accurately assessing a problem that often occurs outside of teacher observation (Miller & Prinz, 1991). *Group Contingencies to Reduce Stealing*, the only intervention with a classwide focus that could be located for this book, combines differential reinforcement of other behavior (DRO) with response cost and is designed for situations in which teachers are unable to determine which students are stealing in the classroom. Under the DRO condition, reinforcement is delivered to the entire class contingent on the nonoccurrence of stealing.

THE GOOD BEHAVIOR GAME

Overview

The Good Behavior Game is a simple but highly effective intervention that uses team competitiveness to reduce disruptive behavior in the classroom. Students are divided into two teams that compete for rewards or privileges, based on which team receives the fewer number of demerits for rule infractions. If both teams receive fewer than a predetermined number of demerits, both teams earn the reward. Critical components in reducing disruptive behavior appear to be the assignment of consequences, the criteria set for winning, and the division of students into teams. Direct feedback alone, that is, placing marks on the chalkboard for breaking class rules, does not affect behavior. Included here is a response cost variation, in which teams are awarded a set number of points at the beginning of the game that are deducted for rule infractions. The intervention has been successfully implemented in regular elementary grade classrooms and classes for emotionally disturbed adolescents.

Purpose

To reduce disruptive classroom behavior using a team competition strategy.

Materials

1. Posterboard chart displaying classroom rules, such as:
    a. Talk only when you have the teacher's permission.
    b. Stay in your seat unless you have permission to get up.

   c. Keep from disturbing others.

   d. Be polite and kind to others.

2. Posterboard chart or section of the chalkboard divided into two sections designated "Team 1" and "Team 2," listing team members' names, if desired, with a column for each day of the week

3. Stars or stickers (optional)

4. Victory tags, consisting of name tags with adhesive backs or circles of colored construction paper with "winner" stickers affixed to them and threaded with yarn, to be worn around the neck (optional)

Observation (Select One or Both)

Option 1

1. Select an instructional period during which students are the least productive and the most disruptive.

2. Using a *Classwide Scanning Form* with a 3- or 5-minute interval, scan the room at the end of each interval, starting with the front of the room and ending with the back, and tally the number of students in each of the following behavior categories:

   a. *On-task behavior*, defined as asking or answering lesson-oriented questions, writing when requested, looking at the teacher during presentations, and any other behavior relevant to the lesson;

   b. *Off-task behavior*, defined as sitting without having appropriate materials at hand, looking at nonlesson materials, and looking around the room after assignments have been made;

   c. *Disruptive behavior*, defined as any behavior disrupting instruction or the on-task behavior of other students, such as inappropriate verbal or motor behavior, failing to follow directions, and aggression.

3. Conduct these observations for 30 to 45 minutes for 4 to 7 days.

Option 2

1. Using a *Group Event Recording Form*, record the frequencies of two or three disruptive behaviors, such as getting out of seat, name calling, and failing to follow directions, during a selected instructional period for a small group of students or the entire class for 4 to 7 days.

Procedure

1. Select an instructional period during which students are especially disruptive and unproductive.

2. Introduce the intervention by telling students that they will be playing a game to help everyone get more out of the subject during which the game will be played.

3. Explain and demonstrate the following procedures, including the criterion for the maximum number of demerits permitted to earn the reward and rewards for the winning team(s), such as wearing victory tags for the rest of the day, extra recess, lining up first for lunch, or extra computer time. If both teams

win, possible rewards include viewing a videotape, 15 minutes of free time, homework passes, or a special art project at the end of the day. If desired, also permit team members to put a star or sticker beside their names on a chart posted at the front of the room.

4. Divide the class into two teams. Be sure to divide disruptive students between the teams. For convenience, use rows or desk groupings to assign teams. Allowing teams to select names fosters team spirit and facilitates encouraging or reprimanding the teams.

5. Display a chart or a section of the chalkboard visible to all students with "Team 1" and "Team 2" (or the names of the teams) written on it. Review the classroom rules at the beginning of the game and record a demerit beside the team name each time any member of a team breaks a rule.

6. Tally demerits at the end of the instructional period and declare the team with the fewer number of demerits as the winner. If neither team exceeds the predetermined limit, both teams are winners.

7. Gradually lower the limit for demerits or extend the period during which the game is played.

8. Initially, deliver rewards daily and then fade them to once a week. Record the number of demerits earned daily by each team on a chart or a section of the chalkboard and deliver the reward to teams meeting the criterion on 4 out of 5 days.

9. Occasionally, chronically disruptive or unproductive students will declare that they do not want to play the game and will deliberately violate the rules. If this occurs, explain that it is not fair to penalize an entire team because one member will not control himself or herself. Create a third team consisting of the problem student or students and add a negative contingency. For example, require any losing teams to remain 5 minutes after school or deduct 5 minutes of recess for each mark scored over the criterion.

10. If desired, expand the game to other instructional periods after students become accustomed to the procedure.

Evaluation (Select One or Both)

Option 1
1. Compare the classwide percentages of students exhibiting on-task, off-task, and disruptive behavior before and after implementation.

Option 2
1. Compare the frequencies of the target disruptive behaviors for the small group of students or the entire class before and after implementation.

Variations

Variation 1
1. Begin the target period with a certain number of credits per team, such as 10.
2. Set a minimum criterion for winning, such as five credits.

3. Remove one credit each time a member of a team breaks the rules.
4. Deliver the reward to teams that meet or exceed the criterion. If both teams meet or exceed the criterion, both teams are winners.

Variation 2
1. For a variation of this intervention specifically designed for use in special classes, see *Improving Media Center Behavior with the Good Behavior Game*.

Notes

1. If students are seated by tables rather than at individual desks, creating as many teams as there are tables facilitates monitoring demerits or credits and delivering rewards.
2. Teachers sometimes express concern about monitoring only inappropriate behavior. In that event, *The Good Behavior Game Plus Merit*, which provides bonuses for appropriate behavior, can be substituted.
3. Field testing suggests that the response cost variation (Variation 1) that removes credits for misbehavior is more effective than the original procedure of recording demerits.

Sources

Barrish, H. H., Saunders, M., & Wolf, M. M. (1969). Good behavior game: Effects of individual contingencies for group consequences on disruptive behavior in a classroom. *Journal of Applied Behavior Analysis, 2,* 119–124. Copyright 1969 by the Society for the Experimental Analysis of Behavior. Adapted by permission.

Harris, V. W., & Sherman, J. A. (1973). Use and analysis of the "good behavior game" to reduce disruptive classroom behavior. *Journal of Applied Behavior Analysis, 6,* 405–417. Copyright 1973 by the Society for the Experimental Analysis of Behavior. Adapted by permission.

RED LIGHT/GREEN LIGHT

Overview

This adaptation of *The Good Behavior Game* provides continuous visual cues to encourage appropriate academic and social behavior in the context of a group-oriented contingency system. Providing visual cues for behavior is especially helpful for young children, who often have difficulty attending to oral directions. Field testing indicates that this strategy is effective in increasing academic productivity as well as reducing off-task and disruptive behavior in prekindergarten and primary grade classrooms.

Purpose

To reduce off-task and disruptive behavior by combining visual cues for appropriate behavior with group-oriented contingencies.

Materials

1. Posterboard chart with a list of classroom rules, such as:
   a. Raise your hand to talk.
   b. Stay in your seat unless you have permission to get up.
   c. Be kind and helpful to others.
   d. Use inside voices to talk.
2. This intervention requires a flannelboard or posterboard chart and red, yellow, and green flannel or paper circles, three sets per team. Display a rating grid on the flannelboard or chart as follows:
   a. Use flannel or paper strips to create a grid with three rows (one for each color) and three or four columns.
   b. In the first column of the grid, list as many numbers as there are teams.
   c. Place a set of colored flannel or paper circles near the flannelboard or chart. Tape will be needed to affix the paper circles to the chart.
   d. Alternatively, create a "stoplight" from flannel or construction paper for each team to which circles can be affixed. (Thanks to Kathy Mang, prekindergarten teacher at Immaculate Conception School, for this variation.)
3. Stickers, "Good Day" awards (see *Reducing Rule Violations with Good Day Awards*), or victory tags, consisting of circles of colored construction paper with or without "winner" stickers, hung around the neck with yarn (optional)

Observation (Select One or More)

Option 1
1. Select an instructional period during which students are the least productive and the most disruptive.
2. Using a *Classwide Scanning Form* with a 3-, 5-, or 10-minute interval, scan the room at the end of each interval, starting with the front of the room and ending with the back, and tally the number of students who are either on-task or off-task as follows:
   a. *On-task behavior* is defined as working on the task or activity at hand, looking at the teacher during presentations, and any other behavior relevant to the lesson or activity.
   b. *Off-task behavior* is defined as sitting without having appropriate materials at hand, looking at noninstructional materials, or any behavior disrupting the on-task behavior of other students, such as inappropriate verbal or motor behaviors.
3. Conduct these observations for 30 to 45 minutes for 4 to 7 days.

Option 2
1. Using a *Group Event Recording Form*, tally the number of disruptive behaviors during one or more periods for the entire class or a group of selected students for 4 to 7 days. *Disruptive behaviors* are defined as verbal or physical aggression, noncompliance, or any other behaviors that interfere with the on-task behavior of other students.

Option 3
1. Record percent correct scores on daily classwork assignments for the entire class or a group of selected students in one or more academic areas for 5 to 10 days.

Procedure

1. Select a time for implementation, such as the morning work period or an instructional period when students are especially unproductive and disruptive.
2. Divide the class into two or more teams. If the students are seated at tables, use tables as teams. Be sure to distribute the most disruptive students among teams.
3. Explain to the students that they will be playing a game during that period to help everyone get the most out of that subject or activity.
4. Post the list of classroom rules and lead a discussion of the purpose of each rule.
5. Explain that you will be observing the teams and using the flannel board, chart, or stoplights to rate their behavior as follows:
   a. Teams following the rules receive a green light ("GO"), indicating that they should continue their good behavior.
   b. Teams that break a rule receive a yellow light ("WARNING"), indicating that they are being warned to stop the inappropriate behavior.
   c. Teams that continue to break a rule or display any aggressive behaviors receive a red light ("STOP").
   d. Teams ending the rating period on green are winners.
   e. All teams can win or lose.
6. Begin the game by placing a green circle in the first column of the rating grid next to each team number or on each stoplight. Every 20 to 30 minutes, or at the end of an activity, rate each team's behavior by attaching a circle to the grid or stoplight.
7. Briefly state why each team is receiving that particular rating. If the rating is unchanged, state why the rating is the same. If a team or team member displays any aggressive behavior or highly disruptive behavior before the regular rating time, immediately change the rating for that team.
8. Teams ending the rating period on green receive rewards at the end of the day or at the end of the period, such as victory tags, stickers, extra recess, or lining up first for lunch, recess, or dismissal.

Evaluation (Select One or More)

Option 1
1. Compare classwide percentages of students displaying on-task and off-task behavior during the selected period before and after implementation.

Option 2
1. Compare the frequency of disruptive behaviors for the entire class or for the target students during the selected period(s) before and after implementation.

Option 3

1. Compare percent correct scores on daily classwork assignments for the entire class or the group of selected students in one or more academic areas before and after implementation.

Variations

1. To encourage rapid transitions between activities, add a rule about transitions (e.g., "Make quick and quiet transitions") and rate teams on those behaviors as well.
2. Reward winning teams with principal attention (see *Encouraging Academic Achievement with Principal Praise*).

Notes

1. Victory tags are especially valued as reinforcers by young children and make practical rewards because they can be reused.
2. During the field testing, many teachers have found this strategy so effective and easy to implement that they use it throughout the school day.

Sources

Barrish, H. H., Saunders, M., & Wolf, M. M. (1969). Good behavior game: Effects of individual contingencies for group consequences on disruptive behavior in a classroom. *Journal of Applied Behavior Analysis, 2*, 119–124. Copyright 1969 by the Society for the Experimental Analysis of Behavior. Adapted by permission.

Harris, V. W., & Sherman, J. A. (1973). Use and analysis of the "good behavior game" to reduce disruptive classroom behavior. *Journal of Applied Behavior Analysis, 6*, 405–417. Copyright 1973 by the Society for the Experimental Analysis of Behavior. Adapted by permission.

THE GOOD BEHAVIOR GAME PLUS MERIT

Overview

This intervention, a variation of *The Good Behavior Game*, combines group contingencies for reducing disruptive behavior with a bonus for positive academic or social behavior. It is especially useful with students who become discouraged or argumentative when corrected because the opportunity to remove demerits and regain access to rewards is built into the procedure. The strategy has been successful not only in reducing disruptive behavior but also in improving assignment completion and increasing active participation for behaviorally disordered students in regular classroom placements. A response cost variation is included in which teams are awarded a set number of credits that are subsequently deducted for rule infractions.

Purpose

To reduce disruptive behavior and increase academic productivity by encouraging positive team competition.

Materials

1. Posterboard chart with a list of classroom rules, such as:
   a. Raise your hand and wait to be recognized when you want to talk.
   b. Keep from making too much noise.
   c. Stay in your seat unless you have permission to get up.
   d. Keep from moving around too much while seated.
   e. Keep from tattling on other students.
2. Posterboard chart or section of the chalkboard listing the ways students can earn merit points, such as completing work at 75% accuracy or better, being especially polite and helpful, and participating actively in class discussions
3. 100–200 3″ × 5″ index cards with the words "one merit" printed on each

Observation (Select One or More)

Option 1
1. Record percent correct scores on classwork assignments for the entire class or a small group of students during a selected instructional period for 5 to 10 days or for several weeks.

Option 2
1. Using a sheet of paper attached to a clipboard, record the frequency of active classroom participation for the entire class or a small group of students during a selected instructional period for 5 to 10 days. *Active classroom participation* is defined as giving a correct answer in response to a teacher-initiated question or contributing an appropriate statement or question to class discussion.

Option 3
1. Using a *Classwide Scanning Form* with a 3-, 5-, or 10-minute interval, scan the room, starting with the front and ending with the back, and tally the number of students exhibiting on-task, off-task, and disruptive behavior as defined below.
   a. *On-task behavior* is defined as working on the task at hand, looking at the teacher during presentations, and any other behavior relevant to the lesson.
   b. *Off-task behavior* is defined as sitting without having appropriate materials at hand, looking at noninstructional materials, and looking around the room after assignments have been made.
   c. *Disruptive behavior* is defined as any behavior disrupting the on-task behavior of other students, such as inappropriate verbal or motor behaviors.
2. Conduct these observations during a selected instructional period for 30 to 45 minutes for 4 to 7 days.

Option 4

1. Using a sheet of paper attached to a clipboard, record the number of classroom rule infractions during a selected instructional period for the entire class or a group of the most disruptive students for 4 to 7 days.

Procedure

1. Select a time for implementation, such as the period when students are most disruptive, least productive, and/or participate least often in class discussions.
2. Divide the class into two teams. Be sure to distribute the most disruptive students between teams. If desired, have the teams select names.
3. Set a criterion for winning the game, such as no more than five demerits.
4. Explain to the students that they will be playing a game during the period to help everyone get the most out of that subject.
5. Explain the game, review the classroom rules, and post the charts listing the classroom rules and ways to earn merit points.
6. In a section of the chalkboard visible to all students, write "Team 1" and "Team 2" (or the names of the teams) and record a demerit beside the team name every time any member of a team breaks a rule.
7. During the selected period, give merit cards to students who display the designated positive behaviors. At the end of the period, have students hold up their merit cards for you to count. Erase one demerit from the chalkboard for every five merits earned by a team. Collect the merit cards for future use.
8. Teams earning less than five demerits receive rewards at the end of the period or the end of the day, such as 10 minutes of free time, time to listen to tapes, homework passes, or extra recess. Both teams can win or lose.

Evaluation (Select One or More)

Option 1

1. Compare percent correct scores on classwork assignments for the entire class or the target students during the selected instructional period before and after implementation.

Option 2

1. Compare the frequency of active classroom participation for the entire class or the target students during the selected instructional period before and after implementation.

Option 3

1. Compare classwide percentages of students exhibiting on-task, off-task, and disruptive behavior during the selected instructional period before and after implementation.

Option 4

1. Compare the frequency of rule infractions for the entire class or the group of the most disruptive students during the selected instructional period before and after implementation.

Variations

Variation 1
1. Begin the period with a certain number of credits per team, such as 10.
2. Set a minimum criterion for winning, such as five credits.
3. Remove one credit each time a member of a team breaks the rules.
4. Restore one credit for every five merit points earned.
5. Deliver rewards or privileges to teams that have the designated number of credits remaining at the end of the implementation period. If both teams meet or exceed the predetermined criterion, both teams are winners.

Variation 2
1. Combine this intervention with *Teaching Transition Time* by awarding merit points for making quick and quiet transitions between activities.

Variation 3
1. Instead of distributing merit cards for positive behavior, record merit points in the form of "plus" marks (+) on the chalkboard next to team names. Erase one demerit for every five earned merits.

Variation 4
1. As behavior improves, post the winning team(s) for an entire week and give a reward to teams meeting the criterion for 4 out of 5 days. Or use principal attention (see *Encouraging Academic Achievement with Principal Praise*) as a Friday reward for teams achieving this level of performance.

Note

This has been one of the most popular interventions in the field testing. Teachers find it very easy to use and often develop their own creative variations. Most teachers prefer to record merit points on the chalkboard rather than to distribute merit cards. As with *The Good Behavior Game*, the response cost variation (Variation 1) appears to be more effective than the original.

Source

Darveaux, D. X. (1984). The good behavior game plus merit: Controlling disruptive behavior and improving student motivation. *School Psychology Review, 13,* 510–514. Copyright 1984 by the National Association of School Psychologists. Adapted by permission.

THE RESPONSE COST RAFFLE

Overview

This intervention combines a response cost procedure with a classroom raffle system to reduce disruptive behavior. Although the target of this intervention is inappropriate behavior, removing "raffle tickets" for lack of progress on assignments and emphasizing to students that they must work on classroom tasks can also have positive effects on academic performance. Originally implemented with small groups of elementary and junior high school students in regular education and resource room settings, it is adapted here for classwide use.

Purpose

To decrease disruptive behavior by providing opportunities to earn rewards for appropriate classroom behavior.

Materials

1. *Reinforcement Menus*, one per student (optional)
2. Posterboard chart with a list of rewards or "raffle prizes"
3. Slips of paper or "raffle tickets" with student names printed on them, five per student per day
4. Box with top for raffle tickets
5. Tape, if desired, for taping tickets to student desks
6. Raffle prizes, such as candy bars, bubble gum, homework passes, fast food certificates, and inexpensive school supplies
7. Slips of colored construction paper, five per student table, with a different color for each table (see Variation 2)
8. Plastic or paper cups, one per student table (see Variation 2)

Observation (Select One or Both)

1. Calculate the average percentage of classwork completed by the entire class during a selected instructional period for 5 to 10 days by calculating the percentage completion rate for each student, summing those rates, and then dividing by the total number of students.
2. Using a *Group Event Recording Form*, record the frequency of three or four disruptive behaviors (calling out, being out of seat, verbal aggression, throwing objects, etc.) that occur during a selected instructional period for 4 to 7 days.

Procedure

1. Explain to students that they will be playing a raffle to help them get more out of their studies during a selected instructional period. Explain the target behaviors that you wish to decrease (calling out, getting out of seat, etc.) and the behaviors you wish to increase (working quietly, being polite to others, etc.).
2. Using *Reinforcement Menus* if desired, help students develop a list of raffle prizes and write the list of rewards on the chart.
3. Explain the raffle procedure, and have the students role play how to behave when a raffle ticket is removed.
4. At the beginning of the selected instructional period, give students five "raffle

tickets" (slips of paper with their names on them), and have them place or tape the tickets on their desks.

5. Whenever a student engages in an undesired target behavior, state what the specific misbehavior is and remove the ticket.
6. If a student responds negatively to the removal of a ticket, remove another ticket. Do this as long as the student responds inappropriately. If the student continues to behave inappropriately and has no tickets left, deliver some negative consequence, such as requiring the student to complete a "Solving My Own Problems Essay" (see *Eliminating Disruptive Lunchroom Behavior with Mediation Essays*) or taking away recess time.
7. Five minutes before the end of the period, collect all tickets remaining on students' desks. Write "group" on two of these tickets, indicating that the entire class wins a prize if one of these tickets is chosen.
8. Place all the tickets in a box.
9. On Friday of each week, conduct the raffle by drawing one ticket from the box and declaring the winner.
10. The winner selects a prize from the posted list of individual rewards.
11. If a group ticket is chosen, the winning student selects from group prizes, such as a classroom game, popcorn party, music time, free time, or a video or movie.
12. Discard the rest of the tickets and begin the raffle procedure again at the beginning of the next class period during which the raffle is in operation.

Evaluation (Select One or Both)

1. Compare the average percentage of classwork completed by the entire class during the selected instructional period before and after implementation.
2. Compare the frequency of disruptive behaviors during the selected instructional period before and after implementation.

Variations

Variation 1
1. Conduct the raffle on a daily rather than weekly basis.

Variation 2
1. For students seated at tables rather than individual desks, place a plastic or paper cup containing five colored tickets on each table, with a different color for each table. Different colors are used to prevent students from taking other teams' tickets to replace their own.
2. Remove a ticket for each incident of misbehavior as described above.
3. At the end of the period, place all remaining tickets in the box and add two tickets of a different color to serve as group tickets. Being careful not to look at the box (to avoid seeing the ticket colors), draw a ticket.
4. Deliver the reward to all members of the team whose ticket is drawn or to the entire class, if one of the group tickets is drawn.

Notes

1. Although neither of the original research studies reported negative student reactions to the withdrawal of tickets, negative responses were occasionally observed during field testing. Modeling appropriate responses to ticket removal when the intervention is introduced and consistently delivering consequences if students display inappropriate reactions help to ensure smooth implementation.
2. To facilitate ticket making, have students write their names on five slips of paper at the beginning of the period. Or have students write their names five times on a sheet of paper that can be duplicated and cut into tickets for future use.

Sources

Proctor, M. A., & Morgan, D. (1991). Effectiveness of a response cost raffle procedure on the disruptive classroom behavior of adolescents with behavior problems. *School Psychology Review*, *20*, 97–109. Copyright 1991 by the National Association of School Psychologists. Adapted by permission.

Witt, J. C., & Elliott, S. N. (1982). The response cost lottery: A time efficient and effective classroom intervention. *Journal of School Psychology*, *20*, 155–161. Copyright 1982 by Elsevier Science, Ltd, Oxford, England. Adapted by permission.

COUNTDOWN TO FREE TIME

Overview

A wide variety of strategies have been used to modify the behavior of children with Attention-Deficit/Hyperactivity Disorder (ADHD). Traditional behavior therapy methods as well as contingency management interventions for ADHD youngsters often require extensive teacher training, special equipment, and high adult–child ratios. This intervention is designed to reduce off-task behavior and improve academic productivity by combining a simple response cost procedure with a novel visual cuing device in the form of a flip chart. In the original study, one target student used a flip chart similar to the teacher's chart to monitor his own behavior, while the second target student viewed a desktop electronic counter with a digital display that was activated by the teacher. In this classwide adaptation, students use index cards to match teacher ratings.

Purpose

To increase on-task behavior in students with attentional problems with a response cost procedure.

Materials

1. Flip chart on stand or easel
2. 21 posterboard cards or large sheets of paper numbered in descending order from 20 to 0, with the numerals large enough to be visible to all students, with holes punched in them and hung on the flip chart

3. 3″ × 5″ index cards, one per student per period of implementation
4. Tape

Observation (Select One or More)

Option 1
1. Select an instructional period during which students are especially inattentive and disruptive, such as morning seatwork.
2. Using a *Classwide Scanning Form* with a 5-minute interval, scan the room at the end of each interval, starting with the front of the room, and tally the number of students who are either on-task or off-task as follows:
   a. *On-task behavior* is defined as attending to the assignment or activity.
   b. *Off-task behavior* is defined as visual nonattention to the assignment, unless the student is talking to the teacher or has a hand raised.
3. Conduct these observations for 20 to 30 minutes for 4 to 7 days.

Option 2
1. Using a *Group Event Recording Form*, tally the number of out of seats or call-outs for the entire class or a small group of students during the selected instructional period for 4 to 7 days.

Option 3
1. Record percent correct scores for classwork during the selected instructional period for the entire class or a small group of students for 5 to 10 days.

Procedure

1. Display the flip chart with the number 20 showing and tell students that they can earn up to 20 minutes of free time for working hard during the selected instructional period.
2. Explain that you will be looking around the room at regular intervals. If you see that all students are working on their assignments, you will not subtract any time. If one or more students is not working, however, you will flip a card over on the chart to indicate that 1 minute of free time has been lost.
3. Distribute the index cards and have students tape the cards to the top of their desks. Demonstrate how to print the numerals from 20 to 0 in descending order on the cards and help students number their cards.
4. Tell students that during the target period they should occasionally look at the flip chart and the number displayed and cross off numbers on their own charts to match the class chart. Demonstrate how to check the class chart and mark student cards.
5. Review rules and procedures for the free-time period. For example, students may talk quietly, draw, read books brought from home, listen to music, work in centers, or work on the classroom computers.
6. Conduct the instructional period as usual. If you are working with a small group while other students are completing independent seatwork, place the

chart next to the small-group table or activity so that you can flip cards without having to walk to the front of the room.

7. At the end of the target period, praise the class for working hard and award the amount of free time corresponding to the number displayed on the chart.

Evaluation (Select One or More)

Option 1
1. Compare classwide percentages of students displaying on-task and off-task behavior during the selected instructional period before and after implementation.

Option 2
1. Compare the frequency of out of seats or call-outs for the entire class or the small group of students during the selected instructional period before and after implementation.

Option 3
1. Compare percent correct scores for classwork completed during the selected instructional period for the entire class or the small group of students before and after implementation.

Variations

Variation 1
1. Instead of using a flip chart, list numbers from 20 to 0 on the chalkboard, and cross off a number in descending order each time you reprimand a student for unproductive or disruptive behavior.
2. Award the amount of free time corresponding to the highest number remaining on the board.

Variation 2
1. List numbers from 20 to 0 on the chalkboard, with the highest number corresponding to the minutes usually allowed for recess time.
2. Cross off a number each time you reprimand a student for unproductive or disruptive behavior.
3. Award the number of minutes of recess corresponding to the highest number remaining at the end of the period.

Notes

1. Teachers in the field testing have preferred Variation 2 for use during morning seatwork and small-group instruction.
2. In the original study, the response cost contingency with a free-time reinforcer was superior to Ritalin in improving academic productivity and on-task behavior in target students.

Source

Rapport, M. D., Murphy, H. A., & Bailey, J. S. (1982). Ritalin vs. response cost in the control of hyperactive children: A within-subject comparison. *Journal of Applied Behavior Analysis, 15,* 205–216. Copyright 1982 by the Society for the Experimental Analysis of Behavior. Adapted by permission.

PUBLIC POSTING TO DECREASE DISRUPTIVE BEHAVIOR

Overview

This all-positive intervention uses an independent group contingency system to decrease inappropriate behavior. Students accumulate points toward weekly rewards by displaying prosocial behaviors during specific time intervals. This strategy is especially useful for self-contained classes or classes organized in "blocks" because monitoring intervals are set at 45 minutes. It also provides a systematic basis for awarding conduct grades because the frequencies of the target social behaviors are recorded as part of the intervention procedures.

Purpose

To decrease off-task and disruptive behavior with an all-positive independent group contingency system.

Materials

1. *Reinforcement Menus,* one per student
2. Kitchen timer or wristwatch with buzzer or alarm
3. Posterboard chart listing the classroom rules; rules should consist of prosocial behaviors that are incompatible with the undesired target behaviors, such as:
   a. Raise your hand to get permission to speak.
   b. Stay in your seat without disturbing others.
   c. Pay attention in class.
   d. Finish all your work.
4. Posterboard chart listing student names, with columns for recording checks
5. 8½" × 11" sheet of paper listing student names and attached to a clipboard (optional)
6. Posterboard chart or section of the chalkboard with a list of rewards (optional)

Observation (Select One or Both)

1. Using a sheet of paper attached to a clipboard, record the number of inappropriate behaviors displayed by the entire class or a small group of the most disruptive students during a selected instructional period for 4 to 7 days. *Inappropriate behaviors* are defined as talking without permission during lessons and independent work, getting out of seat without permission, not paying attention

to teacher presentations, failing to work on class assignments, and disturbing others.

2. Using a sheet of paper attached to a clipboard, record the number of reprimands you deliver to the entire class or a small group of the most disruptive students during a selected instructional period for 4 to 7 days.

Procedure

1. Display the charts with the classroom rules and student names where all students can easily see them. Review the rules and explain that you will be placing checks at regular intervals next to the names of students who are following the rules during the selected instructional period(s).
2. Using *Reinforcement Menus*, help students generate a list of rewards, ranked in order of preference, such as listening to tapes, having a popcorn party, watching a video, or having free time. Write the list on the chalkboard or on a posterboard chart.
3. Divide the time during which the intervention will be used into 45-minute intervals. (For the entire school day, this will be about seven intervals.)
4. Set the timer or your wristwatch to go off every 45 minutes. If desired, attach a sheet of paper listing the classroom rules and student names to a clipboard and carry it with your teaching materials. Transfer checks to the public classroom chart at a convenient time.
5. Record behavior as follows:
   a. If a student has followed at least two of the rules during the interval, put a check by his or her name on the chart.
   b. Only one check can be earned per interval.
   c. Each student can earn a maximum of seven checks daily (one for each of the intervals).
6. Set an initial criterion for earning the reward, such as five checks daily on 4 out of 5 days.
7. Help students select a reward at the beginning of the week, and award the chosen reinforcement on Fridays to students who meet the criterion. Students who do not achieve the criterion must continue working on their academic tasks.
8. As student behavior improves, gradually raise the criterion for earning the reward.

Evaluation (Select One or Both)

1. Compare the frequency of inappropriate behaviors displayed by the entire class or the small group of the most disruptive students during the selected instructional period before and after implementation.
2. Compare the frequency of reprimands delivered to the entire class or the small group of the most disruptive students during the selected instructional period before and after implementation.

Variation

Use the intervention only during morning seatwork and reduce the monitoring interval to about 15 to 20 minutes, depending on the length of the seatwork period.

Notes

1. Activity rewards, such as watching videos or having a popcorn party, are especially appropriate for this intervention but are most easily delivered if students who failed to meet the criterion can be supervised elsewhere. If two or more teachers share responsibility for a group of students, as in "block" teaching, students not achieving the criterion can be sent to another classroom to work on academic tasks while the rest participate in the rewarding activity.
2. In the original study, students sometimes became disruptive when they realized that they had failed to earn a check during an interval and when they realized they had lost the opportunity to earn the weekly reward. To prevent the possible escalation of misbehavior under these circumstances, provide a negative consequence for disruptive behavior, such as 10 minutes subtracted from recess.

Source

Brantley, D. C., & Webster, R. E. (1993). Use of an independent group contingency management system in a regular classroom setting. *Psychology in the Schools, 30,* 60–66. Copyright 1993 by John Wiley & Sons, Inc. Adapted by permission.

THE STAR CHART

Overview

Chronically disruptive students can severely interfere with the academic productivity of other pupils and create a negative classroom climate. Rather than targeting disruptive behavior directly, this intervention reduces it by reinforcing completion of academic work. Students earn free time at the end of an instructional period by completing classwork at a predetermined level of accuracy. Posting stars for work completion on a publicly displayed chart adds visual reinforcement for positive behavior. In the original study, both independent and interdependent group contingencies were successful in reducing the disruptive behavior of remedial reading middle school students, with the interdependent contingency being slightly more effective. Because students and teachers strongly preferred the independent contingency, however, the interdependent format is presented as a variation.

Purpose

To reduce disruptive behavior and increase academic productivity using a free-time contingency.

Materials

1. Posterboard chart listing each student's name down the left-hand side, with columns for the days of the week
2. Gold stars or stickers

Observation (Select One or Both)

Option 1
1. Select an instructional period during which students are especially unproductive and disruptive.
2. Using a *Classwide Scanning Form* with a 5-minute interval, scan the room at the end of each interval, starting with the front of the room and ending with the back, and tally the number of students with appropriate or inappropriate behavior as follows:
   a. *Appropriate behavior* is defined as being seated or at the chalkboard and doing assigned work.
   b. *Inappropriate behavior* is defined at being out of seat, talking to peers, calling out, and any other behavior that cannot be classified as appropriate.
3. Conduct observations for 30 to 45 minutes for 4 to 7 days.

Option 2
1. Using a *Group Event Recording Form*, tally the number of target disruptive behaviors (e.g., out of seats, call-outs, verbal and physical aggression) for the entire class during a selected instructional period.
2. Conduct these observations for 30 to 45 minutes for 4 to 7 days.

Procedure

1. Select an instructional period during which students are especially disruptive and unproductive.
2. Tell the students that they are going to have an opportunity to earn free time at the end of the period for working hard during the rest of the time.
3. Tell students to bring their classwork to you for checking when they complete it. Students who get most of the problems or exercises correct will be permitted to put a star next to their names on the chart.
4. Explain that beginning about 10 minutes before the end of the period (or some appropriate length of time), every student who has earned a star will receive free time for the rest of the period.
5. Discuss with students permissible activities during free time, such as going to the media center, drawing, working in centers, and using classroom computers.
6. Tell the students that those who do not earn a star will have to continue working and will not receive free time.
7. At regular intervals during the work period, remind students of the free-time contingency and encourage them to work hard.
8. At the end of the work period, read the names of the students who have received stars, and award free time accordingly.

Evaluation (Select One or Both)

Option 1

1. Compare classwide percentages of students displaying appropriate and inappropriate behavior during the selected instructional period before and after implementation.

Option 2

1. Compare the frequency of target disruptive behaviors for the entire class during the selected instructional period before and after implementation.

Variation

Follow the procedure as described above but explain to students that they must work together as a group to earn free time. If every student earns a star during the work period, the whole class will receive free time for the rest of the period. If anyone fails to earn a star, all students will have to continue working and will not receive any free time. Because some pupil harassment was observed during the interdependent group contingency in the original study, demonstrate and have students role play examples of positive peer support for work completion. If desired, provide a negative consequence for peer harassment, such as loss of access to free time for the harassing student for the following day or the rest of the week.

Note

This intervention depends on the teacher's ability to check assignments during the class period in order to award the stars and free time accurately. In the original study, an aide was present to assist with checking. If an aide is not available, use this intervention in conjunction with *Checking Stations* to facilitate rapid checking of assignments. Alternatively, award stars for work completion only and deliver a longer free-time period at the end of the week for students who achieve a predetermined level of accuracy on the first 4 days' assignments.

Source

Page, D. P., & Edwards, R. P. (1978). Behavior change strategies for reducing disruptive classroom behavior. *Psychology in the Schools, 15*, 413–418. Copyright 1978 by John Wiley & Sons, Inc. Adapted by permission.

USING PEER MONITORS TO IMPROVE ON-TASK BEHAVIOR

Overview

Peer-mediated interventions offer several advantages over traditional contingency management strategies, including increased freedom from supervision for teachers and enhanced feelings of competence and self-control for students. In this intervention, students earn points from peer monitors for productive behavior during independent seatwork, with the roles of peer monitor and peer earner alternated every other day. The strategy is effective in reducing off-task and disruptive behavior and increasing work completion rates regardless of whether students serve as peer monitors or point earners. Originally implemented with two target students and three peer partners in a fifth-grade mathematics class, it has been adapted here for classwide use.

Purpose

To reduce inappropriate behavior and increase academic productivity through peer monitoring of classroom behavior.

Materials

1. Posterboard chart listing student names, with columns for displaying points earned per day
2. $8\frac{1}{2}'' \times 11''$ sheets of paper printed with the "Good Behavior Checklist" and "Good Work Checklist," one per student pair per day (see Figure 5.1)

Observation (Select One or Both)

1. Using a sheet of paper attached to a clipboard, tally the number of reprimands delivered to the entire class or a small group of the least productive students during an independent seatwork period for 4 to 7 days.
2. Record percent correct scores on assignments during an independent seatwork period for the entire class or a small group of the least productive students for 5 to 10 days.

Procedure

1. Tell the students that they are going to learn an exciting and rewarding way of helping each other to do better in their studies during the seatwork period.
2. Conduct a training session that includes a demonstration of the peer monitoring procedures, appropriate student behaviors during peer monitoring, and how to record points on the classroom chart. Have students practice the monitoring procedures as described below and provide feedback and praise.
3. Divide the students into pairs. Explain that one student is a peer monitor and the other a point earner.
4. Explain that both peer monitors and point earners are responsible for completing their own class assignments.
5. Three times at unpredictable intervals during the target period, have the peer monitors complete the Good Behavior Checklist and review it with the point earners.
6. At the end of the period, have peer monitors evaluate their partners' work by counting the number of "yes" responses earned on the Good Behavior Checklist. Also have peer monitors complete the Good Work Checklist and record the total number of "yes" responses for both checklists.
7. If the point earners meet the criterion (12/15 "yes" responses), have the mon-

itors record a point next to their names on the chart posted at the front of the classroom.

8. Do not provide feedback to peer monitors regarding the accuracy of their evaluations. Instead, instruct them to set a good example for the point earners, and thank them each day for completing their monitor duties.
9. Alternate peer monitor and point earner roles every other day.
10. Periodically review peer monitor ratings, and talk privately with students whose ratings appear to be inaccurate.
11. After four sessions of serving as point earners, students may exchange their points for a reward, such as free time, listening to tapes, homework passes, or using classroom computers. To earn the reward, point earners must meet the criterion number of daily points for three of the four sessions.

Evaluation (Select One or Both)

1. Compare the frequency of reprimands delivered to the entire class or the small group of the least productive students during the independent seatwork period before and after implementation.
2. Compare percent correct scores on assignments completed during the independent seatwork period for the entire class or the small group of the least productive students before and after implementation.

Variations

Variation 1
1. Require every point earner in the class to meet the criterion number of daily points for three of the four sessions.
2. If the criterion is met, deliver a group activity reward to the entire class, such as a popcorn party or a video presentation.

Variation 2
1. Implement the procedure with a small group of the most disruptive and unproductive students rather than the entire class.
2. Alternate the roles of peer earner and peer monitor as described above, but record points privately rather than on a public chart.
3. Provide the rewarding activity for the entire class if the point earners meet the criterion.

Note

This intervention is easiest to implement during an instructional period in which seatwork is highly structured and easy to score, such as mathematics or spelling.

Source

Stern, G. W., Fowler, S. A., & Kohler, F. W. (1988). A comparison of two intervention roles: Peer monitor and point earner. *Journal of Applied Behavior Analysis, 21,* 103–109. Copyright 1988 by the Society for the Experimental Analysis of Behavior. Adapted by permission.

GOOD BEHAVIOR CHECKLIST

Is your partner:

First rating
1. Sitting in the chair?	Yes	No
2. Being quiet?	Yes	No
3. Working on the assignment?	Yes	No

Second rating
1. Sitting in the chair?	Yes	No
2. Being quiet?	Yes	No
3. Working on the assignment?	Yes	No

Third rating
1. Sitting in the chair?	Yes	No
2. Being quiet?	Yes	No
3. Working on the assignment?	Yes	No

Total number of "yeses" ____

GOOD WORK CHECKLIST

Did your partner:

1. Put his or her name on the assignment?	Yes	No
2. Put the date on the assignment?	Yes	No
3. Write the page and problem numbers on the assignment?	Yes	No
4. Erase mistakes neatly or have no mistakes?	Yes	No
5. Write his or her answers so you can read and understand your partner's work?	Yes	No
6. Complete the problems?	Yes	No
If not, how many problems were done?	____	

Total number of "yeses" ____

Total good behavior and good work "yeses" ____

FIGURE 5.1. Point earners' checklists for *Using Peer Monitors to Improve On-Task Behavior*. Adapted from Stern, Fowler, and Kohler (1988, p. 105). Copyright 1988 by the Society for the Experimental Analysis of Behavior. Adapted by permission.

REDUCING DISRUPTIVE BEHAVIOR WITH SELF-MANAGED RESPONSE COST

Overview

Helping students learn to manage their own behavior is an important goal for teachers of any grade or subject. Self-management of behavior increases student independence and self-reliance and helps ensure that newly learned behaviors will transfer to other settings and situations. In this intervention, students are taught to observe their classroom behavior using individual response cost systems. In the original study with two learning-disabled students, the teacher removed strips of construction paper taped to the students' desks for incidents of inappropriate behavior. In this classwide adaptation, index cards for recording behavior have been substituted, and students mark their own cards for rule infractions.

Purpose

To reduce disruptive and noncompliant behavior with a self-managed response cost system.

Materials

1. Posterboard chart with a list of classroom rules, such as:
   a. Stay in your seat unless you have permission to get up.
   b. Keep from calling out to the teacher or classmates.
   c. Raise your hand and wait to be called on to speak.
2. This intervention requires 3" × 5" index cards, one per student per week. List the days of the week down the left side, and make five rows of open circles going across the card to correspond to each day. The number of circles in each row should be one more than the permitted number of rule infractions. For example, if students are allowed to break the rules seven times during the intervention period and still receive reinforcement, there should be eight circles in each row.
3. Tape
4. Grab bag containing a variety of reinforcers, such as stickers, pencils, erasers, homework passes, and wrapped candy
5. Purchased or teacher-made award certificates (see Variation 2)

Observation (Select One or Both)

Option 1
1. Using a *Group Event Recording Form*, tally the number of out of seats and call-outs for the entire class or a group of the most disruptive students during a selected instructional period for 4 to 7 days.

Option 2
1. Using a sheet of paper attached to a clipboard, record the number of rule infractions for the entire class or a group of the most disruptive students during a selected instructional period for 4 to 7 days.

Procedure

1. Explain to the students that they will be learning a new way of managing their own behavior so that they can get more out of their lessons.
2. Review the classroom rules, the intervention procedures, and the rewards for following the rules. Display an index card and demonstrate how to cross out a circle for a rule infraction. Explain that students who complain or argue when instructed to cross out a circle will be required to cross out two circles.

3. Have students tape the index cards to the left-hand side of their desks or table area.
4. If a student breaks a rule, signal to that student to cross out a circle on the card for that day. Students who have any uncrossed circles remaining at the end of the period are eligible to draw a reward from the grab bag.
5. Raise the criterion by decreasing the number of circles on cards as students successfully decrease their frequency of rule infractions.

Evaluation (Select One or Both)

Option 1
1. Compare the frequency of out of seats and call-outs for the entire class or a group of the most disruptive students during the selected instructional period before and after implementation.

Option 2
1. Compare the frequency of rule infractions for the entire class or a group of the most disruptive students during the selected instructional period before and after implementation.

Variation

Instead of using a grab bag to dispense daily reinforcers, prepare or purchase "good notes" or award certificates to be sent home to parents at the end of the week for students meeting the criterion each day.

Note

To facilitate implementation, have students make their own cards and tape them on their desks at the beginning of the week.

Source

Salend, S. J., & Allen, E. M. (1985). Comparative effects of externally managed and self-managed response-cost systems on inappropriate classroom behavior. *Journal of School Psychology, 23,* 59–67. Copyright 1985 by Elsevier Science Ltd, Oxford, England. Adapted by permission.

SELF-MANAGED BEHAVIOR RATINGS

Overview

In traditional self-management strategies, students are rewarded with points and backup reinforcers for behaving appropriately and evaluating themselves accurately. After disruptive behavior has been reduced, the token program is then gradually withdrawn, leaving self-evaluation and praise as reinforcers. In contrast, this intervention uses self-management as the initial strategy for reducing disruptive behavior. The advantage of initiating a token program using self-evaluation is that students may learn to manage their own behavior more rapidly. Originally used with junior high school special education students in a resource room, it is adapted here for regular classroom use.

Purpose

To reduce disruptive behavior using a self-rating procedure.

Materials

1. Posterboard chart with a list of classroom rules, such as:
   a. Keep your attention on the teacher and your own work.
   b. Keep from disturbing others.
   c. Follow the teacher's directions.
   d. Stay in your seat unless you have permission to get up.
   e. Raise your hand and wait to be called upon before talking.
2. Posterboard chart displaying the point system
3. Point cards, consisting of 8½″ × 11″ sheets of paper with self-ratings, one per student per day (see Figure 5.2)
4. Backup reinforcers such as snacks, inexpensive school supplies, and magazines
5. Red felt-tip pen

Observation (Select One or Both)

Option 1
1. Select an instructional period during which students are especially unproductive and disruptive.
2. Using a *Group Interval Recording Form* with a 10-second interval and beginning at the left side of the room, glance at each student at 10-second intervals and code behavior as on-task, off-task, or disruptive until one rating is made for each student.
   a. *On-task behavior* is defined as working on assignments, following teacher directions, or waiting quietly.
   b. *Off-task behavior* is defined as not looking at the assigned task longer than 5 seconds and/or working on something other than the assigned task.
   c. *Disruptive behavior* is defined as talking without permission, being out of seat without permission, throwing objects, and/or interrupting the teacher during a class discussion without first raising a hand.
3. Conduct these observations for 20 to 30 minutes for 4 to 7 days.

Option 2
1. Using a *Group Event Recording Form*, tally the frequency of the following disruptive behaviors during the selected instructional period for 4 to 7 days:

    a. Out-of-seat behaviors
    b. Verbal aggression (cursing, making threatening statements)
    c. Physical aggression (hitting, pushing, throwing objects)
    d. Call-outs

Procedure

1. Display and discuss the classroom rules with the students.
2. Explain that they will be able to earn rewards for positive behavior by rating their own behavior on a 0- to 5-point scale at regular intervals (e.g., every 15 minutes for a 45-minute period).
3. Display on a chart and discuss the following rating criteria for the point system:
   a. 5 = excellent: following the rules and working on assigned tasks throughout the entire period (no warnings or reminders needed);
   b. 4 = very good: following the rules and working on assigned tasks throughout the entire period with the exception of one minor infraction (one reminder);
   c. 3 = average: following the rules and working on assigned tasks without any serious offenses (two reminders);
   d. 2 = below average: following the rules and working on assigned tasks for about half of the period (three reminders);
   e. 1 = poor: following the rules and working on tasks for about half of the period (four reminders);
   f. 0 = unacceptable: failing to follow the rules or work on assigned tasks for any of the period (more than four reminders).
4. Tell students that you will be rating their behavior on the same scale and matching their ratings with yours.
5. Explain the matching procedure as follows:
   a. When student and teacher ratings match exactly, the student receives the number of points corresponding to the rating, plus a bonus point (e.g., if both the student and teacher ratings are 3s, the student receives a 4).
   b. When the student rating is within 1 point of the teacher rating, the student receives the number of points corresponding to the teacher rating (e.g., if the student rating is 4 and the teacher rating is 3, the student receives a 3).
   c. If there is more than a 1-point difference between the ratings, the student receives no points.
6. Explain that students may exchange points for a variety of rewards at the end of the period (or day). Help students develop a set of rewards and create a chart on the chalkboard listing the number of points required for each reward, such as 1 to 3 points for wrapped candy, 4 to 9 points for a juice box, and 10 to 15 points for school supplies or a magazine.
7. At the beginning of the target period, give students a point card on which to record their self-ratings. At the end of each interval, instruct students to mark their self-ratings with a pen or pencil. Move around the classroom and mark your rating on the same card with a red felt-tip pen.

8. Check point cards at the end of the period and deliver rewards according to the posted point system.
9. When the majority of students are receiving ratings of *4* or *5* for each interval on 3 consecutive days and are receiving bonus points for perfect matches, increase the length of the marking interval to 30 minutes or a time corresponding to two intervals per target period. Redo the point cards to include two rather than three ratings.
10. As student behavior continues to improve, match ratings only once, at the end of the period, and redo the point cards accordingly.

Evaluation (Select One or Both)

Option 1
1. Compare classwide rates of on-task, off-task, and disruptive behavior during the target period before and after implementation.

Option 2
1. Compare the frequency of out-of-seat behaviors, verbal aggression, physical aggression, and call-outs during the target period before and after implementation.

Variations

1. Implement the strategy with a small group of disruptive students rather than the entire class. Train peers to perform the matching tasks, and provide rewards for the entire class based on the criteria for behavior and matching described above.
2. Match ratings only once at the end of the period, and add the contingency that 80% of all student ratings must be within 1 point of teacher ratings for any rewards to be delivered. This variation is especially appropriate for large classes.

Note

Including a training session with modeling and guided practice for making self-ratings and responding to teacher matching is essential for smooth implementation.

Source

Smith, D. J., Young, K. R., West, R. P., Morgan, D. P., & Rhode, G. (1988). Reducing the disruptive behavior of junior high school students: A classroom self-management procedure. *Behavioral Disorders, 13,* 231–239. Copyright 1988 by The Council for Exceptional Children. Adapted by permission.

SELF-EVALUATION CARD

Name _____ Date _____

1st Rating
Poor   Excellent

0   1   2   3   4   5   Points _____

                                                   + Bonus _____

                                                   = Total _____

2nd Rating
Poor   Excellent

0   1   2   3   4   5   Points _____

                                                   + Bonus _____

                                                   = Total _____

3rd Rating
Poor   Excellent

0   1   2   3   4   5   Points _____

                                                   + Bonus _____

                                                   = Total _____

FIGURE 5.2. Self-evaluation point card for *Self-Managed Behavior Ratings*. From Smith, Young, West, Morgan, and Rhode (1988, p. 234). Copyright 1988 by The Council for Exceptional Children. Reprinted by permission.

REDUCING RULE VIOLATIONS WITH GOOD DAY AWARDS

Overview

Although regular communication with parents can enhance the effectiveness of school interventions, the complexity of many strategies with a parent component makes them unsuitable for classwide implementation. In contrast, this simple, all-positive school–home note system can easily be implemented with an entire class on a daily basis. Most suitable for students in self-contained prekindergarten through third-grade classes, it requires few materials and no parent contact other than an initial explanatory letter. In this adaptation, a public posting component has been substituted for individual records kept on each child to encourage positive peer pressure and facilitate teacher monitoring of rule infractions.

Purpose

To reduce classroom disruptive behavior with an all-positive school–home note system.

Materials

1. Posterboard chart listing five classroom rules, with numbers, such as:
   1. Ask permission if you wish to leave your seat.
   2. Ask permission to talk in class.

3. Keep your attention on the teacher and your work.
4. Keep from disturbing others.
5. Listen quietly when others are talking.

2. Posterboard chart or section of the chalkboard with a list of the numbers of the classroom rules and space for student initials to be placed beside the numbers; to assist young students in remembering the rules, paste or draw a simple picture representing each rule next to the number of that rule

3. Purchased award certificates or 8½" × 11" sheets of paper, with the following printed on them:

GOOD DAY AWARD

Presented to: _____

Date: _____

Signed: _____

4. Stickers for attaching to awards (optional)
5. Introductory parent letter, one per student (see Figure 5.3)

Observation (Select One or Both)

1. Using a sheet of paper with a list of student names attached to a clipboard, record the number of times you reprimand a small group of the most disruptive students during a selected instructional period for 4 to 7 days.

2. Using a sheet of paper attached to a clipboard, record the number of rule violations for the entire class during the instructional period in which students are most disruptive for 4 to 7 days.

Procedure

1. Prior to the first day of implementation, have students take home the introductory parent letters.

2. Review the classroom rules with students. Display the Good Day Awards, and say that you are looking forward to sending them home with students who follow the rules.

3. Display the chart or point out the section of the chalkboard with the list of rule numbers, and explain that you will be writing the initials of students who break rules next to the rule they violated as a reminder to try harder.

4. Set a criterion for earning an award, such as following four of five rules during the day.

5. When students break a rule, first give a verbal warning. If students do not respond in 5 seconds, write their initials next to that rule on the chart or chalkboard. When recording rule violations, state the rule that was broken, but do not make further comments.

6. At the end of the day, distribute Good Day Awards to students who have met the criterion, praise them for earning the awards, and encourage those who did not receive an award to try harder the next day.

7. As student behavior improves, fade the awards to a weekly system and send a second parent letter describing the change.

School Letterhead

Date:

Dear parent:

I am pleased to tell you that our class will be beginning a new program on (date of implementation) to help students get the most out of their lessons. Each day I will be sending home a Good Day Award with every child who has followed our classroom rules. To earn an award, students must follow at least 4 out of 5 rules during the day. Our classroom rules are as follows:

1. Ask permission if you wish to leave your seat.
2. Ask permission to talk in class.
3. Keep your attention on the teacher and your work.
4. Keep from disturbing others.
5. Listen quietly when others are talking.

When your child brings home a Good Day Award, please praise him or her. If you wish, give your child a small reward or privilege of your choice. If your child does not receive an award, encourage him or her to try harder at school the next day.

Thank you for your support of our efforts to help all our students achieve their maximum potential in school. Please feel free to call me if you have any questions about the program.

Sincerely yours,

Name of teacher

FIGURE 5.3. Introductory parent letter for *Reducing Rule Violations with Good Day Awards.* Adapted from Taylor, Cornwell, and Riley (1984). Copyright 1984 by John Wiley & Sons, Inc. Adapted by permission.

Evaluation (Select One or Both)

1. Compare the frequency of reprimands delivered to the small group of the most disruptive students during the selected instructional period before and after implementation.
2. Compare the frequency of rule violations for the entire class during the selected instructional period before and after implementation.

Variation

For implementation with a small group of students rather than the entire class, explain the procedure privately and keep a record of rule violations on a clipboard.

Notes

1. For ease of implementation, prepare a supply of signed Good Day Awards, ready for distribution to students achieving the criterion at the end of the day.

2. If some students consistently have difficulty achieving the criterion and receiving Good Day Awards, parent consultation is strongly recommended to promote collaborative problem solving and to design additional interventions.

Source

Taylor, V. L., Cornwell, D. D., & Riley, M. T. (1984). Home-based contingency management programs that teachers can use. *Psychology in the Schools, 21,* 368–374. Copyright 1984 by John Wiley & Sons, Inc. Adapted by permission.

ENHANCING THE EFFECTIVENESS OF SCHOOL–HOME NOTES WITH RESPONSE COST

Overview

Studies have repeatedly demonstrated the importance of negative consequences for maintaining appropriate behavior in the classroom. At home, parents often use removal of privileges to reduce children's misbehavior. Unlike most school–home note systems, which require parents to provide only positive consequences, this intervention incorporates a response cost contingency to improve students' classroom behavior. In the original study, a school–home note without response cost did not produce improvements in on-task behavior, whereas the addition of the response cost contingency resulted in marked increases in attentiveness and decreases in disruptive behavior. First used with three fourth graders, the intervention is adapted here for classwide implementation with the addition of a self-managed response cost contingency.

Purpose

To reduce disruptive behavior using a school–home note system with a response cost contingency.

Materials

1. Posterboard chart listing numbered classroom rules, such as:
    1. Keep your attention on the teacher and your own work.
    2. Keep from disturbing others.
    3. Follow the teacher's directions.
    4. Stay in your seat unless you have permission to get up.
    5. Raise your hand and wait to be called upon before talking.
2. Introductory parent letter, one per student (see Figure 5.4)
3. School–home notes, one per student per day (see Figure 5.5)
4. Black felt-tip pen (see Variation 1)

Observation (Select One or Both)

Option 1

1. Using a *Classwide Scanning Form* with a 3-minute interval, scan the classroom from left to right and tally the number of students in each of the following behavior categories:
   a. *On-task behavior*, defined as looking at or working on assigned tasks;
   b. *Off-task behavior*, defined as being seated at a desk but not looking at or working on assigned tasks;
   c. *Disruptive behavior*, defined as being out of seat without permission, making noise, or engaging in any other behavior not approved by the teacher.
2. Conduct these observations for 30 to 45 minutes for 4 to 7 days during a selected instructional period, such as morning seatwork.

Option 2

1. Using a *Group Event Recording Form*, record the frequencies of two or three disruptive behaviors, such as being out of seat, talking out, or physical aggression for the entire class or a small group of the most disruptive students during a selected instructional period.
2. Conduct these observations for 30 to 45 minutes for 4 to 7 days.

Procedure

1. Prior to implementation, send home the introductory parent letter and a copy of the school–home note with all students.
2. Explain to students that you will be sending a note home every day to their parents to help encourage them to do their best work.
3. Explain to students that you will put the notes on their desks and rate their behavior at the end of the target period (such as morning seatwork). Tell them that you are asking their parents to review the notes daily with them and praise them for positive behaviors.
4. Display the chart with the classroom rules and review them with students.
5. Demonstrate the rating and response cost procedures and model appropriate student reactions.
6. When students break a rule, give them a warning, and if they do not comply in 5 seconds, instruct them to cross off a "smiley face" on the note. Give a specific, calmly stated reprimand that describes the infraction.
7. At the end of the day, rate each student's behavior and have students take the notes home.

Evaluation (Select One or Both)

Option 1

1. Compare classwide percentages of students displaying on-task, off-task, and disruptive behavior during the selected instructional period before and after implementation.

Option 2

1. Compare the frequencies of the target behaviors for the entire class or the small group of the most disruptive students during the selected instructional period before and after implementation.

Variations

1. To avoid disrupting ongoing instruction, use a signal rather than a verbal reprimand to indicate to students that they should cross off a smiley face. For example, hold up one finger to indicate that students have broken classroom rule number 1, two fingers to indicate that they have broken rule number 2, and so on.

School Letterhead

Date:

Dear parent:

Beginning on ____ (date of implementation), I will be using a school–home note to provide more information to you about your child's academic and social progress. Each day I will send home a note rating your child's progress in completing classwork and using class time well. The note also shows five "smiley faces." If one or more of these smiley faces is crossed off, this means that your child has broken a classroom rule one or more times. Our classroom rules are as follows:

1. Keep your attention on the teacher and your own work.
2. Keep from disturbing others.
3. Follow the teacher's directions.
4. Stay in your seat unless you have permission to get up.
5. Raise your hand and wait to be called upon before talking.

Please go over the note each day with your child. Praise your child for positive behaviors and talk with your child about how he or she can improve any negative behaviors. You may also wish to give your child rewards or privileges for positive behaviors, such as playing a game with your child, reading your child a story, or providing a special snack or extra television or video game time. Review these rewards each week with your child to make sure that they are still effective in encouraging positive behaviors.

Please feel free to call me at school if you have any questions about the school–home notes. A copy of the note is included for your information. I am looking forward to working together with you to help your child do his or her best in school.

Sincerely yours,

Name of teacher

FIGURE 5.4. Introductory parent letter for *Enhancing the Effectiveness of School–Home Notes with Response Cost.* Adapted from McCain and Kelley (1994). Copyright 1994 by The Haworth Press. Adapted by permission.

SCHOOL–HOME NOTE

Name _____ Date _____

1. Completed Classwork Satisfactorily	YES	SO-SO	NO
2. Used Classtime Well	YES	SO-SO	NO

Teacher Comments: _____
_____
_____

Parent Comments: _____
Parent Initials: _____

FIGURE 5.5 School–home note for *Enhancing the Effectiveness of School–Home Notes with Response Cost.* From McCain and Kelley (1994, p. 33). Copyright 1994 by The Haworth Press. Reprinted by permission.

2. If the intervention will be implemented with a small group of students rather than the entire class, cross off the smiley faces yourself rather than having students do so.

Notes

1. Provide a negative contingency, such as 10 minutes deducted from recess, for students who fail to take notes home, and send the notes a second time.
2. In addition to its superior effectiveness, the response cost note was preferred over the traditional school–home note by all of the students and parents in the original study.
3. Additional consultation with the parents of students who consistently receive poor reports is strongly recommended to encourage parental collaboration and develop alternative interventions.

Source

McCain, A. P., & Kelley, M. L. (1994). Improving classroom performance in underachieving preadolescents: The additive effects of response cost to a school–home note system. *Child and Family Behavior Therapy, 16,* 27–41. Copyright 1994 by The Haworth Press. Adapted by permission.

GROUP CONTINGENCIES TO REDUCE STEALING

Overview

Stealing from teachers or peers can pose serious classroom management problems. Determining whether theft has actually occurred and identifying the responsible party can be difficult and time-consuming. Traditional strategies such as teacher-delivered lectures on honesty often not only fail to solve the problem but disrupt instruction and can contribute to a negative classroom environment. Rather than requiring identification of the individual perpetrator, this intervention uses a group contingency to target stealing. In the original study, the teacher left the room to provide an opportunity for students to return stolen items. To avoid having to leave students unsupervised, this adaptation substitutes an alternative procedure, in which the teacher withdraws to another part of the classroom to permit replacement of missing items.

Purpose

To reduce classroom stealing by using a group contingency procedure.

Materials

None

Observation (Select One or Both)

1. Record the number of items stolen during the school day for one or more weeks.
2. Record the number of complaints of theft each day for one or more weeks.

Procedure

1. Explain to the students that several items in the classroom belonging to the teacher, school, or other students (as appropriate) have been reported missing.
2. Tell the students that if you do not notice anything missing during the morning and if nothing is reported taken, they will have 10 minutes of free time at the end of the morning work period.
3. If nothing has been reported stolen by the end of the morning period, praise students for being honest and award the 10 minutes of free time.
4. If something has been reported stolen or if you have noticed that something has been taken, say:

> "I know that _____ is missing. If the person who took it returns it by putting it on my desk some time before snack [lunch], then you will be able to talk during snack [lunch] as usual. If _____ is not returned before that time, you will have to sit quietly while you eat your snack [lunch] and put your heads down on your desks after you finish [have silent lunch for the en-

tire period]. I will be working at the reading table [or some other place across the room from the teacher's desk] for a few minutes so that the person will have a chance to return what is missing."

5. Make no comment if students return items and permit talking during snack or lunch as described above.
6. As incidents of stealing decrease, provide free time on a weekly rather than daily basis.

Evaluation (Select One or Both)

1. Compare the number of items stolen before and after implementation.
2. Compare the number of complaints of theft before and after implementation.

Variation

Extend the intervention period to include the entire school day and deliver the free-time reward as an end-of-the-day activity. As stealing decreases, provide free time as a Friday afternoon activity.

Notes

1. In the original study, a lecture on stealing was followed by an increase in the number of items taken.
2. Although in the original study, neither the researchers or the teacher observed any negative peer pressure, teachers should take precautions to prevent hostile comments or retaliation. To minimize this possibility and help maintain a positive classroom atmosphere, combining this intervention with a strategy that focuses on positive social behaviors, such as *Increasing Cooperative Behavior with Sharing Time* or *Promoting Positive Behavior through Attribution,* is recommended.
3. In the case of a single student who frequently steals from other children or the teacher and has been identified as responsible for the thefts, parent consultation and referral to a mental health professional are strongly recommended in addition to classroom interventions.

Source

Switzer, E. B., Deal, T. E., & Bailey, J. S. (1977). The reduction of stealing in second graders using a group contingency. *Journal of Applied Behavior Analysis, 10,* 267–272. Copyright 1977 by the Society for the Experimental Analysis of Behavior. Adapted by permission.

INTERVENTIONS TO IMPROVE BEHAVIOR IN SPECIAL CLASSES AND LESS STRUCTURED SITUATIONS

Managing student behavior during special classes and less structured school situations can be especially problematic for teachers. Teachers of special classes, such as art, music, or media, typically see their students less often than regular classroom teachers and have access to fewer contingencies to maintain appropriate behavior. Performance in "specials" may be ungraded or viewed as less important by students than performance in their academic classes, further undermining motivation for productive, positive behavior. The potential for disruptive behavior is also heightened because "specials" often require students to move from one part of the school to another and make use of materials and activities that simultaneously increase opportunities for peer interaction and reduce teacher control.

The interventions in this section are designed to promote positive behavior in special classes and other less structured settings, including physical education and recess, the lunchroom, and at rest time. *Charting to Improve Classroom Behavior during Specials* combines a group-oriented, free-time contingency with public posting and is especially useful for special classes that require students to move from one classroom to another. *Improving Media Center Behavior with the Good Behavior Game*, a variation of *The Good Behavior Game* presented in the previous section, can also be adapted to other special class settings.

Recess and physical education classes are especially likely to be the scene of inappropriate behavior because of the increased opportunities for movement and physical contact among students. In addition, recess periods are often scheduled for more than one class at a time, and the supervisors assigned to the playground may not be the staff members who are most familiar with the children. *Reducing Aggressive and Inappropriate Behavior in Physical Education Classes with Sit and Watch* is a variation of the *Sit and Watch: Teaching Prosocial Behaviors* intervention presented in Chapter 3. A peer-monitored variation has been included to reduce teacher supervisory responsibility.

Although students' behavior during the lunch break often presents management problems, very few empirically based interventions designed to reduce disruptive cafeteria behavior have appeared. *Eliminating Disruptive Lunchroom Behavior with Mediation Essays* combines a writing timeout in the form of a "mediation essay" with a self-managed variation that guides students through an analysis of the consequences of their inappropriate behavior. Although it can be implemented by a single teacher, it is much more effective if it is used by all lunchroom supervisors during a particular lunch period or throughout the entire lunchroom program.

Rest time can also be problematic for very young children. *Brag Sheets: Improving Behavior during Rest Time* uses a school–home note to encourage appropriate behavior during nap time. Included in this intervention, which requires no home-based contingencies, is a questionnaire designed to assess parental reactions to the strategy. The questionnaire can be easily adapted for use in evaluating parents' responses to any of the interventions in this book.

CHARTING TO IMPROVE CLASSROOM
BEHAVIOR DURING SPECIALS

Overview

This intervention combines interdependent and independent group contingencies to reduce disruptive behavior and increase on-task behavior. The interdependent system utilizes peer influence to encourage positive group behavior, while the independent contingency discourages a few disruptive students from preventing the entire class from receiving reinforcement. Because of the high degree of behavior monitoring involved, it is most suitable for implementation in a single instructional period such as a "special." It is particularly suitable for special classes that require students to move from one room to another because walking to and from class and clean-up routines are among the monitored behaviors. Originally used with a third-grade art class, the intervention produced dramatic reductions in disruptive behavior and increases in on-task behavior as well as improvement in the amount and quality of work completion.

Purpose

To reduce disruptive behavior and increase on-task behavior in special classes using a free-time contingency.

Materials

1. Posterboard chart listing rules for the special class, such as:
   a. Use materials appropriately.
   b. Walk quietly to and from the special class.
   c. Follow the teacher's instructions.
   d. Use inside voices when you are working.
2. Posterboard chart with numbers in ascending order from 1 to 12 (or some other appropriate number to correspond to one interval for every 5 minutes in the period) down the left side, five columns corresponding to the days of the week for recording checks, and a section for recording student initials
3. 8½" × 11" sheet of paper with a list of the classroom rules and space for recording student initials, one per intervention session (needed if students move from one room to another)

Observation (Select One or More)

Option 1
1. Using a *Classwide Scanning Form* with a 5-minute interval, scan the room during the special class and record the number of students in each of the following categories:

a. *On-task behavior*, defined as working independently, participating in class dis-cussions, following instructions, listening to directions or the lesson, using materials appropriately, walking quietly in line, or any other task-related be-havior;

b. *Off-task behavior*, defined as daydreaming, looking away from the teacher during instruction, talking without permission, or using materials inappro-priately;

c. *Disruptive behavior*, defined as being out of seat without permission, physical contact with other students, talking loudly in class or line, or running or get-ting out of line during transitions.

2. Conduct these observations for 20 to 30 minutes for 4 to 7 days.

Option 2

1. Using a sheet of paper attached to a clipboard, scan the room every 5 minutes during the special class. Put a check on the paper if 80% of the students are on-task, as defined above. Continue to scan and record checks throughout the class period.

2. Conduct these observations for 4 to 7 days. Note that these observations are identical to the scanning procedure used in the intervention.

Option 3

1. Using a *Group Event Recording Form*, record the number of disruptive behaviors, as defined above, for the entire class or a group of selected students for 20 to 30 minutes during the special class for 4 to 7 days.

Procedure

1. Display and post the chart with the classroom rules at the front of the room.

2. Explain to the students that they will have a chance to earn free time at the end of the period by following the rules, paying attention, and working hard. Review the rules, explain the checking procedure described below, and dis-cuss examples of appropriate and inappropriate behaviors during transitions to and from class (if they occur), the class period, and the clean-up period.

3. About every 5 minutes, scan the room and if 80% of students are on-task, as defined above, put a check on the chart and praise the class. (To determine quickly if 80% are on-task, count how many students are present and select the appropriate number to use as the 80% criterion for that day. For example, if 25 students are present, 20 must be on-task.) If less than 80% of the stu-dents are on-task, say nothing and do not award a check.

4. Use the same procedure during transition and clean-up times. If you escort students from their regular class to the specials room and back, carry a sheet of paper listing the rules to record behavior during the transition period.

5. If any students break a rule, record their initials on a section of the chart (or the paper during transitions) next to the appropriate rule and give a quiet rep-rimand.

6. If the same student breaks a rule again, record an × next to the initials and give another quiet reprimand.

7. Students with four or more rule violations during the period lose the next day's recess.

8. If approximately 25% of the students violate the rules or are disruptive during any one period, the entire class loses its chance at earning a check, and all the students must put their heads down for 3 minutes.

9. If the class earns eight or more checks during the period, put a large check mark at the top of the chart. When the class has earned two large checks, award 10 minutes of free time at the end of the period during which students can talk or listen to music.

10. Gradually increase the number of checks that students must earn to receive free time.

Evaluation (Select One or More)

Option 1

1. Compare the percentages of students exhibiting on-task, off-task, and disruptive behavior during the special class before and after implementation.

Option 2

1. Compare the number of checks awarded for on-task behavior during the special class before and after implementation.

Option 3

1. Compare the frequency of disruptive behaviors for the entire class or the group of selected students during the special class before and after implementation.

Variation

Instead of taking away the recess of students who are disruptive four or more times during one period, require them to complete a "Solving My Own Problems Questionnaire" from *Eliminating Disruptive Lunchroom Behavior with Mediation Essays*.

Note

If the same group of students has special classes with several different teachers, implementing the intervention during all special class periods enhances its effectiveness.

Source

Crouch, P. L., Gresham, F. M., & Wright, W. R. (1985). Interdependent and independent group contingencies with immediate and delayed reinforcement for controlling classroom behavior. *Journal of School Psychology, 23,* 177–187. Copyright 1985 by Elsevier Science Ltd, Oxford, England. Adapted by permission.

IMPROVING MEDIA CENTER BEHAVIOR
WITH THE GOOD BEHAVIOR GAME

Overview

Teachers of special classes often have greater problems managing student behavior compared with regular classroom teachers. First, because they usually see students only once a week, they are likely to have fewer and less powerful contingencies for influencing behavior. Second, misbehavior may reflect students' perception of special classes as less important than their academic classes, a perception heightened by the fact that letter grades are often not given for specials. In this adaptation of *The Good Behavior Game* (GBG), a group-oriented contingency is used to reduce disruptive behavior in media center sessions. Unlike the original GBG, this version involves students in defining the rules for appropriate behavior. The strategy can be easily adapted for use in other special classes, such as art or music.

Purpose

To reduce disruptive behavior during media center sessions or other special classes.

Materials

1. Posterboard chart listing the rules for media center sessions (developed during the intervention procedures), such as:
   a. If you talk, talk quietly.
   b. Use media center materials and equipment during the media center period.
   c. Follow all rules for using media center materials and equipment.
   d. Follow directions the first time they are given.
   e. Treat each other with respect at all times.
2. Posterboard chart listing the numbers of class teams down the left side, with a series of columns for recording points
3. Red and blue adhesive name tags or large red and blue stickers, an equal number for each of the two teams (see Variation 2)

Observation (Select One or Both)

Option 1
1. Using a *Group Interval Recording Form* with a 15-second interval, glance at each student in turn and record that student's behavior at the moment of observation as either on-task, off-task, or disruptive as defined below:
   a. *On-task behavior:* asking or answering lesson-oriented questions, writing when requested, looking at the media specialist during presentations, using materials appropriately, or any other behavior relevant to the lesson or activities;
   b. *Off-task behavior:* sitting without having appropriate materials at hand or looking at or playing with nonmedia center materials;

    c. *Disruptive behavior:* any behavior disrupting the on-task behavior of other students, such as talking loudly, failing to follow directions, or aggression.

2. Conduct these observations for 20 to 30 minutes for 4 to 7 days.

Option 2

1. Using a *Group Event Recording Form,* record the frequency of loud talking, failing to follow directions, and aggression for the entire class or a group of selected students during the media center period for 4 to 7 days.

Procedure

1. Tell the students that they will be playing a game to help everyone get more out of the media center period. Help the students select four or five rules for media center behavior. Keep the rules short, simple, and positive. Write the rules on a posterboard chart and post them where all can see.
2. Divide the class into two teams. Be sure that disruptive and inattentive students are divided between the two teams. For convenience, use table or desk groupings to assign teams. Students remain on the teams for four consecutive sessions, after which new teams can be created, if desired.
3. Tell the students that you will be looking up four times during the period (or about every 10 minutes) and will award a team point if each member of that team is following the rules. If any student on that team is not obeying the rules, no point will be given.
4. Set a criterion for winning, such as earning three of four possible points (one point per observation). If both teams meet the criterion, both teams win.
5. At the designated times during the period, look up and award points as described above. Praise any teams that win for that period and encourage non-winning teams to try harder.
6. Record the points earned by each team for four consecutive media center sessions. During the fifth media center session, provide a special activity, such as a special story or video or extra time on media center computers or at listening centers, for any team(s) that have won for three of the four sessions. Require any nonwinning teams to sit quietly at their desks or tables and work on regular media center activities or lessons.

Evaluation (Select One or Both)

1. Compare the percentages of students exhibiting on-task, off-task, and disruptive behavior during the media center period before and after implementation.
2. Compare the frequency of disruptive behaviors for the entire class or the group of selected students during the media center period before and after implementation.

Variations

Variation 1

1. Use principal attention to reward winning teams, as in *Encouraging Academic Achievement with Principal Praise.*

Variation 2

1. This intervention works best when students do not move around the media center too frequently and have assigned seating. If students will be moving around the center for most of the period or do not have assigned seats, divide the class into a "red" and "blue" team at the beginning of the period and have students wear colored name tags or stickers during the period for easy identification.
2. Have students return the tags or stickers at the end of the period, if desired, or provide new tags or stickers for each period.
3. Award team points as described above.

Note

Although in the original study, the regular classroom teacher provided a special art activity or read a story to the winning team(s) at the end of the day, field testing indicates that contingency-based interventions for special classes are more effective when the specials teacher is the reinforcing agent. Moreover, teachers are often reluctant to become involved in another teacher's behavior management program, especially when they must deliver negative consequences (here, withholding the reward from nonwinning teams) for behavior that occurred outside of their supervision.

Source

Fishbein, J. E., & Wasik, B. H. (1981). Effect of the good behavior game on disruptive library behavior. *Journal of Applied Behavior Analysis, 14*, 89–93. Copyright 1981 by the Society for the Experimental Analysis of Behavior. Adapted by permission.

REDUCING AGGRESSIVE AND INAPPROPRIATE BEHAVIOR IN PHYSICAL EDUCATION CLASSES WITH SIT AND WATCH

Overview

Physical education classes and recess are frequent settings for behavior problems because of their open and less structured environments. At the elementary school level, typical behavior problems include verbal and physical aggression, noncompliance, and attention seeking. This strategy, a modification of the *Sit and Watch: Teaching Prosocial Behaviors* intervention, uses contingent observation and a timeout procedure from participation in a desired activity to reduce inappropriate behavior and includes backup contingencies for chronically misbehaving students.

Purpose

To reduce aggressive and inappropriate behavior during physical education and recess periods by using incidental teaching and a timeout procedure.

Materials

1. Posterboard chart with a list of rules for physical education or recess, such as:
   a. Follow the teacher's and aide's directions.
   b. Line up promptly when you are called.
   c. Use equipment safely.
   d. Do your best to participate in every activity.
   e. Play so that everyone can have fun.
2. Timers, two or three per classroom group, selected from these options:
   a. Hourglass devices constructed from two plastic juice bottles fastened together at the top with glue and screws and a hole drilled in the middle to permit sand to flow through; fill the bottles with enough sand to make the time period about 3 minutes
   b. Kitchen timers with bells
   c. Hourglass egg timers filled with sand; the time period for the sand to flow through should be about 3 minutes

Observation (Select One or Both)

1. Using a *Group Event Recording Form*, tally the number of disruptive behaviors that occur during a 20- to 30-minute observation or during the entire physical education or recess period for 4 to 7 days. Disruptive behaviors are defined as:
   a. *Noncompliance*: refusal to follow a request made by a teacher or aide in 5 seconds; continue to score noncompliance until the child complies with the request or the teacher or aide gives a new command and the student complies;
   b. *Aggression:* striking, pushing, or pulling others;
   c. *Throwing objects*: throwing balls or other sports equipment in an unsafe manner or throwing nonsports objects such as rocks and sand.
2. Using a sheet of paper attached to a clipboard, record the number of reprimands delivered by teachers or supervisors during a 20- to 30-minute observation or during the entire physical education or recess period. Repeat these observations for 4 to 7 days.

Procedure

1. At the beginning of the physical education period or in the classroom before recess, explain to students that they will be learning a new strategy to help everyone have more fun during physical education or recess.
2. Display the chart with the rules for physical education or recess and discuss the purpose of each rule.
3. Demonstrate the Sit and Watch procedures and have students role play going to Sit and Watch and using the timers.
4. In the physical education or recess area, place the timers in a designated Sit and Watch location, such as against one side of the gymnasium or on one side of the playground.
5. When a student breaks a rule or engages in unsafe or inappropriate behavior, send the student to the Sit and Watch area. The student must sit down, pick up

one of the timers, turn it over or set it to ring in 3 minutes, and stay there until all the sand has flowed through or the timer has rung. The student is then allowed to rejoin the group.
6. Be sure to monitor the student in the Sit and Watch area and not to place children too closely together when more than one child is removed from the group.
7. Students who are sent to Sit and Watch twice in one period must turn over the timer twice or set the timer for 6 minutes on the second occasion.
8. If students are sent to Sit and Watch three times in one period, they must remain in the Sit and Watch location for the rest of the physical education or recess period.
9. Students who tattle on others or talk to a student in Sit and Watch must go to Sit and Watch.

Evaluation (Select One or Both)

1. Compare the frequency of disruptive behaviors during physical education or recess before and after implementation.
2. Compare the frequency of reprimands issued by teachers or supervisors during physical education or recess before and after implementation.

Variation

During recess periods, use peer "safety monitors" to supervise the timing procedures for students who are sent to Sit and Watch. Conduct a training session that includes demonstrations and role plays of appropriate behavior for monitors and appropriate student responses. Have volunteer teams of safety monitors take turns supervising the Sit and Watch students.

Note

For implementation at recess, this intervention is most effective when it is used by all teachers whose classes are sharing the same playground area.

Source

White, A. G., & Bailey, J. S. (1990). Reducing disruptive behaviors of elementary physical education students with sit and watch. *Journal of Applied Behavior Analysis, 23,* 353–359. Copyright 1990 by the Society for the Experimental Analysis of Behavior. Adapted by permission.

ELIMINATING DISRUPTIVE LUNCHROOM BEHAVIOR WITH MEDIATION ESSAYS

Overview

Disruptive behavior during lunch periods is a common problem in schools. The high frequency of behavior problems is related to the open lunchroom environment, the large number of children in one area, and, often, supervision by aides, parent volunteers, or teachers who have little or no regular contact with the students in their charge and who may be uncertain regarding the specific consequences they can deliver. Solving lunchroom behavior management problems is important not only because students and teachers alike benefit from a peaceful lunch period but also because teachers must often spend precious instructional time reestablishing appropriate behavior if students become disruptive during lunch. In this strategy, misbehaving students are sent to a designated table in the lunchroom to copy a "mediation essay" that guides them through an analysis of the consequences of their inappropriate behavior. In the original study, 18 different essays were constructed, 3 for each of grades 1 through 6 targeting three different disruptive behaviors. This adaptation provides for the construction of two sets of essays targeting three disruptive behaviors, one set for primary grade students and one for upper elementary grade students. A variation presents the essay as a structured questionnaire so that students must analyze the consequences of their misbehavior and generate alternative appropriate behaviors themselves.

Purpose

To eliminate disruptive lunchroom behavior through mediation essays.

Materials

1. Designated mediation table in lunchroom, with a supply of pens or pencils
2. Copies of constructed mediation essays on 8½" × 11" sheets of paper, as follows:
   a. Essays for grades 1 through 3 should be double-spaced, in primer-size type, and less than one page.
   b. Essays for upper grades should be single-spaced, in elite or some other standard size type, and less than one page (see Figure 5.6 for a sample).
3. Copies of the Solving My Own Problems Questionnaire on 8½" × 11" sheets of paper, as follows:
   a. The questionnaire should be single-spaced, in elite or some other standard size type, with three or four blank lines for each question (Figure 5.7).

Observation (Select One or Both)

1. Using a sheet of paper attached to a clipboard, record the frequency of disruptive lunchroom behaviors for the entire lunchroom group, a target class, or a small number of the most disruptive students for 20 to 30 minutes or the entire period for 4 to 7 days. *Disruptive lunchroom behaviors* are defined as talking loudly, being out of seat without permission, throwing or playing with food, pushing, running, or not complying with teacher, aide, or parent volunteer directions.

2. Using a sheet of paper attached to a clipboard, record the number of reprimands you and/or lunchroom supervisors deliver to the entire lunchroom group, a target class, or a small group of the most disruptive students for 20 to 30 minutes for 4 to 7 days.

Procedure

1. Prior to implementation, select three of the most common or troublesome disruptive behaviors and prepare the mediation essays, one for each problem behavior, according to the guidelines described above.
2. On the first day of the intervention, discuss the target disruptive behaviors and procedures with the class as follows:
   a. Explain that students will be learning a new way of behaving better at lunch so that everyone can enjoy the lunch period more.
   b. Explain that each time a student exhibits a disruptive behavior in the lunchroom, he or she will first be asked to improve his or her behavior.
   c. If the student persists after two requests, he or she will be sent to the mediation table to copy an essay. The essay must be returned to you by the end of the lunch period.
3. Use the essay-copying assignment up to three times for each misbehaving student. On the fourth offense, present the questionnaire and have the student compose his or her own responses.

Evaluation (Select One or Both)

1. Compare the frequency of disruptive lunchroom behaviors for the entire lunchroom group, the target class, or the small group of the most disruptive students before and after implementation.
2. Compare the frequency of reprimands you and/or lunchroom supervisors deliver to the entire lunchroom group, the target class, or the small group of the most disruptive students before and after implementation.

Variations

1. Using the Solving My Own Problems Questionnaire, have misbehaving students supply their own answers to the questions for the first and all subsequent offenses. This variation eliminates the need to construct sets of prepared essays.
2. Have chronically misbehaving students take the completed questionnaires home to be signed by their parents and returned.
3. To implement mediation essays in the regular classroom, designate a table or desk in the back of the classroom as the mediation table and place a set of Solving My Own Problems Questionnaires and pencils or pens on it. Send students who display disruptive or inappropriate behavior to the mediation table and have them complete a questionnaire before they return to the ongoing activity.

Notes

1. This intervention is most effective when all lunchroom supervisors are trained in the procedure and all teachers whose students share the same lunch period introduce the intervention in their classrooms prior to implementation and review the procedures periodically.
2. Field testing indicates that mediation essays are also effective as consequences for many of the other interventions in this section, especially when they are sent home to be signed by parents (see Variation 3).

Source

MacPherson, E. M., Candee, B. L., & Hohman, R. J. (1974). A comparison of three methods for eliminating disruptive lunchroom behavior. *Journal of Applied Behavior Analysis*, 7, 287–297. Copyright 1974 by the Society for the Experimental Analysis of Behavior. Adapted by permission.

SOLVING MY OWN PROBLEMS ESSAY

Name of student: _____ Date: _____
Assigned by: _____ Time: _____

What bad choice did I make?

I didn't follow the aide's directions.

What bad things happen when I make that bad choice?

I don't have fun at lunch when I don't follow the aide's directions. I don't get to sit with my friends and talk. I won't have time to go outside after lunch. I have to copy this essay instead.

What would be a good choice for me to make?

I should follow the aide's directions right away.

What good things happen when I make the right choice?

I can do fun things I like at lunch. I can talk and eat with my friends. After lunch I can go outside with the other students. I can play on the playground. My parents will be happy when they hear I am showing good behavior. The other students will want to play with me.

FIGURE 5.6. Sample constructed mediation essay for *Eliminating Disruptive Lunchroom Behavior with Mediation Essays*. Adapted from MacPherson, Candee, and Hohman (1974, p. 290). Copyright 1974 by the Society for the Experimental Analysis of Behavior. Adapted by permission.

SOLVING MY OWN PROBLEMS QUESTIONNAIRE

Name of student: _____ Date: _____

Assigned by: _____ Time: _____

What bad choice did I make?

_____

_____

_____

_____

What bad things happen when I make that bad choice?

_____

_____

_____

_____

What would be a good choice for me to make?

_____

_____

_____

_____

What good things happen when I make that good choice?

_____

_____

_____

_____

FIGURE 5.7. Sample mediation questionnaire for *Eliminating Disruptive Lunchroom Behavior with Mediation Essays*. Adapted from MacPherson, Candee, and Hohman, (1974, p. 290). Copyright 1974 by the Society for the Experimental Analysis of Behavior. Adapted by permission.

BRAG SHEETS: IMPROVING BEHAVIOR DURING REST TIME

Overview

Daily report cards can be an effective method of improving student performance by informing parents about target social and academic behaviors. This intervention has several advantages over traditional school–home notes. Only minimal teacher consultation time is required, and no home contingencies are used. Moreover, unlike most school–home notes, this strategy was originally designed to be used on a classwide basis rather than with one student or a small group. In the original study with a kindergarten class, the target behavior was disruptive behavior during rest period. The daily report cards or "Brag Sheets" can be modified to target a variety of academic and social behaviors for primary and upper elementary grade students. This adaptation includes a home questionnaire assessing parent reactions to the intervention as an option.

Purpose

To reduce disruptive classroom behavior with a daily school–home note.

Materials

1. Introductory parent letter, one per student (see Figure 5.8)
2. 8½″ × 11″ sheets of paper ("Brag Sheets") listing the target disruptive behaviors, one per student per day (see Figure 5.9)
3. Stamp for teacher signature (optional)
4. Parent questionnaire letter and questionnaire, one set per family (optional; see Figures 5.10 and 5.11)

Observation (Select One or Both)

1. Using a sheet of paper attached to a clipboard, record the number of reprimands you deliver during rest time (or another target period) for 4 to 7 days.
2. Using a *Group Interval Recording Form* with a 10-second interval, glance at each student in turn during rest time and record that student's behavior at the moment of observation as either appropriate or inappropriate as defined below:
   a. *Appropriate behavior:* lying quietly on the floor or mat;
   b. *Inappropriate behavior:* any verbal or motor behavior that disturbs the appropriate behavior of other students, such as touching others or talking.

Procedure

1. Explain to the students that you will be using a new way of letting their parents know how well they are doing in school every day.
2. Display the Brag Sheets and explain what each statement means and how students can earn a "yes" for each statement.
3. Send home the first completed Brag Sheets with the students along with an explanatory letter to parents.
4. Mark the Brag Sheets and give them to the students to take home at the end of each day.
5. As student behavior improves, fade the Brag Sheets to weekly.

Evaluation (Select One or More)

1. Compare the frequency of reprimands issued during rest time (or the target period) before and after implementation.
2. Compare classwide rates of appropriate and inappropriate behaviors during rest time before and after implementation.
3. Seven weeks after introducing the program, send home the parent questionnaire letters and questionnaires to assess parent reactions to the Brag Sheets (see Figures 5.10 and 5.11).

School Letterhead

Date:

Dear parent:

Beginning this week, I will be sending home a daily note called a "Brag Sheet" to let you know how your child is progressing in school. Please read the note and review it with your child each day. Tell your child that he or she is doing a good job when you see positive marks ("Yeses"). If your child receives a poor report, please do not punish your child but encourage him or her to do better the next day. Your child's first Brag Sheet is attached.

Please feel free to contact me if you have any questions about the Brag Sheets.

Sincerely yours,

Name of teacher

FIGURE 5.8. Introductory parent letter for *Brag Sheets: Improving Behavior during Rest Time*. Adapted from Lahey, Gendrich, Gendrich, Schnelle, Gant, and McNees (1977). Copyright 1977 by Sage Publications, Inc. Adapted by permission.

BRAG SHEET

Name of student _____ Date _____

	Yes
1. Your child followed instructions well today.	___
2. Your child was a good rester today.	___
3. Your child completed all school work today.	___
4. Your child got along with his or her classmates.	___

We worked on this skill today: _____

_____

Signed _____
         (Name of teacher)

FIGURE 5.9. Daily report card for *Brag Sheets: Improving Behavior during Rest Time*. Adapted from Lahey, Gendrich, Gendrich, Schnelle, Gant, and McNees (1977, p. 388). Copyright 1977 by Sage Publications, Inc. Adapted by permission.

Variation

Use the Brag Sheets with a small group of the most disruptive students rather than with the entire classroom group.

Notes

1. Completing the Brag Sheets requires about 10 minutes for an entire classroom group. Purchasing a stamp for the teacher signature facilitates timely completion.
2. Consultation with the parents of students who often receive poor marks on their Brag Sheets is strongly recommended to encourage parent collaboration and design additional interventions.

Source

Lahey, B. B., Gendrich, J. G., Gendrich, S. I., Schnelle, J. F., Gant, D. S., & Mc-Nees, M. P. (1977). An evaluation of daily report cards with minimal teacher and parent contacts as an efficient method of classroom intervention. *Behavior Modification, 1*(3), 381–394. Copyright 1977 by Sage Publications, Inc. Adapted by permission.

School Letterhead

Date:

Dear parent:

As you know, for the past several weeks, I have been using Brag Sheets in the classroom to provide you with more information about your child's progress in school. I am very interested in your opinion of the Brag Sheet program and would appreciate your answering the questions on the attached survey. Please return the completed questionnaire to school with your child. Thank you very much for your participation.

Sincerely yours,

Name of teacher

FIGURE 5.10. Parent questionnaire letter for *Brag Sheets: Improving Behavior during Rest Time.* Adapted from Lahey, Gendrich, Gendrich, Schnelle, Gant, and McNees (1977). Copyright 1977 by Sage Publications, Inc. Adapted by permission.

PARENT BRAG SHEET QUESTIONNAIRE

	Very much	Much	Somewhat	Not at all
1. How much do you feel the Brag Sheet has improved communication between you and your child's teacher?	1	2	3	4
2. Has the Brag Sheet given you a better picture of your child's progress in school?	1	2	3	4
3. How much do you feel your child's school performance has improved as a result of the Brag Sheet?	1	2	3	4
4. How much do you think your child likes the Brag Sheet?	1	2	3	4
5. How much do you feel your child's attitude toward school has improved as a result of the Brag Sheet?	1	2	3	4
6. Do you see the Brag Sheet and the incentive it provides as an important part of your child's education?	1	2	3	4
7. How much has your behavior toward your child in terms of incentives and rewards changed as a result of the Brag Sheet?	1	2	3	4

8. How often did you receive the Brag Sheet?
   (1) Every day or almost every day
   (2) Two or three times a week
   (3) One time each week
   (4) Rarely or never

9. Which of the following report systems would you prefer now?
   (1) Daily Brag Sheet
   (2) Weekly Brag Sheet
   (3) Six-week report cards
   (4) Nine-week report cards

FIGURE 5.11. Parent questionnaire for *Brag Sheets: Improving Behavior during Rest Time.* Adapted from Lahey, Gendrich, Gendrich, Schnelle, Gant, and Mc-Nees, (1977, p. 389). Copyright 1977 by Sage Publications, Inc. Adapted by permission.

INTERVENTIONS TO DECREASE VERBAL
AND PHYSICAL AGGRESSION AND INCREASE
COOPERATIVE BEHAVIOR

Students who are physically or verbally aggressive or who refuse to comply with teacher directions can be extremely disruptive to ongoing instruction and can create tension-filled classroom environments (Blase, 1986). Designing effective interventions to help students manage negative emotions and cooperate with adults and peers is critical not only to creating an orderly and collaborative learning environment but to the long-term prognosis of aggressive and defiant children. Conduct problems early in life are quite stable over time (Koot & Verhulst, 1992; Loeber, 1982; Olweus, 1979) and put children at risk for a host of negative developmental outcomes, including peer rejection, school failure, delinquency, and substance abuse (e.g., Coie, Lochman, Terry, & Hyman, 1992; Hinshaw, 1992b; Kupersmidt & Coie, 1990; Loeber, 1990; Tremblay et al., 1992).

The importance of early intervention is underscored by research demonstrating the rapidity with which a vicious cycle of ineffective child behavior, teacher and peer rejection, and school and social failure can be set in motion. Many aggressive and defiant children have acquired their inappropriate behavioral patterns in homes where parents have failed to teach age-appropriate ways of managing negative emotions and have inadvertently reinforced coercive interactional patterns (Patterson, Reid, & Dishion, 1992). When these children enter school, they are likely to continue to engage in similar coercive interactions with their teachers and classmates (Forehand & Wierson, 1993; Reid & Patterson, 1991). Because their inappropriate behavior interferes with their ability to succeed academically and to form positive relationships with adults and peers, they fail to earn the typical school reinforcements of good grades, positive peer attention, and teacher praise. Deprived of these rewards and increasingly isolated from positive social models, they gravitate to groups of rejected youngsters like themselves who do not require them to display the appropriate behaviors they have failed to acquire (Dishion, Patterson, Stoolmiller, & Skinner, 1991). Patterson and his colleagues (1992) describe this phenomenon as "limited shopping," indicating that the development of antisocial behaviors increasingly restricts the number and quality of the social settings available to these youngsters. Over time, the limited shopping situation becomes more pronounced, so that children participate in fewer positive social experiences and spend more time associating with deviant peers who provide modeling and encouragement for antisocial behaviors.

As the vicious cycle progresses, children's membership in these antisocial peer groups contributes to an escalation of aggressive and defiant behaviors and to the development of an antisocial identity in which conforming to deviant peer norms overrides the desire to conform to classroom and school norms (Forehand & Wierson, 1993; Loeber, 1990; Patterson et al., 1992). Under these circumstances, the power of school personnel to influence student behavior in positive directions is severely compromised. When teachers attempt to intervene on behalf of these children, the reinforcement they have to offer for appropriate behavior is far less powerful than that provided by the deviant peer group for antisocial actions, such as disrupting class, defying authority figures, or bullying other students (Dishion et al., 1991; Forehand & Wierson, 1993). Moreover, after the elementary grades, children may become so entrenched in the antisocial peer group that they have difficulty altering their image with teachers and peers even if they are taught more appropriate ways of behaving (Webster-Stratton, 1993). Many of the interventions in this section were originally designed for use during the preschool and primary grade years, while children are still susceptible to adult influence and before they have become irrevocably attached to deviant peers. Moreover, several interventions use peer-mediated strategies to provide group influence and support for positive behaviors.

In designing classroom interventions for aggressive and noncompliant children, consultants should carefully assess the need for adjunctive academic interventions. Although it is not clear whether poor school achievement precedes or follows disruptive behavior problems, students with a combination of learning and behavior problems are especially at risk for the development of aggressive and antisocial behavior and require a comprehensive set of interventions targeting both sets of problems (Hinshaw, 1992a, 1992b; Tremblay et al., 1992). Indeed, research (Coie & Krehbiel, 1984) documents that interventions promoting academic success for aggressive and defiant children can not only increase achievement but also improve classroom behavior, student–teacher relationships, and peer sociometric status.

Importance of School-Based Interventions

Many programs designed to modify aggressive and defiant behavior and improve social competence have attempted to do so through interventions delivered outside of the classroom, such as family-focused treatment in clinic settings. Although many of these treatment programs have had short-term positive effects on children's home behavior, long-term results have been disappointing, and gains have often failed to generalize to the school setting and to peer relationships (Kazdin, 1987; Webster-Stratton, 1993). Moreover, because most of these approaches have been based on treatment of individual families with individual therapists, they are time consuming and costly. In contrast, school-based interventions can directly address the risk factors of academic failure and rejection by teachers and classmates before children become attached to deviant peer groups that promote antisocial attitudes and behaviors.

The classroom is the ideal environment for helping children learn to manage negative feelings and acquire prosocial behaviors because skills are taught and practiced in the setting in which they will be used. Rather than removing aggressive children from the classroom for individual or small-group training, as many programs have done, interventions should be integrated into the regular curriculum, not only to teach prosocial behaviors in the setting in which they will be used but also to prevent socially competent peers from rejecting socially inept children and driving them further into deviant peer group membership (Webster-Stratton, 1993). Moreover, given the increasing prevalence of conduct problems among children (American Psychiatric Association, 1994), implementing classwide strategies to reduce aggression and increase social competence should be a high priority for school consultants.

Types of Social Competence Problems

Social competence problems can result from two types of deficits: *acquisition deficits* or *performance deficits*, either of which may be accompanied by interfering problem behaviors, such as anxiety or aggression, that prevent the acquisition or performance of social skills (Gresham, 1981; Gresham & Elliott, 1990). Students with acquisition deficits have failed to acquire certain social skills in their repertoires, lack a particular step necessary for performing the skill, or execute the skill ineffectively (Gresham, 1995). Strategies such as direct instruction, modeling, coaching, and rehearsal are especially useful for these kinds of social skills problems (Elliott, Gresham, & Heffer, 1987). In contrast, students with social performance deficits possess the requisite social skills but for a variety of reasons fail to perform them. Many more children have performance deficits than have acquisition deficits (Gresham, 1995). Interventions targeting social performance deficits are designed to increase the frequency with which students display the desired behaviors, typically by manipulating antecedents or consequences to encourage satisfactory levels of performance (Elliott, Gresham, & Heffer, 1987).

Diverse learners, including disadvantaged and disabled children, are especially in need of interventions designed to enhance social competence. Children living in poor urban environments, who are often exposed to violent models of behavior, may have few opportunities to learn and practice cooperating with others and to receive reinforcement for engaging in socially effective behaviors (Barnett & Carey, 1992). In addition, although there is little evidence supporting the notion that social skills deficits constitute a specific learning disability, learning-disabled, behavior-disordered, and mildly mentally retarded children generally have poorer social skills and are more often rejected by their peers, compared with their nondisabled classmates (Gresham, 1992; Merrell, Johnson, Merz, & Ring, 1992). Children with ADHD may be especially at risk for impaired peer relationships because of their impulsivity, hyperactivity, and other socially aversive behaviors. Although medication may decrease these behaviors, ADHD children also need interventions that promote social competence because medication does not generate the kinds of socially appropriate behaviors that lead to peer acceptance (Landau & Moore, 1991). Interventions that assist diverse learners in acquiring and performing effective social behaviors can not only prevent inappropriate special education placements but also enhance the likelihood that students who are already placed can be successfully mainstreamed (Gresham, 1981; Knoff, 1988).

Overview of Interventions

The interventions in this section use a variety of techniques, including feedback, social recognition, and contingent reinforcement, to help children manage negative emotions and acquire and practice prosocial behaviors. Providing immediate feedback to students with social competence problems is an especially important aspect of intervention design. The failure of socially rejected children to modify their ineffective behaviors may in part be related to the fact that they seldom receive specific feedback about their social behaviors (Coie, 1990). Two interventions combine feedback with direct instruction, the first in the form of teacher-delivered instruction (*Using Verbal Instructions to Reduce Aggressive Behavior*), and the second by means of peer-mediated instruction (*Decreasing Inappropriate Verbalizations with a Peer Confrontation System*).

Two other powerful reinforcers for prosocial behavior are teacher and peer recognition. Because socially inept children are likely to abandon the effort to behave appropriately if they do not receive reinforcement for their efforts, implementing strategies that prompt teachers and peers to observe and validate small positive behavior changes may be critical to treatment success. By establishing a daily forum for acknowledging appropriate social behavior, *Increasing Cooperative Behavior with Sharing Time* provides children with regular reinforcement and encouragement for effective behavior. *Reinforcing Cooperative Play for Preschoolers* combines social reinforcement in the form of teacher and peer attention with a group-oriented token economy system to prompt prosocial behavior.

Differential reinforcement of low rates of responding (DRL) procedures are used in two interventions to reduce verbal aggression. DRL involves delivering reinforcement either for a reduction in the frequency of an undesired response within a given time period or for an increase in the amount of time that elapses between responses. *Using DRL to Decrease Negative Verbalizations* combines DRL with an interdependent group contingency, whereas *Decreasing Inappropriate Verbalizations with a Group Timeout Ribbon* incorporates a visual cue within a token economy system to prompt students to refrain from the target negative behaviors.

USING VERBAL INSTRUCTIONS TO REDUCE AGGRESSIVE BEHAVIOR

Overview

Many interventions designed to alter students' social interactions use contingency management, such as timeout and response cost, to control behavior. In contrast, this strategy uses direct verbal instruction to modify aggressive behavior and teach children more positive ways of relating to each other. Instructions include three concepts: (1) the harm that results from aggression, (2) its ineffectiveness in interpersonal relationships, and (3) positive methods of solving conflicts. Significant decreases in aggressive behavior, accompanied by significant increases in positive behavior, have been reported for preschoolers during free play periods. In the original study, the teacher practiced at home with scripts before implementation and taught the concepts in individual 10-minute sessions to the most aggressive students in a day care group. Adapted here for classwide implementation, the strategy can be used to target verbal and physical aggression in primary and upper elementary grade classrooms with age-appropriate modifications in the scripts.

Purpose

To reduce aggressive behavior and increase positive social interactions using direct verbal instruction.

Materials

None

Observation (Select One or Both)

Option 1
1. Select a free play period, center time, or some other period during which students are interacting socially.
2. Using a *Group Interval Recording Form* with a 5-second interval, observe each student in turn and categorize behavior as follows:
   a. *Aggressive behavior*, defined as physical aggression, verbal abuse, taking away or not sharing toys or materials, and playful fighting;
   b. *Positive active behavior*, defined as playing cooperatively with at least one other

child, working with others on the assigned activity, and playing/working alone;

c. *Inactive behavior*, defined as passive observation of others, resting alone, and daydreaming.

3. Conduct these observations during the selected period for 20 to 30 minutes for 4 to 7 days.

Option 2

1. Using a *Group Event Recording Form*, tally the frequency of two categories of aggressive behaviors for the entire class or a small group of students during a free play period, center time, or some other period for 4 to 7 days as follows:
   a. *Physical aggression*, defined as taking away or not sharing toys, playful fighting, physically threatening another student, or hitting;
   b. *Verbal aggression*, defined as verbally abusing or verbally threatening another student.
2. Conduct these observations for 30 to 45 minutes for 4 to 7 days.

Procedure

1. Lead a class discussion about aggression and its negative effects, focusing on the three concepts presented below.
2. During the discussion, ask the students leading questions and encourage the desired response, prompting if children do not respond or respond inappropriately. Use the sample scripts as guides.
3. Teach the following three concepts, in the order presented:

Concept 1: Aggression hurts others and makes them unhappy.

> TEACHER: How will other students feel if you hit or yell at them?
> STUDENT: They will be upset.
> TEACHER: Do you remember how you felt when someone hit you?
> STUDENT: I felt bad.
> TEACHER: Can you enjoy school and do your work when you are unhappy?
> STUDENT: No.

Teacher summarizes: When we work and play together, we all want to enjoy ourselves. When another student hits us or yells at us, we don't have fun. So we should not yell and hit and take things from others because then they won't be able to feel good.

Concept 2: Aggression does not solve problems and only makes others angry.

> TEACHER: After you hit or yelled at another student, did that student want to be your friend?
> STUDENT: No.
> TEACHER: What happens to children who always fight with others or call them names?
> STUDENT: Nobody wants to be their friend.

TEACHER: Do you think those children will be happy at school?
STUDENT: No.

Teacher summarizes: You should not hit others or call them names or take their things because that doesn't help you at all. Others won't share with you, they won't want to be your friend, and they won't like to play with you. So you won't be happy at school.

Concept 3: Positive ways to solve conflicts are sharing, taking turns, and working and playing together.

TEACHER: Suppose you're working at a center with another student and you both want to have a good time. What should you do?
STUDENT: Share the materials.
TEACHER: Suppose you have just one ball at recess and three other students want to play with it and have fun. What can you do?
STUDENT: You can take turns playing with the ball, or you can play a game together.
TEACHER: Suppose you have just one jump rope and lots of students want to jump. What can you do?
STUDENT: You can take turns turning the rope and jumping.

Teacher summarizes: If you want to have fun working and playing at school and want your classmates to be happy, too, you should share, take turns, and play together. Then everybody will be happy, and we will have lots of fun at school.

Evaluation (Select One or Both)

Option 1
1. Compare classwide rates of aggressive behavior, positive active behavior, and inactive behavior during the selected period before and after implementation.

Option 2
1. Compare the frequency of physical and verbal aggression for the entire class or the small group of students during the selected period before and after implementation.

Variation

Implement the intervention during a sharing and discussion period, such as circle time for primary grades and class forums for upper elementary grades. Review the concepts periodically to reinforce learning.

Note

In adapting the language in the scripts to the grade in which the intervention is being implemented, emphasize playing cooperatively for younger students and working cooperatively for older students.

Source

Zahavi, S., & Asher, S. R. (1978). The effect of verbal instructions on preschool children's aggressive behavior. *Journal of School Psychology, 16,* 146–153. Copyright 1978 by Elsevier Science Ltd, Oxford, England. Adapted by permission.

DECREASING INAPPROPRIATE VERBALIZATIONS WITH A PEER CONFRONTATION SYSTEM

Overview

Teachers have long recognized the power of peer influence to shape student behavior in either positive or negative directions. This intervention uses a naturally occurring behavior—peer confrontation—to target inappropriate behavior. The teacher guides students in challenging their own classmates to be aware of their inappropriate behavior and its effects on others and in offering suggestions for positive alternatives. Instead of simply suppressing inappropriate behavior, the intervention teaches children constructive ways of dealing with peer-related problem situations. Originally used with a small group of emotionally disturbed primary grade students in a self-contained special education classroom, it is adapted here for regular classroom implementation.

Purpose

To decrease inappropriate verbalizations using a teacher-directed peer confrontation system.

Materials

None

Observation (Select One or Both)

1. Using a sheet of paper attached to a clipboard, record the number of inappropriate verbalizations during a selected instructional period for the entire class or a small group of students for 4 to 7 days. *Inappropriate verbalizations* are defined as any verbalization that occurs without teacher permission, such as name calling, tattling, or teasing.
2. Using a sheet of paper attached to a clipboard, record the number of reprimands you issue in response to inappropriate verbalizations, defined as above, for the entire class during a selected instructional period for 4 to 7 days.

Procedure

1. Introduce the strategy to the students by telling them that they will be learning a new way to help each other get along better at school. Conduct a training

session that reviews the following procedures and provides opportunities for students to role play various situations and receive feedback.
2. When a student makes an inappropriate verbalization, ask the class the following questions:
   a. _____ seems to be having a problem. Who can tell _____ what the problem is?
   b. Can you tell _____ why that is a problem?
   c. Who can tell _____ what he or she needs to do to solve the problem?
3. Following each question, select a volunteer to respond. Praise students for appropriate responses to the questions.
4. Praise the student who made the inappropriate verbalization for accepting and engaging in the positive behavior alternatives suggested by his or her peers.

Evaluation (Select One or Both)

1. Compare the frequency of inappropriate verbalizations during the selected instructional period for the entire class or the small group of students before and after implementation.
2. Compare the frequency of reprimands issued in response to inappropriate verbalizations during the selected instructional period before and after implementation.

Variation

Divide the class into teams based on seating arrangements. When a student makes an inappropriate verbalization, invite members of that team to respond. Because group responding is confined to one area of the classroom, this variation interferes less with ongoing instructional activities, such as independent seatwork.

Notes

1. In the original research study, target students sometimes reacted negatively to peer feedback at first by making inappropriate comments or nonsense sounds and covering their ears. These negative side effects decreased as the intervention proceeded. Modeling appropriate responses to peer feedback before implementation helps to minimize these negative side effects.
2. Teachers may express concern that having students discuss each other's inappropriate behaviors, even in a teacher-directed system, may inadvertently reinforce those behaviors by providing additional attention. In this event, *Using DRL to Decrease Negative Verbalizations* can be suggested.

Source

Bellafiore, L. A., & Salend, S. J. (1983). Modifying inappropriate behaviors through a peer-confrontation system. *Behavioral Disorders, 8,* 274–279. Copyright 1983 by The Council for Exceptional Children. Adapted by permission.

INCREASING COOPERATIVE BEHAVIOR WITH SHARING TIME

Overview

Originally used in a kindergarten classroom, this intervention relies on a naturally occurring reinforcer—peer reporting—to increase prosocial responses. Students are encouraged during a daily sharing time to report the cooperative and friendly behaviors of their peers, who receive a sticker or badge in acknowledgment. As the intervention proceeds, the extrinsic rewards are withdrawn and only peer praise is used. Positive peer reporting has been found to be highly effective in reducing aggression and increasing cooperative play. Teachers also report general behavioral improvement, including increased sharing, greater concern for the needs of others, and more frequent peer contacts with socially isolated children.

Purpose

To increase cooperative behavior and decrease aggression through peer reporting of positive social actions.

Materials

1. "Happy face" badges, consisting of circles of yellow posterboard or construction paper with "smiley faces" drawn with a black felt-tip marker and holes for threading yarn so the badges can be worn around the neck, one per student

Observation (Select One or More)

Option 1

1. Using a modified *Classwide Scanning Form* with a 1-minute interval, conduct 15-minute observations during a free play period for 4 to 7 days as follows:
   a. Count the number of students present in the room or play area at the end of a 1-minute interval and then immediately count the number of students playing cooperatively with each other.
   b. *Cooperative play* is defined as play that involves sharing materials, taking turns, and/or making positive verbalizations.
   c. Calculate the percentage of students engaged in cooperative play for each 1-minute interval. For example, if there are 20 students in the play area and 15 are playing cooperatively, the percentage of students in cooperative play for that interval is 75%.
   d. Calculate the median percentage of students engaged in cooperative play for each 15-minute observation period.

Option 2

1. Using a *Group Event Recording Form*, count the number of aggressive behaviors for the entire class or a group of the most disruptive students during a free play period, center time, or another period for 20 to 30 minutes for 4 to 7 days. *Ag-*

gressive behaviors are defined as hitting, pushing, throwing objects at others, or verbally or physically attacking others.

Option 3
1. Using a sheet of paper attached to a clipboard, record the number of "tattling" behaviors during a free play period or the entire school day for 4 to 7 days. *Tattling behaviors* are defined as any student complaints about the verbal or physical behavior of a classmate.

Procedure

1. Tell the class that during a sharing time each day, every student will have the chance to name a classmate who has been friendly to him or her at play period (or during the school day) and to describe the friendly behavior.
2. Conduct a sharing time period when you permit the students named by their peers as being friendly to take a happy face badge from a hook on the wall or shelf and wear it for the rest of the day.
3. Encourage children not to describe their own friendly acts and do not dispense the badges for self-reports.
4. If a student cannot remember the name of someone who was friendly to him or her, say, "Perhaps tomorrow you will be able to name someone."
5. After 8 days or when aggressive behavior has been substantially reduced, discontinue using the happy face badges.

Evaluation (Select One or More)

Option 1
1. Compare the median percentage of students engaged in cooperative play during the free play period before and after implementation.

Option 2
1. Compare the frequency of aggressive behaviors for the entire class or the group of the most disruptive students during the selected period before and after implementation.

Option 3
1. Compare the frequency of tattling behaviors during the free play period or the entire school day before and after the intervention.

Variation

One of the most popular interventions in the field testing, this strategy lends itself to many variations. For example, have students draw names and write a brief essay to complete a complimentary sentence stem about the student whose name was drawn, such as "I liked it when you . . . ." Then have them illustrate their compositions. As the final activity on Friday, have students read their compositions aloud and present them to their classmates. Thanks to John Daly, fourth-grade teacher at Immaculate Conception School, for this variation.

Notes

1. In the original study, a reversal period in which students were asked to report the names of children who were unfriendly and to describe the unfriendly acts resulted in dramatic increases in aggressive acts and decreases in cooperative acts.
2. This strategy can be easily modified for implementation in primary and elementary grade classrooms that include sharing time or group discussions as part of the daily or weekly routine. If the curriculum includes peer tutoring or other cooperative learning activities, students can be encouraged to name peers who were especially helpful or friendly during these times as well as during recess or physical education class. In upper elementary grade classrooms, use teacher and peer recognition as reinforcement and omit the victory badges.

Source

Grieger, T., Kauffman, J. M., & Grieger, R. M. (1976). Effects of peer reporting on cooperative play and aggression of kindergarten children. *Journal of School Psychology*, *14*, 307–313. Copyright 1976 by Elsevier Science Ltd, Oxford, England. Adapted by permission.

REINFORCING COOPERATIVE PLAY FOR PRESCHOOLERS

Overview

Free play periods in preschool settings provide opportunities for children to share toys and activities and interact verbally and physically with each other. For youngsters who have not developed positive interpersonal skills, such as taking turns and cooperating with others, these less structured times can lead to aggressive, uncooperative behaviors that elicit negative reactions from teachers and classmates and interfere with a positive classroom climate. In the original study, praise and a token system were used to reinforce cooperative play for a small group of behavior-problem preschoolers, with tokens recorded on charts worn by the students. This adaptation employs a team format to facilitate implementation with an entire classroom group, and the individual format is included as a variation.

Purpose

To increase cooperative behavior among preschoolers through a team-oriented token economy system.

Materials

1. "Happy face" charts, consisting of yellow sheets of construction paper, with intervals marked by lines corresponding to the number of minutes spent in the

play activity (e.g., 15 intervals for 15 minutes), threaded with yarn, one for each team captain or each target student (see Variation 2)
2. Small happy face stickers with adhesive backs that can be easily attached to and removed from charts
3. Large happy face stickers
4. Posterboard chart listing team names, with space for affixing stickers (see Variation 1)
5. Individual team badges, consisting of colored circles of construction paper, threaded with yarn, with a different color for each team (see Notes)

Observation (Select One or Both)

Option 1
1. Using a *Group Interval Recording Form* with a 10-second interval, glance at each student in turn and code behavior according to the following categories:
   a. *Cooperative play*, defined as sharing an activity, toy, or conversation with another child or group of children;
   b. *Verbal or physical aggression*, defined as pushing, hitting, or verbally or physically threatening another child or adult.
2. Conduct these observations for 20 to 30 minutes during a free play or center activity period for 4 to 7 days.

Option 2
1. Record the number of timeouts served by the entire class or a small group of children during a free play or center activity period for 4 to 7 days. A *timeout* is defined as 3 minutes of sitting in a timeout chair as a consequence for acts of verbal or physical aggression.

Procedure

1. Tell the students that they will be using happy face charts to remind them to play and work cooperatively with each other during free play, center activity, or some other group interaction period.
2. Lead a discussion of what it means to work and play cooperatively and have students role play various interactional situations, such as sharing toys and center materials.
3. Divide the class into four or five teams based on seating arrangements.
4. Designate a "good manners captain" for each team and give the captain a happy face chart to wear. Rotate captains every day.
5. Tell the children that you will be rewarding cooperative working and playing in each group by putting stickers on the captains' charts during the target period. Explain that teams earning at least eight stickers (or some appropriate number) can trade them for 10 minutes of extra outdoor recess and large happy face stickers to wear during the day.
6. At regular intervals (beginning with 5-minute intervals) during the target period, praise children individually and as a group for cooperative play (e.g., "I like the way Team 3 members are using their center!"), and place happy face

stickers on the charts of captains whose teams are engaging in cooperative behavior.

7. If students display uncooperative or aggressive behavior during the interval, prompt them to engage in cooperative behavior and remind them of the extra recess and stickers they can earn.

8. At the end of the period, count the happy faces on each chart and praise the teams for their efforts to share and work well with others. Give all the members of teams meeting the criterion a large happy face sticker to wear for the rest of the day.

9. Groups that do not earn enough tokens to go outside are allowed to look at books or to engage in a less desired indoor activity.

10. Remind students of the rewards for cooperative play at the beginning of each target period. Gradually increase the criterion to 12 or more stickers as cooperative behavior increases.

11. As students become more successful in playing cooperatively, continue providing verbal praise and the outside play reward, but discontinue the happy face charts and stickers.

Evaluation (Select One or Both)

Option 1

1. Compare the percentages of children exhibiting cooperative play and verbal or physical aggression during the free play or center activity period before and after implementation.

Option 2

1. Compare the number of timeouts served by the entire class or the small group of children during a free play or center activity period before and after implementation.

Variations

1. Instead of placing stickers on captains' charts, post a chart listing the teams at the front of the room and place stickers on the chart. Color code the stickers to assist students in monitoring their team's progress. Provide rewards to winning teams as described above.

2. Give each target student an individual chart and award stickers on an individual basis. Increase monitoring intervals to 10 or 15 minutes and adjust the criterion accordingly.

Notes

1. This intervention is most easily implemented when students are playing or working in small groups in a designated area of the room. If students will be moving around the room, use Variation 1 and hang team badges around their necks to assist in team identification.

2. In the original study, outdoor recess was used as the primary backup reinforcer.

For this reward, an aide or other staff member is needed to supervise students who do not meet the criterion and must remain indoors. If an aide is not available, permit members of winning teams to take home their happy face stickers or a good day award (see *Reducing Rule Violations with Good Day Awards*).

Source

Wolfe, V. V., Boyd, L. A., & Wolfe, D. A. (1983). Teaching cooperative play to behavior-problem preschool children. *Education and Treatment of Children, 6,* 1–9. Copyright 1983 by Pressley Ridge School. Adapted by permission.

USING DRL TO DECREASE NEGATIVE VERBALIZATIONS

Overview

Name calling, teasing, and other negative verbal comments among students can disrupt instruction and contribute to a hostile classroom climate. This intervention applies a differential reinforcement of low rates (DRL) procedure to decrease negative peer verbal interactions. In a DRL procedure, reinforcement is delivered contingent upon a reduction in an undesirable behavior within a particular time period or an increase in the amount of time that passes between occurrences of that behavior. Here DRL is delivered within an interdependent group contingency to create peer pressure for appropriate social behavior. Rapid and significant decreases in negative student verbalizations have been reported with this intervention. Originally used in a special education resource room setting with a small group of junior high school students, it is adapted here for total classroom use.

Purpose

To reduce negative verbalizations among students by using a DRL procedure.

Materials

1. Posterboard chart listing class rules, such as:
   a. Follow the teacher's directions.
   b. Keep from disturbing others while they are working.
   c. Use polite and friendly language.
   d. Respect the teacher, other students, and yourself.
2. Posterboard chart or section of the chalkboard with a line graph for displaying the daily number of negative remarks
3. Posterboard chart or section of the chalkboard with a bar graph for recording extra daily negative remarks
4. *Reinforcement Menus*, one per student
5. Reinforcers, such as juice boxes, candy, inexpensive school supplies, and homework passes
6. Slips of paper describing reinforcers, in a hat or box (see Note)

Observation (Select One or Both)

Option 1

1. Using a sheet of paper attached to a clipboard, record the number of negative verbalizations for the entire class or a small group of students for 20 to 30 minutes during a selected instructional period.
2. *Negative verbalizations* are defined as teasing, name-calling, threatening, or any other unfriendly or aggressive verbalization.
3. Conduct these observations for 4 to 7 days.

Option 2

1. Using a *Classwide Scanning Form*, scan the classroom every 5 minutes during a selected instructional period and record the number of students in each of the following categories:
   a. *Cooperative classroom behavior*, defined as working alone or with others on assigned tasks in a way that does not disturb others;
   b. *Negative verbal behavior*, defined as teasing, name-calling, threatening, or any other unfriendly or aggressive verbalization;
   c. *Disruptive classroom behavior*, defined as behavior that interferes with ongoing instruction and/or the work of other students, such as pushing, out-of-seat behavior, calling out to the teacher, or talking loudly.
2. Conduct these observations for 20 to 30 minutes for 4 to 7 days.

Procedure

1. Explain to the students that they will be able to earn rewards by working together to create a positive classroom climate that supports everyone's learning.
2. Explain that they can earn rewards if the group as a whole makes five or less teasing or name-calling comments during the period. Using *Reinforcement Menus*, help students develop a list of reinforcers from which they can select each day.
3. Post and discuss the classroom rules. Using data obtained during the observation period as a guide, tell the students the maximum number of teasing/name-calling comments allowed for the group to obtain the reward for that day.
4. Make a mark on the chalkboard for every negative verbalization. Do not discuss these remarks or reprimand students who make them. Record the number of negative remarks made each day on a line graph on a chart or the chalkboard so that the class can observe its progress.
5. If the group as a whole does not exceed the criterion number of negative remarks, permit each student to select a reward at the end of the period.
6. To prevent the number of negative verbalizations from increasing if the day's limit is exceeded, give a larger group reward, such as 15 minutes of free time or a popcorn party at the end of the week, if the class has five or less "extra" negative remarks for the week. Record the extra remarks on a bar graph on the chalkboard so that students can monitor their progress during the week.
7. As student interactions become more positive, decrease the permitted number

of negative verbalizations per day. Also decrease the permitted number of "extra" negative comments.

Evaluation (Select One or Both)

Option 1
1. Compare the frequency of negative verbalizations for the entire class or the small group of students during the selected instructional period before and after implementation.

Option 2
1. Compare classwide percentages of students exhibiting cooperative classroom behavior, negative verbal behavior, and disruptive behavior during the selected instructional period before and after implementation.

Variations

1. As improvement continues, record the number of negative comments in a notebook and inform students near the end of the period whether or not they have earned the reward.
2. Use principal attention (see *Encouraging Academic Achievement with Principal Praise*) as an additional reward for an exceptionally positive week.

Note

To facilitate delivery of daily rewards, write descriptions of the daily reinforcers on slips of paper and place them in a hat or box. Have a student draw a slip each day and give all students the same reward.

Source

Zwald, L., & Gresham, F. M. (1982). Behavioral consultation in a secondary class: Using DRL to decrease negative verbal interactions. *School Psychology Review*, *11*, 428–432. Copyright 1982 by the National Association of School Psychologists. Adapted by permission.

DECREASING INAPPROPRIATE VERBALIZATIONS WITH A GROUP TIMEOUT RIBBON

Overview

Inappropriate student verbalizations, such as calling out, teasing or joking with peers, and making excessive noise, are frequent problems in elementary and middle school classrooms. This strategy uses an interdependent group-oriented timeout ribbon in conjunction with a token economy system to reduce inappropriate verbalizations. In a timeout ribbon procedure, the target student wears a ribbon or object that serves as a discriminative stimulus for reinforcement. As long as the student behaves appropriately, the student may wear the ribbon and receive reinforcement. If the student engages in inappropriate behavior, the ribbon is removed and access to reinforcement is denied. In the original study, the group-oriented timeout ribbon was successful in reducing negative verbalizations with small groups of students in resource room settings. Moreover, the decreases in negative verbalizations were accompanied by improvements in the quality and quantity of classwork. Here the strategy is used to target a variety of inappropriate social behaviors in regular classroom groups.

Purpose

To reduce inappropriate verbalizations or other inappropriate social behaviors by using a group-oriented timeout procedure within a token economy system.

Materials

1. Posterboard chart listing the classroom rules; rules should target each undesired behavior and be stated in a positive format, such as:
   a. Raise your hand and wait to be called upon before speaking.
   b. Use polite and kind words to others.
   c. Keep from making too much noise.
   d. Stay in your seat unless you have permission to get up.
2. 14″ × ½″ red ribbon, shaped into a loop with the ends pointed down
3. *Reinforcement Menus*, one per student (optional)
4. Portable easel or bulletin board
5. Posterboard chart or section of the chalkboard listing the number of points necessary to purchase each backup reward
6. Posterboard chart, chart on a section of the chalkboard, or glass jar with marbles or colored chips for recording the number of points earned each day (see variation)

Observation (Select One or Both)

Option 1

1. Using a sheet of paper attached to a clipboard, record the number of inappropriate verbalizations (or other target inappropriate social behaviors) for the entire class during a selected instructional period. *Inappropriate verbalizations* are defined as student verbalizations that occur without teacher permission, such as calling out, teasing or verbally threatening peers, or making comments that disrupt ongoing instruction.
2. Divide the number of inappropriate verbalizations by the number of minutes per period to obtain the number of inappropriate verbalizations per minute.
3. Conduct these observations for 4 to 7 days.

Option 2
1. Using a *Classwide Scanning Form*, scan the room from left to right every 5 minutes during a selected instructional period and record the number of students in each of the following behavior categories:
   a. *Appropriate classroom behavior*, defined as behavior that does not interfere with ongoing instruction or the learning of other students and does not include any inappropriate classroom behavior as defined below;
   b. *Inappropriate classroom behavior*, defined as calling out, teasing or verbally threatening peers, or any other verbal or motor behavior that disrupts ongoing instruction.
2. Conduct these observations for 30 to 45 minutes for 4 to 7 days.

Procedure

1. Attach the ribbon to an easel or portable bulletin board placed in front of the teacher's desk and in full view of all the students.
2. Explain to the students that the ribbon will help them get more out of the instructional period by reminding them to follow the classroom rules. Display the chart with the rules, review them, and have students provide examples of appropriate and inappropriate verbalizations.
3. Explain that while students refrain from breaking the rules they will be able to earn points at regular intervals that they can then exchange for rewards.
4. If desired, distribute *Reinforcement Menus* and help the class select group-oriented reinforcers.
5. Tell students that they will receive 1 point for every 5 minutes they refrain from breaking the rules. Explain how many points are needed to earn each reward and display the chart listing those values (e.g., 10 points = 5 minutes of free time, 25 points = music time, 100 points = 15 minutes of free time, 300 points = a popcorn party, etc.).
6. Each time a student breaks a rule, remove the ribbon from the easel or bulletin board. When the class displays appropriate behavior for 5 minutes, return the ribbon and award a point for every 5 minutes students are following the rules.
7. If a student breaks a rule during the timeout period, extend the period until the group has exhibited 5 minutes of appropriate behavior and then restore the ribbon.
8. At the beginning of implementation, exchange points for reinforcers on a daily basis. As the target behaviors diminish, increase the time interval required for earning points. After additional improvement, make the exchange on a weekly basis.

Evaluation (Select One or Both)

Option 1
1. Compare the frequency of inappropriate verbalizations per minute during the selected instructional period before and after implementation.

Option 2

1. Compare the percentages of students exhibiting appropriate and inappropriate classroom behavior during the selected instructional period before and after implementation.

Variation

Record points earned by dropping marbles or colored chips in a large glass jar displayed on the teacher's desk. This variation is especially appropriate for primary grade classes.

Notes

1. Although the original study did not report negative peer interactions during the removal of the timeout ribbon for rule infractions, negative peer pressure is a potential side effect of any interdependent group contingency. Teaching the strategy using *Say Show Check: Teaching Classroom Procedures*, stressing group cooperation and support, and reviewing appropriate responses to the removal of the timeout ribbon as necessary are recommended to minimize this possibility.
2. By extending the length of the interval required to earn points, this intervention can be implemented during larger blocks of time, such as the morning seatwork period or the entire day, with the daily reward as the last activity.

Source

Salend, S. J., & Gordon, B. D. (1987). A group-oriented timeout ribbon procedure. *Behavioral Disorders, 12*, 131–137. Copyright 1987 by The Council for Exceptional Children. Adapted by permission.

SUPPLEMENTARY READINGS

Elksnin, L. K., & Elksnin, N. (1995). *Assessment and instruction of social skills* (2nd ed.). San Diego, CA: Singular Publishing Group.

The authors emphasize the use of a developmental perspective in assessing and teaching social skills. Included are descriptions of formal and informal approaches to social skills assessment and reviews of several rating scales and checklists. Comprehensive reviews of commercially published social skills curricular programs and guidelines for evaluating these programs are also included. Separate chapters present strategies for very young children, elementary grade children, and adolescents.

Gresham, F. M., & Elliott, S. N. (1991). *Social skills intervention guide: Practical strategies for social skills training*. Circle Pines, MN: American Guidance Service.

An extension of the Social Skills Rating System (SSRS) by the same authors, this book describes a program for teaching social skills to children between 6 and 16 years of age. Included are 43 lessons designed to enhance skills in the five domains assessed by the SSRS (cooperation, assertion, responsibility, empathy, and self-control). Implementation issues, such as selecting and grouping students for training, establishing group rules, and monitoring student progress, are also discussed.

Jones, V. F., & Jones, L. S. (1995). *Comprehensive classroom management: Creating positive learning environments for all students* (4th ed.). Boston: Allyn & Bacon.

This text includes several chapters that focus on solving individual and group behavior problems, including step-by-step procedures for responding to disruptive and defiant behavior. A variety of forms for self-assessment, school–home communications, and student behavior management are included. An entire chapter is devoted to schoolwide behavior management programs.

Rathvon, N. (1996). *The unmotivated child: Helping your underachiever become a successful student.* New York: Simon & Schuster.

Written from an attachment theory perspective, this book focuses on helping parents and teachers work collaboratively to assist children in developing and practicing effective academic and social behaviors at school. Strategies for dealing with the school misbehavior that often accompanies underachievement are presented.

Shapiro, E. S., & Cole, C. L. (1994). *Behavior change in the classroom: Self-management interventions.* New York: Guilford Press.

This book presents guidelines for designing and implementing self-management interventions in the schools. It includes reviews of contingency-based and cognitive-based approaches, interventions for students with severe disabilities, implementation issues, and seven case studies demonstrating the application of self-management strategies to academic, behavior, and social skills problems. A variety of reproducible charts and sample forms are provided.

Wolfgang, C. H. (1996). *The three faces of discipline for the elementary school teacher: Empowering the teacher and students.* Needham Heights, MA: Allyn & Bacon.

Wolfgang, C. H., & Wolfgang, M. E. (1995). *The three faces of discipline for early childhood: Empowering teachers and students.* Needham Heights, MA: Allyn & Bacon.

Designed for teachers and administrators, these companion volumes present what the authors describe as the "three faces of discipline": the relationship–listening face, based on Rogerian theory; the confronting–contracting face, based on Glasser's Reality Therapy and Adlerian theory; and the rules and consequences face, based on assertiveness training and behavior modification. The authors arrange behavior management strategies from these models along a power continuum of teacher action and demonstrate the application of different management methods depending on the misbehavior.

References

◆

Aaron, B. A., & Bostow, D. E. (1978). Indirect facilitation of on-task behavior produced by contingent free-time for academic productivity. *Journal of Applied Behavior Analysis, 11*, 197.

Aaron, P. G. (1995). Introduction to mini-series: Recent advances in reading instruction and remediation. *School Psychology Review, 24*, 327–330.

Aaron, P. G., & Joshi, R. M. (1992). *Reading problems: Consultation and remediation.* New York: Guilford Press.

Abramowitz, A. J., O'Leary, S. G., & Futtersak, M. W. (1988). The relative impact of long and short reprimands on children's off-task behavior in the classroom. *Behavior Therapy, 19*, 243–247.

Abramowitz, A. J., O'Leary, S. G., & Rosén, L. A. (1987). Reducing off-task behavior in the classroom: A comparison of encouragement and reprimands. *Journal of Abnormal Child Psychology, 15*, 153–163.

Acker, M. M., & O'Leary, S. G. (1987). Effects of reprimands and praise on appropriate behavior in the classroom. *Journal of Abnormal Child Psychology, 15*, 549–557.

Adams, M. J. (1990). *Beginning to read: Thinking and learning about print.* Cambridge, MA: MIT Press.

Adams, R. S., & Biddle, B. J. (1970). *Realities of teaching: Explorations with video tape.* New York: Holt, Rinehart & Winston.

Agostin, T. M., & Bain, S. K. (1997). Predicting early school success with developmental and social skills screeners. *Psychology in the Schools, 34*, 219–228.

Alessi, G. J. (1980). Behavioral observation for the school psychologist: Responsive-discrepancy model. *School Psychology Review, 9*, 31–45.

Alessi, G. (1988). Diagnosis diagnosed: A systemic reaction. *Professional School Psychology, 3*, 145–151.

Algozzine, B., O'Shea, D. J., Crews, W. B., & Stoddard, K. (1987). Analysis of mathematics competence of learning disabled adolescents. *Journal of Special Education, 21*, 97–107.

Algozzine, B., Ysseldyke, J. E., & Christenson, S. (1983). An analysis of the incidence of special class placement: The masses are burgeoning. *Journal of Special Education, 17*, 141–147.

Algozzine, B., Ysseldyke, J. E., & Hill, C. (1982). Psychoeducational decision making as a function of the amount of information reviewed. *Psychology in the Schools, 19,* 328–334.

Allen, C. T., & Forman, S. G. (1984). Efficacy of methods of training teachers in behavior modification. *School Psychology Review, 13,* 26–32.

Allington, R. L. (1983a). Fluency: The neglected reading goal. *The Reading Teacher, 36,* 556–561.

Allington, R. L. (1983b). The reading instruction provided readers of differing reading abilities. *Elementary School Journal, 83,* 548–559.

Allington, R. L. (1984). Content coverage and contextual reading in reading groups. *Journal of Reading Behavior, 16,* 85–96.

American Psychiatric Association. (1994). *Diagnostic and statistical manual of mental disorders* (4th ed.). Washington, DC: Author.

American Psychological Association. (1981). Specialty guidelines for delivery of services. *American Psychologist, 36,* 639–685.

American Psychological Association. (1992). Ethical principles of psychologists and code of conduct. *American Psychologist, 47,* 1597–1611.

Anderson, C. W., & Smith, E. L. (1984). Children's preconceptions and content-area textbooks. In G. G. Duffy, L. R. Roehler, & J. Mason (Eds.), *Comprehension instruction: Perspectives and suggestions* (pp. 187–201). New York: Longman.

Anderson, L. M. (1981). Short-term student responses to classroom instruction. *Elementary School Journal, 82,* 97–108.

Anderson, L. (1984a). The environment of instruction: The function of seatwork in a commercially developed curriculum. In G. G. Duffy, L. R. Roehler, & J. Mason (Eds.), *Comprehension instruction: Perspectives and suggestions* (pp. 93–103). New York: Longman.

Anderson, L. M. (1984b). What are students doing when they do all that seatwork? In C. W. Fisher & D. C. Berliner (Eds.), *Perspectives on instructional time* (pp. 189–202). New York: Longman.

Anderson, L. M., Brubaker, N. L., Alleman-Brooks, J., & Duffy, G. G. (1985). A qualitative study of seatwork in first-grade classrooms. *Elementary School Journal, 86,* 123–140.

Anderson, L. M., Evertson, C. M., & Brophy, J. E. (1979). An experimental study of effective teaching in first-grade reading groups. *Elementary School Journal, 79,* 193–223.

Anesko, K. M., & O'Leary, S. G. (1982). The effectiveness of brief parent training for the management of children's homework problems. *Child and Family Behavior Therapy, 4,* 113–126.

Anesko, K. M., Schoiock, G., Ramirez, R., & Levine, F. M. (1987). The Homework Problem Checklist: Assessing children's homework difficulties. *Behavioral Assessment, 9,* 179–185.

Arlin, M. (1979). Teacher transitions can disrupt time flow in classrooms. *American Educational Research Journal, 16,* 42–56.

Armbruster, B. B. (1984). The problem of "inconsiderate text." In G. G. Duffy, L. R. Roehler, & J. Mason (Eds.), *Comprehension instruction: Perspectives and suggestions* (pp. 202–217). New York: Longman.

Armbruster, B. B., & Gudbrandsen, B. (1986). Reading comprehension instruction in social studies programs. *Reading Research Quarterly, 21,* 36–48.

Axelrod, D., Hall, R. V., & Tams, A. (1979). Comparison of two common classroom seating arrangements. *Academic Therapy, 15,* 29–36.

Ayllon, T., & Roberts, M. D. (1974). Eliminating discipline problems by strengthening academic performance. *Journal of Applied Behavior Analysis, 7,* 71–76.

Bahr, M. W. (1994). The status and impact of prereferral interventions: "We need a better way to determine success." *Psychology in the Schools, 31,* 309–318.

Barnett, D. W., & Carey, K. T. (1992). *Designing interventions for preschool learning and behavior problems.* San Francisco: Jossey-Bass.

Beal, C. R., Garrod, A. C., & Bonitatibus, G. J. (1990). Fostering children's revision skills through training in comprehension monitoring. *Journal of Educational Psychology, 82,* 275–280.

Bear, G. C., & Richards, H. C. (1980). An interdependent group-oriented contingency system for improving academic performance. *School Psychology Review, 9,* 190–193.

Beck, I. L., Perfetti, C. A., & McKeown, M. G. (1982). Effects of long-term vocabulary instruction on lexical access and reading comprehension. *Journal of Educational Psychology, 74,* 506–521.

Becker, W. C., Madsen, C. H., Arnold, C. R., & Thomas, D. R. (1967). The contingent use of teacher attention and praise in reducing classroom behavior problems. *Journal of Special Education, 1,* 287–307.

Bennett, N., & Blundell, D. (1983). Quantity and quality of work in rows and classroom groups. *Educational Psychology, 3,* 93–105.

Bergan, J. R. (1977). *Behavioral consultation.* Columbus, OH: Merrill.

Bergan, J. R., & Kratochwill, T. R. (1990). *Behavioral consultation and therapy.* New York: Plenum Press.

Berliner, D. C. (1981). Academic learning time and reading achievement. In J. T. Guthrie (Ed.), *Comprehension and teaching: Research reviews* (pp. 203–226). Newark, DE: International Reading Association.

Berliner, D. D. (1988). Effective classroom management and instruction: A knowledge base for consultation. In J. L. Graden, J. E. Zins, & M. J. Curtis (Eds.), *Alternative educational delivery systems: Enhancing instructional options for all students* (pp. 309–325). Washington, DC: National Association of School Psychologists.

Blase, J. (1986). A qualitative analysis of sources of teacher stress: Consequences for performance. *American Educational Research Journal, 23,* 13–40.

Bossard, M. D., & Gutkin, T. B. (1983). The relationship of consultant skill and school organization characteristics with teacher use of school based consultation services. *School Psychology Review, 12,* 50–56.

Bradley-Johnson, S., & Lesiak, J. L. (1989). *Problems in written expression: Assessment and remediation.* New York: Guilford Press.

Brantley, D. C., & Webster, R. E. (1993). Use of an independent group contingency management system in a regular classroom setting. *Psychology in the Schools, 30,* 60–66.

Bridge, C. A., & Hiebert, E. H. (1985). A comparison of classroom writing practices, teachers' perceptions of their writing instruction, and textbook recommendations on writing practices. *Elementary School Journal, 86,* 155–172.

Broden, M., Bruce, C., Mitchell, M. A., Carter, V., & Hall, R. V. (1970). Effects of teacher attention on attending behavior of two boys at adjacent desks. *Journal of Applied Behavior Analysis, 3,* 205–211.

Brooks, D. M. (1985). The teacher's communicative competence: The first day of school. *Theory into Practice, 24,* 63–70.

Brophy, J. (1981). Teacher praise: A functional analysis. *Review of Educational Research, 51,* 5–32.

Brophy, J. (1986). Teacher influences on student achievement. *American Psychologist, 41,* 1069–1077.

Brophy, J. (1988). Educating teachers about managing classrooms and students. *Teaching and Teacher Education, 4,* 1–18.

Brophy, J. E., & Good, T. L. (1986). Teacher behavior and student achievement. In M. C. Wittrock (Ed.), *Handbook of research on teaching* (3rd ed., pp. 328–375). New York: Macmillan.

Brophy, J. E., & Rohrkemper, M. M. (1981). The influence of problem ownership on teachers' perceptions of and strategies for coping with problem students. *Journal of Educational Psychology, 73,* 295–311.

Broughton, S. F., & Hester, J. R. (1993). Effects of administrative and community support on teacher acceptance of classroom interventions. *Journal of Educational and Psychological Consultation, 4,* 169–177.

Broughton, S. F., & Lahey, B. B. (1978). Direct and collateral effects of positive reinforcement, response cost, and mixed contingencies for academic performance. *Journal of School Psychology, 16,* 126–136.

Brown, J., Gable, R. A., Hendrickson, J. M., & Algozzine, B. (1991). Prereferral intervention practices of regular classroom teachers: Implications for regular and special education preparation. *Teacher Education and Special Education, 14,* 192–197.

Budd, K. S., Leibowitz, J. M., Riner, L. S., Mindell, C., & Goldfarb, A. L. (1981). Home-based treatment of severe disruptive behaviors: A reinforcement package for preschool and kindergarten children. *Behavior Modification, 5,* 273–298.

Cameron, J., & Pierce, W. D. (1994). Reinforcement, reward, and intrinsic motivation: A meta-analysis. *Review of Educational Research, 64,* 363–423.

Carlberg, C., & Kavale, K. (1980). The efficacy of special versus regular class placement for exceptional children: A meta-analysis. *Journal of Special Education, 14,* 295–309.

Carnine, D. (1994). Introduction to the mini-series: Diverse learners and prevailing, emerging, and research-based educational approaches and their tools. *School Psychology Review, 23,* 341–350.

Carnine, D., Jones, E. D., & Dixon, R. (1994). Mathematics: Educational tools for diverse learners. *School Psychology Review, 23,* 406–427.

Carter, J., & Sugai, G. (1989). Survey on prereferral practices: Responses from state departments of education. *Exceptional Children, 55,* 298–302.

Cawley, J. F., & Miller, J. H. (1989). Cross-sectional comparisons of the mathematical performance of children with learning disabilities: Are we on the right track toward comprehensive programming? *Journal of Learning Disabilities, 22,* 250–254, 259.

Chalfant, J. C., & Pysh, M. V. (1989). Teacher assistance teams: Five descriptive studies on 96 teams. *Remedial and Special Education, 10,* 49–58.

Chalfant, J. C., Pysh, M. V., & Moultrie, R. (1979). Teacher assistance teams: A model for within-building problem solving. *Learning Disability Quarterly, 2,* 85–96.

Chinn, P. C., & Hughes, S. (1987). Representation of minority students in special education classes. *Remedial and Special Education, 8,* 41–46.

Christenson, S., Ysseldyke, J. E., Wang, J. J., & Algozzine, B. (1983). Teachers' attributions for problems that result in referral for psychoeducational evaluation. *Journal of Educational Research, 76,* 174–180.

Clarizio, H. F., & Halgren, D. W. (1993). Stability of special education placements: Data-based policy consultation. *Journal of Educational and Psychological Consultation, 4,* 49–67.

Clark, F., & Clark, C. (1989). *Hassle-free homework: A six-week plan for parents and children to take the pain out of homework.* New York: Doubleday.

Clay, R. A. (January, 1998). New laws aid children with disabilities. *APA Monitor,* p. 18.

Coates, D., Renzaglia, G. J., & Embree, M. C. (1983). When helping backfires: Help and helplessness. In J. D. Fisher, A. Nadler, & B. M. DePaulo (Eds.), *New directions in helping: Vol 1. Recipient reactions to aid* (pp. 251–275). New York: Academic Press.

Coie, J. D. (1990). Toward a theory of peer rejection. In S. R. Asher & J. D. Coie (Eds.), *Peer rejection in childhood* (pp. 365–401). Cambridge: Cambridge University Press.

Coie, J. D., & Krehbiel, G. (1984). Effects of academic tutoring on the social status of low-achieving, socially rejected children. *Child Development, 55,* 1465–1478.

Coie, J. D., Lochman, J. E., Terry, R., & Hyman, C. (1992). Predicting early adolescent disorders from childhood aggression and peer rejection. *Journal of Consulting and Clinical Psychology, 60,* 783–792.

Conoley, J. C., & Conoley, C. W. (1992). *School consultation: Practice and training* (2nd ed.). Boston: Allyn & Bacon.

Crouch, P. L., Gresham, F. M., & Wright, W. R. (1985). Interdependent and independent group contingencies with immediate and delayed reinforcement for controlling classroom behavior. *Journal of School Psychology, 23,* 177–187.

Curtis, M. J., Zins, J. E., & Graden, J. L. (1987). Prereferral intervention programs: Enhancing student performance in regular education settings. In C. A. Maher & J. E. Zins (Eds.), *Psychoeducational interventions in the schools: Methods and procedures for enhancing student competence* (pp. 7–25). Elmsford, NY: Pergamon Press.

Deci, E. L. (1971). Effects of externally mediated rewards on intrinsic motivation. *Journal of Personality and Social Psychology, 18,* 105–115.

Deci, E. L., & Ryan, R. M. (1987). The support of autonomy and the control of behavior. *Journal of Personality and Social Psychology, 53,* 1024–1037.

Delquadri, J. C., Greenwood, C. R., Stretton, K., & Hall, R. V. (1983). The peer tutoring spelling game: A classroom procedure for increasing opportunity to respond and spelling performance. *Education and Treatment of Children, 6,* 225–239.

Delquadri, J., Greenwood, C. R., Whorton, D., Carta, J. J., & Hall, R. V. (1986). Classwide peer tutoring. *Exceptional Children, 52,* 535–542.

Deno, S. L. (1985). Curriculum-based measurement: The emerging alternative. *Exceptional Children, 52,* 219–232.

Deno, S. L. (1986). Formative evaluation of individual student programs: A new role for school psychologists. *School Psychology Review, 15,* 358–374.

Deno, S. L., Marston, D., & Mirkin, P. (1982). Valid measurement procedures for continuous evaluation of written expression. *Exceptional Children, 48,* 368–371.

Deno, S. L., & Mirkin, P. K. (1977). *Data-based program modification: A manual.* Reston, VA: Council for Exceptional Children.

Deno, S. L., Mirkin, P. K., & Chiang, B. (1982). Identifying valid measures of reading. *Exceptional Children, 49,* 36–45.

Deno, S. L., Mirkin, P. K., Lowry, L., & Kuehnle, K. (1980). *Relationships among simple measures of spelling and performance on standardized achievement tests* (Research Report No. 21). Minneapolis: University of Minnesota, Institute for Research on Learning Disabilities. (ERIC Document Reproduction Service No. ED 197 508)

Deno, S. L., Mirkin, P. K., & Wesson, C. (1984). How to write effective data-based IEPs. *Teaching Exceptional Children, 16,* 99–104.

Deshler, D. D., Schumaker, J. B., Alley, G. R., Warner, M. M., & Clark, F. L. (1982). Learning disabilities in adolescent and young adult populations: Research implications. *Focus on Exceptional Children, 15,* 1–12.

Dishion, T. J., Patterson, G. R., Stoolmiller, M., & Skinner, M. L. (1991). Family, school, and behavioral antecedents to early adolescent involvement with antisocial peers. *Developmental Psychology, 27,* 172–180.

Dougherty, E. H., & Dougherty, A. (1977). The daily report card: A simplified and flexible package for classroom behavior management. *Psychology in the Schools, 14,* 193.

DuPaul, G. J., Rapport, M. D., & Perriello, L. M. (1991). Teacher ratings of academic skills: The development of the Academic Performance Rating Scale. *School Psychology Review, 20,* 284–330.

Durkin, D. (1978–1979). What classroom observations reveal about reading comprehension instruction. *Reading Research Quarterly, 14,* 481–533.

Edgar, E., & Hayden, A. H. (1984–1985). Who are the children special education should serve and how many children are there? *Journal of Special Education, 18,* 523–539.

Elliott, S. N. (1988). Acceptability of behavioral treatments: Review of variables that influence treatment selection. *Professional Psychology: Research and Practice, 19,* 68–80.

Elliott, S. N., Gresham, F. M., & Heffer, R. W. (1987). Social-skills interventions: Research findings and training techniques. In C. A. Maher & J. E. Zins (Eds.), *Psychoeducational interventions in the schools: Methods and procedures for enhancing student competence* (pp. 141–159). New York: Pergamon Press.

Elliott, S. N., & Treuting, M. V. (1991). The Behavior Intervention Rating Scale:

Development and validation of a pretreatment acceptability and effectiveness measure. *Journal of School Psychology, 29*, 43–51.

Elliott, S. N., Turco, T. L., & Gresham, F. M. (1987). Consumers' and clients' pretreatment acceptability ratings of classroom group contingencies. *Journal of School Psychology, 25*, 145–153.

Elliott, S. N., Witt, J. C., Galvin, G. A., & Moe, G. L. (1986). Children's involvement in intervention selection: Acceptability of interventions for misbehaving peers. *Professional Psychology: Research and Practice, 17*, 235–241.

Elliott, S. N., Witt, J. C., Galvin, G. A., & Peterson, R. (1984). Acceptability of positive and reductive behavioral interventions: Factors that influence teachers' decisions. *Journal of School Psychology, 22*, 353–360.

Elliott, S. N., Witt, J. C., & Kratochwill, T. R. (1991). Selecting, implementing, and evaluating classroom interventions. In G. Stoner, M. R. Shinn, & H. M. Walker (Eds.), *Interventions for achievement and behavior problems* (pp. 99–135). Silver Spring, MD: National Association of School Psychologists.

Emmer, E. T., Evertson, C. M., & Anderson, L. M. (1980). Effective classroom management at the beginning of the year. *Elementary School Journal, 80*, 219–231.

Emmer, E. T., Evertson, C. M., Clements, B. S., & Worsham, M. E. (1997). *Classroom management for secondary teachers* (4th ed.). Boston: Allyn & Bacon.

Englemann, S., Carnine, D., & Steely, D. G. (1991). Making connections in mathematics. *Journal of Learning Disabilities, 24*, 292–303.

Evertson, C. M. (1985). Training teachers in classroom management: An experimental study in secondary school classrooms. *Journal of Educational Research, 79*, 51–58.

Evertson, C. M. (1989a). Classroom organization and management. In M. C. Reynolds (Ed.), *Knowledge base for the beginning teacher* (pp. 59–70). New York: Pergamon Press.

Evertson, C. M. (1989b). Improving elementary classroom management: A school-based training program for beginning the year. *Journal of Educational Research, 83*, 82–90.

Evertson, C. M., & Emmer, E. T. (1982). Effective management at the beginning of the school year in junior high classes. *Journal of Educational Psychology, 74*, 485–498.

Evertson, C. M., Emmer, E. T., Clements, B. S., & Worsham, M. E. (1994). *Classroom management for elementary teachers* (3rd ed.). Boston: Allyn & Bacon.

Evertson, C. M., Emmer, E. T., Sanford, J. P., & Clements, B. S. (1983). Improving classroom management: An experiment in elementary school classrooms. *Elementary School Journal, 84*, 173–188.

Fairchild, T. N., & Zins, J. E. (1986). Accountability practices of school counselors: A national survey. *Journal of Counseling and Development, 65*, 196–199.

Fantuzzo, J. W., Davis, G. Y., & Ginsburg, M. D. (1995). Effects of parent involvement in isolation or in combination with peer tutoring on student self-concept and mathematics achievement. *Journal of Educational Psychology, 87*, 272–281.

Fantuzzo, J. W., King, J. A., & Heller, L. R. (1992). Effects of reciprocal peer tutoring on mathematics and school adjustment: A component analysis. *Journal of Educational Psychology, 84*, 331–339.

Fantuzzo, J. W., & Rohrbeck, C. A. (1992). Self-managed groups: Fitting self-management approaches into classroom systems. *School Psychology Review, 21,* 255–263.

Felton, R. H., & Pepper, P. P. (1995). Early identification of phonological deficits in kindergarten and early elementary children at risk for reading disability. *School Psychology Review, 24,* 405–414.

Filby, N. N., & Cahen, L. S. (1985). Teacher accessibility and student attention. In C. W. Fisher & D. C. Berliner (Eds.), *Perspectives on instructional time* (pp. 203–215). New York: Longman.

Fish, M. C., & Mendola, L. R. (1986). The effect of self-instruction training on homework completion in an elementary special education class. *School Psychology Review, 15,* 268–276.

Fisher, C. W., Berliner, D. C., Filby, N. N., Marliave, R., Cahen, L. S., & Dishaw, M. M. (1980). Teaching behaviors, academic learning time, and student achievement: An overview. In C. Denham & A. Lieberman (Eds.), *Time to learn* (pp. 7–32). Washington, DC: National Institute of Education.

Flugum, K. R., & Reschly, D. J. (1994). Prereferral interventions: Quality indices and outcomes. *Journal of School Psychology, 32,* 1–14.

Foorman, B. R. (1995). Research on "the great debate": Code-oriented versus whole language approaches to reading instruction. *School Psychology Review, 24,* 376–392.

Forehand, R., & Wierson, M. (1993). The role of developmental factors in planning behavioral interventions for children: Disruptive behavior as an example. *Behavior Therapy, 24,* 117–141.

Friedman, D. L., Cancelli, A. A., & Yoshida, R. K. (1988). Academic engagement of elementary school children with learning disabilities. *Journal of School Psychology, 26,* 327–340.

Friend, M., & Bauwens, J. (1988). Managing resistance: An essential consulting skill for learning disabilities teachers. *Journal of Learning Disabilities, 21,* 556–561.

Fuchs, D., & Fuchs, L. S. (1989). Exploring effective and efficient prereferral interventions: A component analysis of behavioral consultation. *School Psychology Review, 18,* 260–279.

Fuchs, D., Fuchs, L. S., & Bahr, M. W. (1990). Mainstream assistance teams: A scientific basis for the art of consultation. *Exceptional Children, 57,* 128–139.

Fuchs, D., Fuchs, L. S., Bahr, M. W., Fernstrom, P., & Stecker, P. M. (1990). Prereferral intervention: A prescriptive approach. *Exceptional Children, 56,* 493–513.

Fuchs, D., Fuchs, L., Gilman, S., Reeder, P., Bahr, M., Fernstrom, P., & Roberts, H. (1990). Prereferral intervention through teacher consultation: Mainstream assistance teams. *Academic Therapy, 25,* 263–276.

Fuchs, D., Fuchs, L. S., Harris, A. H., & Roberts, P. H. (1996). Bridging the research-to-practice gap with mainstream assistance teams: A cautionary tale. *School Psychology Quarterly, 11,* 244–266.

Fuchs, D., Fuchs, L. S., Reeder, P., Gilman, S., Fernstrom, P., Bahr, M., & Moore, P. (1989). *Mainstream assistance teams: A handbook on prereferral intervention.* Nashville, TN: Peabody College of Vanderbilt University.

Fuchs, L. S., & Deno, S. L. (1982). *Developing goals and objectives for educational programs*

[Teaching guide]. Minneapolis: University of Minnesota, Institute for Research on Learning Disabilities.

Galagan, J. E. (1985). Psychoeducational testing: Turn out the lights, the party's over. *Exceptional Children, 52,* 288–299.

Gallup, A. (1984). The Gallup poll of teachers' attitudes toward the public schools. *Phi Delta Kappan, 66,* 97–107.

Gambrell, L. B., Pfeiffer, W. R., & Wilson, R. M. (1985). The effects of retelling upon reading comprehension and recall of text information. *Journal of Educational Research, 78,* 216–220.

Gardner, R. III, Heward, W. L., & Grossi, T. A. (1994). Effects of response cards on student participation and academic achievement: A systematic replication with inner-city students during whole-class science instruction. *Journal of Applied Behavior Analysis, 27,* 63–71.

Gartner, A., & Lipsky, D. K. (1987). Beyond special education: Toward a quality system for all students. *Harvard Educational Review, 57,* 367–395.

Gentile, C. (1992). *Exploring new methods for collecting students' school-based writing. NAEP's 1990 portfolio study.* Princeton, NJ: Educational Testing Service.

Gerber, M. M., & Semmel, M. I. (1984). Teacher as imperfect test: Reconceptualizing the referral process. *Educational Psychologist, 19,* 137–148.

Germann, G., & Tindal, G. (1985). An application of curriculum-based assessment: The use of direct and repeated measurement. *Exceptional Children, 52,* 244–265.

Gettinger, M. (1988). Methods of proactive classroom management. *School Psychology Review, 17,* 227–242.

Glass, G. V. (1983). Effectiveness of special education. *Policy Studies Review, 2,* 65–78.

Good, T. L. (1983). Classroom research: A decade of progress. *Educational Psychologist, 18,* 127–144.

Graden, J. L., Casey, A., & Bonstrom, O. (1985). Implementing a prereferral intervention system: Part II. The data. *Exceptional Children, 51,* 487–496.

Graden, J. L., Casey, A., & Christenson, S. L. (1985). Implementing a prereferral intervention system: Part I. The model. *Exceptional Children, 51,* 377–384.

Graham, S. (1983). Effective spelling instruction. *Elementary School Journal, 83,* 560–567.

Graham, S. (1990). The role of production factors in learning disabled students' compositions. *Journal of Educational Psychology, 82,* 781–791.

Graham, S., Harris, K. R., & MacArthur, C. A. (1993). Improving the writing of students with learning problems: Self-regulated strategy development. *School Psychology Review, 22,* 656–670.

Graham, S., & Miller, L. (1979). Spelling research and practice: A unified approach. *Focus on Exceptional Children, 12,* 1–16.

Greenwood, C. R. (1991). Longitudinal analysis of time, engagement, and achievement in at-risk versus non-risk students. *Exceptional Children, 57,* 521–535.

Greenwood, C. R., Carta, J. J., & Hall, R. V. (1988). The use of peer tutoring strategies in classroom management and educational instruction. *School Psychology Review, 17,* 258–275.

Greenwood, C. R., Carta, J. J., & Maheady, L. (1991). Peer tutoring programs in the regular education classroom. In G. Stoner, M. R. Shinn, & H. M. Walker (Eds.), *Interventions for achievement and behavior problems* (pp. 179–200). Silver Spring, MD: National Association of School Psychologists.

Greenwood, C. R., & Delquadri, J. (1988). Code for Instructional Structure and Student Academic Response (CISSAR). In M. Hersen & A. S. Bellack (Eds.), *Dictionary of behavioral assessment* (pp. 120–122). New York: Pergamon Press.

Greenwood, C. R., Delquadri, J. C., & Hall, R. V. (1984). Opportunity to respond and student academic performance. In W. L. Heward, T. E. Heron, D. S. Hill, & J. Trap-Porter (Eds.), *Focus on behavior analysis in education* (pp. 58–88). Columbus, OH: Merrill.

Greenwood, C. R., Delquadri, J. C., & Hall, R. V. (1989). Longitudinal effects of classwide peer tutoring. *Journal of Educational Psychology, 81,* 371–383.

Greenwood, C. R., Dinwiddie, G., Terry, B., Wade, L., Stanley, S. O., Thibadeau, S., & Delquadri, J. C. (1984). Teacher- versus peer-mediated instruction: An ecobehavioral analysis of achievement outcomes. *Journal of Applied Behavior Analysis, 17,* 521–538.

Greenwood, C. R., Terry, B., Utley, C. A., Montagna, D., & Walker, D. (1993). Achievement, placement, and services: Middle school benefits of ClassWide Peer Tutoring used at the elementary school. *School Psychology Review, 22,* 497–516.

Gresham, F. M. (1981). Assessment of children's social skills. *Journal of School Psychology, 19,* 120–133.

Gresham, F. M. (1989). Assessment of treatment integrity in school consultation and prereferral intervention. *School Psychology Review, 18,* 37–50.

Gresham, F. M. (1992). Social skills and learning disabilities: Causal, concomitant, or correlational? *School Psychology Review, 21,* 348–360.

Gresham, F. M. (1995). Best practices in social skills training. In A. Thomas & J. Grimes (Eds.), *Best practices in school psychology—III* (pp. 1021–1030). Washington, DC: National Association of School Psychologists.

Gresham, F. M., & Elliott, S. N. (1990). *Social Skills Rating System.* Circle Pines, MN: American Guidance Service.

Gresham, F. M., Gansle, K. A., Noell, G. H., Cohen, S., & Rosenblum, S. (1993). Treatment integrity of school-based behavioral intervention studies: 1980–1990. *School Psychology Review, 22,* 254–272.

Gresham, F. M., & Kendell, G. K. (1987). School consultation research: Methodological critique and future research directions. *School Psychology Review, 16,* 306–316.

Gresham, F. M., & Lopez, M. F. (1997). Social validation: A unifying concept for school-based consultation research and practice. *School Psychology Quarterly, 11,* 204–227.

Grossen, B., & Carnine, D. (1991). Strategies for maximizing reading success in the regular classroom. In G. Stoner, M. R. Shinn, & H. M. Walker (Eds.), *Interventions for achievement and behavior problems* (pp. 333–355). Silver Spring, MD: National Association of School Psychologists.

Gutkin, T. B., & Curtis, M. J. (1990). School-based consultation: Theory, techniques, and research. In T. B. Gutkin & C. R. Reynolds (Eds.), *The handbook of school psychology* (2nd ed., pp. 577–611). New York: Wiley.

Gutkin, T. B., Henning-Stout, M., & Piersel, W. C. (1988). Impact of a district-wide behavioral consultation prereferral intervention service on patterns of school psychological service delivery. *Professional School Psychology, 3,* 301–308.

Hall, R. V., Panyan, M., Rabon, D., & Broden, M. (1968). Instructing beginning teachers in reinforcement procedures which improve classroom control. *Journal of Applied Behavior Analysis, 1,* 315–322.

Harrington, R. G., & Gibson, E. (1986). Preassessment procedures for learning disabled children: Are they effective? *Journal of Learning Disabilities, 19,* 538–541.

Harris, A. J., & Jacobson, M. D. (1972). *Basic elementary reading vocabularies.* New York: Macmillan.

Harris, A. M., & Cancelli, A. A. (1991). Teachers as volunteer consultees: Enthusiastic, willing, or resistant participants? *Journal of Educational and Psychological Consultation, 2,* 217–238.

Harris, J., Wilkinson, S. C., Trovato, J., & Pryor, C. W. (1992). Teacher-completed Child Behavior Checklist ratings as a function of classroom-based interventions: A pilot study. *Psychology in the Schools, 29,* 42–52.

Hay, W. M., Hay, L. R., & Nelson, R. O. (1977). Direct and collateral changes in on-task and academic behavior resulting from on-task versus academic contingencies. *Behavior Therapy, 8,* 431–441.

Hayeck, R. A. (1987). The teacher assistance team: A pre-referral support system. *Focus on Exceptional Children, 20,* 1–7.

Hayes, J. R., & Flower, L. S. (1986). Writing research and the writer. *American Psychologist, 41,* 1106–1113.

Heller, L. R., & Fantuzzo, J. W. (1993). Reciprocal peer tutoring and parent partnership: Does parent involvement make a difference? *School Psychology Review, 22,* 517–534.

Heller, M. S., & White, M. A. (1975). Rates of teacher verbal approval and disapproval to higher and lower ability classes. *Journal of Educational Psychology, 67,* 769–800.

Heward, W. L., Heron, T. E., Gardner, R. III, & Prayzer, R. (1991). Two strategies for improving students' writing skills. In G. Stoner, M. R. Shinn, & H. M. Walker (Eds.), *Interventions for achievement and behavior problems* (pp. 379–398). Silver Spring, MD: National Association of School Psychologists.

Hillocks, G. (1987). Synthesis of research on teaching writing. *Educational Leadership, 44,* 71–82.

Hinshaw, S. P. (1992a). Academic underachievement, attention deficits, and aggression: Comorbidity and implications for intervention. *Journal of Consulting and Clinical Psychology, 60,* 893–903.

Hinshaw, S. P. (1992b). Externalizing behavior problems and academic underachievement in childhood and adolescence: Causal relationships and underlying mechanisms. *Psychological Bulletin, 111,* 127–155.

Hobbs, N. (1966). Helping disturbed children: Psychological and ecological strategies. *American Psychologist, 21,* 1105–1115.

Hooper, S. R., Swartz, C. W., Montgomery, J. W., Reed, M. S., Brown, T. T., Wasileski, T. J., & Levine, M. D. (1993). Prevalence of writing problems across middle school samples. *School Psychology Review, 22,* 610–621.

Howell, K. W., Fox, S. L., & Morehead, M. K. (1993). *Curriculum-based evaluation: Teaching and decision making* (2nd ed.). Pacific Grove, CA: Brooks/Cole.

Idol, L. (1987). Group story mapping: A comprehension strategy for both skilled and unskilled readers. *Journal of Learning Disabilities, 20,* 196–205.

Idol, L. (1993). *Special educator's consultation handbook* (2nd ed.). Austin, TX: PRO-ED.

Johnson, L. J., Pugach, M. C., & Hammittee, D. J. (1988). Barriers to effective special education consultation. *Remedial and Special Education, 9,* 41–47.

Johnson, T. C., Stoner, G., & Green, S. K. (1996). Demonstrating the experimenting society model with classwide behavior management interventions. *School Psychology Review, 25,* 199–214.

Juel, C. (1988). Learning to read and write: A longitudinal study of 54 children from first through fourth grades. *Journal of Educational Psychology, 80,* 437–447.

Juel, C. (1996). Beginning reading. In R. Barr, M. L. Kamil, P. B. Mosenthal, & P. D. Pearson (Eds.), *Handbook of reading research* (Vol. 2, pp. 759–788). Mahwah, NJ: Erlbaum.

Kavale, K. (1990). Effectiveness of special education. In T. B. Gutkin & C. R. Reynolds (Eds.), *The handbook of school psychology* (2nd ed., pp. 870–898). New York: Wiley.

Kazdin, A. E. (1987). Treatment of antisocial behavior in children: Current status and future directions. *Psychological Bulletin, 102,* 187–203.

Keith, T. Z. (1982). Time spent on homework and high school grades: A large-sample path analysis. *Journal of Educational Psychology, 74,* 248–253.

Kelley, M. L. (1990). *School-home notes: Promoting children's classroom success.* New York: Guilford Press.

Kelley, M. L., & Stokes, T. F. (1982). Contingency contracting with disadvantaged youths: Improving classroom performance. *Journal of Applied Behavior Analysis, 15,* 447–454.

Knoff, H. M. (1988). Effective social interventions. In J. L. Graden, J. E. Zins, & M. J. Curtis (Eds.), *Alternative educational delivery systems: Enhancing instructional options for all students* (pp. 431–453). Washington, DC: National Association of School Psychologists.

Kohler, F. W., Schwartz, I. S., Cross, J. A., & Fowler, S. A. (1989). The effects of two alternating peer intervention roles on independent work skills. *Education and Treatment of Children, 12,* 205–218.

Koot, H. M., & Verhulst, F. C. (1992). Prediction of children's referral to mental health and special education services from earlier adjustment. *Journal of Child Psychology and Psychiatry, 33,* 717–729.

Kounin, J. (1970). *Discipline and group management in classrooms.* New York: Holt, Rinehart & Winston.

Kratochwill, T. R., & Bergan, J. R. (1990). *Behavioral consultation in applied settings: An individual guide.* New York: Plenum Press.

Kruger, L. J., Struzziero, J., Watts, R., & Vacca, D. (1995). The relationship between organizational support and satisfaction with teacher assistance teams. *Remedial and Special Education, 16,* 203–211.

Kulberg, J. M. (1993). What school psychologists need to know about writing disabilities. *School Psychology Review, 22,* 682–683.

Kupersmidt, J. B., & Cole, J. D. (1990). Preadolescent peer status, aggression, and school adjustment as predictors of externalizing problems in adolescence. *Child Development, 61,* 1350–1362.

Lahey, B. B., Gendrich, J. G., Gendrich, S. I., Schnelle, J. F., Gant, D. S., & McNees, M. P. (1977). An evaluation of daily report cards with minimal teacher and parent contacts as an efficient method of classroom intervention. *Behavior Modification, 1,* 381–394.

Landau, S., & Moore, L. A. (1991). Social skills deficits in children with attention-deficit hyperactivity disorder. *School Psychology Review, 20,* 235–251.

Lentz, F. E., Jr. (1988). On-task behavior, academic performance, and classroom disruptions: Untangling the target selection problem in classroom interventions. *School Psychology Review, 17,* 243–257.

Lentz, F. E., Jr., & Shapiro, E. S. (1986). Functional assessment of the academic environment. *School Psychology Review, 15,* 346–357.

Lepper, M. R., Greene, D., & Nisbett, R. E. (1973). Undermining children's intrinsic interest with extrinsic rewards: A test of the "overjustification" hypothesis. *Journal of Personality and Social Psychology, 28,* 129–137.

Levine, F. M., & Anesko, K. M. (1987). *Winning the homework war.* New York: Prentice Hall.

Levine, F. M., & Fasnacht, G. (1974). Token rewards may lead to token learning. *American Psychologist, 29,* 816–820.

Lieberman, L. (1983). The homework solution. *Journal of Learning Disabilities, 16,* 435.

Lipsky, D. K., & Gartner, A. (1987). Capable of achievement and worthy of respect: Education for handicapped students as if they were full-fledged human beings. *Exceptional Children, 54,* 69–74.

Loeber, R. (1982). The stability of antisocial and delinquent child behavior: A review. *Child Development, 53,* 1431–1446.

Loeber, R. (1990). Development and risk factors of juvenile antisocial behavior and delinquency. *Clinical Psychology Review, 10,* 1–41.

Lordeman, A. M., & Winett, R. A. (1980). The effects of written feedback to parents and a call-in service on student homework submission. *Education and Treatment of Children, 3,* 33–44.

Lovitt, T. C., & Horton, S. V. (1991). Adapting textbooks for mildly handicapped adolescents. In G. Stoner, M. R. Shinn, & H. M. Walker (Eds.), *Interventions for achievement and behavior problems* (pp. 439–471). Silver Spring, MD: National Association of School Psychologists.

MacPherson, E. M., Candee, B. L., & Hohman, R. J. (1974). A comparison of three methods for eliminating disruptive lunchroom behavior. *Journal of Applied Behavior Analysis, 7,* 287–297.

Madden, N. A., & Slavin, R. E. (1983). Mainstreaming students with mild handicaps: Academic and social outcomes. *Review of Educational Research, 53,* 519–569.

Madsen, C. H., Jr., Becker, W. C., & Thomas, D. R. (1968). Rules, praise, and ignoring: Elements of elementary classroom control. *Journal of Applied Behavior Analysis, 1,* 139–150.

Madsen, C. H., Jr., Becker, W. C., Thomas, D. R., Koser, L., & Plager, E. (1968). An analysis of the reinforcing function of "sit-down" commands. In R. K. Parker (Ed.), *Readings in educational psychology* (pp. 265–278). Boston: Allyn & Bacon.

Marks, E. S. (1995). *Entry strategies for school consultation.* New York: Guilford Press.

Marston, D. B. (1989). A curriculum-based measurement approach to assessing academic performance: What it is and why do it. In M. R. Shinn (Ed.), *Curriculum-based measurement: Assessing special children* (pp. 18–78). New York: Guilford Press.

Marston, D., & Magnusson, D. (1985). Implementing curriculum-based measurement in special and regular education settings. *Exceptional Children, 52,* 266–276.

Marston, D., & Magnusson, D. (1988). Curriculum-based measurement: District level implementation. In J. L. Graden, J. E. Zins, & M. J. Curtis (Eds.), *Alternative educational delivery systems: Enhancing instructional options for all students* (pp. 137–172). Washington, DC: National Association of School Psychologists.

Martens, B. K., Witt, J. C., Elliott, S. N., & Darveaux, D. X. (1985). Teacher judgments concerning the acceptability of school-based interventions. *Professional Psychology: Research and Practice, 16,* 191–198.

McCain, A. P., & Kelley, M. L. (1994). Improving classroom performance in underachieving preadolescents: The additive effects of response cost to a school–home system. *Child and Family Behavior Therapy, 16,* 27–41.

McLeod, T., & Armstrong, S. (1982). Learning disabilities in mathematics—Skill deficits and remedial approaches at the intermediate and secondary level. *Learning Disability Quarterly, 5,* 305–311.

McGill-Franzen, A., & Allington, R. L. (1991). Every child's right: Literacy. *The Reading Teacher, 45,* 86–90.

McKee, W. T., Witt, J. C., Elliott, S. N., Pardue, M., & Judycki, A. (1987). Practice informing research: A survey of research dissemination and knowledge utilization. *School Psychology Review, 16,* 338–347.

Medland, M. B., & Stachnik, T. J. (1972). Good-behavior game: A replication and systematic analysis. *Journal of Applied Behavior Analysis, 5,* 45–51.

Medway, F. J. (1979). Causal attributions for school-related problems: Teacher perceptions and teacher feedback. *Journal of Educational Psychology, 71,* 809–818.

Meichenbaum, D. H., & Goodman, J. (1971). Training impulsive children to talk to themselves: A means of developing self-control. *Journal of Abnormal Psychology, 77,* 115–126.

Menlo, A., & Johnson, M. C. (1971). The use of percentage gain as a means toward the assessment of individual achievement. *California Journal of Educational Research, 22,* 193–201.

Merrell, K. W., Johnson, E. R., Merz, J. M., & Ring, E. N. (1992). Social competence of students with mild handicaps and low achievement: A comparative study. *School Psychology Review, 21,* 125–137.

Meyers, B., Valentino, C. T., Meyers, J., Boretti, M., & Brent, D. (1996). Implementing prereferral intervention teams as an approach to school-based consultation in an urban school system. *Journal of Educational and Psychological Consultation, 7*, 119–149.

Miller, R. L., Brickman, P., & Bolen, D. (1975). Attribution versus persuasion as a means for modifying behavior. *Journal of Personality and Social Psychology, 31*, 430–441.

Miller, G. E., & Prinz, R. J. (1991). Designing interventions for stealing. In G. Stoner, M. R. Shinn, & H. M. Walker (Eds.), *Interventions for achievement and behavior problems* (pp. 593–616). Silver Spring, MD: National Association of School Psychologists.

Moskowitz, G., & Hayman, J. L., Jr. (1976). Success strategies of inner-city teachers: A year-long study. *Journal of Educational Research, 69*, 283–289.

Mullis, I. V. S., Campbell, J. R., & Farstrup, A. E. (1993). *NAEP 1992 reading report card for the nation and the states.* Washington, DC: National Center for Education Statistics, Report No. 23-ST06.

Mullis, I. V. S., Dossey, J., Owen, E. H., & Phillips, G. W. (1993). *NAEP 1992 mathematics report card for the nation and the states.* Washington, DC: National Center for Education Statistics, Report No. 23-ST02.

Mullis, I. V. S., & Jenkins, L. B. (1988). *The science report card: Elements of risk and recovery. Trends and achievement based on the 1986 national assessment.* Princeton, NJ: Educational Testing Service, Report No. 17-S-01.

National Association of School Psychologists. (1986). *Intervention assistance teams: A model for building level instructional problem solving.* Silver Spring, MD: Author.

National Association of School Psychologists. (1992a). *Principles for professional ethics.* Silver Spring, MD: Author.

National Association of School Psychologists. (1992b). *Professional conduct manual.* Silver Spring, MD: Author.

National Association of School Psychologists. (1992c). *Standards for the provision of school psychological services.* Silver Spring, MD: Author.

National Association of School Psychologists. (1995). Position statement: Students with emotional/behavioral disorders. In A. Thomas & J. Grimes (Eds.), *Best practices in school psychology—III* (pp. 1219–1221). Washington, DC: Author.

National Association of School Psychologists/National Coalition of Advocates for Students. (1985). *Advocacy for appropriate educational services for all children.* Washington, DC: National Association of School Psychologists.

National Coalition of Advocates for Students. (1987). *Rights without labels.* Washington, DC: Author.

National Commission on Excellence in Education. (1983). *A nation at risk: The imperative for educational reform.* Washington, DC: Author.

Neilsen, A., Rennie, B., & Connell, A. (1982). Allocation of instructional time to reading comprehension and study skills in intermediate grade social studies classrooms. In J. A. Niles & L. A. Harris (Eds.), *New inquiries in reading research and instruction* (pp. 81–84). Rochester, NY: National Reading Conference.

Nelson, J. R., Smith, D. J., Taylor, L., Dodd, J. M., & Reavis, K. (1992). A statewide survey of special education administrators regarding mandated prereferral interventions. *Remedial and Special Education, 13*, 34–39.

Newman, J. L. (1993). Ethical issues in consultation. *Journal of Counseling and Development, 72,* 148–156.

Okyere, B. A., & Heron, T. E. (1991). Use of self-correction to improve spelling in regular education classrooms. In G. Stoner, M. R. Shinn, & H. M. Walker (Eds.), *Interventions for achievement and behavior problems* (pp. 399–413). Silver Spring, MD: National Association of School Psychologists.

O'Leary, K. D., Kaufman, K. F., Kass, R. E., & Drabman, R. S. (1970). The effects of loud and soft reprimands on the behavior of disruptive students. *Exceptional Children, 37,* 145–155.

Olweus, D. (1979). Stability of aggressive reaction patterns in males: A review. *Psychological Bulletin, 86,* 852–875.

Olympia, D. E., Sheridan, S. M., & Jenson, W. (1994). Homework: A natural means of home–school collaboration. *School Psychology Quarterly, 9,* 60–80.

Ownby, R. L., Wallbrown, F., D'Atri, A., & Armstrong, B. (1985). Patterns of referrals for school psychological services: Replication of the referral problems category system. *Special Services in the Schools, 1,* 53–66.

Paine, S. C., Radicchi, J., Rosellini, L. C., Deutchman, L., & Darch, C. B. (1983). *Structuring your classroom for academic success.* Champaign, IL: Research Press.

Parmar, R. S., & Cawley, J. F. (1993). Analysis of science textbook recommendations provided for students with disabilities. *Exceptional Children, 59,* 518–531.

Paschal, R. A., Weinstein, T., & Walberg, H. J. (1984). The effects of homework on learning: A quantitative synthesis. *Journal of Educational Research, 78,* 97–104.

Patterson, G. R., Reid, J. B., & Dishion, T. J. (1992). *A social interactional approach: Vol 4. Antisocial boys.* Eugene, OR: Castalia.

Petty, W. T., & Finn, P. J. (1981). Classroom teachers' reports on teaching written composition. In S. M. Haley-James (Ed.), *Perspectives on writing in grades 1–8* (pp. 19–33). Urbana, IL: National Council of Teachers of English.

Pfiffner, L. J., Rosén, L. A., & O'Leary, S. G. (1985). The efficacy of an all-positive approach to classroom management. *Journal of Applied Behavior Analysis, 18,* 257–261.

Piersel, W. C., & Gutkin, T. B. (1983). Resistance to school-based consultation: A behavioral analysis of the problem. *Psychology in the Schools, 20,* 311–320.

Pigott, H. E., Fantuzzo, J. W., & Clement, P. W. (1986). The effects of reciprocal peer tutoring and group contingencies on the academic performance of elementary school children. *Journal of Applied Behavior Analysis, 19,* 93–98.

Ponti, C. R., Zins, J. E., & Graden, J. L. (1988). Implementing a consultation-based service delivery system to decrease referrals for special education: A case study of organizational considerations. *School Psychology Review, 17,* 89–100.

Porter, A. (1989, June–July). A curriculum out of balance: The case of elementary school mathematics. *Educational Researcher, 18,* 9–15.

Prasse, D. P. (1995). School psychology and the law. In A. Thomas & J. Grimes (Eds.), *Best practices in school psychology—III* (pp. 41–50). Washington, DC: National Association of School Psychologists.

Pressley, M., & Wharton-McDonald, R. (1997). Skilled comprehension and its development through instruction. *School Psychology Review, 26,* 448–466.

Proctor, M. A., & Morgan, D. (1991). Effectiveness of a response cost raffle procedure on the disruptive classroom behavior of adolescents with behavior problems. *School Psychology Review, 20,* 97–109.

Pugach, M. C. (1985). The limitations of federal special education policy: The role of classroom teachers in determining who is handicapped. *Journal of Special Education, 19,* 123–137.

Rader, H. (1975). The child as terrorist: Seven cases. *School Review, 84,* 5–41.

Raschke, D. (1981). Designing reinforcement surveys—Let the student choose the rewards. *Teaching Exceptional Children, 14,* 92–96.

Reid, J. B., & Patterson, G. R. (1991). Early prevention and intervention with conduct problems: A social interactional model for the integration of research and practice. In G. Stoner, M. R. Shinn, & H. M. Walker (Eds.), *Interventions for achievement and behavior problems* (pp. 715–739). Silver Spring, MD: National Association of School Psychologists.

Reschly, D. (1980). School psychologists and assessment in the future. *Professional Psychology, 11,* 841–848.

Reschly, D. J. (1988). Special education reform: School psychology revolution. *School Psychology Review, 17,* 459–475.

Reynolds, M. C., Wang, M. C., & Walberg, H. J. (1987). The necessary restructuring of special and regular education. *Exceptional Children, 53,* 391–398.

Robinson, P. W., Newby, T. J., & Ganzell, S. L. (1981). A token system for a class of underachieving hyperactive children. *Journal of Applied Behavior Analysis, 14,* 307–315.

Rosemond, J. (1990). *Ending the homework hassle: Understanding, preventing, and solving school performance problems.* Kansas City: Andrews and McMeel.

Rosén, L. A., O'Leary, S. G., Joyce, S. A., Conway, G., & Pfiffner, L. J. (1984). The importance of prudent negative consequences for maintaining the appropriate behavior of hyperactive students. *Journal of Abnormal Child Psychology, 12,* 581–604.

Rosenfield, S. A. (1987). *Instructional consultation.* Hillsdale, NJ: Erlbaum.

Rosenfield, S. A., & Gravois, T. A. (1996). *Instructional consultation teams: Collaborating for change.* New York: Guilford Press.

Rosenshine, B. V. (1980). How time is spent in elementary classrooms. In C. Denham & A. Lieberman (Eds.), *Time to learn* (pp. 107–126). Washington, DC: National Institute of Education.

Roser, N., & Juel, C. (1982). Effects of vocabulary instruction on reading comprehension. In J. A. Niles & L. A. Harris (Eds.), *New inquiries in reading research and instruction* (pp. 110–118). Rochester, NY: National Reading Conference.

Ross, R. P. (1995). Implementing intervention assistance teams. In A. Thomas & J. Grimes (Eds.), *Best practices in school psychology—III* (pp. 227–237). Washington, DC: National Association of School Psychologists.

Roth, K. J., Smith, E. L., & Anderson, C. W. (1984). Verbal patterns of teachers: Comprehension instruction in the content areas. In G. G. Duffy, L. R. Roehler, & J. Mason (Eds.), *Comprehension instruction: Perspectives and suggestions* (pp. 281–293). New York: Longman.

Sanford, J. P., & Evertson, C. M. (1981). Classroom management in a low SES junior high: Three case studies. *Journal of Teacher Education, 32,* 34–38.

Sarason, S. B., & Doris, J. (1979). *Educational handicap, public policy, and social history: A broadened perspective on mental retardation.* New York: Macmillan.

Schumaker, J. B., Deshler, D. D., Alley, G. R., & Warner, M. M. (1983). Toward the development of an intervention model for learning disabled adolescents. *Exceptional Education Quarterly, 4,* 45–74.

Schumaker, J. B., Deshler, D. D., & McKnight, P. C. (1991). Teaching routines for content areas at the secondary level. In G. Stoner, M. R. Shinn, & H. M. Walker (Eds.), *Interventions for achievement and behavior problems* (pp. 473–494). Silver Spring, MD: National Association of School Psychologists.

Schumaker, J. B., Hovell, M. F., & Sherman, J. A. (1977). An analysis of daily report cards and parent-managed privileges in the improvement of adolescents' classroom performance. *Journal of Applied Behavior Analysis, 10,* 449–464.

Schwartz, B. (1990). The creation and destruction of value. *American Psychologist, 45,* 7–15.

Shapiro, E. S. (1987). Intervention research methodology in school psychology. *School Psychology Review, 16,* 290–305.

Shapiro, E. S. (1996a). *Academic skills problems: Direct assessment and intervention* (2nd ed.). New York: Guilford Press.

Shapiro, E. S. (1996b). *Academic skills problems workbook.* New York: Guilford Press.

Shapiro, E. S., & Cole, C. L. (1994). *Behavior change in the classroom: Self-management interventions.* New York: Guilford Press.

Shapiro, E. S., & Goldberg, R. (1986). A comparison of group contingencies for increasing spelling performance among sixth-grade students. *School Psychology Review, 15,* 546–557.

Shapiro, E. S., & Lentz, F. E., Jr. (1986). Behavioral assessment of academic skills. In T. R. Kratochwill (Ed.), *Advances in school psychology* (Vol. 5, pp. 87–139). Hillsdale, NJ: Erlbaum.

Shepard, L. A. (1987). The new push for excellence: Widening the schism between regular and special education. *Exceptional Children, 53,* 327–329.

Sheridan, S. M., Kratochwill, T. R., & Elliott, S. N. (1990). Behavioral consultation with parents and teachers: Delivering treatment for socially withdrawn children at home and school. *School Psychology Review, 19,* 33–52.

Shinn, M. R. (Ed.). (1989). *Curriculum-based measurement: Assessing special children.* New York: Guilford Press.

Shinn, M. R., Good, R. H. III, Knutson, N., Tilly, W. D. III, & Collins, V. L. (1992). Curriculum-based measurement of oral reading fluency: A confirmatory analysis of its relation to reading. *School Psychology Review, 21,* 459–479.

Shinn, M. R., & Marston, D. (1985). Differentiating mildly handicapped, low-achieving, and regular education students: A curriculum-based approach. *Remedial and Special Education, 6,* 31–38.

Shinn, M. R., Nolet, V., & Knutson, N. (1990). Best practices in curriculum-based measurement. In A. Thomas & J. Grimes (Eds.), *Best practices in school psychology—II* (pp. 287–307). Washington, DC: National Association of School Psychologists.

Shinn, M. R., Ysseldyke, J. E., Deno, S. L., & Tindal, G. A. (1986). A comparison of differences between students labeled as learning disabled and low achieving on measures of classroom performance. *Journal of Learning Disabilities, 19,* 545–552.

Short, E. J., & Ryan, E. B. (1984). Metacognitive differences between skilled and less skilled readers: Remediating deficits through story grammar and attribution training. *Journal of Educational Psychology, 76,* 225–235.

Sindelar, P. T., Griffin, C. C., Smith, S. W., & Watanabe, A. K. (1992). Prereferral intervention: Encouraging notes on preliminary findings. *Elementary School Journal, 92,* 245–259.

Sindelar, P. T., & Stoddard, K. (1991). Teaching reading to mildly disabled students in regular classes. In G. Stoner, M. R. Shinn, & H. M. Walker (Eds.), *Interventions for achievement and behavior problems* (pp. 357–378). Silver Spring, MD: National Association of School Psychologists.

Skrtic, T. M. (1991). The special education paradox: Equity as the way to excellence. *Harvard Educational Review, 61,* 148–206.

Smith, B. M., Schumaker, J. B., Schaeffer, J., & Sherman, J. A. (1982). Increasing participation and improving the quality of discussions in seventh-grade social studies classes. *Journal of Applied Behavior Analysis, 15,* 97–110.

Smith, D. J., Young, K. R., West, R. P., Morgan, D. P., & Rhode, G. (1988). Reducing the disruptive behavior of junior high school students: A classroom self-management procedure. *Behavioral Disorders, 13,* 231–239.

Smyth, W. J. (1985). A context for the study of time and instruction. In C. W. Fisher & D. C. Berliner (Eds.), *Perspectives on instructional time* (pp. 3–27). New York: Longman.

Solomon, D., & Kendall, A. J. (1976). Individual characteristics and children's performance in "open" and "traditional" classroom settings. *Journal of Educational Psychology, 68,* 613–625.

Stahl, S. A., & Fairbanks, M. M. (1986). The effects of vocabulary instruction: A model-based meta-analysis. *Review of Educational Research, 56,* 72–110.

Stahl, S. A., & Kuhn, M. R. (1995). Does whole language or instruction matched to learning styles help children learn to read? *School Psychology Review, 24,* 393–404.

Stainback, W., & Stainback, S. (1984). A rationale for the merger of special and regular education. *Exceptional Children, 51,* 102–111.

Stanley, S. O., & Greenwood, C. R. (1983). How much "opportunity to respond" does the minority disadvantaged student receive in school? *Exceptional Children, 49,* 370–373.

Stanovich, K. E. (1986). Matthew effects in reading: Some consequences of individual differences in the acquisition of literacy. *Reading Research Quarterly, 21,* 360–407.

Stanovich, K. E. (1993–1994). Romance and reality. *The Reading Teacher, 47,* 280–291.

Steege, M. W., & Wacker, D. P. (1995). Best practices in evaluating the effectiveness of applied interventions. In A. Thomas & J. Grimes (Eds.), *Best practices in school psychology—III* (pp. 625–636). Washington, DC: National Association of School Psychologists.

Stein, M., Dixon, R. C., & Isaacson, S. (1994). Effective writing instruction for diverse learners. *School Psychology Review, 23,* 392–405.

Stern, G. W., Fowler, S. A., & Kohler, F. W. (1988). A comparison of two intervention roles: Peer monitor and point earner. *Journal of Applied Behavior Analysis,*
21, 103–109.

Stoddard, B., & MacArthur, C. A. (1993). A peer editor strategy: Guiding learning-disabled students in response and revision. *Research in the Teaching of Eng-*
lish, 27, 76–103.

Strain, P. S., Lambert, D. L., Kerr, M. M., Stagg, V., & Lenkner, D. A. (1983).
Naturalistic assessment of children's compliance to teachers' requests and
consequences for compliance. *Journal of Applied Behavior Analysis, 16,*
243–249.

Sturge, C. (1982). Reading retardation and antisocial behavior. *Journal of Child*
Psychology and Psychiatry, 23, 21–31.

Taylor, V. L., Cornwell, D. D., & Riley, M. T. (1984). Home-based contingency
management programs that teachers can use. *Psychology in the Schools, 21,*
368–374.

Thomas, D. R., Becker, W. C., & Armstrong, M. (1968). Production and elimina-
tion of disruptive classroom behavior by systematically varying teacher's behavior. *Journal of Applied Behavior Analysis, 1,* 35–45.

Thomas, J. D., Presland, I. E., Grant, M. D., & Glynn, T. L. (1978). Natural rates
of teacher approval and disapproval in grade-7 classrooms. *Journal of Applied*
Behavior Analysis, 11, 91–94.

Thorpe, H. W., Chiang, B., & Darch, C. B. (1981). Individual and group feedback
systems for improving oral reading accuracy in learning disabled and regular
class children. *Journal of Learning Disabilities, 14,* 332–334, 367.

Thurlow, M. L., & Ysseldyke, J. E. (1982). Instructional planning: Information collected by school psychologists vs. information considered useful by teachers.
Journal of School Psychology, 20, 3–10.

Tindal, G., & Hasbrouck, J. (1991). Analyzing student writing to develop instructional strategies. *Learning Disabilities Research and Practice, 6,* 237–245.

Tremblay, R. E., Masse, B., Perron, D., Leblanc, M., Schwartzman, A. E., & Led-
ingham, J. E. (1992). Early disruptive behavior, poor school achievement,
delinquent behavior, and delinquent personality: Longitudinal analyses. *Jour-*
nal of Consulting and Clinical Psychology, 60, 64–72.

Turco, T.. L., & Elliott, S. N. (1986). Assessment of students' acceptability ratings
of teacher-initiated interventions for classroom misbehavior. *Journal of School*
Psychology, 24, 277–283.

Turco, T. L., & Elliott, S. N. (1990). Acceptability and effectiveness of group contingencies for improving spelling achievement. *Journal of School Psychology, 28,*
27–37.

Van Houten, R., Hill, S., & Parsons, M. (1975). An analysis of a performance
feedback system: The effects of timing and feedback, public posting, and
praise upon academic performance and peer interaction. *Journal of Applied*
Behavior Analysis, 8, 449–457.

Van Houten, R., Nau, P. A., MacKenzie-Keating, S. E., Sameoto, D., & Colavecchia, B. (1982). An analysis of some variables influencing the effectiveness of
reprimands. *Journal of Applied Behavior Analysis, 15,* 65–83.

Veenman, S. (1984). Perceived problems of beginning teachers. *Review of Educational Research, 54,* 143–178.

Von Brock, M. B., & Elliott, S. N. (1987). Influence of treatment effectiveness information on the acceptability of classroom interventions. *Journal of School Psychology, 25,* 131–144.

Wagner, R. K., & Torgesen, J. K. (1987). The nature of phonological processing and its causal role in the acquisition of reading skills. *Psychological Bulletin, 101,* 192–212.

Walberg, H. J., Paschal, R. A., & Weinstein, T. (1985). Homework's powerful effects on learning. *Educational Leadership, 42,* 76–79.

Weade, R., & Evertson, C. M. (1988). The construction of lessons in effective and less effective classrooms. *Teaching and Teacher Education, 4,* 189–213.

Webster-Stratton, C. (1993). Strategies for helping early school-aged children with oppositional defiant and conduct disorders: The importance of home-school partnerships. *School Psychology Review, 22,* 437–457.

Weinstein, C. S. (1977). Modifying student behavior in an open classroom through changes in the physical design. *American Educational Research Journal, 14,* 249–262.

Weinstein, C. S. (1979). The physical environment of the school: A review of the research. *Review of Educational Research, 49,* 577–610.

Weinstein, C. S. (1996). *Secondary classroom management: Lessons from research and practice.* New York: McGraw-Hill.

Wheldall, K., Morris, M., Vaughan, P., & Ng, Y. Y. (1981). Rows versus tables: An example of the use of behavioral ecology in two classes of eleven-year-old children. *Educational Psychology, 1,* 171–184.

White, A. G., & Bailey, J. S. (1990). Reducing disruptive behaviors of elementary physical education students with sit and watch. *Journal of Applied Behavior Analysis, 23,* 353–359.

White, M. A. (1975). Natural rates of teacher approval and disapproval in the classroom. *Journal of Applied Behavior Analysis, 8,* 367–372.

White, P. L., & Fine, M. J. (1976). The effects of three school psychological consultation modes on selected teacher and pupil outcomes. *Psychology in the Schools, 13,* 414–420.

Wickstrom, K. R., & Witt, J. C. (1993). Resistance within school-based consultation. In J. E. Zins, T. R. Kratochwill, & S. N. Elliott (Eds.), *Handbook of consultation services for children: Applications in educational and clinical settings* (pp. 159–178). San Francisco: Jossey-Bass.

Will, M. C. (1986). Educating children with learning problems: A shared responsibility. *Exceptional Children, 52,* 411–416.

Will, M. (1988). Educating students with learning problems and the changing role of the school psychologist. *School Psychology Review, 17,* 476–478.

Williams, P. L., Lazer, S., Reese, C. J., & Carr, P. (1995). *NAEP 1994 U.S. history: A first look. Findings from the National Assessment of Educational Progress.* Washington, DC: Office of Educational Research and Improvement, U.S. Department of Education.

Winett, R. A., & Winkler, R. C. (1972). Current behavior modification in the classroom: Be still, be quiet, be docile. *Journal of Applied Behavior Analysis, 5,* 499–594.

Witt, J. C. (1986). Teachers' resistance to the use of school-based interventions. *Journal of School Psychology, 24,* 37–44.

Witt, J. C., & Elliott, S. N. (1982). The response cost lottery: A time efficient and effective classroom intervention. *Journal of School Psychology, 20,* 155–161.

Witt, J. C., & Elliott, S. N. (1985). Acceptability of classroom intervention strategies. In T. R. Kratochwill (Ed.), *Advances in school psychology* (Vol. 4, pp. 251–288). Hillsdale, NJ: Erlbaum.

Witt, J. C., Hannafin, M. J., & Martens, B. K. (1983). Home-based reinforcement: Behavioral covariation between academic performance and inappropriate behavior. *Journal of School Psychology, 21,* 337–348.

Witt, J. C., & Martens, B. K. (1983). Assessing the acceptability of behavioral interventions used in classrooms. *Psychology in the Schools, 20,* 510–517.

Witt, J. C., & Martens, B. K. (1988). Problems with problem-solving consultation: A re-analysis of assumptions, methods, and goals. *School Psychology Review, 17,* 211–226.

Witt, J. C., Martens, B. K., & Elliott, S. N. (1984). Factors affecting teachers' judgments of the acceptability of behavioral interventions: Time involvement, behavior problem severity, and type of intervention. *Behavior Therapy, 15,* 204–209.

Witt, J. C., Moe, G., Gutkin, T. B., & Andrews, L. (1984). The effect of saying the same thing in different ways: The problem of language and jargon in school-based consultation. *Journal of School Psychology, 22,* 361–367.

Witt, J. C., & Robbins, J. R. (1985). Acceptability of reductive interventions for the control of inappropriate child behavior. *Journal of Abnormal Child Psychology, 13,* 59–67.

Wolf, M. M. (1978). Social validity: The case for subjective measurement or how applied behavior analysis is finding its heart. *Journal of Applied Behavior Analysis, 11,* 203–214.

Wolfe, V. V., Boyd, L. A., & Wolfe, D. A. (1983). Teaching cooperative play to behavior-problem preschool children. *Education and Treatment of Children, 6,* 1–10.

Wolfgang, C. H. (1996). *The three faces of discipline for the elementary school teacher: Empowering the teacher and students.* Needham Heights, MA: Allyn & Bacon.

Wood, J. W., Lazzari, A., Davis, E. H., Sugai, G., & Carter, J. (1990). National status of the prereferral process: An issue for regular education. *Action in Teacher Education, 12,* 50–56.

Yeaton, W. H., & Sechrest, L. (1981). Critical dimensions in the choice and maintenance of successful treatment: Strength, integrity, and effectiveness. *Journal of Consulting and Clinical Psychology, 49,* 156–167.

Ysseldyke, J., Algozzine, B., & Epps, S. (1983). A logical and empirical analysis of current practice in classifying students as handicapped. *Exceptional Children, 50,* 160–166.

Ysseldyke, J. E., Algozzine, B., Shinn, M. R., & McGue, M. (1982). Similarities and differences between low achievers and students classified learning disabled. *Journal of Special Education, 16,* 73–85.

Ysseldyke, J. E., & Christenson, S. L. (1988). Linking assessment to intervention. In J. L. Graden, J. E. Zins, & M. J. Curtis (Eds.), *Alternative educational delivery systems: Enhancing instructional options for all students* (pp. 91–109). Washington, DC: National Association of School Psychologists.

Ysseldyke, J. E., Christenson, S., Pianta, B., & Algozzine, B. (1983). An analysis of teachers' reasons and desired outcomes for students referred for psychoeducational evaluation. *Journal of Psychoeducational Assessment, 1,* 73–83.

Ysseldyke, J. E., Christenson, S. L., Thurlow, M. L., & Bakewell, D. (1989). Are different kinds of instructional tasks used by different categories of students in different settings? *School Psychology Review, 18,* 98–111.

Ysseldyke, J. E., Pianta, B., Christenson, S., Wang, J. J., & Algozzine, B. (1983). An analysis of prereferral interventions. *Psychology in the Schools, 20,* 184–190.

Ysseldyke, J. E., & Thurlow, M. L. (1984). Assessment practices in special education: Adequacy and appropriateness. *Educational Psychologist, 19,* 123–136.

Ysseldyke, J. E., Thurlow, M., Graden, J., Wesson, C., Algozzine, B., & Deno, S. (1983). Generalizations from five years of research on assessment and decision making: The University of Minnesota Institute. *Exceptional Education Quarterly, 4,* 75–93.

Zins, J. E., & Barnett, D. W. (1983). Report writing: Legislative, ethical, and professional challenges. *Journal of School Psychology, 21,* 219–227.

Zins, J. E., Curtis, M. J., Graden, J. L., & Ponti, C. R. (1988). *Helping students succeed in the regular classroom: A guide for developing intervention assistance programs.* San Francisco: Jossey-Bass.

Zins, J. E., & Fairchild, T. N. (1986). An investigation of the accountability practices of school psychologists. *Professional School Psychology, 1,* 193–204.

Index

♦

Absenteeism, 145
Academic achievement
  evaluation of changes in, 47–48
  proactive classroom management and,
    61–62, 94–97
Academic engagement rates
  defined, 61
  diverse learners and, 62. *See also* Student
    engagement rates
Academic interventions
  for academic productivity, 117–142
  evaluating, 115–117
  for homework completion, 143–158
  for mathematics performance, 186–
    205
  overview of, 113–114
  for reading performance, 158–186
  for science performance, 233–236,
    249–254
  for social studies performance, 233–
    249
  targets of, 114–115
  for written language performance,
    206–233
  See also specific types
Academic Performance Rating Scale
  (APRS), 116–117
Academic problems, types of, 114–115
Academic productivity interventions
  Classwide Peer Tutoring, 122–125
  The Daily Assignment, 119–122
  *Encouraging Academic Achievement with
    Principal Praise*, 140–142
  *Improving Academic Productivity with
    Performance Feedback*, 136–138
  *Increasing Academic Performance by Reinforcing
    Correct Answers*, 128–131
  *Join the Team: Reciprocal Peer Tutoring to
    Raise Achievement*, 126–128
  overview of, 117–119
  Self-Monitoring to Improve Work Completion,
    138–140
  *Stop the Clock: Improving Productivity during
    Small-Group Instruction*, 133–136
  *Winning the Recess Game: Raising Class
    Averages with a Free-Time Contingency*,
    131–133
Achenbach Teacher Report Form (TRF),
  49
Active Teaching of Classroom Rules, 74–76
ADHD. *See* Attention-Deficit/
  Hyperactivity Disorder
Administrators, support of intervention
  assistance programs, 24–25
Aggressive behavior
  consequences of, 314–315
  effects of school-based interventions on,
    315–316
  See also Verbalizations, negative,
    interventions for
Aggressive behavior interventions
  evaluating, 257–258
  overview of, 317–318
  *Decreasing Inappropriate Verbalizations with a
    Peer Confrontation System*, 321–322
  *Increasing Cooperative Behavior with Sharing
    Time*, 323–325
  *Using Verbal Instructions to Reduce Aggressive
    Behavior*, 318–321
  See also Disruptive behavior
    interventions; Physical education
    interventions
Art classes. *See* Special classes interventions
Assessing Available Instructional Time, 64–67
Assessing Student Engagement Rates, 67–69
Assessments
  in special education programs, problems
    with, 2–5

See also Evaluation; National Assessment
of Educational Progress; Needs
assessments
Attention-Deficit/Hyperactivity Disorder
(ADHD)
behavioral interventions, 272–275
social competence problems and, 317

Behavior
effects of groups on, 60–61
evaluation of changes in, 48–53
prosocial, teaching of, 108–111
See also Aggressive behavior;
Verbalizations, negative, interventions
for
Behavior Intervention Rating Scale (BIRS),
30
Behavioral interventions
for aggressive behavior, 315–333
for disruptive behavior, 258–296
evaluating, 257–258
for increasing on-task behavior, 88–92,
258–295
for less structured situations, 305–313
for lunchrooms, 305–309
for media centers, 301–303
need for, 256
overviews of, 256–260, 296–298,
317–318
for recess and physical education,
303–305
for rest time, 309–313
for social competence problems,
315–333
for special classes, 296–305
Behavioral Observation of Students in
Schools (BOSS), 63–64
*Brag Sheets: Improving Behavior during Rest
Time,* 297–298, 309–313
Buckley Amendment. *See* Family Education
Rights and Privacy Act

CBM. *See* Curriculum-based measurement
*Charting to Improve Classroom Behavior during
Specials,* 297–300
Checking Stations, 86–88, 279
Children's Intervention Rating Profile
(CIRP), 30–31
Classroom environment, seating
arrangements and, 70–73
Classroom management. *See* Proactive
classroom management
Classroom rules and procedures,
establishing, 73–78
Classwide Engagement Rate Recording Form, 69

Classwide peer tutoring, 56–57, 63,
118–119
Classwide Peer Tutoring, 118–119, 122–125,
167, 169
Classwide scanning, 50, 52–53
Classwide Scanning Form, 52
Code for Instructional Structure and
Student Academic Response
(CISSAR), 63
Communication. *See* Teacher–student
communication
Composition Strategy Development in Writing,
216, 229–233
Conflict resolution, 104–106
Consultants
choosing interventions and, 17–18
collaborating with teachers, 28–29
developing administrative support and,
24
effective skills of, 20–21, 28
ethical responsibilities of, 37
evaluating interventions and, 29–31, 45
in the intervention assistance process,
33–35
intervention integrity and, 31–33
participation in interventions, 23–24
scheduling problems and, 27–28
teacher resistance and, dealing with it
effectively, 21–23
teacher training and, developing formats
for, 24–27
Content area interventions, 233–254
Cooperative behavior interventions,
323–328
Countdown to Free Time, 259, 272–275
*The Coupon System: Decreasing Inappropriate
Requests for Teacher Assistance,* 86,
88–90
*Cover, Copy, and Compare: Increasing Math
Fluency,* 187, 191–194
Cover, copy, and compare strategy, 187,
191–194, 235–236, 246–249
Critical thinking map, 238–243
Curriculum-based assessment (CBA), 115
Curriculum-Based Mathematics Probes, 188–191
Curriculum-based measurement (CBM)
for academic interventions, 47–48,
115–116
for mathematics interventions, 188–191
for reading interventions, 160–164
for spelling interventions, 208–210
for writing interventions, 217–219
Curriculum-Based Oral Reading Probes,
160–164
Curriculum-Based Spelling Probes, 208–210
Curriculum-Based Written Expression Probes,
217–219

The Daily Assignment, 117, 119–122
Daily report cards, 147–150, 309–313
Decoding, 165
*Decreasing Inappropriate Verbalizations with a
  Group Timeout Ribbon,* 318, 330–333
*Decreasing Inappropriate Verbalizations with a
  Peer Confrontation System,* 317, 321–322
Desk arrangements, 70–73
Diagnosis, problems with, 2–3
Differential reinforcement of low rates
  procedure (DRL), 317–318, 328–330
Discussions, interventions to promote,
  243–246
Disruptive behavior
  effects of academic interventions on,
  114
  managing, 256–257
  See also Aggressive behavior; Verbaliza-
  tions, negative, interventions for
Disruptive behavior interventions
  Countdown to Free Time, 272–275
  *Enhancing the Effectiveness of School–Home
  Notes with Response Cost,* 291–294
  evaluating, 257-258
  The Good Behavior Game, 260–263
  The Good Behavior Game Plus Merit, 266–269
  Group Contingencies to Reduce Stealing,
  295–296
  overview of, 258–259
  Public Posting to Decrease Disruptive Behavior,
  275–277
  Red Light/Green Light, 263–266
  *Reducing Disruptive Behavior with Self-
  Management Response Cost,* 282–284
  *Reducing Rule Violations with Good Day
  Awards,* 288–291
  The Response Cost Raffle, 269–272
  Self-Managed Behavior Ratings, 284–288
  The Star Chart, 277–279
  *Using Peer Monitors to Improve On-Task
  Behavior,* 279–282
  See also Aggressive behavior
  interventions; Physical education
  interventions
DRL. *See* Differential reinforcement of low
  rates procedure

Ecological perspective, 7–8, 11, 22–23, 38
Editing skills, interventions, 216, 222–229
Educational reform, effects on special
  education, 4
Education of All Handicapped Children
  Act. *See* Public Law 94-142
*Eliminating Disruptive Lunchroom Behavior with
  Mediation Essays,* 245, 297, 305–309
*Encouraging Academic Achievement with Principal
  Praise,* 119, 140–142

*Enhancing the Effectiveness of School–Home
  Notes with Response Cost,* 260, 291–294
Evaluation
  of academic interventions, 115–117
  of available instructional time, 64–66
  of behavioral interventions, 257–258
  of changes in academic behavior, 47–48
  of changes in student behavior, 48–53
  classwide scanning, 50, 52–53
  ethical issues in, 39
  event recording, 49–50
  home-based strategies in, 54
  interval recording, 49–51
  of intervention acceptability, 30–31
  in intervention assistance programs, 9,
  14, 34–35
  of mathematics interventions, 188–191
  methods and measures in, 47
  momentary time sampling, 49–50
  narrative recording, 67
  of proactive classroom management
  interventions, 63–68
  rationale for, 46–47
  of reading interventions, 160–164
  resistance to, 45–46
  of science interventions, 236
  of social studies interventions, 236
  of spelling interventions, 208–210
  of student engagement rates, 67–69
  of writing interventions, 216–217
  See also Assessments
Evaluation measures
  Assessing Available Instructional Time,
  64–67
  Assessing Student Engagement Rates, 67–69
  Behavioral Observation of Students in
  Schools (BOSS), 63–64
  Classwide Scanning Form, 62
  Code for Instructional Structure and
  Student Academic Response
  (CISSAR), 63
  Curriculum-Based Mathematics Probes,
  188–191
  Curriculum-Based Oral Reading Probes,
  160–164
  Curriculum-Based Spelling Probes, 208–210
  Curriculum-Based Written Expression Probes,
  217–219
  Group Event Recording Form, 50
  Group Interval Recording Form, 50
  Homework Problems Checklist (HPC),
  117
  Quality Evaluation Measure for Written
  Products, 217
  Schedule Analysis Form, 66
  Social Skills Rating System, (SSRS)
  257–258

Event recording, 49–50
Expectations, communicating, 101–107

Family Education Rights and Privacy Act
  (FERPA), 38
Feedback
  in academic productivity interventions,
    119, 136–138
  in science interventions, 249–251
Fluency. *See* Mathematics fluency; Reading
    fluency
Free-time contingencies
  in behavioral interventions, 272–275,
    277–279, 298–300
  in mathematics interventions, 204–205

Game-like interventions
  for academic productivity, 90–92, 119,
    126–128, 131–133
  for disruptive behavior, 260–272
  for homework completion, 150–152
  for social studies, 236–238
  for spelling, 210–213
  for transitions, 80–82
Geography interventions, 235–236,
    246–249
The Good Behavior Game, 258, 260–263
The Good Behavior Game Plus Merit, 23–24,
    56, 144, 150–151, 258–259,
    266–269
Grades. *See* Public posting strategies
Group contingencies
  limiting reward satiation in, 42–43
  peer harassment and, 36
Group Contingencies to Reduce Stealing, 260,
    295–296
Group Event Recording Form, 50
Group Interval Recording Form, 51
Groups, effects on individual student
    behavior, 60–61
Group Story Mapping, 174–175, 177–180

Home-based evaluation strategies, 54
Home-based interventions
  for academic productivity, 119–122
  for mathematics, 199–204
  for disruptive behavior, 259–260
  See also School–home note interventions
Homework
  assessing homework problems, 117
  benefits of, 143
  passes, 42, 43
Homework interventions
  *Improving Homework Compliance with Public
    Posting and Group Contingencies*, 144,
    150–152

*Improving Homework Submission with
    School–Home Notes*, 144–146
Self-Instruction to Improve Homework Completion,
    155–158
Self-Managed Teams to Monitor Homework,
    152–155
Homework Problems Checklist (HPC), 117

IAPs. *See* Intervention assistance programs
IATs. *See* Intervention assistance teams
*Improving Academic Productivity with Performance
    Feedback*, 119, 136–138
*Improving Achievement and Behavior with
    Contingent Praise*, 94–97
*Improving Homework Compliance with Public
    Posting and Group Contingencies*, 144,
    150–152
*Improving Homework Submission with
    School–Home Notes*, 144–146
*Improving Math Completion Rates and Accuracy
    with Free Time*, 188, 204–205
*Improving Math Performance with Explicit
    Timing*, 187, 194–195
*Improving Math Performance with Reciprocal Peer
    Tutoring and Parental Involvement*, 188,
    199–204
*Improving Media Center Behavior with the Good
    Behavior Game*, 297, 301–303
Improving Participation in Social Studies Classes,
    235, 243–246
*Improving Science Test Grades with Public
    Posting*, 144, 150, 236, 249–251
*Improving Social Studies Homework Compliance
    with the Tic–Tac–Toe Game*, 235–238
*Improving Understanding of Textual Material in
    Social Studies with a Critical Thinking
    Map*, 235, 238–243
*Improving Writing Revision Skills by Monitoring
    Comprehension*, 216, 222–226
Incentive systems. *See* Rewards
*Increasing Academic Performance by Reinforcing
    Correct Answers*, 119, 128–131
*Increasing Cooperative Behavior with Sharing
    Time*, 317, 323–325
*Increasing Homework Completion with a Daily
    Report Card*, 143–144, 147–150
*Increasing Spelling Performance with Group
    Contingencies*, 201, 214–215
*Increasing Writing Productivity with Self-
    Monitoring*, 216, 219–222
Individualized Education Plan (IEP), 35
Individuals with Disabilities Education Act
    (IDEA), 39
Instructional time
  devoted to mathematics, 187
  devoted to reading , 159
  devoted to science, 233–234

Instructional time *(continued)*
    devoted to vocabulary, 170
    devoted to writing, 206
    evaluating available time, 64–67
    percentage of total school time, 62
Interval recording, 49–51
Intervention assistance programs (IAPs)
    assessing intervention integrity and, 31
    characteristics of, 7–8
    current status of, 6–7
    documenting, 38–39
    goals of, 10
    guidelines for success of, 21–33
    implementation of, 25–27
    legal and ethical considerations in,
        35–40
    measures of effectiveness in, 46–47
    problems with, 8–10
    steps in developing, 33–35
    studies of, 8–10
Intervention assistance teams (IATs)
    documentation and, 38–39
    intervention assistance process and,
        33–35
    training for, 24–25
Intervention packages, 54–57
Interventions
    acceptability of, 29–31
    case examples, 54–57
    classroom resources and, 13–14
    consultants and, 17–18
    criteria for selection, 10–14
    criticism of, 4–5
    designing, 28–29
    ecological perspective in, 11
    ethical considerations in, 35–40
    evaluation of, 9, 14, 34–35, 39, 44–54
    format of, 14–16
    goals of, 32–33
    group-oriented perspective in, 12
    implementation, 34
    integrity of, 31–33
    introducing to a class, 32
    legal considerations in, 35–40
    parents and, 17, 37–38
    proactive approach in, 11–12
    problems with, 9
    referrals for additional services, 39–40
    rewards and, 14, 40–44
    side effects of, 36
    targets of, 16–17
    See also specific interventions
Intervention targets, 16–17
    of academic interventions, 114–115
    case examples, 55–56
    ethical issues and, 35–36
    student selection of, 38

*Join the Team: Reciprocal Peer Tutoring to Raise
    Achievement*, 118, 126–128

Learning disabilities
    lack of consensus in defining, 3
    overidentification of, 3–4
    proactive interventions for
        learning-disabled students, 62
    social skills deficits and, 316–317
Least restrictive environment (LRE)
    principle, 7
"Limited shopping" concept, 314
Listening Previewing, 165, 168–170
Lotteries, 42–43
Lunchroom interventions
    overview, 297
    *Eliminating Disruptive Lunchroom Behavior
        with Mediation Essays*, 305–309

Mathematics
    achievement, deficits in, 186
    curriculum weaknesses and, 187
    instruction, problems in, 187
Mathematics fluency
    evaluating, 188–191
    interventions, 191–195
    problems in, 186
Mathematics interventions
    *Cover, Copy, and Compare: Increasing Math
        Fluency*, 187, 191–194
    evaluating, 188–191
    *Improving Math Completion Rates and
        Accuracy with Free Time*, 188, 204–205
    *Improving Math Performance with Explicit
        Timing*, 187, 194–195
    *Improving Math Performance with Reciprocal
        Peer Tutoring and Parental Involvement*,
        188, 199–204
    overview of, 187–188
    *Reciprocal Peer Tutoring to Improve Math
        Achievement*, 187, 195–199
"Matthew effects," 160
Media center. *See* Special classes
    interventions
Mediation essays, 305–309
Metacognitive skills, reading interventions
    and, 181–183
Momentary time sampling, 49–50
Motivation, intrinsic, 40
Music classes. *See* Special classes
    interventions

Narrative recording, 67
National Assessment of Educational
        Progress (NAEP)
    in geography achievement, 233
    in math achievement, 186

in reading achievement, 160
in science achievement, 233–234
in U.S. history achievement, 233
in writing achievement, 206
Needs assessments, 26–27

Observations
assessing reliability of, 53
conducting, 23
enhancing interventions with, 32
methods and measures, 49–53
On-task behavior
academic interventions and, 114
proactive classroom management and,
85–86
See also Disruptive behavior
Oral reading probes, 160–164

Parents
in home-based evaluation strategies, 54
homework interventions and, 143–144
in the intervention assistance process, 26,
37–40
mathematics interventions and, 199–204
reading interventions and, 168
See also School–home note interventions
Peer confrontation system, 321–322
Peer Editing, 216, 222–226
Peer harassment with group contingencies,
36
Peer-mediated interventions
disruptive behavior and, 257
for improving cooperative behavior,
323–325
for improving social competence,
321–325
for increasing on-task behavior, 279–282
for reading comprehension, 175,
183–186
for reducing inappropriate requests for
help, 88–90
for transitions, 82–85
for writing, 222–226
See also Peer tutoring
Peer-Monitored Transitions, 78, 82–85
Peer monitors, 82–85, 279–282
Peer tutoring
in spelling interventions, 210–213
in vocabulary interventions, 171–173
See also Classwide peer tutoring;
Reciprocal peer tutoring
Peer Tutoring in Sight Words, 171–173
The Peer Tutoring Spelling Game, 207, 210–213
Percentage gain, 48
Phonological awareness skills, 158
Physical education interventions
overview, 297

*Reducing Aggressive and Inappropriate Behavior
in Physical Education Classes with Sit and
Watch*, 303–305
See also Special classes interventions
Praise
characteristics of effective, 93–94
by principals in academic interventions,
140–142
proactive intervention for, 94–97
in science interventions, 249–251
Prereading strategies, 174–177
Preschool
behavioral interventions, 263–266,
288–292, 303–305, 309–313,
318–321, 325–328
intervention packages, case example,
54–55
proactive interventions,
76–78, 80–82, 108–111
Principals
in academic productivity interventions,
140–142
in behavioral interventions, 269, 302
importance as supporters of IAPs, 24
Proactive classroom management
classroom environment and, 70–73
classroom rules and procedures in,
73–78
diverse learners and, 62
evaluating, 63–68
importance of, 61–63
overview of, 60–61
prosocial behavior and, 108–111
seatwork and, 85–92
teacher–student communication in,
93–107
teacher training in, 62–63
transitions and, 78–85
Proactive classroom management
interventions
Active Teaching of Classroom Rules, 74–76
Checking Stations, 86–88
*The Coupon System: Decreasing Inappropriate
Requests for Teacher Assistance*, 88–90
critical tasks of, 68, 70
evaluating, 63–68
*Improving Achievement and Behavior with
Contingent Praise*, 94–97
Peer-Monitored Transitions, 82–85
Problem-Solving Student Conferences, 104–
107
*Promoting On-Task Behavior with a Circular
Desk Arrangement*, 71–73
*Promoting Positive Behavior through
Attribution*, 102–104
*Say Show Check: Teaching Classroom
Procedures*, 76–78

Proactive classroom management
    interventions *(continued)*
  *Short, Soft, and Close: Delivering Effective
    Reprimands,* 99–101
  Sit and Watch: Teaching Prosocial Behaviors,
    108–111
  Speeding Up Transitions: Beat the Buzzer,
    80–82
  *The Study Game: Increasing Productivity
    during Seatwork,* 90–92
  Teaching Transition Time, 78–80
Problem-Solving Student Conferences, 102,
    104–107
*Promoting On-Task Behavior with a Circular
    Desk Arrangement,* 71–73
Promoting Positive Behavior through Attribution,
    102–104
Public Law 94-142, 3, 7, 206
Public posting strategies
  in academic productivity interventions,
    131–132, 136
  in behavioral interventions, 259–260,
    275–277
  in homework interventions, 150–152
  in science interventions, 249–251
Public Posting to Decrease Disruptive Behavior,
    259, 275–277

Quality Evaluation Measure for Written
    Products, 217

Raffle games, 269–272
Reading
  achievement, deficits in, 160
  consequences of poor, 159–160
  effects on social studies and science
    achievement, 234
  importance of, 158–159
Reading comprehension
  effects on social studies and science
    achievement, 234
  failure to teach, 174
  schema theory and, 174–175, 177
  social studies interventions and, 234,
    236–243
  writing interventions and, 226–229
Reading comprehension interventions
  Group Story Mapping, 177–180
  overview of, 174–175
  Reconciled Reading, 175–177
  Story Retelling, 183–185
  Using Story Grammar to Aid Comprehension,
    181–183
Reading fluency
  evaluating, 160–164
  problems in, 114

Reading fluency interventions
  Listening Previewing, 168–170
  overview of, 165
  Repeated Readings, 165–168
Reading interventions
  for comprehension, 174–186
  evaluating, 160–164
  for fluency, 165–170
  need for, 158–160
  overview of, 165
  for vocabulary, 170–173
Reading vocabulary interventions
  overview of, 170–172
  Peer Tutoring in Sight Words, 171–173
Recess interventions
  overview of, 297
  *Reducing Aggressive and Inappropriate Behavior
    in Physical Education Classes with Sit and
    Watch,* 303–305
Reciprocal peer tutoring
  in academic productivity interventions,
    126–128
  in mathematics interventions, 195–204
  overview of, 118–119
*Reciprocal Peer Tutoring to Improve Math
    Achievement,* 187, 195–199
Reconciled Reading, 174–177
Red Light / Green Light, 55, 258, 263–266
*Reducing Aggressive and Inappropriate Behavior in
    Physical Education Classes with Sit and
    Watch,* 297, 303–305
*Reducing Disruptive Behavior with Self-Managed
    Response Cost,* 259, 282–284
Reducing Rule Violations with Good Day Awards,
    55, 259–260, 288–291
Reinforcement Menu, 41
Reinforcers. *See* Rewards
Reinforcing Cooperative Play for Preschoolers, 317,
    325–328
Repeated Readings, 165–169
Report cards. *See* Daily report cards
Reprimands, 97–101
Response cards, in science interventions,
    251–254
Response cost
  in behavioral interventions, 259–260,
    263, 266, 269–272, 282–284,
    291–294
  in proactive interventions, 88–90
The Response Cost Raffle, 31, 259, 269–272
Rest time interventions
  *Brag Sheets: Improving Behavior during Rest
    Time,* 309–313
  overview of , 297–298
  Revision skills, in writing interventions,
    216, 222–229
Rewards, 40–44

Say Show Check: Teaching Classroom Procedures, 32, 74, 76–78

Schedule Analysis Form, 66

School–home note interventions
for academic productivity, 119–122
for disruptive behavior, 259–260, 288–294
for homework, 143–150
overview of, 117–118
for rest time, 309–313

Science
achievement, deficits in, 233
deficiencies in textbooks, 234–235
instruction, problems in, 233–235
reading deficits and performance in, 234

Science interventions
evaluating, 236
Improving Science Test Grades with Public Posting, 249–251
overview of, 233–236
Using Response Cards to Improve Participation and Achievement in Science, 251–254

Seating arrangements, 70–73

Seatwork interventions, 85–92

Self-instruction interventions
for homework, 155–158
for social studies, 246–249

Self-Instruction to Improve Homework Completion, 144, 155–158

Self-Managed Behavior Ratings, 259, 284–288

Self-Managed Teams to Monitor Homework, 144, 152–155

Self-management strategies
in academic productivity interventions, 138–140
in behavioral interventions, 259, 282–288
in homework interventions, 144, 152–158
in mathematics interventions, 195–199
in proactive interventions, 86–88
self-instruction training and, 155–156
in social studies interventions, 246–249
in writing interventions, 219–222, 226–229
See also Self-regulated strategy development in writing interventions

Self-Monitoring to Improve Work Completion, 119, 138–140

Self-regulated strategy development in writing interventions, 229–233

Short, Soft, and Close: Delivering Effective Reprimands, 55, 98–101

Sit and Watch: Teaching Prosocial Behaviors, 55, 108–111

Small-group instruction interventions, 90–92, 133–136

Social competence
effects of school-based interventions on, 315–317
interventions, 108–111, 315–333
problems in, 314–317

Social Skills Rating System, (SSRS) 257–258

Social studies
achievement, deficits in, 233
deficiencies in textbooks, 234–235
instruction, problems in, 234–235

Social studies interventions
evaluating, 236
Improving Participation in Social Studies Classes, 243–246
Improving Social Studies Homework Compliance with the Tic–Tac–Toe Game, 236–238
Improving Understanding of Textual Material in Social Studies with a Critical Thinking Map, 238–243
overview of, 235–236
Using Cover, Copy, and Compare to Improve Geography Accuracy, 246–249

Social validity, 36

Special classes interventions
Charting to Improve Behavior during Specials, 298–300
Improving Media Center Behavior with the Good Behavior Game, 301–303
overview of, 296–297
Reducing Aggressive and Inappropriate Behavior in Physical Education Classes with Sit and Watch, 303–305

Special education
criticisms of, 2–5
revolution in delivery systems, 5–6

Speeding Up Transitions: Beat the Buzzer, 78, 80–82

Spelling
achievement, deficits in, 207
instruction, problems in, 207

Spelling interventions
evaluating, 208–210
Increasing Spelling Performance with Group Contingencies, 214–215
overview of, 207
The Peer Tutoring Spelling Game, 210–213

The Star Chart, 259, 277–279

Stealing, 260
interventions, 295–296

Stop the Clock: Improving Productivity during Small-Group Instruction, 119, 133–136

Story grammar, 181–183, 229–233

Story mapping, 174–175, 177–180

Story Retelling, 175, 183–186
Student conferences, solving classroom
    problems with, 102, 104–107
Student engagement rates
    for diverse learners, 62
    during independent seatwork, 85–86
    evaluating, 67–69
Student participation
    science interventions and, 251–254
    seating arrangements and, 70–73
    social studies interventions and, 243–
    246
Student problems, teachers' perspective on,
    21–22
*The Study Game: Increasing Productivity during
    Seatwork,* 86, 90–92

Tardiness, 145
Teacher assistance teams, 7
Teachers
    challenges facing, 1–6
    collaborating with school consultants,
    28–29
    concerns with rewards, 41
    difficult-to-teach students and, 1–2
    in IAP implementation, 26–27
    interviewing, 116
    introducing interventions to a class, 32
    perspectives on student problems, 21–22
    resistance to evaluation of interventions,
    45–46
    resistance to intervention assistance
    programs, 22
    scheduling time for school consultants,
    27–28
    special education programs and, 4–5
Teacher–student communication
    communicating positive expectations,
    101–107
    delivery of praise in, 93–97
    delivery of reprimands in, 97–101
Teacher training, 10, 24–27, 62–63
Teaching Transition Time, 56, 78–80, 269
Timeout, 303–305, 330–333

Token economies, 41, 325–328, 330–333
Transitions
    behavior interventions, 266, 269,
    298–300
    proactive interventions, 78–85

*Using Cover, Copy, and Compare to Improve
    Geography Accuracy,* 235–236, 246–249
Using DRL to Decrease Negative Verbalizations,
    318, 328–330
*Using Peer Monitors to Improve On-Task
    Behavior,* 259, 279–282
*Using Response Cards to Improve Participation
    and Achievement in Science,* 235, 251–254
Using Story Grammar to Aid Comprehension,
    175, 181–183
*Using Verbal Instructions to Reduce Aggressive
    Behavior,* 317–321

Verbalizations, negative, interventions for,
    321–322, 328–333. *See also* Aggressive
    behavior interventions; Disruptive
    behavior interventions

*Winning the Recess Game: Raising Class Averages
    with a Free-Time Contingency,* 119,
    131–133
Workshops, in IAP implementation, 25–27
Written language
    achievement, deficits in, 206
    shift in instruction, 215–216
    See also Spelling
Written language interventions
    evaluating, 216–219
    Composition Strategy Development in Writing,
    227–233
    *Improving Writing Revision Skills by
    Monitoring Comprehension,* 222–226
    *Increasing Writing Productivity with Self-
    Monitoring,* 219–222
    overview of, 215–216
    Peer Editing, 222–226
    See also Spelling interventions